Z9631

SAM MILLER

Sam Miller was born and brought up in London. He studied History at Cambridge University and Politics at London University's School of Oriental and African Studies, before joining the BBC in 1986, for which he has worked, on and off, ever since. In the early 1990s he was the BBC World Service TV and radio correspondent in Delhi, and on his return to the UK in 1993 was the presenter of the BBC's current affairs programme, *South Asia Report*. Later he became the head of the Urdu service and subsequently Managing Editor, South Asia. He was posted back to Delhi in 2002 and has remained there ever since. He is the author of *Delhi: Adventures in a Megacity* (2009) and *Blue Guide: India* (2012).

SAM MILLER

A Strange Kind of Paradise

India Through Foreign Eyes

VINTAGE BOOKS
London

2 4 6 8 10 9 7 5 3 1

Vintage
20 Vauxhall Bridge Road,
London SW1V 2SA

Vintage is part of the Penguin Random House group of companies
whose addresses can be found at global.penguinrandomhouse.com

 Penguin
Random House
UK

First published in Vintage in 2015
First published in hardback by Jonathan Cape in 2014

www.vintage-books.co.uk

A CIP catalogue record for this book is
available from the British Library

ISBN 9780099555865

Printed and bound by Clays Ltd, St Ives Plc

MIX
Paper from
responsible sources
FSC
www.fsc.org   FSC® C018179

Penguin Random House is committed to a sustainable future
for our business, our readers and our planet. This book is
made from Forest Stewardship Council® certified paper

To Tony Mango

And to my parents without whom I would still be nothing;

And, finally, to my smiling and thoughtful grown-up children, to the woman who wasn't an apple, to the radiant one, and to anybody who has been happily lost in a foreign land.

Contents

Prologue

MY FIRST VISIT to India was as a wedding guest. I was the brother of the bride, and was expected to be on my best behaviour. I was also by then, in a way that threatened to complicate the nuptials, the boyfriend of the groom's sister. As I flew in to Bombay, I felt no great rush of excitement about visiting India for the first time, no sense of my Indian destiny. My thoughts were for my girlfriend — and for some Portuguese custard tarts that I was carrying in my hand luggage.  She was already in India and I would be seeing her at her home in Bombay for the first time. I was concerned that it might not be easy for us to spend time alone together. And the tarts, *pastéis de nata*, were from our favourite London café and I had stepped on them while climbing over my sleeping neighbour to get to the toilet.

I had decided some years earlier, in an off-handedly decisive way, that India was not for me. I'd encountered several 'India bores' at university; non-Indian acquaintances who had spent their 'year off' backpacking, or in an ashram — being ill or cheated most of the time, as far as I could tell. Then there was the teenage friend who had volunteered to help modernise an Indian village, and I'm afraid I laughed out loud when I heard that the villagers had thrown a dead rat into her tent. Her brother followed her out to India — and was very proud of having survived on less than one pound a day, and briefly came to believe that he was a lesser Hindu god. Another friend had nursed a companion who almost died of dysentery — and she told me in forensic detail how every day she would clean her friend's

1

bloodied sheets. I, meanwhile, was interested in somewhere else — the area that people older than me knew as the Levant. I learned Arabic, studied Middle Eastern politics and lived briefly in Syria. I was a trainee journalist with the BBC, and the Middle East was to be my area of expertise. Instead, it was my sister who fell for India, and for an Indian who was studying in Britain — who swept her off on long, tiring holidays. I obediently shuffled through their pretty photographs of Rajasthani lakes and Goan beaches — slowing down briefly when I saw an image of his sister, with a sunbeam smile for the camera, talking on the phone.

Of Indian history and culture I knew very little. I had not read Tagore or Narayan or Rushdie. I had never visited a Hindu temple — and could never remember whether Shiva was the creator or the destroyer, or both. I was unable to assume the lotus position. I did not care for the music of Ravi Shankar. I had not watched a Satyajit Ray film, or a Hindi movie. The spate of Raj nostalgia that had marked the early 1980s in Britain had largely passed me by, and I did not watch *The Jewel in the Crown* or *The Far Pavilions*. My family, so far as I then knew, had no historical connections with India. My views and images of India, such as I had, were largely childhood ones, conjured up by the eloquent rhythms of the *Just So Stories* and *The Jungle Book*, and by Tintin's occasional appearances in the subcontinent. As a politics student and then a journalist, I was of course aware of India's recent tribulations, the assassination of Indira Gandhi, and her replacement by the boyish Rajiv Gandhi — but of not much more than that.

The plane arrived in Bombay in the middle of the night, and I could see little of the city from the air. But standing on the tarmac, waiting for the bus, I could taste the hot damp air as if it were the breath of earth, coiling around me. I was miraculously vacuumed out of the airport into a car bearing diplomatic number plates and a Greek flag, and driven off. I gazed in silence out of the window, transfixed — looking at the people asleep on the pavement. The

2

traffic slowed, and I could see flames dancing in the distance. As the car edged closer, I saw that dozens of huts were on fire. The police had partly blocked the road and were staring, like me, at the flames. No one in the car knew what was happening.

We reached the groom's house, and I placed the mangled custard tarts next to my groggily supine lover. I was packed off to a different bed, disappointed to be given a berth in what had become a temporary male dormitory, and listened to the sounds of gentle snoring and of waves breaking in the distance.

~

Reader, I married her. Two decades later, I live in India — a long-term resident with no current plans to leave. I am far from alone. India has a more diverse collection of foreign residents than at any time in its history. And there are almost certainly a greater number of foreigners in India than ever before,[1] and definitely more tourists. We came here to visit and live for a huge range of different reasons — as diplomats, pilgrims, entrepreneurs, students, missionaries, patients, artists, wastrels, journalists, holiday-makers, drug-users, soul-searchers, refugees, prostitutes, fortune-hunters, wanderers, job-seekers — and occasionally, like me, as a lover and a spouse.

We all have our patchwork ideas of India, our notions and opinions and prejudices — often fallacious and absurd — of

[1] Official figures on the number of foreigners living in India are confidential — possibly, a civil servant at the Ministry of Home Affairs told me, because no one has got round to adding them up. But there are estimated to be about five hundred thousand legally resident foreigners in the country. There is an uncountable and probably very large population of illegal Bangladeshi migrants — figures of up to ten million are sometimes mentioned. Comparisons with the past are hard to make because of the problems of defining both nationality and the borders of India at particular points in history. But it still seems hard to refute the proposition that there are more foreigners living in the country than ever before.

this enormous, disparate country, which is, as I take pleasure in reminding newcomers, bigger in population than all but its own continent: Asia. It is a place onto which foreigners have projected their own exotic fantasies and fears, their explanatory and simplifying schemata. And they seem never quite to make up their minds — as they swing from one extreme to the other — whether this country is actually a land of great wealth or of appalling poverty, of spiritual renunciation or of unabashed materialism, of fasting or of gluttony, of erotic sophistication or of sexual puritanism, of corruption or of moral superiority. They probably fail to admit that it might be all these things, and, even more so, everything in between.

There is nothing new to this. The earliest surviving descriptions of India by foreigners, all Greeks, from more than two thousand years ago, were of a fantasy land at the edge of the known world; a land of mystery and miracles, and some distinctly unusual behaviour. There were tales of killer ants that dig for gold; of humans with giant ear lobes that could be used as sleeping bags, a land where it would be unthinkable not to eat one's recently deceased parents, and where fountains spouted molten gold.

Ever since, we foreigners have been pretty credulous. The Indian Rope Trick — where a magician throws a rope into the air, which is climbed by a small boy who then disappears — was the invention of an American journalist, who actually admitted that he made it all up. That has not stopped visitors to India from claiming that they have seen it actually happen. When my wife first travelled abroad she would regularly get asked if she went to school on an elephant — and whether India had any cars. And one acquaintance of mine seemed aggrieved that she had travelled the full length of the country and never seen anyone sleeping on a bed of nails.

The world does now, at least, know more about India than it did in the past. Images of a large white tomb, popularly known as the Taj Mahal, adorn tea-bag boxes and restaurant menus all over the world. Bollywood song-and-dance routines have become internationally chic. India is purported to be a land of computer whiz-kids; and it has come to control the formerly very British sport of cricket. Poverty, of course, has given it another kind of fame, complete with a deceased celebrity

in the form of the saint-designate Mother Teresa, a fame richly embellished by an Oscar-winning movie like *Slumdog Millionaire*. India is no longer on the periphery.

The first visitors to India

The subject of India's prehistory is a battleground where nationalists, racists, religious fundamentalists, archaeologists and geneticists club each other over the head with their respective wisdoms. They tend not to listen to each other. And one can take one's pick. I prefer the geneticists — largely because the archaeologists have discovered so little — and the others have too many axes to grind. I get a certain restrained pleasure from telling Indian racists that, according to the latest evidence from DNA analysis, the first Indians came from Africa, and even more pleasure from telling European racists that their ancestors probably came from Africa by way of India. The unlikely mastermind of these discoveries is a bespectacled Estonian geneticist called Toomas Kivisild who writes frighteningly abstruse but very short academic papers on the subject, often with more than a dozen collaborators. The photograph on his university website profile shows him as a genial fellow, standing in an Indian street market with an auto-rickshaw and a cartload of mangoes as a backdrop. His pioneering research since 1999 seems to have convinced his peers that the first modern humans arrived in India more than fifty thousand years ago, and that most of the world's non-African population are their descendants.

Those earliest visitors to India are thought to have taken what's become known as the 'southern route' out of Africa, following the coastline from the Horn of Africa — at a time when sea levels were much lower than today. They were 'beachcombers', proclaims one historian, often foraging and hunting inland, but remaining close to the coast, edging their way, incredibly slowly, around the Arabian Sea. The archaeological remains of their settlements, according to this theory, are now under the sea — probably lost for ever. And it's hard to imagine how we might ever know what they thought of India.

The earliest inscriptions, probably dating back three thousand years, may possibly, one day, give us some clues. The undeciphered symbols etched into hundreds of stone  tablets dug up during excavations at 'Indus Valley' sites in Pakistan and India are both one of the world's great unsolved mysteries and a cause of recent nationalistic friction. The past is rarely dead in India. Three western academics[2] declared in 2004 that these symbols were not a language, and that the Indus Valley civilisation was not literate. This provoked further attempts by Indian researchers to prove that the symbols were a form of writing, partly through computer analysis, but we're

[2] The three academics, Steve Farmer, Richard Sproat and Michael Witzel — respectively a comparative historian, a linguist and an Indic philologist — have offered a prize of ten thousand dollars to anyone who can refute their thesis. See http://www.safarmer.com/indus/prize.html.

still no nearer knowing what those symbols might mean.

A little over two hundred years ago, western philologists were startled to discover that the languages of north India were related to most European languages, and that Sanskrit and ancient Greek appeared to be cousins. The explanation that emerged for this became known as the 'Aryan Invasion Theory', a nineteenth-century proposition according to which an early Indo-European language was brought to India by foreigners: horse-riding, pale-skinned Aryans who conquered the north of the country, subjugated the existing population or drove them into southern India. The supporters of this theory found part of their evidence in ancient Sanskrit texts, particularly in what appeared to be the description of an Aryan victory over a flat-nosed, dark-skinned enemy. They also pointed out that both tigers and rice were absent from the earliest of the texts, the *Rigveda* — an unlikely omission, unless of course the invaders had brought the hymns of the *Rigveda* with them from a land without rice and tigers. Much of this literary evidence has now been discounted, and what were thought to be the earliest descriptions of India by foreigners, are now seen as ambiguously indigenous accounts. And the supporters of the theory tend now to talk about a gradual migration rather than an invasion. But the linguistic and DNA evidence does demonstrate links between India and the rest of the world that pre-date recorded history. And for this reason we are never likely to find out what the early foreigners thought of the subcontinent.

An ancient Greek

Tony Mango was only seventy-two when I first met him at the breakfast table of my girlfriend's house in Bombay.[3] I had woken

[3] The city's name was formally changed, in English, to Mumbai, in 1996. Both names are in everyday conversational use, and visiting foreigners will often be corrected, whichever one they say. I still say Bombay to most of my friends and family, but use Mumbai for official purposes. I've used Bombay

late, stumbling down the wooden spiral staircase around which the house appeared to have been built. I swept past a striking collection of colourful 1960s' designer furniture, white walls covered in modern Indian art, and, smelling the sea air, opened a glass sliding-door into the garden. I was in a strange kind of paradise, surrounded by gently swaying coconut palms that all leaned steeply towards the sea. I went to a low garden wall, some three metres above the beach. I sat on the wall, looking out at a magnificent panorama — a small fishing village to my left, with distant high-rises in both directions, a long, yellow, sandy beach that swept round in a semi-circle, forming a broad bay with coloured fishing boats bobbing close to the shore, white-tipped waves audibly breaking twenty metres away. There were women paddling in the water in their saris, young men playing cricket as if their futures depended on it. So this is India, I said in a pompous inner voice, admitting to myself that this was not quite what I had been expecting from Bombay. I then looked down and was startled to see a darkish, uncircumcised willy being waggled dry; its owner, relieving himself against the garden wall, quite unaware of my presence. I recoiled, launching myself backwards, embarrassed by my embarrassment and looked towards the house. A European man was sitting at a table in the garden watching me. He beckoned me over.

I introduced myself, knowing this must be my girlfriend's Greek stepfather. Without waiting for me to answer his question about whether I'd slept well, he informed me that a horizontal strip of white tiles, with religious images, had been embedded, a little below penis-level, along the beach side of the garden wall;

(and Calcutta and Madras) in this book, since I am largely dealing with a period when those were the names that were used most commonly in English. Some older English-language names, such as Cawnpore (Kanpur), or Cape Comorin (Kanyakumari) have fallen out of general use, while other recent changes such as Mysuru for Mysore or Odisha for Orissa have been slow to catch on.

tiles with images of Shiva, Jesus, Koranic calligraphy, a Sikh guru, the Buddha and a Zoroastrian angel. But it hadn't really worked. The urinators simply passed along the wall to a spot where someone else's religious symbol had been placed. And someone had broken the 'Muslim' tiles — a Hindu extremist, he supposed. He invited me to order breakfast, the first of many hundreds of meals I would eat in this house. I wasn't used to ordering breakfast, certainly not at someone's home, and most hotels had buffets, anyway. He bellowed for a servant, 'Mohaaan', and somehow I ended up with a masala omelette, with onions, tomatoes and a few chillies.

'Pass the newspaper, Tom,' he said in a quite affable manner. I was about to say, 'Actually, my name is Sam'; but I couldn't quite work out the tone of voice in which I should deliver this statement. I was very keen not to leave the wrong impression. Maybe, I would mention it to my girlfriend, later — and she could tell him, whisper it in his ear.

'His name is Sam, not Tom,' she said, over lunch, in that forthright public manner that I had come to love. 'Tom . . . Dick . . . Harry,' he muttered back, wickedly, just within earshot. For Tony Mango, I was just the latest in a series of suitors of

9

his stepdaughter whom he could tease. A previous boyfriend, called Iqbal, not famous for passing his exams, was known by Tony as mini-IQ. I hadn't come out of it too badly. I supposed he would call the next one Dick. His own name, he told me later that day, had been changed from Mangos, which he rhymed with 'loss', because when he first came to India, everyone either pronounced it mongoose or mango, and the latter seemed the preferable option. It was a typical Tony story, delivered with a self-deprecatory laugh, and not entirely true — since I later found out that his UK-based cousins were all called Mango as well.

For his ninetieth birthday in 2005, I was the master of ceremonies, at a party that took place in the same Bombay

garden. After a lot of coaching, I narrated Tony's long life story, with the help of a slide show that he had put together: the tale of how he was born in Constantinople in 1915 under the Ottoman Empire, evacuated to Geneva during the First World War, went to work in Britain and then sailed to India in 1938 to work for a Greek trading company. In 1965 he was made the Honorary Greek Consul in Bombay, and remained in post, with a brief intermission, until his death — the doyen of the diplomatic community. He would rescue spaced-out Athenian students who'd been mugged or had taken overdoses, help Greek traders clear customs, and set about trying, not very successfully, to plant olive orchards and manufacture feta cheese. It also gave him access to imported foreign wine, and the right to park his car, so long as it flew the Greek flag, almost anywhere he wanted — which is why I had so easily escaped the crowds at Bombay airport. And on the morning after my arrival he began answering my questions about everything I had seen and heard and smelled in my first twelve hours in his adopted country. He was the first of my India guides — explaining caustically, for instance, that those burning huts on the side of the road were an Indian version of town planning. They had been deliberately set on fire by the authorities — 'slum clearance, you see'.

Tony Mango was proud of his Greek ancestry, and talked of other Greeks who'd preceded him in India, of the nineteenth-century Sanskritist Galanos and of course, Alexander the Great, who had reached India's borders more than two millennia earlier — India's most famous visitor until the Beatles turned up in 1968.[4] By the time he was ninety, Tony would always refer to himself, to me, as 'the ancient Greek' — though he never really seemed to get much older. In May 2008, he fell ill while on holiday in Greece. At the time I heard of his illness, I was delivering a lecture to a group of travel writers about ancient Greek accounts of India, a subject Tony and I had often discussed, and I asked my wife to carry a packet to him, with a letter and a copy of my talk — some hospital reading matter, I said. She took it to him the day he became unconscious, his heart and lungs having conspired against him and each other, and he died several days later at the age of ninety-two. The packet was returned to me unopened, a reminder of Tony, and all of the things I'd forgotten to ask and to tell him.

That talk — an introduction to some of the often very funny and sometimes sensible things that the earliest Greeks thought of India — became the kernel of a larger project which then grew into this book. It's an attempt to understand how the Greeks, the Romans, the Chinese, the Arabs, Africans, Europeans and Americans — everyone really, except for Indians themselves, came to construct their ideas of India. And it is also an attempt to explain how those ancient and recent imaginings still help to

---

[4] It is possible to argue, if one is feeling particularly pedantic, that the Buddha should be seen as a visitor. He was almost certainly born just across the border in what is now Nepal.

define how the world sees this country that has become my home.

Many of these imaginings have borne little relation to reality, and many of those who were responsible for these imaginings never even travelled to India. Knowledge and experience have never been particularly well regarded as qualifications for writing about India. And so this has also become an investigation in the history of stereotypes, and in the history of the imagination. It is also a strangely skewed history of India, viewed through a series of foreign prisms, including my own. It touches, intermittently, upon my own twenty-five-year connection with India, but it is, in essence, the tale of a 2500-year engagement between foreigners and India that begins with the ancient Greeks.

More ancient Greeks

Scylax was a sailor, the greatest seafarer of his age[5] — and the first visitor to India whose name has survived. He lived five hundred years before Jesus Christ, a Greek in the service of the Persian King Darius the Great, whose empire stretched from Egypt to the borders of India. Scylax returned from a scouting trip down the Indus with some wondrous and dubious tales of strange tribes, and the even stranger uses they made of their extremities. Among the people he is said to have met were the *Skiapodes* or shadow-feet, whose feet were so large and flat that

[5] Original versions of Scylax's journey have not survived, but his travels are referred to by, among others, Herodotus, Aristotle and Strabo. And his name became an eponym for almost any great traveller in the centuries after his death. In the fourth century BC, a guide to the Mediterranean coastline was published under his name, except it wasn't written by him, and the anonymous author is known to this day as Pseudo-Scylax. According to Herodotus' account of Scylax's travels, he sailed down the Indus into the Arabian Sea, a feat copied by Alexander the Great two centuries later. Darius ruled over a large number of Greek speakers in what is now Turkey — including the province of Caria where Scylax seems to have been born. Darius later invaded mainland Greece, finally being defeated at Marathon, approximately 26 miles 385 yards from Athens.

they could take shelter from the midday sun by lying down and sticking them up in the air. Then there were the *Monophthalmoi*, rather like the Cyclops of Greek legend, who had a single eye in the middle of their foreheads, and, my favourite, the *Enotikoitoi* or ear sleepers, whose ears were so big and pendulous that they could curl them around their bodies and use them as sleeping bags. For the ancient Greeks, India became a place of marvels and freaks beyond the known world, rather as modern societies have imagined strange creatures who inhabit other galaxies. The tales of Scylax were a kind of *Star Trek* of their day, an accessible and popular mixture of science and fantasy.[6]

For almost two centuries, we have no further accounts of Greeks, or anyone else, actually travelling to India. However, this was no impediment to what became a flurry of almost psychedelic writing about India and its curiosities. From this period came the story of vicious giant ants that dig for gold (Herodotus), of how south Indian males ejaculate black semen (Herodotus again), and, most imaginatively, from the writings of the Greek physician Ctesias, who claims that in India there is a tiny bird which buries its excrement, and if you just so happen to find it and eat a piece the size of a sesame grain, you will be dead by sunset.[7] Not everything is invention. Both Herodotus

[6] His original words have not survived, but a series of descriptions taken from Scylax are found in the writing of others. He also described India as having, rather puzzlingly, the shape of an artichoke — which could possibly have been a description of the Indus delta, through which he sailed as he headed for the Arabian Sea. Strictly speaking, if he never got beyond the Indus delta, now in Pakistan, then he never entered what is modern India.

[7] Ctesias lived in Persia for several years, as the personal physician of King Artaxerxes II, and would have had contact with travellers to India, and Indian visitors to Persia. He describes dog-headed humans, pygmy men who grow their beards so long that they can be used as clothes, and affirms that it never rains in India. Unwisely, Ctesias says he has told 'the perfect truth', adding that he himself had seen with his own eyes some of the things he describes, and had been informed of the rest by eye-witnesses. He says that he has omitted many far more marvellous things, for fear that those

and Ctesias do accurately portray India as a hugely populous and varied country and one with great natural riches. It's even been argued that some of the more bizarre stories have been transmogrified in translation and over time, and that the giant ants were actually marmots whose burrowing brought nuggets of gold to the surface. Or that the story is really a metaphor for India as a land of riches — something which would remain a key motif of descriptions of India until modern times. And I suppose it's only a little far-fetched to argue that the buried bird shit was really a poisonous truffle, and that one ought to forgive Herodotus, who did not have an easy way of confirming for himself the colour of Indian sperm.

The second visitor to India whose name we know was a certain Alexander of Macedon, whose tutor, Aristotle, would have acquainted him with these early texts, and who crossed the Indus in 326 BC, with a much depleted army. Alexander wanted to conquer the heartland of India and reach the Ganges and what he called the Eastern Ocean. But his army wanted to go no further — possibly scared off by the tales of strange creatures who lived in India. Alexander feared a mutiny and turned back somewhere close to the modern Indo-Pakistan border, leaving behind a Greek toehold on the subcontinent. He then sailed, Scylax-like, down the Indus, and headed west, eventually dying in Babylon at the age of thirty-two. Alexander's journey has remained ever since one of the world's great stories, undisputed in its key elements, but also much mythologised. For the myth-makers and romantics, India remained an unknown land at the edge of the world — and Alexander was labelled as the man who had conquered the known world. But for his generals who ruled the newly-conquered lands after his death, India was very much a

who had not seen them might think that his account was untrustworthy. The second-century AD satirist Lucian is very rude about Ctesias, imagining him on an island (with Herodotus), where the greatest torments were reserved for those who had told lies, and written 'mendacious histories'.

real place, just beyond their borders. They knew that Alexander had wished to conquer India, and they had held him back. One of those generals, Seleucus, who became the ruler of Alexander's eastern empire, never lost interest in India, particularly as a potential source of elephants and aphrodisiacs. A generation after the death of Alexander he sent an ambassador to the court of the most powerful of the Indian kings, Chandragupta, founder of the Mauryan Empire. The ambassador, an Ionian Greek called Megasthenes, visited the Mauryan capital, Pataliputra, now known as Patna, and it is his extraordinary writings that provide us with the first significant account of India written by a foreigner.

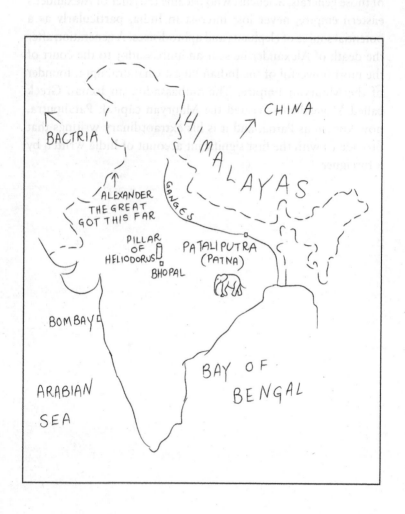

CHINA

HIMALAYAS

BACTRIA

ALEXANDER
THE GREAT
GOT THIS FAR

GANGES

PILLAR
OF
HELIODORUS

PATALIPUTRA
(PATNA)

BHOPAL

BOMBAY

BAY OF
BENGAL

ARABIAN
SEA

Chapter One: *In which the Author plumbs Patna's hidden depths, learns about Ashoka the Greek, and dreams of a dreadlocked Doppelgänger*

IN THE HEART of modern Patna, the capital of Bihar, until recently India's most despised state,[1] is arguably the country's least impressive major archaeological site. A mosquito-ridden tract of grass and swampland, as big as four tennis courts, is all that is still visible of Pataliputra, the first great Indian city and capital of the Mauryan Empire of Ashoka the Great. An empire whose dominance over the subcontinent was arguably greater than at any time since, including the Mughal and British periods. There is one broken column that has been dug up and

[1] In the 1990s and early 2000s, Bihar became — because of corruption, lawlessness and poverty — the epitome of all that was wrong with India. The favourite political joke of the time was that Pakistan could have Kashmir after all, so long as they took Bihar as well. Things have improved somewhat in recent times, with the election and re-election of a reforming state government.

is on display — but the main excavation is in the marshiest part of the site and the column stumps are all under muddy water. It is, however, possible to *feel* some of the stumps, a kind of archaeological toe-Braille, by removing one's footwear and paddling through the marshland — and I was able to foot-grope a couple of Mauryan column-stumps with my toes. Once the water reached my knees, I pulled back — despite the encouragement of an exuberant bystander who indicated with his arms that I should breaststroke my way through the giant Pataliputra puddle.

The bystander turned out to be a gardener, whose breath and clothes were sour with alcohol, and who had great tufts of hair growing horizontally out of his ears — which appeared to have been combed and gelled into unnatural straightness. He started telling me about the politics of Bihar, apologising for its thieving politicians — and said that corruption was why no one had bothered to drain the site of Ashoka's palace. It's been 'sanctioned', he assured me, using the English word, but then gave a despairing shrug of his shoulders — as if he knew it would never happen. He rattled on, listing the politicians he blamed for the ills of Bihar, choice curses accompanying every name. But I only had eyes for his ears, and he caught me staring at them. He smiled back at me, and began stroking the tufts as if they were objects of distinction. He told me that everyone he knew wanted to leave Bihar, but that it had once been home to the greatest and richest of civilisations. He sniffled, as if on the point of tears — and then tried to sell me a small terracotta head, one inch high, of a woman with a pinched nose and unruly hair. Mauryan, he insisted, but it looked a little too perfect to me, as if freshly moulded. I said so, and he looked at me apologetically, as if to say 'well, I have to make money somehow', but did not say a word. He then lifted his hand high, and dashed the terracotta head against a paving stone. It broke into many pieces. He strode off, and I headed towards a small building with a large sign that

18

said, misleadingly, 'Museum'. Inside were four laminated black-and-white photos of the excavations, and a single empty display case, with a sign that read 'terracotta figurines'.

A detailed description survives of Patna under the first Mauryan emperor, one of those rare accounts that cuts a small window through the opaque haze of ancient history. And the account itself has a peculiarly peripatetic history. It was written by Megasthenes, who travelled to Patna 2300 years ago, as an ambassador of the Seleucid Empire, founded by one of Alexander the Great's generals. The full text does not survive. Instead, there are dozens of long and short quotations from his *Indika*, reproduced or summarised in works of the Roman period. Some of these much later works set out to demonstrate that Megasthenes was a fantasist. He was one of the principal targets of the more-than-forthright geographer Strabo, who, writing during the lifetime of Jesus Christ, said that 'generally speaking, the men who hitherto have written on the affairs of India are a set of liars'.

Like other early Greeks writing about India, Megasthenes wrote at length about strange monsters and half-humans who lived in India — and by Strabo's more rationalist times, India had become more than a place of fantasy, and was no longer seen as being beyond the edge of the known world. Megasthenes' reputation was damaged in the Roman period, his original text was lost, and he was largely forgotten until the eighteenth century.[2] He was 'rediscovered' by Orientalists, mainly servants of the British East India Company, who busied themselves in

[2] The hyper-sceptical historians of the Roman period probably trusted Megasthenes' account of India most — that is, only to a small degree. They tended to dismiss other accounts, such as that of Ctesias, out of hand. Megasthenes emerges as the most important, if slightly unreliable, western source on early India during the late eighteenth century, in large part because of the work of the most influential Orientalist of that period, William Jones.

India with the task of classifying everything and everybody that came their way. The ancient Roman geography books that quoted Megasthenes were disinterred, and used as if they were moth-eaten travel guides. Sanskrit texts were scanned for further clues, and startling breakthroughs were made in ancient European and Indian chronology. Indian timelines, still seen as largely mythological in the west, could now be synchronised with the early Greek period. The king known by Megasthenes as Sandrocottus, turned out to be, on further investigation and with a little linguo-labial imagination, the same person as Chandragupta — Ashoka the Great's grandfather and founder of the Mauryan Empire. And the city that Megasthenes called Palibothra was the same as the Mauryan capital, Pataliputra — now Patna.

Patna under the early Mauryan emperors was probably the world's most populous city,[3] and Megasthenes was suitably awestruck. He is amazed by India's richness, its fertility, its tigers, by the generosity shown to foreigners, by its abstemious ascetics, its engineers, its musicians and, most of all, by its elephants. Large parts of the surviving fragments of his *Indika* read like a layman's guide to looking after a pet pachyderm. The best treatment for an elephant with a deep and inflamed gash, Megasthenes informs us, is to insert pieces of pork, uncooked and bloody, into the wound; while, less controversially, eye inflammations in elephants should be treated with cow's milk.

Patna, meanwhile, is described as a 'very large and wealthy' city overlooking the Ganges, with 'sumptuous palaces', surrounded by walls more than twenty-nine kilometres in length with a deep, wide defensive moat on the landward side. These walls, continues Megasthenes, a little overwhelmed, have

[3] According to the indomitable urban statistician and heterodox historian Tertius Chandler, Pataliputra was, for more than a century, the most populous city in the world. He claims that Pataliputra took over this position from Alexandria in about 300 BC, and was replaced by the Chinese city of Xian in about 190 BC.

570 towers and no less than forty-six gates — the existence of the walls and several of its gates would later be confirmed by twentieth-century archaeology.[4] Chandragupta had by far the largest standing army in India (and probably the world) with at least 60,000 foot soldiers, 30,000 cavalry and 8000 elephants. Megasthenes describes how the city was organised — with six committees, each with five members, looking after industrial arts, foreigners, birth and death records, trade and commerce, manufacturing and tax collection. There were officials to superintend the rivers, inspect the sluices, construct roads and place milestones at regular intervals along those roads. It's one of the earliest detailed accounts of urban life and government, curiously ignored by the great modern historians of the city.[5] And there's some marvellous detail. Emperor Chandragupta, for instance, had a personal guard consisting of female soldiers, and whenever he travelled outside his palace to dispense justice, a masseur would rub his limbs with wooden rollers.

Although it's the earliest surviving foreign description of India, it is clear from Megasthenes' account that there were lots of other foreign visitors, and more of an infrastructure to care for them than there is now:

Indian officers are appointed whose duty is to see that no foreigner is wronged. Should any of them lose his health, they send physicians to attend him, and if he dies they bury him,

[4] Megasthenes describes Pataliputra as being the shape of a parallelogram with sides eighty stadia by fifteen stadia (roughly 15 kilometres by 2.7 kilometres). The Roman naturalist Aelian said, in what may be a further quote from Megasthenes, that neither Ecbatana nor Susa — the greatest of the ancient Persian cities (modern-day Hamadan and Shush respectively) — could come close to matching Pataliputra for splendour or magnificence.

[5] Pataliputra is almost unmentioned in the classic western studies of the city. It's entirely missing from Mumford's *The City in History*, though there is an un-indexed reference to Ashoka. There is also a very brief reference to the dimensions of Patna in John Reader's *Cities*.

and deliver such property as he leaves to his relatives. The judges also decide cases in which foreigners are concerned with the greatest care and come down sharply on those who take unfair advantage of them.

There are several other sources for this period[6] — and these enable historians both to confirm and to dispute some of the things Megasthenes says, or rather the things his Roman interpolators say he said. And we certainly shouldn't believe everything that's ascribed to him. Slavery and writing did not exist in Mauryan India, according to Megasthenes. We know they both did — though it seems likely that the condition of slaves was less abject than in Greek territories, and that knowledge of writing was limited to the very few. On the other hand, he refers to reeds that secrete a sweet syrup and to 'trees on which wool grows', and one can imagine Megasthenes' detractors scoffing at such fantasies. In fact, these are probably the first references, in western texts, to sugar cane and to cotton — both native to south Asia.

Megasthenes himself, as an ambassador, a traveller, a Greek abroad, barely emerges from the multiplicity of variant texts. And there are some telling mysteries about Megasthenes' mission that we may never be able to solve. We know of a peace treaty between the Indian Mauryans and the Greek Seleucids — as a result of which the latter gave up much of their territory close to India, and received, in return, five hundred elephants. This may explain why elephants were written about at such length by Megasthenes — the Seleucids needed to know how to look after five hundred of them. Most intriguingly, though, as part of the peace treaty, the unnamed daughter of the Seleucid

[6] There is an impressively wide range of Indian sources for this period, including the classic work on Indian statecraft, the *Arthashastra* (which may possibly belong to a later period), the stone-carved edicts of Ashoka, and several Buddhist and Jain texts, as well as other Greek accounts.

emperor was sent to Chandragupta in Patna, possibly under Megasthenes' escort, so that the two imperial houses could be joined in marriage. The implication is that Chandragupta's grandson Ashoka the Great might have been partly Seleucid and that therefore Greek blood might have pulsed through the veins and arteries of India's greatest dynasty.

'He should be called Ashoka the Greek,' Tony Mango once joked to me. He was both proud of and amused by the ubiquity of his fellow countrymen, and he delighted in the ancient Indo-Greek connection. I think I may have offended Tony by responding to his remark with the question, 'What, like "Phil the Greek"?',

referring to the British piss-takers' nickname that served to transform the popular image of Queen Elizabeth's husband from a rather thoughtless aristocratic buffoon to a down-at-heel  spiv.[7] Tony, I think, winced at my remark. As a Greek in British India in the 1930s, he was from a caste apart, neither ruler nor ruled; and he detected a certain understated prejudice against him on the part of some of the British. And the 'Phil the Greek' monicker manages to mock both Greeks and the Duke of Edinburgh. I didn't say to Tony that I thought it of little ultimate

[7] He was born on the Greek island of Corfu as Prince Philip of Greece and Denmark. The last viceroy of India, Lord Mountbatten, was his maternal uncle. Prince Philip has made the headlines several times for what have been seen as insensitive remarks about India and Indians. In August 1999, while touring a Scottish factory and looking at a fusebox, he said, 'It looks as though it was put in by an Indian.' He later explained, 'I meant to say cowboys. I just got my cowboys and Indians mixed up.'

importance whether Ashoka (or the British royal family) was really partly Greek, but the notion of it clearly gives Philhellenes a certain frisson of excitement. For me, I delight in the mixing of bloodlines, noble and ignoble — for no better reason than that it infuriates those who are obsessed with ethnic purity — although I also have a suspicion that widespread miscegenation might contribute to world peace.

We don't know if Ashoka spoke Greek, but he certainly knew people who did. From his capital in Patna, Ashoka ordered that inscriptions be chiselled on rocks and pillars across his realm. Several dozen survive, and are among the earliest deciphered Indian inscriptions. The texts vary, but most refer, indirectly, to Ashoka's conversion to Buddhism — and his wish to see others follow him on the same true path. Most of the edicts are in ancient Indian languages. But some were also written in Greek[8] (and in Aramaic — which would be the mother tongue of Jesus of Nazareth more than 250 years later). It would be another two millennia before a European would learn to write in an Indian language.

Ashoka's edicts also record that he sent ambassadors to five named Greek kings (one in Asia, two in North Africa and two in Europe) with the aim of converting them to Buddhism — he refers to it as 'conquest by dharma'. Of what happened to Ashoka's ambassadors, there is no trace; they disappear from history. They may have died en route, or never actually left Patna, or they may, on the other hand, have even set up Buddhist communities in Greek territories, for all we know — and we know very little. However, it is clear that like Alexander,

[8] More than fifty Ashokan edicts, chiselled on rocks, pillars and cave walls, have been found in India, Nepal, Pakistan and Afghanistan. They used a variety of scripts — including, to the amazement of western archaeologists, Greek and Aramaic. The Buddha, or specifically Buddhist beliefs, are not referred to in the edicts, and some historians argue that Ashoka may not have considered himself a Buddhist.

roughly sixty years earlier, Ashoka saw himself at the centre of a shrunken world, where interaction between the people of different continents was normal and good practice. These two 'Greats' of Classical civilisation had a knowledge of and an interest in other lands that would put several modern 'world' leaders to shame. The grand scale of their ambition and their self-confidence is hard to over-estimate.

The longevity and varied nature of the early Greek connection with India has been largely forgotten. It is usually limited to the brief Alexander episode and the stories that it later spawned.[9] Even though Alexander and his army never actually made it beyond the Indus valley, and even though his presence in the subcontinent is unmentioned in contemporary Indian texts. In fact, the Greek connection lasted almost eight hundred years. That's a longer period than from the arrival of the first European colonists in India in 1498 to the current day. And it is not as if the ancient Greeks didn't leave their mark — as any numismatist or historian of ancient art will tell you. Thousands of coins have been found that were minted by Indo-Greek kings who ruled a series of principalities on the borderlands that now form Pakistan and Afghanistan — many of them with bilingual inscriptions in Greek and an Indian language. There are so many of them that they can be picked up on eBay for less than twenty dollars

[9] The Roman histories of the Alexander period provide early references to widow-burning, later best known as suttee or *sati*. There was also great interest in the gymnosophists, or naked philosophers (*gymnos* means naked in Greek), whom Alexander was said to have met near the Indus. One of them, Calanus, is described as having travelled westwards with Alexander's army — and committed suicide in Susa by building a funeral pyre and setting it alight. He impressed the Greeks by not flinching in the fire. He is quoted as saying to Alexander — as the pyre burned — 'see you in Babylon', usually interpreted as a prediction of Alexander's death. It is not clear who the gymnosophists were — possibly either the naked Hindu ascetics known as Naga sadhus or Digamber Jain monks (*digamber* means sky-clad), who to this day do not wear clothes.

apiece. And there is, as I write, a guide price of two hundred dollars (lower bids accepted) for a silver tetradrachm of Demetrius I, who converted, like several other Indo-Greek kings, to Buddhism and is portrayed, jowled but firm of chin, with an elephant headdress on the front, and with the words ΒΑΣΙΛΕΩΣ ΔΗΜΗΤΡΙΟΥ[10] on the back, next to an image of a naked Heracles crowning himself and carrying a lion-skin. Then there is what has become known simply as 'Gandhara art' — a sublime syncretic blossoming of sculpture, derived from both Greek and Indian figurative traditions, and available, at a price, at gandhara.com.au, a Sydney-based online gallery. There are dozens of heavenly beings and buddhas-in-waiting dressed *à la grecque*, with gently pleated robes, finely chiselled European noses, twirled moustaches, and dozens of tiny coils of hair. Several of them, we are informed, are of museum-quality, and prices can be obtained on request. And there are scores of little heads, not dissimilar to the one that was smashed to the ground by the modern guardian of Pataliputra.

There's one other souvenir of the ancient Indo-Greek connection, that you can't buy and isn't even in a museum — and which became an unlikely object of veneration. It stands, unshaded, in a field of grass in the centre of India. A Greek ambassador, whose name, Heliodorus, means gift of the sun, left it there more than two thousand years ago as a gift for the kings of a forgotten dynasty. The pillar of Heliodorus is a tall sandstone column, six and a half metres high. When the British archaeologist Alexander

[10] Transliterated as *Basileos Demetriou*, meaning 'of King Demetrius'. He — or successor kings known as Demetrius II and Demetrius III — appears to be the same as the king known in Indian sources as Dharmamitra, who invaded what is now Bihar in the second century BC.

Cunningham chanced upon it in 1887, the entire pillar was covered in a thick vermilion paste made of red lead and oil, and it was a place of Hindu pilgrimage. The pilgrims had smeared the paste onto the pillar as a mark of devotion. And the deity was the pillar itself — known as Khambh Baba.[11] Cunningham wanted to scrape the paste off, but villagers persuaded him not to do so. 'I was very unwillingly obliged to be content with the examination of the red surface,' he declared in his notes, and wandered off, having dated the pillar to the Gupta period around the fourth century AD. A less obliging British visitor, an engineer called Lake, returned to the pillar two years later and began scraping the paste

off. Underneath, written in Brahmi script, was an inscription which would stun Edwardian historians of India. The inscription gave the name of the donor, Heliodorus — a clearly Greek name. It described him as the ambassador of the Greek King Antialcidas of Taxila — which meant that Cunningham's date for the pillar was wrong by almost half a millennium and that it had been erected in about 110 BC. It proved that two hundred years after Alexander, Greeks were travelling deep into the interior of India — far from the traditional international trade routes along the coast or down the great rivers of the north. But the descriptions also astonished historians by describing Heliodorus as a devotee

[11] *Khambh* means pillar and *baba* is a term of respect often used for saints and ascetics.

of the god Vishnu — and this challenged the widely held belief that Hinduism had never allowed foreigners to convert.

Heliodorus' pillar attracts few visitors these days. Bhopal is the nearest city, which despite being one of India's prettiest state capitals, ranks — as a result of the industrial disaster of 1984 — next to Chernobyl at the top of any list of unlikely tourist hubs. Even closer to the pillar are the great Buddhist hilltop stupa of Sanchi, and the superb rock-cut temples of Udayagiri. But in the full hour I spent at the pillar not a soul came — tourist or pilgrim. The only human presence was an old woman, so deeply wrinkled that half her face was in permanent shadow, and who was wrapped up tightly in a red blanket, as if she was preparing to hibernate. The pillar is part of the huge modern empire ruled by the Archaeological Survey of India, and it stands alone like an enormous sundial in a scrappy patch of green meadow down a country lane close to the River Bes. The pillar itself is a complex piece of ancient stonework. Its lower portion, on which the inscription is still clearly visible, is octagonal. Higher up each facet is bisected, and bisected again, so that the column becomes sixteen-sided, then thirty-two-sided and finally, the upper portion of the column is circular. On top of the pillar, hard to make out because of its height, are a bell-shaped capital and a broken abacus with what looks like the image of a goose and some flowers. Originally, the pillar would have been surmounted by the image of a man-eagle god. The inscription describes the pillar as a *Garuda-dhvajo* — a Garuda column — of which many other later examples survive. Garuda is the eagle god, after whom Indonesia — with its own strong Hindu tradition — named its national airline. In India, Garuda is most often portrayed anthropomorphically as a hunchback with wings and a huge beaked nose. He is the mount or vehicle of Vishnu and is often seen bearing the weight of a much larger Vishnu on his shoulders, and struggling, it always seems, to flap his wings.

Most archaeological sites like these have a watchman, who will point out, for a small fee, things that a visitor might otherwise miss, and supply some often entirely spurious information — usually about a long-distance secret tunnel. Here there was no one but the old woman who alternately lay and sat on the grass, with, I thought, the distracted look of dementia in her eyes. In fact, she turned out to be more sane and articulate than me. I paced around the compound measuring with my full stride the dimensions of the site, looking, I suppose, a little like a jackbooted soldier on parade — and this clearly intrigued her. She beckoned me over with a wave of her arm, and that simplest of Hindi words, *ao*, 'come'. She had disturbed my stride count, and I had to restart my march. When I'd finished I went over to her. She made me sit and explain what I was doing there. Once I had justified my strange behaviour to her in my verb-deficient, gender-ignorant Hindi, she began telling me her story. She was dying, she told me before anything else, and she was in pain and always uncomfortable. She liked to spend her last days here, in the open. Her grandson would come and fetch her in the evenings when the sun was setting. She remembered that when she moved nearby as a newly-wed, many people came to pray at the pillar. There was a small hut next to the pillar where the priest used to live — but the government broke it down. There were newer temples in the town, and people liked to go there now.

'Why did they pray at the pillar?' I asked.

'They believed that the pillar was once a human being. I believed it too. They said that a long time ago, a great king came here with an army and met a saint called Hirapuri who was very holy. Hirapuri refused food and drink for six months every year. The king was so impressed by Hirapuri that he asked if he could stay with him. Hirapuri said yes, he could stay, but that if he did so, then he would never be able to leave, not for all eternity. The king agreed and was transformed into the pillar, Khambh Baba. Everyone used to know the story of the pillar, but now it's forgotten. No one's interested now.' She fell into a thoughtful silence, before resuming, looking straight into my eyes as if performing an act of confession. 'I believed it with all my heart. Then they knocked down the priest's hut and told the priest to leave. Then I began to wonder if it was true. Now, I think it's really just an old pillar — but I still sometimes pray here, and leave some flowers. Nobody comes much any more, just a few foreigners — like you. There's a gardener, but he's useless and drunk most of the time — and the goats eat the grass.' She shifted uncomfortably on the ground.

I began writing up her story in my notebook, repeating the key statements back to her. 'What,' I asked, as an afterthought, 'was the king's name?' Without hesitation, she responded 'Sikandar'. A chill ran through me. Sikandar is the Hindi (and Persian) form of the name Alexander. 'Unani?' I asked, using the old Hindi (and Persian) word for Greek, from the same root as 'Ionian'. Yes, she nodded. I could hardly believe it. The pillar had been worshipped as an incarnation of Alexander the Great. How had the archaeologists and historians missed this extraordinary fact? It implied that the local population had known, long before the deciphering of the inscription, that the pillar had a Greek connection. It indicated that there were, after all, Indian sources for Alexander's Indian adventures that hadn't been drawn from European accounts. I imagined myself dazzling the academic world with my monograph on a hitherto unknown Alexandrine tradition in central India. I began asking my interlocutor how old she was and how long she had lived near the pillar. She couldn't answer either question with precision, but she said she had moved here when she got married, and that her second child — her only son — was born before the British left. I calculated that this probably meant she was born in the mid or late 1920s. So it seemed highly likely that she would have learned the story from village elders who would have been born long before 1909, when the inscription was deciphered, and the Greek connection discovered. But could she remember, I asked, after all these years, who first told her the story?

'Everyone knew the story, old and young. There was a special festival for Khambh Baba each year. And everyone knew about Hirapuri and the pillar.'

'But what about Sikandar?'

She smiled, broadly. 'Oh that. I learned about that just now. A month ago.'

'What do you mean?'

'A man like you,' she pinched the skin of my forearm, as if to see if its colour were real, 'came here, on his own — like you. His Hindi was very good, better than yours, and he wore orange clothes. His hair was matted like Lord Shiva's.' She laughed out loud. 'And he had a beard. He said he was a Hindu, and that he loved Krishna. He was the person who told me that the king's name was Sikandar, and that he came from Greece.' She could remember nothing more about her previous visitor, and was clearly exhausted by our conversation.

I left confused and a little crestfallen. My imagined academic triumph was clearly stillborn. I had unfairly assumed that archaeologists had failed to interview the locals properly. And so it seemed the story of the pillar being an incarnation of Alexander the Great was a piece of fiction newly spread by a foreigner. I now wonder whether he just made the story up, or if someone had told him that Alexander had been turned to stone. And I have become a little obsessed by this foreigner — and he is beginning to haunt me. Everywhere I go, I expect to find a Hindi-speaking white man with dreadlocks; a story-telling Krishna devotee, dressed in orange. He even appears occasionally in my dreams, ashen-faced, looking like a younger, more handsome version of myself. He is becoming my alter ego. He is deeply spiritual and I am not; he believes in miracles and I do not; he sees simplicity where I see nuance. He inhabits a very different India from the one I know.

31

An Early Intermission

I FIRST MET Shireen at just after 7pm on Tuesday the 18th of August 1987. I was less than three metres from the precise spot at which I had appeared on this earth a quarter of a century earlier. She was 7191 kilometres from home. I opened the front door of my parents' house in London, and was immediately blinded by the evening sun reflecting off the white skirt and blouse[1] of my future wife, who was dressed as if she was auditioning for the role of Sandy in the film *Grease*. Except, unlike Olivia Newton-John, her hair was black, so black and voluminous, that it seemed to swallow the sunlight — like an eclipse. For a moment it seemed as if all that hair could leave little room for a face, but as my eyes corrected for the sunlight I made out a quizzical smile, beaming brown eyes and a pert nose. Her mother stood behind, sari-clad, and pushed her daughter forward.

It was less than a week before the UK leg of the marriage of Shireen's brother to my sister — and we were regularly thrust into each other's company over the next few days. It did not take us long to fall for each other, to the bemusement of both our families, and of ourselves. Ten days later she moved into my flat. Our early conversations had a strange interplanetary feel to them. We were from worlds that intellectually were very

[1] Shireen informs me, as is her wont, that my memory is at fault here. She was all in white, she insists, but in Indian clothes — a long, white *salwar kameez* with *dhoti*-style trousers — and wouldn't have dreamed of wearing western clothes for her first visit to her brother's parents-in-law's house. She insists that she was wearing what became known as her Olivia Newton-John outfit, in which the white skirt had denim patches and metal studs, at our second meeting. It is possible, of course, that she is right, and I am wrong — though her assertions on the subject have done nothing to eradicate my clear memories of her, and what she was wearing, on that balmy summer evening.

alike, but also startlingly different, at a more prosaic level. Her first language was English, she had read more British poetry than me, and had far superior table manners. But she lightly sprinkled her sentences with words of Hindi and Gujarati, had never made herself a cup of tea, had never seen a vacuum cleaner, and was totally flummoxed when I told her I was going on holiday to Pakistan. 'What? On your way to India?' 'No, I'm just going to Pakistan.' 'But why would anyone go all the way to Pakistan and not to India?' India, quite understandably, was the centre of her world, indeed *the* world. It was, until then, somewhere on my periphery, a blackish hole, a large place of which I knew little.

We swapped stories of childhood, and we seemed to be as much separated by time as by distance. She appeared to have had something close to a British upper middle-class Edwardian childhood in Britain, complete with servants, ancient nursery rhymes ('Grace had an English heart', 'Naughty, sporty college boy'[2]) and a home where grown-ups and children ate separately. Brown stew and Irish stew were among the dishes that appeared each week on the nursery menu. In fact, I would later realise that I was learning more about the Parsis, the community of Zoroastrian Indians she belonged to, than about the country she lived in. Some aspects of her Parsi life were harder to fathom. She had drunk cow's urine during her coming-of-age ceremony, her dead relatives were normally left out in the sun to be picked at by vultures — and her brothers bore the names of ancient Persian kings. I felt unable to match these exotic customs with anything of more than passing interest. Though the British bath-tub was to Shireen a curious foreign horror, a means

[2] The first song is better known as *The Ballad of Grace Darling*, about a nineteenth-century Englishwoman who saved the crew of a sinking ship. Wordsworth and Swinburne wrote poems about Grace Darling. The second song is better known as *When It's Night-time in Italy* written in 1923 and later performed by the Everly Brothers.

only, she insisted, of wallowing in one's own filth. She had a point. She would pinch and fondle the fruit in Portobello Market, much to the exasperation of the stall-holders, and once in a supermarket, I found her tasting tubes of previously unopened cheese spread. 'You can't do that,' I said, agitated, and pulled her away, worried that she might be arrested, even deported. She was unabashed, unapologetic. 'But how can you buy something you haven't tasted? They weren't very good, anyway. My stepfather wants to make cheese spread in India and I thought I might send some to him.'

I began picking up a curious medley of semi-intimate vocabulary from Gujarati and Hindi — *bagal* was armpit, *nunga* was naked, *susu* was piss, *saas ki budbu* was bad breath, *sipla* was cissy — none of which were of much use outside our relationship — and replaced words that both of us knew perfectly well in English. I found these words more exotic, sensual, than their Anglo-Saxon equivalents, though, in fact, most of them belonged to the realm of baby talk, something I only realised when we had children of our own.

Together we watched an English-language film called *The*

Householder,[3] set in Delhi, about a young Indian couple learning to fall in love with each other. Theirs was an arranged marriage, and the husband complains incessantly about his wife's domestic incompetence, demanding that the house be 'spick and span', and inviting his tyrannical mother to stay in order to teach his wife household skills. The words 'spick and span' became our joke — Shireen had no desire to be a domestic goddess, and she was so caustic about an Indian meal I once made that I have hardly cooked since. It's not surprising then that we ate out a lot. And as an ostensibly feminist English male, I even allowed her to pay for the odd meal. She informed me after paying for one dinner that the restaurant bill amounted to more than three months' salary of her beloved Manga, the servant who had played a central role in bringing her up, particularly after the early death of her father. It was my first sense of how different India's economy was from the ones I knew. I suddenly thought of myself as rich. Most foreigners visiting modern India feel the same, and many find the sight of widespread poverty deeply unsettling. There can be no greater contrast with how most ancient visitors to India felt — who almost universally saw it as a land of untold wealth.

[3] *The Householder* was filmed in 1962. Although it's about a north Indian couple in an arranged marriage, in other ways, the film is a discreet testament to miscegenation. It was the first film made by Bombay-born Ismail Merchant and California-born James Ivory — whose film and personal partnership survived until Merchant's death in 2005. The stars were Leela Naidu, whose mother was French and father was Indian, and Shashi Kapoor, who would marry the British actress Jennifer Kendal. The screenplay was written by Ruth Prawer Jhabvala, born in Germany, and married to a Parsi architect. I've written at length about the film in a previous book, *Delhi: Adventures in a Megacity*.

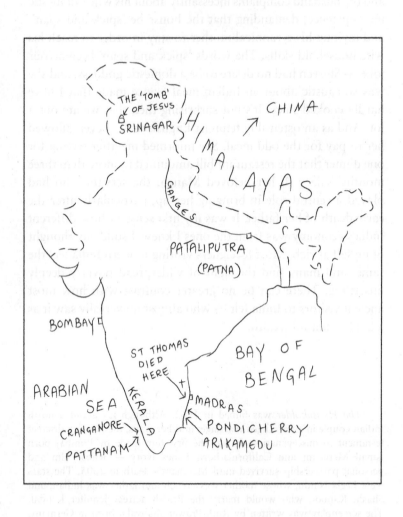

THE 'TOMB'
OF JESUS

SRINAGAR

CHINA

HIMALAYAS

GANGES

PATALIPUTRA
(PATNA)

BOMBAY

ST THOMAS
DIED
HERE

BAY OF
BENGAL

ARABIAN
SEA

KERALA

MADRAS

CRANGANORE

PONDICHERRY

PATTANAM

ARIKAMEDU

*Chapter Two: In which the Author
visits the tomb of Jesus, identifies the
forearm of Doubting Thomas, and
ponders the relationship between
chicken's milk and Indian mushrooms*

IN THE BACKSTREETS of downtown Srinagar, the summer capital
of Indian Kashmir, is an old and not very impressive building
known as the Rozabal shrine. On my first visit in 2008, the taxi
circled around, the driver asking for directions several times,
before we could find it — a minor Muslim tomb in a city of
many mosques and mausoleums. The Rozabal shrine was on a
street corner, a modest stone building with a multi-tiered green
roof. A watchman let me inside and allowed me to inspect, but
not photograph, the smaller wooden chamber within. It had a
perforated screen like a trellis, and through the gaps I could see
a gravestone covered in a green cloth. A year later, the shrine
was firmly shut, its gate padlocked, because it had attracted
too many visitors. The grave contains, according to an eclectic
combination of New Age Christians, heterodox Muslims and
da Vinci codistas, the mortal remains of another candidate for
the most important visitor of all time to India. A non-European
who could pull rank on both Alexander the Great and the Beatles
for international renown and popularity.[1] The tomb is officially
the burial site of Youza Asaph, a medieval Muslim preacher.

---

[1] The Beatles visited Delhi briefly in 1966 on a stopover from a disastrous
visit to the Philippines, and then had a much longer and rather controversial
stay at Rishikesh in 1968 (see Chapter 14). Only George Harrison made
it to Kashmir, where Ravi Shankar taught him to play the sitar. It is not
known if he visited the Rozabal shrine. John Lennon famously said, in
1966, that the Beatles were 'more popular than Jesus'.

But a growing number of people believe that this is the tomb of Jesus of Nazareth.

'What else could they do? They had to close it. It was becoming a security problem,' Riaz told me. He was back in Srinagar from London where he was studying. His family home almost overlooks the tomb — and he was witheringly dismissive of the notion that Jesus was buried there. 'First, it was just a story spread by the local shopkeepers — because some mad professor[2] had said it was Jesus' tomb. They thought it would be good for business. Tourists would come, after all these years of violence that had scared foreigners away. And then it got into *Lonely Planet*, and too many people started coming here. And

---

[2] In fact, the notion that Jesus died in Kashmir appears to date back to the late nineteenth century. Nikolai Notovitch, a Russian traveller visiting a Buddhist monastery in Ladakh, claims to have been shown an ancient biography of Jesus describing his life and death in India. The derivative 2008 best-selling book, *The Rozabal Line*, by the Indian writer Ashwin Sanghi, uses the Rozabal legend to create a *Da Vinci Code*-like thriller about the life and bloodline of Jesus.

one foreigner ...' — he gave me an apologetic look — 'broke off a bit from the tomb to take home with him. So that's why it's closed now.'[3] On cue, a couple of unwashed and exhausted Australians appeared, carrying the latest edition of the *Lonely Planet* guide to India, which, sure enough, carried the tale of Jesus' tomb, with some caveats about crackpots and blasphemy. They asked me to take a photo of them outside the shrine — but did not seem desperately disappointed that it was closed, and they had no intention of hacking off part of the grave as a souvenir. The tomb of Jesus was just another place to tick off on their tourist-in-India must-visit list.

The ruins of a Buddhist monastery at Harwan in a spectacular location halfway up a mountainside on the northern outskirts of Srinagar are not yet mentioned in *Lonely Planet*. It's a spot that was until recently out of bounds, because, as a senior police officer told me, it was 'infested with terrorists'. But the watchman seemed prepared for the arrival of mass tourism, with his  fifty words of English, and his hidden stock of pieces of ancient terracotta tiles for sale. He informed me that Jesus was among the religious leaders who attended the fourth Buddhist

[3] The fourteenth-century armchair traveller, Sir John Mandeville (see Chapter 5), described how visitors to Jesus' 'other' tomb, in the Church of the Holy Sepulchre in Jerusalem used to break off bits of stone from the structure — until a wall was built around it.

Council[4] in AD 80, and even pointed to the place where he sat.

The stories of Jesus in India, which largely date back to the late nineteenth century, are not just aimed at gullible tourists. They need to be seen in the wider context of attempts to explain some of the striking similarities between Christianity and Buddhism, a matter of great interest to nineteenth-century scholars, and to the desire among some proselytising Christians (and one sect of Muslims), to root the story of Jesus in Indian soil. They talk of the missing years of Jesus, unmentioned in the gospels or the Koran, between the ages of twelve and thirty — when, they argue, he was in India, picking up Buddhist ideas. Others have argued, just as implausibly, that he came to Britain, a theory that was in vogue when William Blake asked,

> And did those feet in ancient time
> Walk upon England's mountains green?
> And was the Holy Lamb of God
> On England's pleasant pastures seen?[5]

[4] The fourth Buddhist Council in Kashmir is often described as the moment when a schism emerged in Buddhism between the Hinayana and Mahayana schools. The former aimed to preserve the original non-theistic teachings of the Buddha, while the Mahayana school incorporated new ideas and turned the Buddha and other enlightened beings into semi-deities. The Hinayana school would dominate in Sri Lanka and south-east Asia, while the Mahayana teachings would spread to Tibet, China and north-east Asia. The previous Buddhist council was held in Pataliputra in about 250 BC and may even have been presided over by Ashoka.

[5] Blake's poem refers to an obscure tradition that a youthful Jesus accompanied his tin-trading uncle, Joseph of Arimathea, to the tin mines of Cornwall. These traditions also talk of Joseph of Arimathea returning to England with the Holy Grail, the chalice that Jesus had used at the Last Supper — and which became the subject of a series of medieval legends and a Monty Python film. Blake's poem was set to music in the early twentieth century, and as *Jerusalem*, became an unofficial English (rather than British) national anthem. It was also adopted by revolutionaries and socialists as an anti-capitalist hymn, with its reference to 'dark satanic mills', and its promise of a new Jerusalem.

These aren't traditions that have entirely died out. The US-based Christian sect known as the Church Universal and Triumphant is the best-known modern supporter of the belief that Jesus lived in Kashmir (though they don't believe he died there). Its members also claim that its founder, the aptly-named Mark Prophet, was a reincarnation of the poet Longfellow, the Arthurian knight Sir Lancelot, and the Egyptian Pharaoh Akhenaten.[6] In Islam, in which Jesus is the penultimate prophet, there is also a minority tradition adopted by the heterodox Ahmadiyya sect, whose theology largely dates from the nineteenth century, that Rozabal contains the grave of Jesus — and that Jesus is in fact the long-awaited future Buddha, otherwise known to Buddhists as the Maitreya.

The suggestion that Jesus lived in India tends to be dismissed out of hand by professional historians, sometimes with loud guffawing. However, there's a deeper, longer, more plausible tradition that it wasn't Jesus who was the first Christian to come to India but someone who knew his body intimately. St Thomas[7] is best known in the west as Doubting Thomas, the

[6] They suffered a major setback when their prophecy that a worldwide nuclear war would break out in 1990 did not take place. The Church Universal and Triumphant followed many of the ideas of Madame Blavatsky whose India-based Theosophical Movement believed in 'Ascended Masters', all famous people from history who lived on (and on), reincarnated as modern spiritual leaders. Mark Prophet's wife, Elizabeth Clare, was said to be a reincarnation of queens Nefertiti, Guinevere and Marie Antoinette.

[7] St Thomas the Apostle is not to be confused with the European St Thomases — Aquinas or à Becket or More. He was a Palestinian carpenter who, according to some traditions, was Jesus' twin brother. Both the Greek (*didyma*) and Aramaic (*ta'uma*) versions of Thomas' name mean twin. Philip Pullman ransacked this tradition for his 2010 book about the Virgin Mary's twin boys, *The Good Man Jesus and the Scoundrel Christ*. There's also an early tradition that another apostle, St Bartholomew, came to India. Both Bartholomew and Thomas were born as Jews, but according to Jewish tradition, the first Jews came to India earlier than them. There's even a community of nine thousand people known as the Bnei Menashe living in north-east India who claim descent from one of the lost tribes of Israel, sent into captivity by the Babylonians more than seven hundred years before the birth of Christ.

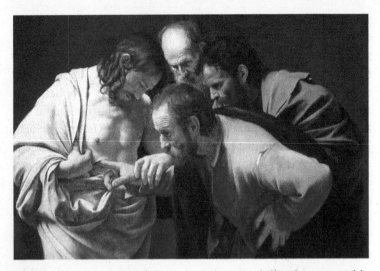

apostle who — in one of Caravaggio's most chillingly memorable images — stuck his finger into Jesus' gaping chest wound to see if it was real. For most Indian Christians, he is the man who introduced Christianity to India. The Thomas Christians of Kerala, now split into seven sects, and known as the Nasranis (derived from Nazareth), claim to be descendants of the apostle's earliest converts. They believe that Thomas arrived in coastal Kerala in AD 52, at a place called Cranganore — where a church keeps part of the arm that touched Christ. And they believe that Thomas was killed, martyred for his beliefs, twenty years later, on a hill that overlooks the runway of Madras airport, close to the eastern coast of India.

A bizarrely entertaining account of Thomas' travels and death in India, deserving of a wider readership and a modern translation, has survived in a non-canonical early Christian text known as the *Acts of Thomas*. Several early versions of the text have survived in Aramaic and Greek, the oldest of which is thought to date back to at least the third century AD, and possibly earlier. In the *Acts*, we hear how a man-servant who strikes Thomas at a feast because he doesn't join in the festivities then goes outside to fetch some water, where he is killed and torn to pieces by a lion. The man-servant's severed hand is then dragged into the banquet hall, as Thomas had earlier prophesied, by a black dog.[8] Thomas later encounters a talking serpent, who has killed a handsome young man whom he caught having sex with a beautiful girl. He challenges the serpent to show his powers by sucking the venom out of the dead man who lies, purple, by the roadside. In doing so, the serpent swallows his own venom and explodes, while the young man comes back to life and falls at Thomas' feet. This is all quite apart from the more everyday matters of raising the dead and battling Satan — which he accomplishes with considerable success.

St Thomas comes across, in the *Acts of Thomas*, as a deeply gloomy and humourless character — a curmudgeon of the highest order. He rants about the awfulness of children[9] and his main contribution to Christian theology is to demand that even married couples should give up sexual intercourse — a strategy adopted by several Christian sects which all, for obvious reasons, quickly died out. He is sent to India to convert, to preach hellfire but not — as in the Jesus-in-Kashmir myth — to learn. India, he declares, in his only general comment on his new country, is a 'land of error'.

His gloominess may have been compounded by the fact that Thomas never wanted to go to India in the first place. Indeed

---

[8] There is a fine painting of this scene by Luca di Tommè in the Scottish National Gallery in Edinburgh. It's one of a series of four paintings about Thomas in India by the fourteenth-century Sienese master — which shows that the non-canonical stories of Thomas were known in the medieval period.

[9] Thomas is quoted as saying, '[Most] children become useless, oppressed of devils, some openly and some invisibly, for they become either lunatic or half-withered or blind or deaf or dumb or paralytic or foolish; and if they be sound, again they will be vain, doing useless or abominable acts, for they will be caught either in adultery or murder or theft or fornication, and by all these will ye be afflicted.'

he is a pretty strong candidate for the most reluctant visitor to India of all time. He travels there under quite extraordinary circumstances — sold as a slave by, of all unlikely slave-traders, Jesus Christ. According to the *Acts of Thomas*, the apostles draw lots to see where in the world they each should go to spread the word of Christianity. Thomas picks India, his short straw, and then announces to his fellow apostles that he is not willing to go there. He gives all kinds of excuses — about being weak of flesh and not being able to travel, and of not having the appropriate linguistic skills. Jesus appears to him in the night and orders him to go to India, and Thomas refuses a second time, declaring, 'Whither thou wouldst send me, send me, but elsewhere, for unto the Indians I will not go.' In order to force Thomas to go to India, Jesus comes to earth to sell him as a slave to an Indian merchant for three silver coins. Thomas, the story continues, is then taken on board a ship to the east.

Thomas is a builder, a jack of all trades, who can make everything from ploughs to temples — and on arrival in India is asked by a king, called Gundaphar,[10] to build a palace. Thomas promises to do so, and the king gives him money to pay for the construction work. But Thomas builds absolutely nothing and instead gives the money to the poor and the sick. The king turns up at the building site and asks Thomas, 'Where is the palace?' to which the apostle responds, 'You cannot see it now, only when you have departed from this world.' The king, unsurprisingly, is more than a little unhappy and decides to have Thomas skinned alive and then burned. However, before Thomas can be kebabed, the king's brother dies, and he sees the magnificent palace awaiting the king in heaven. God restores the brother

[10] The name Gundaphar or Gudnaphar used in the *Acts of Thomas* has been tentatively identified with one of a series of kings called, in Latin, Gondophares. In the early Christian era, they ruled the Indo-Parthian Empire in what is now Pakistan and Afghanistan. They are thought to have been Zoroastrians.

to the mortal world, where he is able to tell the king about the heavenly palace. Thomas is set free. He advises everyone to forswear fornication and continues on his Indian travels — until he convinces one queen too many that she should give up sex. Her king orders the apostle to be killed. He is lanced to death in AD 72 on St Thomas Mount, clearly visible as you fly into Madras airport, and home now to a church, a seminary, several religious bookshops and a snack-bar. There's a special warning against any kind of petting or intimacy — in the form of a large signboard in English declaring that 'the holiness of this place does not permit the pairs to misuse this place for their merriment'. Thomas would have approved.

The putative appearance of the coitophobe apostle in southern India coincides with a sudden spurt in commercial intercourse between India and the west. Visitors to the museum in the former French colony of Pondicherry, three hours' drive south of Thomas' place of martyrdom, can see dozens of pieces of amphora that once contained wine, olive oil and fish paste from different parts of the Roman Empire, including Spain, Italy and Greece. They were dug up in the 1940s by an eminent British archaeologist who had been allowed to excavate in French territory in India, and who announced that he'd uncovered a first-century AD Roman settlement at Arikamedu on the Coromandel coast. This seems to have been a bit of late colonial, Europhile over-excitement, and the site turned out, instead, to have been an impressive, but very Indian, seaport. In the Pondicherry museum is a seemingly insignificant fragment of red pottery, smaller than a one-rupee coin. It is part of the base of a cup stamped with the letters SERT, which has been traced back to a particular workshop, owned by Sertorius, who lived during the first century AD in the Tuscan city of Arezzo. The cup was manufactured at about the time of the crucifixion — making it probably the oldest European artefact in India — apart

from a few Roman coins.[11] About seven thousand kilometres away in the National Museum in Naples is an even more extraordinary exhibit, the earliest dated Indian artefact in Europe, a superbly fashioned image of a woman and her attendants carved onto a tiny piece of ivory. It definitely arrived in Europe before AD 79, because it was unearthed from the volcanic debris of Pompeii, destroyed by the eruption of Vesuvius that year.

The connection between Thomas and these artefacts is the discovery, or possibly rediscovery, of the monsoon trade winds — which suddenly made commerce and travel between India and the west so much quicker and more reliable. Until this period, it was necessary to carry goods overland, or send them hopping from port to port through coastal waters. But a forgotten someone, possibly a Greek navigator called Hippalus in the first century BC, discovered that if you set off across the Indian Ocean from the Arabian peninsula, at the right time of year and in roughly the right direction, you could reduce the duration of your journey to India dramatically. This involved, in a sense, an enormous act of faith — to head out to a place where no land could be seen, nor would be seen for several weeks (the journey took between twenty and forty days) — and it must have tested the nerve of many a traveller.

[11] A bronze statue of Poseidon dug up near Kolhapur may be significantly older, as is a possible Etruscan strainer found in the same place. The earliest Indian objects found elsewhere in the world are peppercorns, placed inside the nostrils of the Egyptian Pharaoh Ramesses II to help the process of mummification, that date back to the Pharaoh's death in 1213 BC.

The fact that Egypt was a Roman province, and had been since the snake-assisted suicide of the last of the Pharaohs, the unforgotten Cleopatra, in 30 BC, meant that there was now a sea route from the Roman Empire to the east.[12]

The development of a trade route between the Roman Empire and India seems to have changed the way India was seen in the western world. It was no longer seen as a semi-mythical land, the edge of the known world — but rather as a real, if rather distant, place which supplied luxury goods — spices, gemstones and ivory — to the Roman Empire. Spices, particularly pepper, were the main imports — and used not only as a flavouring, but as aphrodisiacs and preservatives. They were mixed into perfumes and medicines, and burned in religious rituals. Pliny the Elder,[13] writing at about the time of St Thomas' death in AD 72, complained that in 'no year does India drain off less than 50 million sesterces of our empire's wealth, sending back goods to be sold at a hundred times their original cost'. For Pliny, Indian imports were a wasteful frippery, not a necessity — and he singles out the women of the Roman Empire as the main cause of this waste. Ancient Rome's closest approximation to a novel, *Satyricon* by Petronius, has a marvellously wicked scene where a regular dinner guest at the home of the nouveau-riche former

[12] This trade route was taken over by Arab traders as the Roman Empire declined, and as the navy of the Persian Sassanid Empire took control of much of the Indian Ocean. Direct trade between India and a European power would not resume until the arrival of Vasco da Gama off the coast of Kerala in 1498 (having rounded Africa). Cleopatra was the last of the Ptolemies, who, like the Seleucids, were a Greek dynasty founded by one of Alexander the Great's generals. The Ptolemaic dynasty died with Cleopatra; the last of the Seleucids had been deposed by the Roman general Pompey thirty-three years earlier.

[13] Pliny the Elder died during the eruption of Vesuvius in AD 79 that destroyed Pompeii. According to the account by his nephew, Pliny the Younger, he appeared to have been suffocated by toxic fumes. The word Plinian is used by vulcanologists to describe a particularly violent eruption of a volcano.

slave, Trimalchio, describes his host's culinary peccadilloes. Trimalchio, he says, 'grows everything on his own estate. Wool, citrus, pepper; you can even have chicken's milk if you like . . . And in the last few days, he gave instructions for mushroom seed to be sent from India.'[14]

In the Roman period, India would gain a reputation not only as a source of exotic luxuries, but also as a land of wealth and opportunity, a place where one would escape, rather than encounter, destitution. Another Roman epicurean, the poet Horace, who popularised the phrase *carpe diem*, mocks those who risk their lives to make a quick buck in India: 'You rush, a tireless merchant, to furthest India/ fleeing poverty across the sea, through rocks and fire.' And the poor of India are unmentioned in texts of the period — except, in passing, in the *Acts of Thomas*, as the beneficiaries of the apostle's unbuilt palace.

India was being incorporated in other ways into the Roman world-view — even into its pantheon. The Roman gods, it transpired, had known about India all along, and some of them had even been there. In fact, Megasthenes had referred to the ancient triumphant adventures of the Greek god Dionysus in India, but his Roman avatar, Bacchus, was much more firmly identified with India by writers and by artists. The alcoholic, bibulous, carousing Bacchus is said to have spent several years wandering about Asia, teaching its inhabitants how to make wine — and, almost as an afterthought, conquering India. The triumph of Bacchus, returning from India to the west, is depicted

---

[14] *Satyricon* was probably written in the middle years of the first century AD. Trimalchio's meal is really a piece of performance art, and reaches its climax when a roast boar arrives at the table. It has been stuffed with live birds that fly out when the boar is cut open. F Scott Fitzgerald's extravagant millionaire Jay Gatsby was partly based on Trimalchio, and *Trimalchio* was the original title for the book we now know as *The Great Gatsby*. The epigraph for another literary work of the 1920s, TS Eliot's *The Waste Land*, about the Cumaean Sibyl wishing she was dead, was taken from one of Trimalchio's monologues in *Satyricon*.

on several surviving Roman sarcophagus lids — often in a chariot pulled by elephants and tigers. Bacchus became a central part of a new Roman 'history' of India, the first of several such histories which would be used by foreigners to assert their superiority over India, and sometimes to reinforce their imperial claims. Pliny refers to Bacchus as the first in a line of 153 kings of India — the last of whom, precisely 6451 years and three months later, was Alexander the Great. This trumped-up genealogy can seem quite silly today, but it was a device that enabled the Roman Empire to justify its self-importance and its ambition.

The Alexander story had begun to take on a mythological life of its own. It was no longer believed that Alexander had just reached the borders of India, but that he'd reached the Ganges, and even conquered the entire country. He was on his way to becoming a god, and one of his most fervent devotees was the Emperor Trajan, who dreamed of conquering India. Trajan, born in Spain, was the first Roman emperor not to come from Italy (though he was of Italian stock), and his ambitions were more global than those of his predecessors. Late in life, he invaded what is now Iraq, and planned to head further east. In Babylon, he visits the house in which Alexander died. But his invasion fleet never got beyond the Persian Gulf — and there may never have been any real intention to invade India. The Roman historian Cassius Dio described a wistful, ageing emperor, reaching the Gulf, who 'having caught sight of a ship setting sail for India, said he would have definitely crossed over the seas, were he still young. He began to reflect more, inquiring into the affairs of India, and he deemed Alexander a lucky man.' Trajan died soon after, on the journey back to Rome.

Despite the increasing volume of writing about India in the Roman period, there are very few eye-witness accounts. The *Acts of Thomas* tells us almost nothing about the India that the apostle may have encountered, and was almost certainly written by someone who had never been there. Trajan could only dream of going there. None of the great Graeco-Roman geographers travelled to India, and most of them distrusted contemporary travellers' tales. The rare exception was Ptolemy who went around propositioning sailors with questions about the geography of India, but ended up with a lot of technical information about trade and travel. There is a fascinating anonymous first-hand account of travelling by the monsoon trade winds to India, a kind of sailor's guidebook, known as *The Periplus*.[15] Its author tells us that Indians preferred Italian wines to those from the Middle East, and wanted gold and silver in return for pepper, but he tells us next to nothing about the people he met in India. He does, like his contemporary, Pliny, refer to the wealthy port city of Muziris, on the western coast of India, somewhere in modern Kerala. It's a location that's also referred to in the great Tamil classics of the period — as a place where *yavanas*, a word that originally referred just to Greeks, but which had come to be a general word for foreigners, would arrive in great ships, 'beating the white foam', to buy pepper in return for gold.

The precise location of the lost city of Muziris has been a matter of some dispute, heightened by the recent emergence of Kerala as an important tourist destination. The main candidate for many years has been the town of Cranganore, which was already a pilgrimage centre — and is described in tourist literature as the 'cradle' of three of India's imported religions: Christianity, Judaism and Islam. According to local tradition, India's first mosque was built here in AD 629, three years before the death of the Prophet Muhammad, while the earliest members of Kerala's long-standing Jewish community are said to have arrived here

---

[15] *The Periplus of the Erythraean Sea* was written in about AD 60 by an unknown author who was probably a Roman citizen of Greek origin living in Egypt. It largely contains nautical and market advice for traders buying pepper and other spices. The author believes, like many other Romans, that Alexander reached the Ganges.

more than half a millennium earlier in the aftermath of the destruction by the Romans of the Second Temple in Jerusalem in AD 70. But Cranganore is best known for the St Thomas pilgrimage centre. St Thomas is said to have stepped ashore near Cranganore in AD 52, setting up several churches before crossing to the eastern coast of India, and the hillock now known as St Thomas Mount, where he died twenty years later. The pilgrimage centre, built for the nineteenth centenary of Thomas' arrival in India is in a spectacularly lush location, surrounded by palm trees, overlooking the Kerala backwaters, and best approached by boat. It consists (as at St Thomas Mount) of a church, a bookshop and a snack-bar, but at Cranganore there is also an indoor sound-and-light show, and a small piece of Thomas himself.

I entered the church and queued at the back of a line of American Baptists, visiting India on what they called 'a study tour'. They'd been told by their guide that they would see the finger bone of the apostle, the same finger that he had poked into Jesus' chest cavity. They were tremulously excited by the prospect. We filed past a statue of St Thomas, emerging Hindu-fashion from a lotus flower, and past the tabernacle — a bizarre metre-high cupboard shaped like a medical text-book representation of a sclerotic heart, complete with enlarged arteries, and a *trompe l'oeil* door concealing the communion wine. The relic of Thomas was in a glass case in the altar. Several of the Americans stared reverentially at it, a large bone of the kind a dog might have enjoyed two thousand years ago — fat and tapering and at least four inches long. One of them, a Doubting Thomas, eventually said, 'That's awful long for a finger bone.' He was shushed by one of the others. But he wouldn't stop: 'Maybe the bones got fused together, you know, when he poked Jesus.' There was some keen nodding from the others, as if this might explain why, in fact, the relic looked nothing like a finger. When a priest eventually explained that this wasn't his finger at all, but part of St Thomas' elbow, they all looked a little disappointed. 'But it was the same arm that touched Our Lord,' added the priest, and they cheered up a little. The Doubting Thomas winked at me and said *sotto voce*, 'They don't know their "beeps" from their elbows round here.' I, meanwhile, was pushing my thumb deep into the sinews of my lower and upper arm, to work out exactly which bit of Thomas' elbow was on display. No photographs were allowed, and so I made a quick sketch, and was able, later, with the help of *Gray's Anatomy*, to identify it as part of the ulna, the longer bone in the forearm — with a distinctive triangular spur known as the coronoid process. Most of the rest of the apostle is in a copper urn in the crypt of the cathedral in the Italian city of Ortona.[16]

Six kilometres south of the elbow of St Thomas, on the other side of the Periyar river, are four trenches cut deep into the sandy soil of a small plot of land in Pattanam. It is part of what

---

[16] According to church accounts, the relics of St Thomas were moved from India to Edessa in what is now Turkey in the fourth century, to the Greek island of Chios in the twelfth century and then to Ortona in the thirteenth century. The Ortona church in which the relics were stored was blown up by the Nazis, but the urn containing almost all of St Thomas survived. The ulna of Thomas was presented to the Thomas Christians of Kerala in 1952, on the 1900th anniversary of the saint's arrival on the Malabar coast. The finger of St Thomas, the one that is said to have probed inside the chest wound of Jesus, is in Rome, in the Chapel of Relics in the Basilica of the Holy Cross in Gerusalemme, alongside pieces of wood and nail from the cross, and two thorns from the crown of Jesus.

may become one of India's most important archaeological sites, with early finds that seem to suggest that this, not Cranganore, is the site of the lost city of Muziris. There are dozens of bags of broken pottery sorted according to type and place of origin. Most of the pottery was manufactured in India, but several hundred fragments of Roman amphora have already been found, much more than at Arikamedu near Pondicherry on the east coast. The archaeology students who were working on the site wouldn't answer my questions. They pointed me instead to a small hut, where I would find 'Sir', who turned out to be the chief archaeologist, PJ Cherian. He was a reflective, extremely well-read, betel-nut-chewing Keralite who was camping nearby in the village — and who seemed only moderately pleased to be visited by someone who introduced himself as a journalist.

Cherian explained that they'd originally begun digging near Cranganore under pressure from powerful local politicians who wanted the prestige of Muziris and the potential tourist income to come to their constituency. Almost nothing was found there, and the dig moved across the river to the less glamorous village of Pattanam in a separate constituency in a different district of Kerala — where the archaeologists had wanted to dig in the first place. They soon made some important finds: part of a canoe, a wharf, small iron objects, copper coins, thousands of beads made of glass and semi-precious stones and the extraordinary collection of pottery. Only a tiny percentage of the area has been excavated — and Cherian believes that Pattanam could turn out to be one of the world's great archaeological sites. But progress is slow, funding will be needed for future excavation and villagers are fearful that their land will be taken from them.

When I asked Cherian about whether he was sure this was the Muziris described in Roman writings, he bristled. 'That's the one thing that everyone asks, even Indians . . . especially Indians.' I looked at him quizzically, unsure what I had said that had irritated him so, and waited for him to fill the silence.

'Why,' he eventually asked, 'is everyone so obsessed with the Roman connection? We're not under European rule any more. Why haven't we got over this? Would this happen with a major western archaeological dig? Would it be hijacked by questions of whether it traded with India? Of course not.' I felt slightly embarrassed, as if I'd been outed as an old-fashioned Orientalist. I wanted to tell him that I wasn't an Orientalist, that I was in fact an admirer of Edward Said,[17] almost a follower, but then that would have sounded embarrassingly ingratiating. Instead, I agreed with him, and then began to dig a deep trench for myself. I said I was interested in the Roman connection because Pliny describes Muziris as the greatest commercial city[18] in India, and that trade with India was bankrupting Rome. Cherian raised his eyes heavenwards, and left the hut to spit out the chewed betel nut. He quickly returned, his voice no longer muffled by dozens of small foreign objects in his mouth.

'Pliny,' Cherian responded with a snort, 'was just a journalist [he was actually a naval commander] and he didn't have a clue about economics. But that's not really my point. This dig is about much more than whether this is Muziris. It's about the discovery, perhaps, of a major Indian urban settlement and seaport that dates back more than two thousand years. And yes it would have traded with many places — other parts of India, the Middle East and Persia, Sri Lanka and, yes, Rome. But this obsession with Rome is just too much.'

[17] The Palestinian-American writer Edward Said (1935–2003), author of *Orientalism* (1978), which challenged the ways many westerners had defined and studied 'The Orient' (see Intermission Nine). Among his supporters, Orientalist became a dirty word. Among some of his opponents, Edward Said became a dirty name; the subject of *ad hominem* vilification. He was also a literary critic, a political activist, a member of the Palestinian National Council and a pianist.

[18] He actually uses the word 'emporium' which meant a place set aside for international rather than local trade. It is not cognate with 'empire' which comes from the Latin *imperium*.

'But isn't it also interesting and important,' I responded, 'to examine how foreign views of India have reflected the preoccupations and fantasies of foreigners — even if, especially if, those views are wrong. And we know some of the views of Romans, and almost nothing from elsewhere in the world.'

Cherian nodded, as if to say that there might, after all, be some value in what I was saying. 'Yes, it is important. But in the end,' he said, 'I'm a materialist — I want to find out how people lived.'

'By digging up the past?'

'Yes. While you want to know how people thought.'

'Yes. I do. By trying to make sense of what they wrote, or drew or made. We just have so little evidence from this period, except from the Romans.'

We continued talking — and by the time he showed me around the dig, the trenches were in shadow. It was March, and he'd need to finish digging before the monsoon rains came in late May. The trench would then be filled up again and the land restored to its owners.

Our unlikely meeting in a small hut in rural Kerala ended more than amicably. It was almost, but not quite, a meeting of minds — to the surprise, I think, of us both. It was as if we were on the same side, but playing slightly different games, and I think I probably learned more from Cherian than he did from me. And it's become, for me, one of those percussively unforgettable conversations, memories of which jump out as I write. Principally, it continues to remind me of the extent to which old Orientalist and Eurocentric agendas continue to dominate many Indian historical discussions. But on top of this there is a veneer of nationalism, a modern pan-Indian identity, which has been retrospectively overlaid onto the ancient history of the subcontinent. And, it follows that there is an issue about how 'foreignness' might be defined, and whether a north Indian and a north European might both be foreigners in Kerala. Being a foreigner, and being seen as a foreigner, are subjective matters, ones that are as old as the hills, matters of mood and perception, belonging and nostalgia, language and colour, that long pre-date those key determinants of modern foreignness: one's place of birth and one's passport.

A Second Intermission

MY FIRST WEEK in India had a distinctly sybaritic flavour. There was a lot of gluttony and dope-smoking. The half-hearted attempts of Shireen's family to keep us apart ended when she climbed through the window of the guest house to which I and several others had been consigned on the eve of the wedding of my sister to her brother. And at the wedding itself, I was given what I was told was an important task. It was up to me — as the only male relative of the bride — to explain the Zoroastrian religion, about which I knew next to nothing, to the wedding guests. I was given a long religious text in English to read out which used so much obscure circumlocution and metaphysical jargon that it was almost entirely unintelligible. It spoke, among other things, of Ahura Mazda and the Spentas,[1] who — I later learned — are deities and not, as I joked laboriously and entirely inappropriately, a rock band. Tony Mango was the only one who was amused.

Most of the wedding ceremony was a long blessing in Avestan, a language that no one speaks, and very few understand. My attempts to find out what the prayers meant were in vain; even

[1] Ahura Mazda is the name of God in Zoroastrianism, while the Spentas are lesser deities, immortal beings akin to angels.

the priest could only give me a few generalities about fighting evil and the importance of behaving well and telling the truth. 'Good Thoughts, Good Words, Good Deeds' is the mantra all Parsis learn to describe their faith — to which 'good food' deserves to be added. Not only was the food transcendentally superb, but it was also the main topic of conversation before, during and after the wedding. Indeed it is still discussed in the family as an example of that most splendid of Parsi meals, the *lagan nu bhonu*, or wedding feast.

The rest of the week was a bit of a haze, partly because I was stoned a lot of the time. I was not a regular smoker, and the main effect on me of the powerful Bombay marijuana was a gluttonous silence. I went one afternoon to meet Shireen's aunt, and she would later give my brother-in-law a two-word appraisal of me in English and Gujarati — 'duffer *che*,' she said. He's a duffer. We've teased her about that ever since, but I never felt able to admit to her that I was probably a little stoned. I did no sightseeing while in Bombay, though I do remember being impressed by the ubiquity of the sea, which seemed visible from every apartment block and down every side-street.

I was carted around town by Shireen from house to house, party to party, restaurant to restaurant to be exhibited to her friends. Their world was curiously and unexpectedly recognisable — as if I had travelled backwards in time by a decade. The social circle of westernised Anglophone twenty-somethings into which I had fallen reminded me of Britain's mid-1970s' pre-punk generation. There were a lot of flared trousers and patchwork skirts; drunken parties with better snacks than I'd ever eaten in London. Boys were 'into' heavy metal — and Deep Purple was puzzlingly popular. Girls preferred the Eagles, Elton John and even Lionel Richie. Everyone seemed to know the words, and some would sing them out loud. During the slower songs, couples smooched chastely, more cheek-to-cheek than pelvis-to-pelvis. I heard no Indian music. Many of the people I met were studying abroad, mainly in the US, and were back for the New Year holidays — not sure whether they'd ever return permanently to a country which some of them had openly begun to despise. They complained about Bombay's traffic, its filth, its beggars; and the disorderliness, corruption and backwardness of India.

I remember one party, where I eavesdropped on several complainers, who suddenly froze, when a foreigner — not me but someone's visiting girlfriend — agreed with their grouses, and added several of her own. They made it clear they did not want to hear negative views about their country from a foreigner. She left the group, bemused and close to tears — as someone muttered the words 'colonial mentality'.

I realised that one had to be careful with one's opinions. This was easy for me at the time, because I didn't really have any. I was often asked by Indians, and on my return to the UK, what I thought of India — and I was usually at a loss for words, and said something pretty banal. This was, I like to think, not because I'm a duffer, or even because I am given to humility. I simply didn't know enough. But I had done the basic calculation. This enormous country with fifteen times the population of my own, with dozens of languages, could hardly be appraised on the basis of a brief visit to one of its cities, in which I had mixed, almost entirely, with the grown-up offspring of urban English-speaking plutocrats.

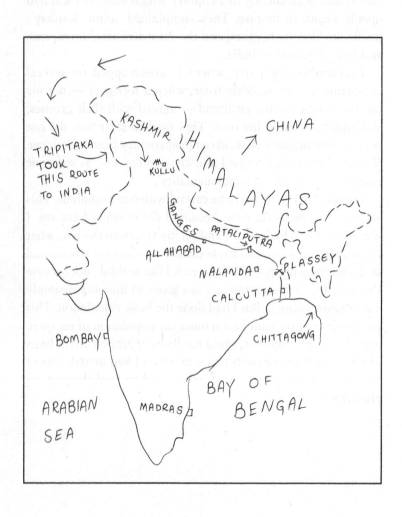

Chapter Three: In which the Author is besotted with a transgendered monk, takes a seventh-century electronic quiz, and is almost very rude to a pretty woman

IN 1979, AT the age of seventeen, I fell in love with a Buddhist monk. Tripitaka was achingly beautiful, soft of cheek, disarmingly naive and priggishly well behaved. At the time, I lived in my parents' home in London and would revise for my final school exams while slumped in front of the TV. I became hooked on a cult Japanese TV series, called *Monkey*, appallingly badly dubbed into English, targeted at ten-year-olds and broadcast by my future employers at the BBC. The series related the adventures of the eponymous Monkey, who, according to the theme tune, was 'born from an egg on a mountain top/the punkiest monkey that ever popped'. In each episode, Monkey and his 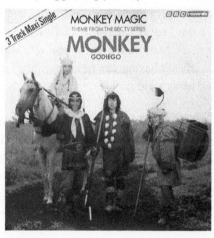 friends Pigsy, Sandy and, yes, Tripitaka would defeat demons and other malefactors as they made their very slow way from China to India in their quest for ancient Buddhist texts, like a less po-faced, martial-arts version of *The Lord of the Rings*. Monkey — who could summon up his cloud chariot with a strange finger waggle that was imitated in school playgrounds across

Britain — was clearly, like Pigsy and Sandy, aimed at younger viewers. But Tripitaka, the monk, was different. Played by the ravishing Japanese actress Masako Natsume, she, or he, became an object of teenage fantasy. As far as I was concerned, she made few concessions to the fact that she was supposed to be playing a male character, although I would later discover that her gender was a matter of some confusion to younger viewers. In the comments section on YouTube, where dozens of clips from the TV series have been uploaded, one fan said,

> I always thought when I was a kid that Tripitaka was cute, but I never wanted to admit it as I thought it was a cute boy . . . Now that I know she was really a woman, I realise I wasn't having gay feelings. (Phew) That can really mess you up as a kid (lol).[1]

Like the Emperor Trajan, the four friends in the TV series never made it to India. The series ended after two seasons, and in 1987, Masako Natsume would meet an early death, eaten away by leukaemia at the age of twenty-seven.

Most of the characters and events in *Monkey* were fictional, but not — as I discovered much later — Tripitaka. He was based

---

[1] The series was hugely popular in Australia where it was known as *Monkey Magic*. Many viewers were confused by Tripitaka's gender, including Val Nobrega, who wrote on the *Monkey Magic* Facebook group, 'Really glad to know Tripitaka was a girl after twenty-odd years of rumours. For the first time in my life I actually thought I was attracted to a guy. Being a gay woman, it raised a few moral "issues" for me. Glad to know my gaydar is actually working fine after all.'

on a real (male) monk who made the long overland journey from China to India in the seventh century AD — to visit the holy sites of Buddhism, and to find ancient Buddhist texts. Tripitaka would also make an extraordinary literary and cultural journey. His biography, based on his fifteen-year trip, was written in his lifetime and his exploits would strike such a chord in China that he would become something of a superhero. By the tenth century, his pilgrimage to India had inspired a series of fantastic legends. His exploits became the subject of several medieval Chinese plays. And then, in the sixteenth century, he reappeared in one of the usually capitalised 'Four Great Classical Novels of Chinese Literature', *Monkey* by Wu Ch'eng En,[2] in which an invented simian companion, not present in the original biography, gave new life to the story of Tripitaka. The original seventh-century biography became known among scholars in India and in the west in the nineteenth century, and a British Sinologist published the first popular translation of *Monkey* in the 1940s, a book which would later become part of the Penguin Classics series. The Japanese TV programmes that I watched as a love-struck teenager were just one of several attempts to make a screen version of *Monkey*.

Most recently and most bizarrely, a fading star of 1990s Britpop, Damon Albarn, formerly lead singer with Blur, collaborated with the Chinese director Chen Shi-Zheng to bring Monkey, Tripitaka, Pigsy and Sandy onto an opera stage. To almost universal astonishment, the opera was rather good, and received more-than-favourable reviews. In these later versions of the Tripitaka story, India is reduced to little more than an empty shell. It is still the destination of the travellers, but apart from being a place of Buddhist learning, has no distinctive features. It is as if the companions are following the Taoist dictum, 'a good

[2] The title *Monkey* was given to the book by its twentieth-century British translator Arthur Waley. In China, it is known as *The Journey to the West* — a title that meant little in the better-known west, but referred to a journey from China that went westwards (and southwards) to India.

traveller has no fixed plans, and is not intent on arriving'. The opposite is true of the original version of the tale.

Tripitaka has had many names and many avatars and is best known to historians, and to millions of Indian schoolchildren, as Hiuen Tsang, though the official romanised spelling of his name has recently been modernised, not entirely helpfully, to Xuanzang.[3] He must rank as one of the most determined travellers of all time, and provides the most detailed descriptions of all the early foreign chroniclers of India. But more than that, he is also a seminal figure in the history of Asia, whose great journeys and writings, barely known in the west, are a reminder of the ancient pre-eminence of India and China; two neighbours who competitively aspire, once again, to global leadership in the twenty-first century. China and India are separated by the world's highest mountain range, which proved an *almost* insuperable disincentive to dialogue until the age of the aeroplane. Contact was rare between the two countries for most of the last two millennia, except during an extraordinary period between the third and seventh centuries AD — when Buddhism spread rapidly through Asia, while remaining strong in the land of its birth. We know the names of more than a hundred Buddhist monks from China who travelled to India in that time span — while the number of named Europeans who came to India in the same period can be counted on the fingers of half a hand.

India was the holy land for China's Buddhists; a place of pilgrimage — their Jerusalem. Buddhism in China dates back to the first century AD, when, at the same time as St Thomas was said to have preached to bemused Indians about the evils of sexual intercourse, the first Indian Buddhist scholars appeared at the court of the Chinese emperor. The emperor, usually known

---

[3] *Tripitaka* literally means 'three baskets' in Sanskrit, a reference to the baskets in which, traditionally, ancient Buddhist scrolls were kept. The monk was born in about AD 602 as Chen Hui, and was later named after the object of his search.

simply as Ming, was an immediate convert, having already had a dream in which the Buddha had appeared before him as a shining golden deity. China, often stereotyped as impervious to foreign ideas, gorged itself on Buddhist beliefs, and before long, Chinese Buddhist monks began making their way to India, to study ancient texts and visit the land in which the Buddha had lived.

Some of the Chinese pilgrims left accounts of their time in India, devoted in part to esoteric doctrinal issues — and they can seem rather like some modern-day 'spiritual' travellers, so keen to find themselves that they barely notice the world around them. But Tripitaka (aka Xuanzang) stands out.[4] His descriptions of India read, in their early twentieth-century translations, like the journals of a time traveller. They contain, for instance, the earliest accounts, in almost Baedeker-style language, of such popular modern tourist destinations as Kashmir and Varanasi. There is more than a stray note of piety, of course, and the monk himself is, as in his later incarnations, sickeningly high-minded about almost everything — but his priggishness is redeemed by plenty of historical detail and great dollops of derring-do.

Tripitaka leaves China in AD 630, heading west on foot and horseback through Central Asia, and is immediately beset by demon robbers; his knee is grazed by an arrow fired by a soldier from a tower. He nearly dies of thirst in the Gobi desert and many of his companions are frozen to death in the Tianshan mountains. There's a significant encounter, in what is now Uzbekistan, when he witnesses the earliest recorded example of anti-Indian racism. A local ruler, the presumably pasty-faced 'Khan of the Western Turks', tells Tripitaka that the heat of India will be too much for a man with his pale skin — and warns him that 'the men there are naked-blacks, without any sense of decorum, and not fit to

[4] The other well-known Chinese traveller to India was Fa Xian who visited the main Buddhist sites more than two hundred years before Tripitaka. Fa Xian spent fifteen years travelling on foot via what is now Afghanistan and returning to China by boat via Sri Lanka and Java.

look at'. The monk does not respond to this provocation and simply declares that he is travelling to India in search of holy relics and Buddhist law — but it was important enough as a conversation for him to recall two decades later. He then travels into Afghanistan, providing the first descriptions of the rock-cut giant Buddhas of Bamiyan, carved a century earlier, and destroyed by the Taliban[5] in 2001.

Tripitaka gives pithy portraits of the people of each region he visits in India. And although there are many dozens of sweeping generalisations, he goes out of his way to differentiate between them, rather than tarring them all with the same brush. The people of the Kullu valley 'are coarse and common in appearance, and are much afflicted with goitre and tumours. Their nature is hard and fierce; they greatly regard justice and bravery.' The northern Indian city of Prayag, now better known as Allahabad, has a 'climate [that] is warm and agreeable; the people are gentle and compliant in their disposition. They love learning, and are very much given to heresy.' Kashmiris, in a stereotype that survives to this day, 'are handsome in appearance, but are given to cunning'. He often sandwiches forceful negative comments ('of a weak pusillanimous disposition'; 'ungainly and revolting'; 'dissolute and cruel'; 'crooked and perverse') with minor praise ('they are faithful to their oaths and promises'; 'they dread the retribution

[5] Tripitaka provides a detailed description of how colourful the Bamiyan Buddhas looked in the seventh century AD, with 'golden hues that sparkle on every side, and precious ornaments that dazzle the eyes by their brightness'. The statues were once covered in stucco that was then painted. After the 2001 destruction of the statues, scientists trawling through the rubble (and in nearby caves) found traces of paint made from oil. Until then, oil paint was seen as a European invention.

of another state of existence'), as if he'd just been forced to attend a training course on giving constructive feedback.

Tripitaka's admiration for the people he meets increases as he nears his destination, the ancient Buddhist sites in what is now known as Bihar — where he hoped to find sacred texts and relics. And it's in modern Bihar, so reviled and so deserving of love, that the Chinese monk lives on, in unexpected ways, both virtually and in person. He briefly visited Ashoka's capital at Pataliputra, carefully inspecting its ruined buildings and ancient walls. Unlike Megasthenes nine hundred years earlier, he did not linger, and travelled instead towards the Buddhist holy places of southern Bihar — and in particular the great seminary at Nalanda. And the monk — or rather part of him — would return, St Thomas-style, to Pataliputra, now Patna, more than 1300 years later. A fragment of Tripitaka's skull was presented to the Indian government by the Chinese in the 1950s, at a time of friendship between the two countries, enabling the relic to survive the iconoclasm of the Cultural Revolution — and it has remained under lock and key in Patna Museum ever since.[6]

Tripitaka then headed south to Bodhgaya, still the best known of all Buddhist sites, and where the Buddha achieved enlightenment beneath a *bodhi* tree. The tree,[7] records Tripitaka,

[6] I have been informed by 'friends' of the museum authorities that the relic is still in the museum. My requests to see the relic, or a photograph of it, have not been answered. And a friend who is aware of the conditions in the museum's store is of the opinion that the skull fragment of Tripitaka may have been mislaid. The relic was brought to India by the twenty-one-year-old Dalai Lama in 1956 as part of a state visit headed by the Chinese premier Chou En Lai. It was a gift to the Indian people, to celebrate the 2500th birth anniversary of the Buddha. Three years later, during the Tibetan uprising, the Dalai Lama would flee across the Himalayas into exile in India.

[7] And it is *still* there, or its descendant is, at the back of the main Bodhgaya temple. A *bodhi* tree is normally defined as a specimen of the Sacred Fig (or *Ficus religiosa*) which has been propagated from the original tree, or is a descendant of the tree beneath which the Buddha achieved enlightenment. In north India, the tree, with its distinctive heart-shaped leaves, is better known as the *peepal*.

is still there, with 'its yellowish-white bark' and 'its shining green leaves' — but it is much shrunken since the time of the Buddha a millennium earlier, and he is told that its upper branches have been hacked away by 'wicked kings'. But his most important destination was the Buddhist seminary at Nalanda, often described as the world's first university.[8] On arriving at Nalanda, his jaw drops; he is awestruck. And on his return to China, many years later, carrying ancient texts and relics from Nalanda, he gives a fine detailed description of the seminary, the high point of his peregrinations, and the place where he lingers longest. He speaks of a great wall surrounding the seminary which housed ten thousand monks, and inside there were multi-storeyed monks' chambers, with 'dragon projections and coloured eaves, the pearl-red pillars carved and ornamented, the richly adorned

---

[8] There are rather too many candidates for this encomium, and it largely depends on how one defines 'university'. The Platonic Academy pre-dates Nalanda by more than three-quarters of a millennium. Taxila, in modern Pakistan, which also pre-dates Nalanda by several centuries, was a Buddhist place of higher education but lacked the lecture halls and student residential quarters found in Nalanda. The oldest place of higher education in the world that is still operating is Bologna University founded in 1088. A new Nalanda University in Bihar was formally constituted in 2010, and is due to admit students in 2014.

balustrades and the roofs covered with tiles that reflect the light in a thousand shades'. And he reserves his most purple prose for the great college at the heart of the complex, with 'fairy-like turrets, like pointed hilltops, congregated together. The observatories appear to be lost in the morning vapours and the upper rooms tower above the clouds.'

Nalanda today is a small, sleepy hamlet with some of India's most extensive early ruins. By the start of the second millennium AD, Buddhism was dying in the land of its birth — in the face of a Hindu revival that managed to incorporate, in part, some Buddhist ideas and icons. Nalanda itself was sacked in the twelfth century by a Muslim warlord, who is said to have ordered his forces to destroy the seminary when he discovered that there was no copy of the Koran in its library. Nalanda never recovered — a Tibetan pilgrim visited in 1235 and found just one monk, ninety years old, amid the ruins, teaching a group of students. The red-brick buildings of Nalanda were transformed gradually, by wind and rain and pollen and seed, into great overgrown mounds, and lay forgotten by all. They were identified in the nineteenth century with the help of an English translation of Tripitaka's words, and a series of excavations in recent decades has revealed the impressive ruins of the most important educational institution of its era.

Nalanda suffers — like so many other great historical sites in the state — from Bihar's ill repute, for which reason it is not on the main international tourist trail. But it still gets thousands of foreign visitors, most of them Buddhist pilgrims from east Asia.[9] And Tripitaka's seventh-century devotion to Nalanda has been reciprocated in the twenty-first century. Pilgrims are led round the modern Xuanzang Memorial Hall, built with Chinese help, and shown huge murals depicting the life of Tripitaka, and a strange

[9] Gaya international airport, just six kilometres from Bodhgaya and sixty-six kilometres from Nalanda is used almost entirely for Buddhist pilgrims from Sri Lanka and east Asia. It was, until sporadic Delhi flights started recently, India's only international airport that had no domestic flights.

statue of the monk wearing a contraption that someone really ought to patent, which combines a backpack with a sunshade. Also in Nalanda is a building that advertises itself as India's first multi-media museum, where visitors can sit down to watch an interactive audio-visual presentation in a small theatre. The virtual guide, a cartoon man with a bald head, a blue shirt and the pectoral muscles of a bodybuilder, is, as you may have guessed, none other than the Chinese monk himself, with the same backpack–sunshade contraption as the statue in the memorial hall. Members of the public are asked difficult questions about Buddhism, in the same way that seventh-century guards tested the knowledge of visitors, including Tripitaka, before they were allowed access to the seminary. I would have been turned away; this was clearly not a place for pleasure-seekers. Among the less obscure questions that flashed up on the computer screen was,

'How does one attain blissful peace?' to which the answer was, rather sadly, 'Everything is changeable, everything appears and disappears and there is no blissful peace until one passes beyond the agony of life and death.'

Visitors to the ruins of Nalanda approach from the east, and first encounter some well-kept lawns, and then a series of old institutional buildings, many of them high-walled, and starkly identical, the first red-brick university. Each building has a courtyard, around which there are small cells where student monks worked and slept, with a shelf for their manuscripts and a wall-niche for a lamp. All around are Buddhist shrines, and the Nalanda site is dominated by an enormous stepped stupa, studded with statuary, whose summit — thirty-one metres above the ground — is shaped like the back of an elephant. One young Indian man tried to attach himself to me as a guide, promising — in return for two hundred rupees — to show me hidden tunnels, and a rather unlikely royal bedchamber. But I wanted to attach myself to a group of smartly dressed east Asians who were wandering slowly and serenely around the site. My would-be guide seemed more than disappointed and, holding my hand a little aggressively, explained that he was a poor man. I began to argue, slightly off the point, that there would hardly have been a royal bedroom in a Buddhist seminary. Our discourse prior to that had been in English, and he was so stunned to hear me speaking in Hindi, that he jumped, almost, I thought, out of his skin. He apologised ingratiatingly, finally letting go of my hand, and scampered off.

I began stalking the east Asians, and eventually went up to a pretty young woman who seemed to be leading the group. She had a slight resemblance to my teenage fantasy-lover, Masako Natsume (aka Tripitaka), and was happy to talk in a faintly flirtatious manner to a stranger. As I chatted with her (they were Thais; they were all on pilgrimage; and, yes, she did know about the Chinese monk, but not about the *Monkey* TV series), her group began to gather round us. She spoke some English, the others did not. I felt I should draw her companions into the conversation and asked her, uncontroversially, to find out what they thought of India. She spoke to them, and they began discussing, very earnestly, with furrowed brows, what to tell me — as if they were trying to reach some kind of consensus. The three words she then uttered offended me so deeply that I'm still struggling to explain my reaction. 'India is dirty,' she said, enunciating each word carefully, but without emotion. An involuntary 'Oh' escaped my lips — and I fell silent, deflated. I had not expected this answer, and now wished I had not asked the question. There would be no more flirting. Her words seemed so dismissive, so stark, so crude. She looked at me, and made no retraction, no qualification. I felt my adopted homeland had been humiliated. I searched for a brilliant reply, to crush her insolence. But nothing came. I'm ashamed to say I felt like cursing her, that the words that came to my mind were 'fuck off back to Thailand', but, thankfully, these words did not issue forth from my lips.

A wave of mild nausea came over me. And I still could not quite understand why I was so upset. After all, many public spaces in India are disgustingly filthy, and I had just seen a used condom, and a freshly-laid human turd, in the ancient monks' cells of Nalanda. It was that she, my ersatz-Tripitaka, and her companions, seemed to have nothing else to say about India. I was used to hearing pieties about the Buddhist holy land, and the usual platitudes about India's spirituality. She finally broke the silence, and her next five words added to my disquietude. 'You are not from India,' she said, as if to ask why I should care so much, and as if to suggest that she would not have said such a thing to someone who was an Indian. She was correct, of course. I'm not from India, but at that moment I felt as defensive of my country of residence as anyone whose family had been here for a hundred generations. 'That's right,' I said, 'but maybe I've lived here too long,' and wandered off, still smarting. I felt she was trying to make me complicit, as a fellow foreigner, in a particular view of India — to be kept as a secret from Indians, for fear of causing offence. And it does cause offence, as Indians will tell me, especially when they're in their cups, and it is an issue about which even I, as a long-term resident, married to an Indian, have learned to watch my words.

A Third Intermission

ON MY SECOND trip to India, like so many visitors before and since, I witnessed a marvel, a miracle. On a Calcutta pavement I saw a handstand being performed by a boy who had no head. I also received my first chilling lesson on the subject of begging. The year was 1989 and I had been sent, alone, to Calcutta by the BBC to make a radio programme marking the three hundredth anniversary of the foundation of the city. It was my first foreign reporting assignment for the BBC, and I'd somehow bullied my bosses into allowing me to make the Calcutta programme as a prelude to the real purpose of my trip — a portrait of Kabul, from which the Soviet army had just withdrawn.

Shireen and I were still together, in a distant, on–off sort of way — and she was incandescent when I said that I was going to India without her. She now lived in Paris, studying French at the Sorbonne, just like — as I often reminded her — Marie-Claire in *Where Do You Go to, My Lovely?*.[1] She was learning the ways of a Parisian bourgeoise, and, more prosaically, how to use a vacuum cleaner ('but where should I have put the water, then?' she asked me over the phone). In the eighteen months since my first visit to India, I had become more than intrigued by her country, and had been transformed, as if by osmosis, into a sentimental Indophile. At the end of my previous trip I'd visited some fantasy fortresses, high on hilltops, deep in the interior,

---

[1]Like the heroine of the Peter Sarstedt song, as well as studying at the Sorbonne, Shireen lived in a fancy apartment off the Boulevard St Michel, and her loveliness did go on and on. But she didn't have a topless swimsuit, possessed no Rolling Stones records, had never met the Aga Khan, and her dancing was more Petula Clark than Zizi Jeanmaire. Peter Sarstedt, I later discovered, was born in Delhi in 1943. Anjan Dutta's Calcutta version of the song has the heroine, renamed Mala, hanging out at the Alliance Française.

which contributed to a romantic dream in which I would spend my life wandering, with my best beloved, through the Indian countryside. Shireen had taught me a few sentences of Hindi, and how to write my name in the Devanagari script used for Hindi. Singing the Indian national anthem, so much more rousing and tuneful than my own, had become my party piece. And I desperately did not want to think ill of anything Indian, least of all Calcutta, for reasons that I will explain.

You see, the city of Calcutta is for many foreigners what the state of Bihar is for many Indians — the subject of morbid nightmares. Generations of British schoolchildren learned about the Black Hole of Calcutta, where, so it was said, 123 British captives suffocated to death in a small unventilated room inside the old Fort.[2] Kipling later bestowed on Calcutta the epithet, 'City of Dreadful Night'[3] — and the name stuck, even though he'd already used it to describe Lahore. Calcutta was then discarded as India's capital by the British in 1911; it was racked by famine and riots in the 1940s, and, at independence, it lost half of its hinterland, which became East Pakistan and later Bangladesh. Its status as the most benighted of basket-cases was assured with the unlikely emergence of a minute Albanian nun, who cared for the dying, as the city's most famous post-independence celebrity.[4]

[2] The captives were detained on the night of 20 June 1756 by the forces of the Nawab of Bengal, Siraj ud-Daula — nicknamed Sir Roger Dowlett by the British. In fact, the number of people who died was probably a lot lower, and not all the casualties were British. But the legend was more important than the truth. A year later, the forces of 'Sir Roger' were defeated by the British at the Battle of Plassey, from when British hegemony in the subcontinent is often dated.

[3] This hyper-promiscuous epithet was borrowed from the Scottish poet James Thomson, who used it to describe his discombobulatingly melancholic vision of London. It was later used by the American short-story writer O Henry to describe New York.

[4] I tried to meet Mother Teresa but she was out of the country. I would, quite literally, bump into her two years later, in Bangladesh, on a staircase in Chittagong airport. I was covering the 1991 Bangladesh cyclone for the

Günter Grass raised the bar of opprobrium still higher when he referred to the city, in words he has never been allowed to forget, as 'a pile of shit'.[5] I was determined to find something nice to say about the city.

I arrived to some disturbingly heavy late monsoon rains. My taxi from the airport broke down, and I had to wade to another vehicle through the rising roadside waters in my socks and trainers. The hotel had lost my booking, the phones didn't work, I couldn't get batteries for my tape recorder that lasted more than twenty minutes, the BBC stringer who was going to arrange my interviews had gone on holiday and a mottled green-blue mould was spreading in an alarming but painless fashion over both my insteps.[6] I felt slightly desperate. I began wandering about the city, often on foot, getting very wet, and visiting a long list of addresses I had been given by friends and fellow journalists. I was welcomed with a warmth that first delighted and then shamed me, especially when I considered how niggardly a welcome a young journalist from Calcutta would almost certainly receive in London. But I would, much later, come to realise that it was my Britishness, and, most important, the fact that I worked for the BBC, that put me in a privileged position which seemed to open all doors.

BBC, while she was giving succour, in her own special way, to its victims. I was running down the stairs and she was walking up — and I'm ashamed to say that I knocked her to the ground. She got up quickly and agreed to my request for an interview. But she then answered every question I asked her with the words 'God Bless You'. I have never been able to find a satisfactory explanation for her behaviour, except possibly the effects of concussion.

[5] The quote is from the German author's 1977 novel, *Der Butt*, translated into English as *The Flounder*. In the same book, Grass refers to Calcutta as 'this crumbling, scabby, swarming city, this city that eats its own excrement . . .'

[6] My fears that I contracted some unusual tropical skin disease were entirely false. A doctor who I visited examined my feet and then, to my surprise, my trainers, and pointed out that the ingress of monsoon water had caused the green dye used in my insoles to spread onto my skin.

However, my BBC identity card was of no use to me when, at a Calcutta metro station, I was arrested by the police for recording the sound of a train without permission. I was taken to a small, unventilated room, and only released when I played the arresting officers a radio interview I'd just recorded with the film director Satyajit Ray, a demigod for most Calcuttans, in which he'd told me to visit the city's metro, the first — as he proudly pointed out — in south Asia.

I stepped outside the station, relieved to be a free man, and there — in front of me — was the marvel. A boy wearing nothing but a pair of ragged green shorts was doing a handstand on what passed for a pavement. It was immediately apparent that he was without a head, and his severed neck appeared to be resting, bloodlessly, on the mud and gravel. Next to him was a large green leaf on which bystanders had thrown a few coins. Of course, I told myself, he must have a head, it's some kind of illusion, or his head must somehow be concealed beneath the pavement. But how, then, did he breathe? I watched, speaking

into my microphone, trying to describe the strangeness of the scene. After about ten minutes, the boy let his legs fall to the ground, and began blindly scrabbling at the stones and earth around his neck. Soon, he freed his head and looked around, a little disappointed at the few coins on the leaf. I rotated my hands inwards in an interrogatory manner, opening my palms to him, as if to ask how he'd performed his miracle. He proudly showed me a small see-through plastic straw which he put up his nose, and which served as a subterranean snorkel. We shared no language, and so I clapped, and he clapped back, and I smiled and so did he, and I laughed and he laughed back, and then put his hand out, and I gave him some money. He ran off. I was dazzled by his athleticism and ingenuity, but didn't then have any sense of what the lives of child street performers might be like. I didn't realise that they usually do not live with their parents, are often run by Fagin-like gang leaders, who beat them, take all their earnings, and who don't let them go to school.

A day later, I visited a leprosy clinic — for Calcutta, in 1989, had the reputation of being the leprosy capital of India. And it was at the clinic that I received my most telling and unexpected lesson about poverty and begging in India. On my arrival, a young doctor was berating a hideously deformed patient of his — which I took, understandably enough, to show a lack of compassion. When the patient had left, I asked him why he was so upset with his patient. He explained to me that leprosy was a totally curable disease, which, if treated early, had only minor symptoms. However, the more deformed his patients were, the more money they could earn as beggars from members of the public, particularly, he said in a withering voice, from 'irresponsible' foreign visitors. The patient who had just left was someone he had helped cure, who had then deliberately re-infected himself and re-opened his wounds in order to increase his earning power. Give to charities, he told me, not to beggars.

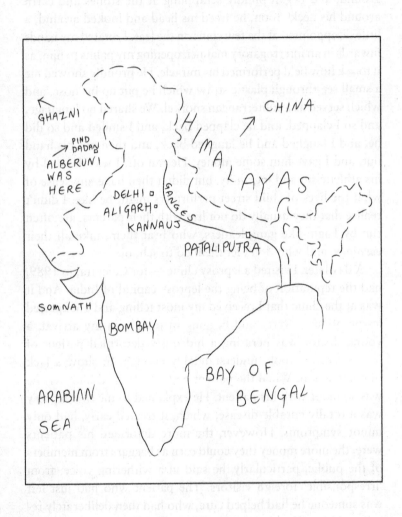

Chapter Four: *In which the Author hears tales of 'Muslim devils', learns the Latin for 'sperm-swallowing eunuch', and reveals the sexual secrets of the good ladies of Kannauj*

'THIS IS THE site of the Hindu holocaust, much worse than the Jewish holocaust,' said the man who had taken pity on me.

I had been attempting to enter a Hindu temple overlooking the sea in Gujarat, in western India, when I was stopped at the security gate. 'No cell phones, no cameras.' There were no lockers nearby — as there are at most temples — and the guard said he couldn't look after my camera and mobile.

'Well, what am I supposed to do?' I said, rather loudly, in Hindi. The guard shrugged his shoulders. A soft-spoken man in a checked shirt came up to me, and addressed me in lightly accented English. 'I will look after your belongings for you. I am anyway waiting for my family. It would be a great misfortune if you came all the way to Somnath and did not go inside.'

The yellow sandstone temple at Somnath is modern, built in the 1950s to an ancient design — and is one of the most important shrines to the god Shiva.[1] As in many Shiva temples, the sanctuary is not occupied by a statue, but by a piece of cylindrical polished stone with a rounded end, the lingam, often

---

[1] Somnath, on the Saurashtra peninsula, is one of the twelve *jyotirlinga*, or a lingam of light. According to the website www.12jyotirlinga.com, a person who has reached a higher level of spiritual attainment will see these linga as 'columns of fire piercing through the earth'. It also provides the text of a poem, referring to each of the *jyotirlinga*, that begins '*Saurashtra Somnatham . . .*' and which, if recited regularly, in the morning and evening, 'washes [away] all the sins committed in the previous 7 births'.

said to represent the erect penis of the god. I joined the queue inside the temple, nodding politely at the lingam, and bent down to allow a priest to daub a spot of red paste on my forehead. Back outside, the soft-spoken man was eager to talk. He wanted to tell me about the Hindu holocaust.

'Do you know what happened here? Fifty thousand Hindus were killed at Somnath by Muslims, and they destroyed the temple. It was the beginning of Muslim rule in India — and after this they killed more than eighty million Hindus,[2] raping Hindu women and forcibly converting them to Islam.'

I must have looked a little incredulous.

[2] The figure of eighty million missing Hindus was first prestidigitated by the historian KS Lal in his *Growth of Muslim Population in Medieval India* (1972). The term Hindu holocaust appears to date from the 1990s and has been popularised by western supporters of Hindu revanchism, such as Koenrad Elst and François Gautier. Elst in particular, in his *Negationism in India* (1992), has compared those who deny the genocide of many millions of Hindus to those who deny the Holocaust. Gautier, meanwhile, is attempting to raise funds for a Hindu Holocaust Museum, to be located in Delhi or Bangalore.

'You do not believe me?'

'Um. No, not really,' I responded apologetically, not wishing to offend someone who had done me a favour, although I was beginning to find his Islamophobia a little distasteful.

'You do not know our history. Muslims have destroyed our country, and they will destroy yours. It all begins, here at Somnath, with Mahmud of Ghazni.'

And he proceeded to list, chronologically, a series of people he referred to as 'Muslim devils': Muhammad of Ghor, Muhammad bin Tughlaq, Timur, Babur, Aurangzeb, Nadir Shah, Jinnah and Osama bin Laden. I knew, from past experience, that there was little point in arguing, in even pointing to the positive Muslim contributions to Indian historical and cultural development, and forced myself to give him a cheerful goodbye wave.

Mahmud of Ghazni must rank as the most unpopular visitor to India of all time. He first turned up in northern India, with his army, and without an invitation, in about the year AD 1000, and returned almost every summer, like an unimaginative tourist, for the next quarter of a century. For Mahmud, India was rich and weak, and ripe for plunder. He carried back to his base in Ghazni, now a provincial capital in Afghanistan, quite stupendous quantities of gold, silver and jewels, most of them seized from temples, as well as many elephants and large numbers of captured Indians, destined to be slaves or soldiers. According to Mahmud's own historians, hundreds of thousands of Hindus were put to death. Mahmud's appalling reputation in modern India rests largely on the destruction by his army, of the temple at Somnath in 1026. In popular demonology, Mahmud has become the archetypal bad Muslim[3] — a figure of hate,

---

[3] Aurangzeb, the last of the great Mughal emperors, has a similar reputation, and indubitably was responsible for ordering the demolition of an uncertain number of Hindu temples. But he also has a reputation for great piety, and visitors to the shrine marking his place of death outside Ahmednagar are told stories of his simplicity and his love for the poor.

particularly among Hindu revivalists. Very few people in India would dream of leaping to the defence of Mahmud, though he has some admirers in Pakistan and Afghanistan. Mainstream Indian historians who have tried to put Mahmud's annual raids into some kind of historical context have been slapped down by the revivalists and charged with being apologists for Muslim aggression. The destruction of the temple of Somnath, almost a millennium ago, is a living political issue, a running sore — in the same way that the Fall of Constantinople and the Battle of Kosovo Polje are remembered by some ultra-nationalist Greeks and Serbs as if they were occasions of recent humiliation, deserving of contemporary revenge.

There seems little doubt, from accounts written by his own courtiers, that Mahmud of Ghazni was, as his detractors eagerly point out, a rapacious warlord and a religious zealot — a man for whom India was simply a source of wealth. But it is also often forgotten that under his rule Ghazni became a major centre of learning.[4] And at Mahmud's court resided one of the greatest scholars of any age, a remarkable man who was the first foreigner to write a work of genuine scholarship about India,[5] a polymath who arguably deserves the slightly dubious accolade of 'the first Orientalist' — and whose work contains uncanny similarities to

[4] Ferdowsi, the author of the Persian-language Iranian national epic, *The Shahnameh*, also lived in Ghazni. Mahmud refused to pay him in full for *The Shahnameh*, and Ferdowsi cursed him with the words 'Heaven's vengeance will not forget. Shrink, tyrant, from my words of fire, and tremble at a poet's ire.' In *The Shahnameh*, Ferdowsi tells the story of Shireen, the Christian queen of Shah Khusro, who murders her rival Maryam. When Khusro dies, and Maryam's son Kobad takes power, Shireen kills herself. Ferdowsi refers to Khusro's enormous harem, and how 'Twelve hundred beauties arrived/ Preceded by sunlike Shireen/ In height a silver column as she walked.'

[5] He was not, though, the first Muslim to write about India. The earliest recorded writings, dated to AD 851, by a Muslim visitor to India are by a trader called Suleiman, who talks of the great wealth of the country, in the form of camels, horses, elephants, gold and silver — though he also refers to a king on the east coast of India who is 'poor and proud'.

those of many British and French Orientalists of the nineteenth and twentieth centuries. Abu Rayhan al-Biruni, better known as Alberuni,[6] was not from Ghazni, but had been brought there forcibly by Mahmud's army from his home town more than one thousand kilometres away in modern-day Uzbekistan.[7] He spent most of his adult life at Mahmud's court in Ghazni, and seems to have accompanied the Ghaznavid army on at least one of its annual forays into India. After the death of Mahmud, he is able to write critically of the invasions, declaring that Mahmud 'utterly ruined the prosperity of the country' and that the people of India 'became like atoms of dust scattered in all directions'. He also describes in some detail how Mahmud ordered the lingam from Somnath to be broken and brought in pieces to Ghazni. Part of the lingam was thrown into the hippodrome, while another part was laid in front of the door of the main mosque, 'on which people rub their feet to clean them from dirt and wet'.

The passages in his book dealing with Mahmud's invasions indicate that Alberuni was no sycophant — unlike many other writers of the period. He was genuinely interested in India, and in Hindus — though he never pretended to be anything other than an intrigued outsider, a God-fearing Muslim studying a culture very different from his own. Alberuni's range and his breadth of inter-cultural knowledge are astonishing. He makes

[6] Alberuni is said to have written more than 130 books, of which all or part of only twenty-two have survived. Among his achievements was that he was able to calculate the radius of the earth to an accuracy of fifteen kilometres by climbing a hill near Pind Dadan, now in Pakistan. Western scientists continued to believe the less accurate calculations of the ancient Greeks, which is one reason why Columbus believed he had reached Asia when he crossed the Atlantic. Unlike his Central Asian contemporary Avicenna, who was also a scientist, Alberuni was little known in the west — and was unmentioned by Dante, who consigned Avicenna to the relatively pleasant outer-most circle of hell.

[7] Alberuni's home town of Kath, now known as Biruney, on the plains south-east of the Aral Sea, is visible from the right-hand side of the plane when flying on the most commonly used air route from Delhi to London.

reference to Homer, Socrates and Pythagoras and a host of other less important figures from ancient Greece and Rome at a time when they were all but forgotten in Europe. And he has a knowledge of the Bible that would shame many modern Christian priests. Like later European Orientalists, he attempts to collect, categorise and catalogue facts and information about India in

an orderly manner — and like many of them he becomes frustrated by what he sees as the fundamental illogicality of Indians. Their scribes, he says, are 'careless' and 'negligent'; their books are 'verbose'; their mathematics and astronomy are a mixture of 'pearls and dung'; their classification of spiritual beings is disorganised and arbitrary; their system for measuring small units of time is 'foolishly painstaking'. He says the popular version of the Hindu religion is full of 'hideous fictions' and 'silly notions'; and he makes the complaint, widely echoed by modern tourists who ask for directions, that Indians hate to say the words 'I do not know'.

Alberuni believes his own religion and culture are superior to those of India, but like many later Orientalists, he is eager to point out that the world also has a lot to learn from India and Indians, and that this knowledge needs to be teased out of them. Indians, he says, are 'by nature niggardly in communicating that which they know, and they take the greatest possible care to withhold it from men of another caste among their own people — still much more, of course, from any foreigner'. He points to old Sanskrit texts which had reverential references to Greek learning — and laments the arrogance of contemporary India. If only they would travel a bit more, he complains, 'they would soon change their minds — for their ancestors were not as narrow-minded as the present generation'.

Alberuni introduces the idea of a kind of Indian exceptionalism, whereby Indians think 'there is no country but theirs, no nation like theirs, no kings like theirs, no religion like theirs, no science like theirs' — and he considers this trait to be 'haughty, foolishly vain, [and] self-conceited'. It's a reaction to Indian exceptionalism that is repeated today — particularly by India's smaller neighbours, though usually *sotto voce*, for fear of some kind of retribution or ostracism.

Alberuni differs in one minor and one major respect from many later Orientalists. First, he was not priggish about describing sexual and bodily functions. The only English-language translation of Alberuni's *al-Hind* was published in 1888, and key passages of the text have been rendered by the translator from Arabic into Latin — presumably to protect under-educated Victorian women and the lower classes from the profanities of medieval India. We learn that the *crepitus ventris*, better known as the common fart, was considered by Indians to be a good omen, while sneezing was a bad omen. Another Latinised sentence refers to the popularity of the woman-on-top sexual position — in which the woman is described as moving 'as if ploughing a field', while the man underneath 'remains completely relaxed'. The next Latinised sentence deals with the prevalence in India of penis-sucking, sperm-swallowing eunuchs (. . . *qui penem bucca devorans semen elicit sorbendum*). Unlike Herodotus, who famously declared that Indian semen was black, Alberuni says little that is easy to contradict. And the female superior position and fellating eunuchs — presumably alien to Alberuni's Ghazni — do both make fleeting appearances in the much earlier Indian work of sexology known as the *Kama Sutra*.

Alberuni's interest was neither prurient nor judgemental, but anthropological, and part of an attempt to set out what he saw as the vast differences between his world and India. He encourages his readers to be open-minded, admitting that many Indian 'customs differ from those of our country and of our time to such a degree as to appear to us simply monstrous'. And, he goes on to argue, in defiance of the conventions of his time, that the perceived strangeness of something rests ultimately on our unfamiliarity with it. This is a remarkably relativist approach, at a time when most scholars were searching for certainty, and for evidence to buttress their own intellectual and religious world-view.

Second, unlike those later Orientalist texts, Alberuni's *al-Hind* was not born out of colonialism. Mahmud of Ghazni, unlike later Muslim invaders, did not incorporate India into his empire. However, the politics of power is central to understanding Alberuni's work — which was only made possible by the superior military strength of Mahmud. It is not absolutely clear how Alberuni gathered such systematic, well-ordered information — in contrast to almost every other foreign writer until the eighteenth century — but it seems likely that his most important sources were Indian prisoners who had been brought by Mahmud's army to Ghazni. Just as Alberuni, too, had been brought there by force. It wasn't quite a dialogue of equals, but between individuals whose status was dependent on the whims of their captors.

At the start of the final paragraph of his book, just before a rousing paean to the oneness of God and to the Prophet Muhammad, Alberuni declares his purpose in writing. He wanted to provide sufficient information 'for anyone who wants to converse with the Indians, and to discuss with them questions of religion, science or literature, on the very basis of their own civilisation'. One might hope that would be at least one of the purposes of any book on India — though this has rarely been the case. Alberuni tries to be even-handed, and is not interested in titillating his audience with marvels. Partly for this reason — and his gritty obsession with the minutiae of Indian science — later readers have tended to describe his writings as boring.

There are many surviving texts by early Muslim writers who talk about India in a manner more entertaining than Alberuni's. They tend to be gossipy and salacious. Elephants, untold wealth and sex are major themes. Captain Buzurg, a tenth-century Persian sailor and fabulist, tells his readers that the good ladies of Kannauj, then a major city on the Ganges, possess labia that are muscular enough to crack an areca nut,[8] while the eleventh-century Moroccan geographer al-Idrisi asserts that in India 'concubinage is permitted with all persons except married

---

[8] Both Cleopatra and the Duchess of Windsor are sometimes said, unverifiably, to have been in possession of similar muscles. Ibn Battuta (see below) refers to a Turkish queen whose vagina, and those of her female progeny, had a 'conformation' like a ring. The sultan, he says, 'finds her every night like a virgin'. According to the Urban Dictionary, an Internet guide to contemporary slang, a 'Hindu massage' is a term for when 'A woman contracts her vaginal muscles around a male's penis during intercourse to bring the male to orgasm.' The dictionary goes on to give this example of how the phrase is used, 'Indira's Hindu massage caused her lover to explode inside her', but gives no explanation of its origin or antiquity. One possible source is the Hindu erotic classic, *The Ananga Ranga*, translated by Sir Richard Burton, in which he describes a sexual position called the *Purushayita* 'in which the woman must ever strive to close and constrict the Yoni until it holds the Linga, as with a finger, opening and shutting at her pleasure, and finally, acting as the hand of the Gopala-girl, who milks the cow. This can be learned only by long practice . . . And she will be pleased to hear that the art once learned, is never lost. Her husband will then value her above all women, nor would he exchange her for the most beautiful Rani (queen) in the three worlds. So lovely and pleasant to man is she who constricts.' Burton goes on to record that 'amongst some races the constrictor vaginæ muscles are abnormally developed. In Abyssinia, for instance, a woman can so exert them as to cause pain to a man, and, when sitting upon his thighs, she can induce the orgasm without moving any other part of her person.'

women; thus a man may have intercourse with his daughter, his sister, or his aunts provided they be unmarried'. It's unlikely that Captain Buzurg enjoyed or endured the attentions of the women of Kannauj — more than nine hundred kilometres from the nearest seaport — and it's pretty clear that al-Idrisi never went anywhere near India at all. But from the late twelfth century there was a sudden spurt of Muslim visitors to India — and many of them stayed on. The invading army of Muhammad of Ghor — another of the many hate figures mentioned by the man who took pity on me at Somnath — conquered Delhi in 1192, and deposited there several of his generals, former slaves of Turkish origins, to rule on his behalf. And so began what would later be known as the Sultanate period, a succession of Muslim dynasties which dominated north Indian politics (until the arrival of the also-Muslim Mughals more than three centuries later), and whose monumental ruins are visible across large parts of the country.

The ethnically Turkish Muslim aristocracy that ruled Delhi in the early years of the Sultanate was gradually diluted. Indian converts and foreign Muslims, including Tajiks from Central Asia and blacks from the east coast of Africa, came to India, and began to be appointed to important positions in the armies and governments of the Sultanate. The defeat of the Christian armies of Europe in the Crusades meant that Muslim rulers controlled a continuous stretch of territory from Morocco to Delhi. And by the fourteenth century, under the Tughlaq dynasty, Delhi had become a magnet for adventurers and opportunists from throughout the Muslim world, in the same way that European mercenaries and fortune-seekers would flock to India four centuries later. The most famous of the fourteenth-century *arrivistes* was the callow Moroccan traveller Ibn Battuta, whose entertaining and often scabrous accounts in his *Rihla*, or Travels, provide an extraordinarily detailed picture of courtly life in Tughlaq Delhi.

The twenty-one-year-old Ibn Battuta left his native

Tangiers[9] in 1325, a newly-qualified Islamic jurist. He meandered his way around the Middle East and Caucasus over the next nine years, performing the Haj twice, encountering many marvels and having lots of sex with slave-girls. In Alexandria, he came across a holy man who prophesied that he would visit, among other places, India, and meet there the holy man's brother — a certain Dilshad. And it's only then that it occurred to Ibn Battuta to go to India, about which he seemed to have few preconceptions. As he neared India, other travellers told him about the Sultan of Delhi, Muhammad bin Tughlaq, who 'makes a practice of honouring strangers, and showing affection to them, and singling them out for governorships or high dignities of state'. He also learned that the Sultan loves getting presents and is extremely generous with return gifts. Indeed, there was a racket at the Indian border — whereby middlemen supply travellers with lavish gifts for the Sultan knowing that they would get even more in return.

So Ibn Battuta borrowed money to buy camels, horses and white slaves for the Sultan, in the expectation that he would make more than enough money to pay his creditors back. And, indeed, on receiving his gifts, the Sultan immediately sent Ibn Battuta several thousand silver dinars, and absurdly large quantities of flour, meat, sugar and areca nuts. A little later, at a time when, Ibn Battuta informs us — in the digressive personal style that would one day become *de rigueur* among travel writers — that he could not sit down because of a boil on his bottom, the Sultan made him a judge. This was an enormously profitable sinecure, and in the long India section of the *Rihla*, there is no reference to him ever actually hearing a case.

Ibn Battuta remained grateful to his patron, but later, at the end of his journey, when he was safely back in the west, close to

[9] The rest of the world would get its revenge on Tangiers' most famous son, when the city became a twentieth-century magnet for such similarly inventive writers as Jean Genet, Paul Bowles, William S Burroughs and the future Indophile Allen Ginsberg.

home, he was able to relate just how nerve-racking it was to work for Muhammad bin Tughlaq. 'This king is, of all men, the most addicted to the making of gifts and to the shedding of blood.' He comes across, in Ibn Battuta's account, as a stereotype of the fabulously rich oriental tyrant — preposterously generous one moment, savagely cruel the next: 'His gate is never without some poor man enriched or some living man executed.' He had gold and silver coins launched into the grasping Delhi crowds from catapults placed on the back of elephants. A turbulent sheikh, who called the Sultan an oppressor, had his mouth prised open with forceps and liquefied human excrement was poured down his throat. The sheikh, who earlier had his beard picked out, hair by hair, was then beheaded. Ibn Battuta was terrified. He used to visit the sheikh, but only, he now pitifully insisted, to see the cave in which he lived. Ibn Battuta was placed under armed guard by the Sultan, and went on a fast, and recited a protective prayer 33,000 times in an attempt to save himself — and was only freed after the sheikh's execution. Eventually, Ibn Battuta decided that it was time to leave Delhi. He swapped clothes with a mendicant, renounced the world, and asked the Sultan's permission to go away on pilgrimage — but the Sultan insisted, to Ibn Battuta's astonishment, that he instead become his ambassador to the king of China, 'for I know your love of travel and of sightseeing'.

Things then got even worse. Ibn Battuta set out with his party of four thousand people, many of them slaves sent as gifts for the king of China, but they didn't get much beyond modern Aligarh, 115 kilometres from Delhi. They were attacked by bandits, his companions seized and killed, and our hero drifted half-naked and starving through the countryside before being rescued.[10]

[10] Ibn Battuta is rescued, in a dream-like sequence, by a man who gives his name as Qalb al-Farih, which he later realises is the Arabic equivalent of the Persian name Dilshad. He is convinced this must be the brother of the Alexandrian holy man who directed him to India. Dilshad literally means Joyous Heart.

The Sultan insisted that Ibn Battuta continue with his mission, and he promised to do so, wandering through India, vaguely attempting to find a boat for China (which he did eventually visit, or at least he says he does — his account of China is suspiciously brief). And as he travelled through India he encountered many marvels and heard about many others — levitating yogis with sandals that also levitate, men with the mouths of dogs, humans that turn into tigers and can extract the heart of a man without leaving a wound, and — in what is now Sri Lanka — monkeys that have sex with women.[11]

A few of these marvels may not have been imaginary. High among these are the Maratha women of western India whom 'God has endowed with special beauty, especially in their noses and eyebrows' and, Ibn Battuta assures us, 'they have, in intercourse, a deliciousness and a knowledge of erotic movements beyond that of other women'. A nineteenth-century Moroccan prince who owned a manuscript of the *Rihla* wrote a marginal note at this point, 'O God, give me a taste of this delight.' The only point at which Ibn Battuta shows much of an interest in the customs and beliefs of the majority population is, perhaps predictably, in a detailed description of the practice of *sati*, when the widows of three 'infidel' men killed in battle are burned to death. About this Ibn Battuta does not comment except to say that the widows chose to be burned, and that he almost fell off his horse while watching, and his companion had to splash water on his face to bring him to his senses. He does talk about food — there are useful descriptions of how to eat a coconut and a mango without making a terrible mess,

[11] A May 2009 article in the British newspaper *The Sun* headlined 'Chimp in Zoo Sex Attack', describes how 'cops are investigating a chimp after it tried to RAPE a female zoo keeper. Terrified Valentina Kirilova had to fight off the sex-crazed primate when he grabbed her as she gave him a banana at Rostov Zoo in Russia.' Chimpanzees are not native to south Asia.

and the earliest recorded mention of that modern staple, the humble samosa.

Ibn Battuta took few notes — and he lost those he did make when he was robbed and stripped to his underwear by Indian pirates. His very detailed account of his journeys is therefore entirely memory-dependent, which might explain some of his exaggerations. But he also clearly wanted to impress people back home, both with his own achievements, and with the way Islam had spread through the east. His dimensions are often awry. Many of the Delhi buildings he describes have survived, including the Alai Minar, an enormous stump of a tower, which would have been the tallest building in the world if it had ever been completed. Ibn Battuta insists that three elephants could walk abreast inside the tower's passage, whereas it would in fact be a struggle for a single elephant of average girth to squeeze through.

I live in Ibn Battuta's Delhi. I am surrounded by the ruins of the city he knew, ruins that I adore, and that are disappearing — and I sometimes feel I am the only one who cares. And I fear that I have become extremely boring on the subject. I wrote about them in a previous book, in particular about how a fourteenth-century mosque was bulldozed to build squash and badminton courts for the 2010 Commonwealth Games. I hoped to cause an outcry. I failed. Part of the reason for this is that so much has survived. The southern quadrant of modern Delhi is full of medieval ruins, hundreds of them — tombs, palaces, fortresses, mosques, wells, pavilions — more than any other city I can think of. Almost anywhere else in the world, many of these ruins would be major tourist attractions.

Take what's left of the Sultan's palace, for instance, where Ibn Battuta witnessed such dramatic extremes of cruelty and largesse. It is now known as Bijay Mandal and consists of a large arched hall, with part of its roof intact, and a raised octagonal pavilion at one end. From my home, it is a short, dangerous

amble across the multi-carriageway Outer Ring Road which was a dirt-track until the 1960s, past a 2008-vintage flyover, not far from the nearest metro station, open to the public since 2010. Bijay Mandal has its uses. It is frequented by drug addicts, card players, young lovers and goats — and is popular with latrine-less locals who use it as a urinal and a shithouse — but I've never, ever, in my half-dozen trips there seen anyone else 'visiting' it; not a single tourist, Indian or foreign. One foreigner who has been to Bijay Mandal, more than once, in fact, is the greatest of modern Ibn Battutistas, Tim Mackintosh-Smith,[12] who described the site as being 'booby-trapped with faeces', but proceeds to soliloquise on the importance of being 'undeterred by the turd', a useful mantra for anyone visiting India's less-heralded historic sites.

[12] Tim Mackintosh-Smith, a sesquipedalian, paronomasiac British resident of Yemen, has written three travel books about Ibn Battuta, whom he refers to as IB or 'The Tangerine', after his home town, Tangiers. William Dalrymple visits Bijay Mandal in his 1993 Delhi travelogue, *City of Djinns*, and either fails to notice the turds that were undoubtedly clinging to his boots, or is too fastidious to mention them.

Many are deterred, but not me. And when I chunter on at Delhi parties about the glorious medieval ruins of south Delhi, I'm chortled at; another foolish foreigner more interested in the past than the future. I'm made to feel that I'm behaving in the way Indians expect foreigners to behave. I have learned to laugh at myself, on this subject at least. I realise that I am a slave to the Picturesque, that quaint aesthetic ideology of the eighteenth century, which led to the construction of new ruins across Europe, and the depiction by western artists of many ancient Indian ones. And I even have a secret sympathy with the artist-clergyman William Gilpin, who suggested that 'a mallet, judiciously used' might render the insufficiently ruined gable of Tintern Abbey, later immortalised by Wordsworth and Turner, more picturesque.

A well-worn ruin has its place in the finest of compositions — and can still make my day. There's a painting on my wall right now, an oil dated 2005, by one of my oldest friends, of the garden of a Delhi house where I once lived. Looming gloriously over the garden's mottled lawn, its shrubbery and its washing line, is a fine piece of Ibn Battuta's Delhi, an enormous jagged eminence, what's left of one of the jambs and the tower of the southern gate of Siri Fort. In 2008, the city authorities took it upon themselves to 'beautify' the walls of Siri, built by Delhi's Khilji dynasty as their capital just a quarter of a century before Ibn Battuta turned up in India. At first I was pleased, because several parts of the wall looked as if they were on the point of collapse, and needed stabilisation before the next monsoon. The undergrowth was cleared, and then the builders turned up. They brought with them lots of broken rocks, similar in size and shape to those used in the wall. They began rebuilding missing parts of the wall, and jagged-edged ruins became smooth-edged surfaces, either parallel or perpendicular to the ground. They added a couple of new bastions to provide additional medieval authenticity. It did all look very neat and tidy, but I was forlorn. I missed my untidy ruins. And I still long to sneak out in the night, armed with a mallet or pickaxe, and return them to their once ruinous state.

A Fourth Intermission

I AM NOT, and have never been, an aficionado of Bollywood. But in Calcutta in 1989, I began watching a Hindi movie that still holds me in thrall. I saw the first half of the film at the home of one of Shireen's college friends, but was asked to leave by her father at midnight — he was clearly uncomfortable with the idea of a stranger sitting up late into the night with his unmarried daughters. In Kabul, a week later, I began — through the eyes of its beleaguered residents, smothered and orphaned and maimed by war — to see India from a very different point of view. For these Afghans, India was a land of peace and plenty and elephants;[1] a place where the children of the rich went to study, and a home to the heroes of the age, more adored than any politicians or religious leaders — the film stars of Bollywood. And to my astonishment, the film I had begun watching in Calcutta was being shown at a cinema in the centre of Kabul. I'd just got a little beyond the point where I had been interrupted in Calcutta — to a dramatic moment where one of the heroes revealed himself to be without arms, both limbs severed at the shoulder — when the film in the projector overheated and caught fire, blotches of vibrant yellow and blackened acetate dancing across the screen. The audience began shouting and throwing things at the screen, including their sandals, which they then doggedly retrieved, as if this were a weekly occurrence, when they realised the film would not restart, and once the management had promised them their money back.

Back in the west, Shireen elected to forego the glamour of Paris and live with me in London. She began a course in child

---

[1] There was even an Indian elephant in the Kabul zoo who responded to simple commands in Hindi, and whom I 'interviewed' along with her keeper.

development, worked in a delicatessen, taught herself to cook simple curries, and scoffed at my attempts to make a westernised, heavily tomato'ed version of dal. We talked about going to live in India, and on a train journey back from Cambridge, to visit my old college, she said that it was time to get married.[2] There was no genuflexion, and I hurriedly agreed to her proposal before she could change her mind. I began reading everything I could about India, from the Ramayana to Rushdie, and forced myself to watch rather dull Bollywood movies — then being shown at the oddest of hours on British TV — as a way of improving my Hindi. But I could not find a copy of the film which had ended so prematurely in Calcutta and Kabul. A colleague of mine at the BBC Hindi service tracked it down, and I finally found out what happened to the armless man, the charmingly drunken ne'er-do-well, the silent handsome one, the widow in white, the loquacious village flirt and Gabbar Singh, quite the nastiest villain I'd ever come across.

At three and a half hours, *Sholay* is not for the faint of heart. It was once described as a Curry Western, a nod to Sergio Leone's Spaghetti Westerns, though it's a failure of imagination not to see it as quite unique. It does draw on a mélange of occidental influences — from Shakespeare to John Wayne via Charlie Chaplin — and then folds them into the song-and-dance structure of a Bollywood film, in a way that could have been a disaster. There's some clammy over-acting, particularly by the ne'er-do-well (with whom I quickly identified), and some terrible filmy clichés and coincidences, but it can still make me laugh and cry more than twenty years later. I adore its cinematographic tricks, its clever self-references — and its angry young heroes, who are, uniquely, both cowboys and Indians. They are also travellers, wandering vagabonds in denim, who have been to big cities, and know a little English.

---

[2] I have a recollection of Shireen using the phrase 'too long we have tarried', as the Pussycat famously said to the Owl, but there is a high chance that this is another example of false memory syndrome.

As I write, I'm flying from Dubai to London, and I've just watched *Sholay* again, probably for the tenth time. I'm not alone. It's usually said to be the most popular Hindi movie of all time, and many Indians can repeat chunks of dialogue and sing the songs from *Sholay*. I can think of no Hollywood equivalent to that. My Indian neighbour on the plane was bemused and delighted at a foreigner watching a Hindi movie, and we had a long discussion about the symmetry between what happened in the film and what happened in real life to the six stars of the film. Most famously, the two leading men — the silent one and the ne'er-do-well — married their respective leading ladies, their *Sholay* girlfriends.[3]

There is not a single foreigner in *Sholay* — unless you count the head of King-Emperor George VI on the silver rupee that plays a decisive role in the dénouement of the film. There is an absurd prison warden, with a Hitler moustache and a Norman Wisdom[4] walk, who keeps declaring that he had been a jailer in British times, as if this might bring him respect. It doesn't. Released in

[3] The wedding of the silent one (Amitabh Bachchan) to the widow in white (Jaya Bhaduri) took place after the film was cast and slightly before shooting began, while the ne'er-do-well (Dharmendra) and the village flirt (Hema Malini) got married several years after the film was released. Bachchan became the best known of all Bollywood stars, and the host of the Indian version of *Who Wants to be a Millionaire*. Dharmendra and Hema Malini both had political careers, as MPs for the Bharatiya Janata Party. The armless man, Sanjeev Kumar, who was said to be besotted with Hema Malini in real life, is usually remembered for having played characters much older than him. He died in 1985 at the age of just forty-seven. Amjad Khan, the villain, went on to star in Satyajit Ray's *The Chess Players* and reprised his Gabbar Singh identity from *Sholay* in a series of advertisements for glucose biscuits.

[4] Norman Wisdom (1915–2010), once described by his fellow Londoner Charlie Chaplin as his 'favourite clown', spent six years in Lucknow in the 1930s as a bandsman with the 10th Hussars, where he won the British army flyweight championship, and where he learned to fall off horses in order to amuse the memsahibs. He would become one of the best-known comics in 1960s' Britain, and later, to his astonishment, a superstar in Stalinist Albania.

1975, *Sholay* is clearly a post-independence movie, but no one has a phone, or catches a plane, or uses an electric gadget. It portrays a world in which English is not understood, except when the scriptwriter wants to joke with the section of his audience that does speak some English. The ne'er-do-well threatens to throw himself off the water-tower when the village flirt refuses to marry him. 'Suicide,' he shouts to the assembled crowd, using the English word. 'What does that mean?' one villager asks another. 'Oh, when the English die they call it suicide.' And as the ne'er-do-well hangs perilously off the water-tower, he declares with remarkable bilingual fairness, '*Is* story *mein*, emotion *hai*, tragedy *hai*, drama *hai*'; which translates, almost obviously, as 'In this story, there are emotions, there is tragedy, there is drama'. But the story he is referring to is both his life story, and the story of the film. And, yes, she agrees to marry him.

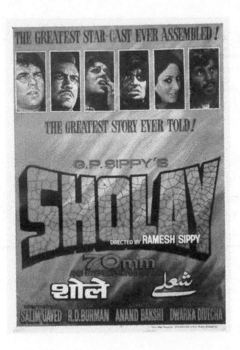

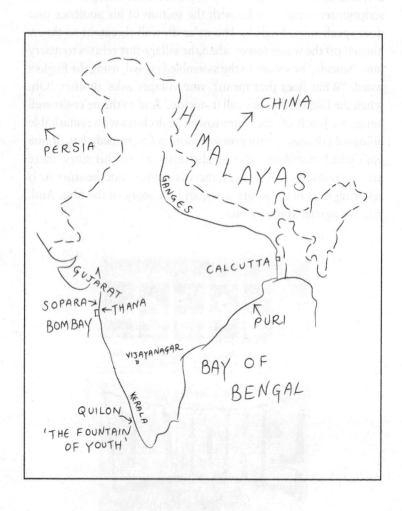

Chapter Five: In which the Author uncovers the fate of the Virgin's girdle, reveals his love of Marvel comics, and reflects on the Indian origins of the juggernaut

'DOT OR FEATHER?' the young American asked me as the air stewardess poured us each a glass of Alsatian Riesling. I looked at him blankly. He pointed to the centre of his forehead, just above the line of his eyebrows, and then touched the back of his head, and drew his hand, fingers pinched together, up above his head. And then I understood. 'Dot,' I answered, smiling.

It was June 2008, the start of Obama's summer of hope. I was travelling to Washington on work, and had been hoping to get some sleep. My garrulous neighbour had been visiting his girlfriend, a fellow American, in Paris — and was now returning home. He'd loved his time in Paris, and told me in almost intimate detail what he'd been up to there. 'Here, let me show you a picture of my girlfriend.' And then he realised he couldn't — it was on his mobile phone, turned off for the duration of the flight. 'She's white, see,' he explained. I nodded sympathetically. 'And sometimes, back home, people aren't very polite. They stare. They weren't like that in France. They didn't seem to notice that she is white and I am black.' I nodded again and suppressed a yawn of tiredness, not boredom. He turned to me. 'You're not like that, are you?' 'No, no,' I said, as the drinks trolley appeared, 'and my wife is Indian.' The stewardess interrupted us, and we both chose white, chuckling as we named our colour. And that's when he asked me, 'Dot or feather?'

Christopher Columbus, who thought he'd reached India

when he landed in the Bahamas[1] in 1492, bears much of the responsibility for the modern confusion between Indian Americans and American Indians — though I've been able to trace the dot/feather trope only back to the early years of this millennium. The UK-born, India-educated, US-based photographer Annu Matthew used it for an exhibit at her 2002 show called 'An Indian from India', while the Brooklyn rapper Jay-Z boasted in his track *Girls, Girls, Girls* released on, of all dates, September 11, 2001:

> I got this Indian squaw. The day that I met her,
> [I] asked her what tribe she [is] with, red dot or feather?
> She said all you need to know is I'm not a ho,
> And to get with me, you better be Chief Lots-a-Dough.

The reference to Indian Indians as 'dots', after the decorative

---

[1] It is not clear which of the Bahamas he landed on, though San Salvador is the most assertive in its claims. Some historians believe that Columbus actually landed first on the orientally-named Grand Turk Island, part of the Turks and Caicos archipelago. The Turks Islands got their name from a plant found there: the Turk's Cap Cactus which has a red tip reminiscent of a Turkish fez.

mark on the foreheads of many Hindu women, is just a little older, going back to the 1980s, when racist gangs, known as 'dot-busters', attacked south Asians living in Jersey City — while the Urban Dictionary, a self-consciously unrestrained online guide to modern slang, refers to 'the Indian Dot', created by a man who touches his penis, bloodied by his partner's period, to her forehead. American Indians have struggled for centuries over how best to describe themselves in English, and there's a hoary joke in which a Native American remarks that 'maybe it's not so bad that we're known as Indians; just imagine if Columbus had been searching for Turkey or the Virgin Islands'. One Native American leader has even claimed, with little obvious evidence, that Columbus wasn't confused at all, and that when he is said to have described the people of North America as 'Indios', he actually said 'in Deos', or 'in God', though it's not totally clear what he might have meant by that.

The roots of the Columbian confusion can be traced back long before the Genoese explorer made landfall in the Americas, and his mistake was not simply to underestimate the circumference of the earth.[2] For more than half a millennium, in what became known as the Dark Ages, there was an extraordinary level of confusion in Europe about where exactly India was located. This is not entirely surprising. With the decline of the Roman Empire, and the emergence of new powers in the Middle East, the old, admittedly tenuous, direct links between the Mediterranean countries and India were snapped. After the sixth-century visit of the Alexandrian monk Cosmas Indicopleustes (literally 'Cosmas who sailed to India') there is a gap of more than half

---

[2] If Columbus had read Alberuni, he'd have found a much more accurate figure for the circumference of the world, and would have realised that he had chanced upon a continent that was not known to Europeans. Six years after Columbus' journey, Vasco da Gama took a Portuguese fleet around the southern tip of Africa and reached India by sea.

a millennium before we get any confirmed travellers to India from the Christian west.[3]

In early medieval Europe, India slipped out of focus, and reverted to its fuzzy pre-Alexandrine identity as a semi-legendary land at the edge of the known world, full of riches, marvels and monsters.[4] India continued to be associated with Alexander and St Thomas, but their stories, too, became more fantastic and complex — with several competing and overlapping spin-off adaptations in different languages and different centuries. Alexander, for instance, was given superhuman powers, conquering the world and exploring beneath the seas, talking to trees — and ruling all of India. The story of St Thomas, meanwhile, is adapted to deal with several loose ends left behind by the New Testament. He, with the other apostles, is magically spirited back to Palestine to attend the death and assumption to heaven of the Virgin Mary. But, according to one version, he doesn't get there in time because he has had to travel all the way from India, and so Mary drops her girdle down upon the panting Thomas, his arms stretched upwards, as she soars up to heaven.[5]

---

[3] There is a later Anglo-Norman tradition that an Anglo-Saxon monk from Dorset called Sigehelm of Sherborne was sent by Alfred the Great to India — and came back bearing gifts. At the Festival of Empire held in London in 1911 to mark the coronation of George V, Alfred the Great's thirty-seventh-generation direct descendant, participants dressed as monks paraded ivory, 'porcelain jars of spicery', silken fabrics, peacocks, apes, and tiger and leopard skins to represent the returning mission of Sigehelm. Alfred the Great, in his translation of the late Roman Christian philosopher Boethius, places India at the far south-east corner of what he called Middle Earth. The latter term would later be used by the Anglo-Saxon scholar Tolkien to describe his land of hobbits, homunculi and other creatures, though Tolkienologists say that he may have lifted the actual words 'Middle Earth' from the poet Cynewulf.

[4] Indirect trade, via Middle Eastern middlemen, continued — and pepper and other Indian spices were widely used in noble and monastic cooking in many parts of Europe.

[5] The Virgin's girdle was not the corset-like undergarment of modern English innuendo, but a belt or sash, sometimes known as a cincture, or

Meanwhile, the story of the Magi, or the Wise Men from the east, who attended the birth of Jesus, is tidied up with the later elaboration that they were three kings who were later converted to Christianity by Thomas when he was travelling to India.[6]

St Thomas and the Magi even had walk-on parts in probably the most important and persistent Christian myth of the medieval period, the legend of Prester John, King of India. The legend was born out of the Crusades, those doomed attempts by Christian Europe to wrest the Holy Lands from Muslim control. Prester John was imagined as the Crusaders' saviour, the ruler of a far-off Christian kingdom, a descendant of the Magi, the protector of the followers of St Thomas, who would, one day, march to the rescue of his western brethren, bearing an emerald sceptre, or cross. Some modern historians argue that Prester John was a deliberate fraud aimed at strengthening the resolve of western Christians in their battles against Islam. Later travellers would go in search of Prester John in India, in Central and east Asia and in Abyssinia. By the time of Shakespeare, who name-checks him in *Much Ado About Nothing*, Prester John is a metaphor for someone who lives at the furthest end of the world. In the early twentieth century, John Buchan made his name as a novelist with an imperial adventure story called *Prester John*, in which the followers of the priest-king, and the quest for his ruby necklace,

zone in Greek, and said in Mary's case to have been made of camel hair. As well as the tradition that Thomas received the girdle because he was late getting there from India, it's also said that, as with the resurrection, Thomas doubted what his eyes were seeing — and that the possession of the Virgin's girdle convinced him that he wasn't imagining things. A piece of Mary's cincture is among the relics held at the Monastery of Vatopedi on Mount Athos.

[6] The Wise Men are only mentioned in St Matthew's Gospel, where they are referred to as Magi, the words normally used to describe Zoroastrian priests. The idea of them as three kings is a later interpolation. The earliest texts do not say how many there were — but that they carried three gifts: gold, frankincense and myrrh.

are transposed to Zululand — while Prester John's most recent appearance in popular literature was as a time-travelling Marvel Comics villain, sporting an electric-yellow apron over his naked legs, who gets to utter the immortal line, 'I have dispensed the powers of my stellar rod in combat with the Fantastic Four'.[7]

The most detailed early account of Prester John is in a famous letter written in Latin and circulated in the 1160s, purporting to come from Prester John himself, and addressed to the Byzantine emperor, Manuel I. The author of the letter, whose real identity is unknown, describes himself, in the regal first-person plural, and in a most boastful manner, as the King of the Three Indias, the ruler of seventy-two principalities, home to elephants, crocodiles and camels, in which pepper grows, and many precious stones can be found. These are lands inhabited, he says, by, among others, cannibals, wild men, horned men, one-eyed men, and men with one eye on the front of their heads and one on the back — and, he adds helpfully, women of a similar kind. 'Our land flows with honey,' he declares, mellifluously, 'and there is milk everywhere,' and he describes a waterless sea, made of sand, complete with tides and waves and tasty fish, as well as a magical fountain which purges Christians and would-be Christians of all their sins. Most important from the Crusaders' point of view, he also claimed to have an army of ten thousand horsemen and one million foot soldiers. So it is hardly surprising that a few

[7] In the Marvel Comics series, Prester John at one point becomes the last inhabitant of the isle of Avalon, known for its apples and its Arthurian connections, in an unlikely conflation of two medieval myths. The Fantastic Four have nothing to do with Enid Blyton's Famous Five, but are the dysfunctional superhero team of Mr Fantastic, the Invisible Woman, the Human Torch and the Thing, who first appeared in comic form two months before my birth. TS Eliot refers to Prester John in the context of a balloon, presumably as a way of not rhyming moon with June, in *Conversation Galante:* 'I observe: "Our sentimental friend the moon!/ Or possibly (fantastic, I confess)/ It may be Prester John's balloon . . ."'

years later, Pope Alexander III[8] sent an envoy, his personal doctor, a man by the name of Philip, on a journey to the east to search for Prester John and inquire about his great riches and enormous army. Philip was carrying a letter from Alexander addressed 'to the very dear John, illustrious and magnificent King of the Indies', which gently chided him for his 'pride in opulence and power' but praised him for his Christian faith and piety. Philip set sail from Venice, reached Palestine and then disappeared.

The phrase 'the Three Indias', and variants in several languages, occur repeatedly in medieval European literature. The location of these Indias, or Indies, as they would increasingly become known, is frustratingly and deliberately imprecise. At times, India simply becomes a metaphor for those parts of the world that are not known to Europeans. According to the letter from Prester John, the India which he rules extends from the Tower of Babel to the wastelands over which the sun rises.[9] Medieval European maps normally show the world as a circle, surrounded by water — with Asia as a semicircular continent at the top, with Europe and Africa as quadrants on the lower left and lower right. At the top of Asia, Paradise is often shown,

[8] Alexander III succeeded Adrian IV, the only English Pope, in 1159 and died in 1181. He had long-running disagreements with Henry II of England over the role of the Church, resulting in a famous murder in a cathedral, the killing of a turbulent priest, another Thomas, soon to become St Thomas à Becket, and about whom TS Eliot would write the play *Murder in the Cathedral*. Alexander also quarrelled with the Holy Roman Emperor Frederick Barbarossa who supported three successive anti-popes. He reached a compromise with Frederick at the third Lateran Council at which he introduced two-thirds voting for future popes, thereby inventing the notion of the super-majority. He also outlawed sodomy by priests.

[9] The Tower of Babel, mentioned in the Book of Genesis, was often identified with the ziggurat of Etemenanki in Babylon in modern-day Iraq, which was destroyed by Alexander the Great. According to the Prester John impersonator, the Lost Tribes of Israel can be found beyond the wastelands over which the sun rises.

and nearby is India — or one part of India. And on one of the most famous maps there are drawings of each of the apostles, next to their place of death — and there is Thomas near the top, next to India and Paradise.

India remained a misty eminence for most medieval Europeans, while its Asiatic neighbour, China, clambered dramatically out of the shadows. In 1221, a gullible bishop had returned to Europe from the disastrous Fifth Crusade with some 'good news'. A certain King David, he said, either the son or grandson of Prester John, he wasn't quite sure which, was advancing on the Saracens, as the Muslims were known in Europe, from the east. He was partly correct. It turned out that there was indeed an enormous army heading rapidly westwards but it was not commanded by a relative of Prester John or any Christian leader, but by a Mongol warlord called Genghis Khan. The Mongol forces veered northwards long before they reached Jerusalem, and instead rampaged around the Ukraine (and a generation later, Poland and Hungary). European emissaries were sent to this new pagan imperial power, partly in an attempt to encourage the Mongol rulers to convert to Christianity[10] and to encourage them to take on the Saracens — and there was significant contact between China and Europe for the first time.[11]

[10] It wasn't absurd of the Europeans to hope that the Mongol emperors would convert to Christianity. Kublai Khan's mother was a Christian, from the Keralt dynasty which had converted to Nestorian Christianity in the eleventh century. Some of Genghis Khan's descendants did convert, but to a different Abrahamic religion — Islam. Timur (or Tamerlane), who led an invasion of India by a Mongol army in 1398, was one of these descendants. Timur's descendant Babur would later become the first Mughal emperor, invading India in 1526. The word Mughal is derived from Mongol.

[11] An ambassador of the Roman Empire was thought to have visited China in AD 166. The controversial American Sinologist Homer H Dubs argued that ten thousand Roman legionaries captured at the battle of Carrhae eventually settled in the village of Liqian in north-west China, where the inhabitants are more European-looking than in neighbouring villages. Recent DNA testing indicates that Dubs' theory is wrong.

In the 1260s, two Venetian traders, the Polo brothers, Nicolo and Maffeo, caught up in fighting in Central Asia, found themselves pushed towards China,  and landed up at the court of Kublai Khan, the grandson of Genghis. Nicolo's son Marco would join them on a second trip to Kublai Khan's summer capital, Shangdu, best remembered and splendidly embellished, thanks to Marco Polo himself, and assorted extras (including Samuel Taylor Coleridge, Citizen Kane, William Dalrymple, Bill Gates and Olivia Newton-John), as Xanadu.[12] It's usually forgotten that Marco Polo also visited India — giving the first detailed account of the south of the country by a foreign visitor. However, his India chapters feel like an extended footnote, and were treated largely as such by Marco Polo's huge medieval readership. His account of his travels was dictated to a fellow jailbird in a prison in Genoa, who then wrote them up in medieval French, and it was so widely copied and translated that more than 140 different early manuscripts have survived — and this may help to explain some of the non sequiturs and digressions. A modern minority insist he never

[12] Coleridge's poem *Kubla Khan*, subtitled 'A Vision in a Dream', begins 'In Xanadu did Kubla Khan/ A stately pleasure-dome decree' and goes on to describe a landscape that is more Quantocks than Inner Mongolia. Citizen Kane's absurdly opulent Gothic palace in the film of the same name, as highly regarded in Hollywood as *Sholay* is in Bollywood, is called Xanadu. William Dalrymple, in his first book, *In Xanadu*, followed in Marco Polo's footsteps — but, curiously for someone who then became besotted with India, ignored Polo's Indian peregrinations. Bill Gates' extravagantly hi-tech home, partly buried beneath the Hollywood hills, is widely known as Xanadu 2.0. It was also the name of a quite appalling Hollywood film, about an eponymous nightclub, starring the unlikely combination of Gene Kelly and Olivia Newton-John.

got beyond the Black Sea — and made the rest of it up, or stole it from other travellers, which would explain why he didn't mention foot-binding, chopsticks, tea-drinking and the Great Wall in his China chapters.

However, Marco Polo's India passages sound genuine enough, with some of the credulity shown by so many visitors, and they're even tinged with some moments of unexpectedly sensible scepticism. Hindu ascetics, whom he refers to as 'Chughis', probably a mishearing of 'yogis', can live for more than 150 years, he informs us unreliably, largely because of their diet of mercury and sulphur. Like several previous visitors, he tells tales of humans with the faces of dogs, and he continues with the unlikely European obsession with the obscure properties of Indian birdshit — which, he insists, is a valuable source of diamonds.[13] But Marco Polo also breaks a taboo, like a magician's assistant revealing the secrets of the trade. He investigates one particular scam aimed at gullible foreigners — the fake pygmy swindle — and reveals all. 'When people bring home pygmies which they allege to come from India,' he declares, 'it is all a lie and a cheat.' He describes how the scamsters catch and kill a kind of small monkey which 'has a face just like a man's'. They dry the monkey skin, pluck and shave its body hair, then stuff it and dress it to look like a little man. Polo assures his readers that 'nowhere in India, nor anywhere else in the world, were there ever men so small as these pretended pygmies'.

In the two hundred years that separate Marco Polo's wanderings and the arrival of Vasco da Gama off India's western coast, there was a steady trickle of clerical and lay visitors from

---

[13] For Ctesias' theory on the poisonous qualities of Indian bird faeces, see Prologue, page 13. According to Marco Polo, in order to get diamonds from deep rock crevasses, Indians throw large pieces of raw animal flesh into them. He says the diamonds stick to the flesh which is then eaten by eagles. The diamonds are then easily obtained from the eagles' faeces. Sometimes they kill the eagles and open their stomachs to find more diamonds.

Europe. Four Catholic missionaries who became famous in Europe as the 'martyrs of Thana'[14] were executed in 1321, on the orders of the local Muslim ruler in Thana, now little more than a suburb of Bombay, after they used rather ill-advised language to describe the Prophet Muhammad. Their bones were spirited away and buried in nearby Sopara by Jordanus of Sévérac, a French friar of the Dominican order who had accompanied the martyrs earlier in their journey. Another European friar, Odoric, who happened to be in western India the following year, and who will play a larger role in this tale, then disinterred the bones and reburied them in China.

Jordanus later wrote a short treatise on India, in which he is repeatedly lost for words about almost everything he sees and tastes. He describes the mango as 'a fruit so sweet and delicious as it is impossible to utter in words', the coconut as 'a wonder! and a thing which cannot be well understood without being witnessed', and the elephant as 'a marvellous thing, who kneels, lies, sits, goes and comes, merely at his master's word. In short, it is impossible to write in words the peculiarities of this animal.' Only at the end of his treatise does he remember his purpose and declares that 'if there were two or three hundred good friars, who would faithfully and fervently preach the Catholic faith, there is not a year which would not see more than ten thousand persons converted to the Christian faith.' The biggest obstacle to converting India to Roman Catholicism is not, he is quite clear, either the idolatrous Indians or Christian 'schismatics', but Islam. 'Among the idolaters,' he assures his European readers, 'a man may with safety expound the Word of the Lord.' But 'the preachers', he says, 'of the perfidious and accursed Saracens' are 'perverting' the heathens of India. He recounts how he

[14] The four were Franciscans — three of them Italian monks, the fourth a lay brother from Georgia. Their purpose was to convert non-Christians as well as indigenous Christians to the Roman Catholic Church. The leader of the four, Thomas of Tolentino, was beatified in the 1890s.

has had four spells in Saracen prisons, where his hair has been plucked out, he has been scourged and stoned, and nine fellow missionaries, including the four martyrs of Thana, have been murdered. According to Jordanus, India is a key battlefield in the post-Crusades war to contain Islam. The dream of previous centuries, of a mysterious Christian kingdom which will one day rise in defence of Christian Europe against the Muslims, and liberate the Holy Land, has evaporated.

And Prester John, according to Jordanus, was never in India (or China), but instead lived in a distant part of Africa. However, Africa, he continues, in one of those seemingly irrational medieval confabulations that would make later historians despair, is also part of India, or part of one of several Indias. It can become hard to follow. Gradually, India came to mean something new, not just a huge swathe of unmapped Asia, including many of its islands, but sometimes part of Africa as well. No wonder Columbus was a little confused.

Friar Odoric of Pordenone, who disinterred the martyrs' bones which Jordanus had earlier buried, also travelled widely in India — and then to China before heading back to his native Friuli in northern Italy. He too dictated the story of his travels, which would, indirectly, be enormously influential. Because Odoric's tales became the most important source for an armchair traveller whose writings were far more popular even than Marco Polo's.

There are more than three hundred surviving early manuscripts of the *Travels of Sir John Mandeville*, in eleven European languages, including Danish, Czech and Irish. His work was used as the main source for the most important maps of the late medieval period. It was consulted by Columbus prior to his departure for what he thought would be India, and was treated for a couple of centuries as the indispensable guide to the east. In fact, it is full of fabulous lies and imaginings, teasingly written as an epic travelogue and a quest; the literary ancestor of *Gulliver's Travels* and

Robinson Crusoe.[15]
Mandeville's *Travels*
contains possibly the
finest collection of
human monsters of
all time — or at least
until Marvel Comics
first appeared at the
start of World War
Two.

Medieval texts had been scoured for strange stories of the east, some of which trace their ancestry back to Classical times. Mandeville's east contains one-eyed flesh-eating giants, headless men with faces on their backs, and, my favourite, an island tribe which subsists on the smell of a certain kind of apple. And, making a comeback, are the men with sleeping-bag ears from Scylax, the gold-digging ants of Herodotus, the waterless but fish-filled sea of Prester John, and, from Odoric, the tale of the discomforts of, presumably, scrotal or testicular elephantiasis. Mandeville describes reaching an island on his way to India where it is so warm that 'men have testicles hanging down to their thighs because of the violent heat', though they apparently know how to 'bind up' their pendulous balls and use 'astringent ointments on them . . . otherwise they could not live'.

Mandeville's 'India', like those of Jordanus and Marco Polo, is formidably vague. But he does refer to real places in what we now refer to as India, and repeats stories that are based on real events and half-truths. Thana, near Bombay, where the four friars were

[15] Even the name Sir John Mandeville is almost certainly an invention. In the text, written in medieval French, Mandeville refers to himself as an 'unworthy' English knight from the city of St Albans, north of London, who travelled to Asia in the 1330s. There is no historical record of such a knight, and plenty of evidence to suggest he didn't exist. Almost all his stories are lifted from other writers, with embellishments.

executed, is inhabited by a wide range of people who worship, among things, fire, snakes, trees and the sun. Further down the coast, pepper and ginger grow. There are Jews and Christians in India, he continues, quite correctly, but he exaggerates their numbers. He claims to have visited the tomb of St Thomas, where, he says, incorrectly, that the apostle's arm 'with the hand which he put into Our Lord's side after the Resurrection . . . lies outside in a reliquary'. He visits the 'Fountain of Youth', which appears to be close to the town of Quilon in modern Kerala, drinking from it three times. Those who drink regularly from the well 'seem always young'.

Mandeville, whoever he may have been, was no bigot, and does not, for instance, echo the Islamophobia of Jordanus, and tells his readers, pointedly, that Muslims believe that Jesus was a great prophet. There are some of the first stumbling attempts by a European to describe the religious beliefs of the people of India. A shadowy, often misleading and exoticised idea of what we now call Hinduism emerges from his text. He describes, appreciatively but inaccurately, how Indians represent their God as half-man and half-ox, 'for man is the loveliest and best creature God made, and the ox the holiest'. Cremation is preferred to burial so that one 'should suffer no pain by being eaten by worms when in the grave'. Ritual suicide plays a major role, as it would for so many later western accounts of Hinduism. He relates how a devotee carrying a knife 'cuts off a piece of his flesh and throws it up to the face of the idol, saying devout prayers and commending himself to his god. And then he strikes himself with the knife in different places until he falls down dead.' Mandeville is almost admiring of this, complaining that Christians would not suffer one-tenth of this pain and mortification 'for love of our Lord Jesus Christ'. And as further evidence he borrows and embellishes Odoric's account of a Hindu religious ceremony, in the form of a street procession, in which devotees maim and kill themselves by throwing themselves beneath the wheels of a chariot bearing a richly adorned idol. They believe, he says, that 'the more pain they suffer for the love of that idol, the more joy they will have in the other world'.

Death by chariot was described in even more painful terms by Nicolo Conti, a Venetian trader, who visited the kingdom of Vijayanagar in southern India in the 1420s, and recorded that not only do devotees, carried away by the fervour of their faith, throw themselves under the chariot wheel, but some of them 'make an incision in their side, and inserting a rope through their body, hang themselves to the chariot by way of ornament'. Conti does not actually say he saw all this happen, and later travellers to Vijayanagar do not refer to death by chariot wheel, or to the rope torture, though they do mention the same ceremony. It is clear that there were some suicides associated with street processions, but not on the scale suggested by the European obsession with the issue. It became one of several oft-repeated, partly true stories about India, an eastern tale to terrify small children, an example of the fanaticism and irrationality of 'idol worshippers', a justification for the 'civilising' influence of the west. And the story of the unstoppable chariot would later be given a name in English, a word derived from Sanskrit, that then took on several new identities of its own — some of them rather unlikely.

In 1965, the cartoonists and story-writers behind Marvel Comics came up with a new villain for their X-Men series. He was a red, muscle-bound superhuman with a spherical head whose special power was that he was 'physically unstoppable once in motion'. He had once been a human until he picked up a magic ruby in a temple and became, thereafter, the Juggernaut. He fought, among others, the Incredible Hulk and Spider-Man and usually lost. He was always a more important villain than, say, Prester John, and he gained new infamy as the result of the X-Men TV cartoon of the 1990s, and then an enormously popular Internet meme, in which the original words of the cartoon film were overdubbed with a spoof dialogue which included multiple repetitions of the phrase 'I'm the Juggernaut, Bitch'. This catch-phrase, which seemed briefly to capture the imagination of a generation, was then adopted by the makers of the X-Men films. It was famously uttered in the 2006 movie *X-Men: The Last Stand* in which the Juggernaut was played by the more-than-rugged former Welsh international footballer Vinnie Jones, best remembered for a photo in which he is pictured squeezing the testicles of the much more famous England striker, Paul Gascoigne. The original comic-book character continued to enthral Marvel readers throughout the first decade of the third millennium, particularly when he fell in love with the She-Hulk, a rather fetching fluorescent-green mutant with gravity-defying breasts.

The Marvel villain is just one of the many avatars of Juggernaut.[16] In Britain, the word 'juggernaut' is a synonym for a very large truck. While in most of the English-speaking world it has become a metaphor for anything that appears unstoppable, such as the 'Obama juggernaut' of 2008, and the Facebook juggernaut of a slightly more recent vintage. But there's another related meaning, used widely in the nineteenth century, and meaning a force or person which demands the blind devotion of its followers. Albert Carr, later to be President Truman's speechwriter, wrote a book called *Juggernaut: The Path of Dictatorship* with a final chapter on Hitler that was published on the eve of the Second World War. Charlotte Brontë comes closest to the original meaning in *Jane Eyre*, in words uttered

---

[16] According to the Urban Dictionary, juggernaut means, 'The manliest state of being. Basically being able to do any of the following: chop down trees with your penis; eat rocks for breakfast and shit out gunpowder: headbutt your front door open, causing it to splinter into pieces; jump off a cliff and break your fall with your face; wrestle sharks; kill a bear with your bare hands.' Jargonaut, meanwhile, is a portmanteau neologism for someone who over-uses linguistic jargon.

by one of the most stinkingly unpleasant characters in Victorian literature. The clergyman-headmaster Mr Brocklehurst has the ten-year-old Jane placed before him, standing on a stool, and tells the assembled teachers and students:

> '[T]his is a sad, a melancholy occasion; for it becomes my duty to warn you, that this girl, who might be one of God's own lambs, is a little castaway: not a member of the true flock, but evidently an interloper and an alien. You must be on your guard against her; you must shun her example; if necessary, avoid her company, exclude her from your sports, and shut her out from your converse. Teachers, you must watch her: keep your eyes on her movements, weigh well her words, scrutinise her actions, punish her body to save her soul: if, indeed, such salvation be possible, for (my tongue falters while I tell it) this girl, this child, the native of a Christian land, worse than many a little heathen who says its prayers to Brahma and kneels before Juggernaut — this girl is — a liar!'

Juggernaut — as Brontë and Brocklehurst knew — is a god. He is actually Jagannath, literally Lord of the Universe, another name for the god Krishna, himself an avatar (in the original sense of the word) of Vishnu. The most well-known temple to Jagannath is in the town of Puri on India's eastern coast, and every year an idol of the god is hauled through the streets of the town on a great chariot. It was here that the British encountered tales, true and not quite so true, of devotees who killed themselves by throwing themselves beneath the chariot wheels, in the manner described by Odoric, Mandeville and Nicolo Conti.

Modern Puri is an uncanny place. It's a beach resort that is full of pilgrims. There's an old railway hotel, famous for its terrible service and its snooker room, which has been tarted up recently. The actual beach is a long, sandy strip, with waves that are magnificent and dangerous. An English friend who went there in the 1970s stayed for a few weeks in a bed-and-breakfast run by an Anglo-Indian woman called Edith, and ate porridge with bananas every morning. My mother, a strong swimmer, went to Puri in the 1980s, and her hotel insisted she was accompanied by a lifeguard whenever she went into the sea. She discovered that the lifeguard could not swim. Perhaps, she thought, he was there to protect her modesty.

Huge numbers of Indians come to Puri — both for the sea and the temple. Foreigners, though, are not allowed inside the high walls of the Jagannath shrine. I tried to inveigle my way in — suggesting, without actually telling a lie, to a tall, shirtless man, a temple official, that I was a Hare Krishna. This was unwise, as I would later discover.

'No foreigners,' he said.

'What? Even Hindu foreigners?'

'No foreigners. Only Hindus.'

There was an extremely short man listening to our stilted exchange. He introduced himself. He was from Calcutta and he'd come to Puri for *darshan*, to see the idol at the Jagannath Temple and to see the beach. I asked him if he was planning to swim in the sea. No, he told me. He didn't know how to swim, but would go in — up to his knees.

'It's dangerous,' he explained, 'to go deep into the water.'

'Suicidal,' I suggested, 'if you can't swim.'

The short man then began to interrogate the temple official on my behalf. I asked whether devotees ever throw themselves under the wheels of the chariot. The official laughed, dismissively, as if he had been asked the question too many times before.

'No. And it was very rare in the old days. Sometimes it happened by accident, the crowds were so big — but now we have lots of security. Sometimes there were people who wanted to die anyway. Maybe they were sick and they thought this was a good way to die.'

'So no one has killed themselves for Jagannath recently?' He looked embarrassed when the short man translated my question.

'Yes, they have.' And he explained. They had not died beneath the wheels of the chariot, the Juggernaut of western usage, but had killed themselves within the temple precincts.

'One man,' he said, 'had thrown himself down a well, and a woman had hung herself from the ceiling of one of the buildings inside the shrine. A man who had climbed the tower of the temple had to be rescued. It's a new thing. Maybe people who want to kill themselves — they like to do it in a holy place.'

And why, I asked him again, through my interlocutor, were foreigners not allowed to enter the temple? There followed a long, bad-tempered discussion which I could not understand. Eventually, the very short man put his hand on my elbow and, as he led me away through the streets of Puri, he began to explain.

'I am sorry,' he said. 'I am sorry as an Indian and as a Hindu, and I do not agree with them. They will not let foreigners in. Not even foreign Hindus. They say that is their tradition and their belief. That only Indians can be Hindus. They are angry because they were forced to allow some Hindus from Indonesia, from Bali, into the temple. He said that many Hare Krishnas try to come in; white people like you, he said. There is one Hare Krishna, he said, an American who dresses like a sadhu, who has married a local girl. He was refused entry — so he is building another Jagannath temple. The temple officials are angry, they think pilgrims will go there. It's not true, they won't go there. Not many at least. But foreign money will go there. The Hare Krishnas are rich.'

'But how,' I asked, 'can they tell when non-Hindu Indians enter the temple?'

'They can't.'

We had reached the road that runs alongside the beach, and he turned to me to say goodbye.

'One last question, please. The Hare Krishna, the American — did he say anything more about him?'

'He had a beard. He spoke good Hindi and Sanskrit. They were amazed by him. That's all.'

'Nothing else. His name?'

'No. Why? Do you know him?'

'No, I haven't met him. But I think we may have an acquaintance in common, an old woman who lives near a pillar — many, many miles from here.'

A Fifth Intermission

THE INDIAN FAMILY with which I had become inextricably entangled were proud Parsis, descendants of migrants from Persia — and followers of one of the world's oldest religions. The first Parsis arrived in India more than a thousand years ago — Zoroastrians fleeing Muslim rule in Persia. They are often held up as an example of how a migrant group can integrate successfully into a host community — but retain their identity. The best-known story about early Parsis tells how, when they arrived by boats on the coast of western India, in Gujarat, they found they had no language in common with the existing inhabitants. The local Gujarati king held out a jug of milk that was full to the brim as a way of saying that there was no room for the migrants in his land. The leader of the Parsis, a priest, poured a spoonful of sugar into the jug, which did not overflow. Rather, the milk was enriched and sweetened. They were allowed to stay.

The Parsis adopted many local customs, and learned Gujarati. Their cuisine — almost as important as their faith — remains a distinctive Indo-Persian hybrid. They kept their religion but agreed not to make converts. This largely explains why they form such a minuscule proportion of the Indian population. I can never become a Parsi, and for the most conservative members of the community the marriages of my wife and mother-in-law to non-Parsis also put them outside the faith. However, I have felt accepted by Parsis, and I became a semi-detached member of the community — just as Tony Mango did before me. I adore their food. Parsi women tend to be admirably voluble. And there's a sweetness and gentleness to many Parsi menfolk that is almost as admirable. I even share a first name with one of the most renowned of modern Parsis,

Sam Manekshaw, India's first Field-Marshal, and can usually pass myself off as a foreign-returned Parsi. I cannot claim to be a believer, but the simplicity of the popular version of the Zoroastrian religion, usually rendered as 'Good Thoughts, Good Words, Good Deeds', appeals to me far more than the austere shalt-nottery of the Ten Commandments.

Shireen and I had a monsoon wedding which took place less than six months after she proposed. The timing was for the convenience of my British friends and relatives who had long summer breaks, and who could therefore combine our marriage ceremony with a proper Indian holiday. It was deeply inconvenient for everyone else because Bombay tends to fall apart during the monsoon. My mother-in-law-designate, almost unique among Parsis in not being an Anglophile, was less than pleased. It anyway seemed an act of parsimony, so to speak, that two of her children should be marrying into just one British family — and now there would be the weather to cope with. The Bombay guests complained a lot about the long journeys along waterlogged roads to Juhu, but it didn't actually rain heavily until the last of three days of celebrations. My friends, who had little sense of the difference between Parsis and Hindus, but had seen several Indian weddings on TV, were hoping I would appear on a horse, even an elephant, during the course of the nuptials. The ceremony — really a blessing — was, in fact, rather subtle and restrained.

It all took place in the same house overlooking the sea where I had spent my first night in India. Shireen underwent a separate ceremony which involved her planting a tree, breaking a coconut and then coming inside to bathe, followed by a sip of cow's urine, the smell of which made her slightly less delectable than usual. We were both in white, Shireen in a sari and me dressed up, as a friend pointed out, as if I was opening the bowling at Lord's. An old man, a Parsi priest, dressed in several layers of

muslin petticoats then sat us down. He stooped over us and threw handfuls of rice at us, and chanted at us in Old Avestan, which no one present understood, including the priest himself. We then ate a very large meal.

There are many myths and misconceptions about the Parsis. The nineteenth-century American novelist Herman Melville portrays them as the devil's children, tail-concealers. Fedallah, his terrifying Parsi mariner in *Moby Dick*, had long, white hair that he tied up, in a most unParsi fashion, as if it were a clothless turban. According to Melville, in what reads like a spoof of the Orientalist romanticisation of the east, Fedallah 'was such a creature as civilised, domestic people in the temperate zone only see in their dreams, and that but dimly; but the like of whom now and then glide among the unchanging Asiatic communities'. The fact that Parsis were widely seen as the most European of Indian ethnic groups makes Melville's purple prose seem doubly absurd. As the early nineteenth-century English traveller Anne Elwood points out, Parsis 'have a number of carriages, give sumptuous entertainments, drink wine, play at cards and appear to assimilate in every respect with the manners of our countrymen, excepting in their form of worship and style of dress'. Another Parsi plays a central role in a nineteenth-century classic novel, Jules Verne's *Around the World in Eighty Days*. Like Melville, Verne never travelled to India but his representation of Parsis as 'the most thrifty, civilised, intelligent, and austere of the East Indians' is not fantastically far from the truth. However, in the character of Aouda, the daughter of a rich Parsi merchant,[1] our credulity is stretched. She is orphaned and married off to a Maharajah — and when he dies, she is expected to join him on his funeral pyre. She is saved by the heroes of the book, the Englishman Phileas Fogg, and his French manservant, Passepartout. And when they finally reach London, Aouda, like another Parsi more than one hundred years later, proposed marriage to her Englishman.

If you ask most foreigners, and quite a lot of Indians, what they know about Parsis you will get a lot of vague looks and inaccurate assertions. They are often described as fire worshippers, and Parsis generally seem to take this in their stride. In fact, Parsi Zoroastrians worship God, whom they call Ahura Mazda; and fire, though central to many Parsi rituals and traditions, is not a deity. All Parsis are not rich, whatever you may be told — though the average per capita wealth must put them among the most affluent communities in India. And they most certainly don't all have long noses — indeed the noses of my in-laws are rather self-effacing. Parsi men are often accused of being rather shy, but the most famous Parsi of the twentieth century hardly fits that description. He was Farrokh Bulsara, a bisexual rock star born in Zanzibar but brought up in India,

[1] She is described in the text as a relative of a real Parsi, Sir Jamsetjee Jeejeebhoy, who was famous for his philanthropic activities. He founded the JJ School of Art, in the grounds of which Rudyard Kipling was born. Kipling's father, Lockwood, was a teacher at the school. The role of Princess Aouda in the Hollywood version of *Around the World in Eighty Days* was played by Shirley MacLaine, who would later become an admirer of Maharishi Mahesh Yogi.

famous for singing *Bohemian Rhapsody* and *Fat-Bottomed Girls*, and better known as Freddie Mercury.

At the time of my wedding I first heard another story about Parsis, an urban legend which several interlocutors swore to be true. They would not make such a claim today. I was told how someone's aunt or cousin was sitting on her Bombay terrace eating breakfast, when a Parsi digit fell onto her plate. Parsis, you see, practise a form of sky-burial, in which the dead are placed in an amphitheatre-like building known as a Tower of Silence, two of which are hidden away from the public gaze on Bombay's Malabar Hill. The bodies are left to be picked clean by vultures — who, I was assured, would drop the occasional Parsi finger or toe as they soared over the mansions and high-rises of south Bombay. This story is no longer told. The reason: the south Asian vulture is now almost extinct. They have been poisoned by the drug Diclofenac, given routinely to Indian cows — whose flesh, in the past, has provided even more nourishment to the vulture community than the Parsis of Bombay. The corpses now rot in the Towers of Silence — and many Parsis were appalled when photographs appeared, showing piles of uneaten bodies. Large reflector mirrors are being brought in to concentrate the power of the sun and speed up the process of decay, and there are plans to set up a special aviary as a Diclofenac-free home for Parsi-eating vultures. Many Parsis are opting for cremation or burial.

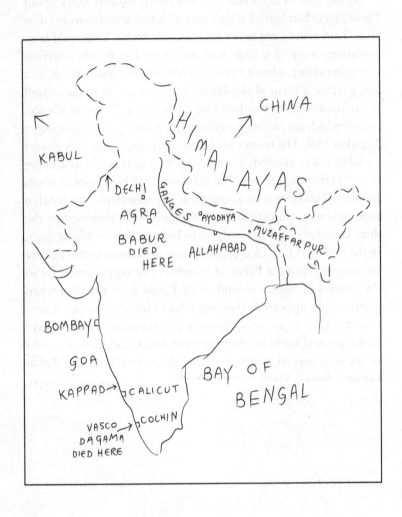

Chapter Six: In which the Author is faintly amused by the banana of Vasco da Gama, the breasts of Venus, and the turds of Babur

I WAS AT a reception in Delhi being addressed by an earnest young marketing manager for an Indian tourism company, her sari pinned, not draped over her shoulder — with a large red *bindi* on her forehead, and a nameplate badge bearing the name Pinky. She was telling me about the limitless potential of tourism in India, particularly its coastline and its golden beaches. 'Northern Kerala,' Pinky was explaining, 'has not yet been discovered by foreigners.'

I smiled at these words, a big smile, as I recollected something I had read earlier that day, and then I chuckled loudly at the delicious irony of what she had just said. So loudly that, I realised later, she must have thought I was laughing in her face — and that I was perhaps a little mad, or very rude. Pinky looked away, briefly, composing herself, and continued with her mini-lecture on why certain Indian beaches, particularly in Goa and southern Kerala, were very popular.

'We have many better beaches than the ones in southern Kerala and Goa, but beach tourists,' she said, 'want seafood and sun and beer and things to buy, small things to take home as a way of saying they have been to India. And most of all they want to be with each other — they do not really come for our culture.'

I nodded in agreement, recounting how on a recent visit to Goa, the beachside shacks had been named after 'The Rover's Return' and 'The Queen Vic', fictional pubs from British TV soap operas. 'And,' I continued, thinking aloud, 'it must make a difference that Goa and southern Kerala both have large local Christian populations.'

Pinky was not impressed by this point. 'You foreigners,' she said, 'always get that wrong. Hindus are easily in the majority in Goa.'

Now it was my turn to compose myself. I wanted to tell Pinky that I knew *that*. And that I hadn't said what she suggested I had said, and that what I had actually said was true. And that I found the vocative phrase 'you foreigners' a bit insulting — as if we were all the same. And I suppose what I really wanted to tell her was that I wasn't just another foreigner, and that I actually knew quite a lot about India, the kind of facts that might win a pub quiz, if they had pub quizzes here — and that I'm a regular non-participating winner of *Kaun Banega Crorepati* (the Indian version of *Who Wants to Be a Millionaire*). I even know northern Kerala quite well. But I could not find the right tone of voice to tell her all this. And so it went unsaid.

And instead I found myself telling her in a convoluted way why I thought her earlier remark about foreigners discovering northern Kerala was so poignant. I had just been reading a book about Vasco da Gama, I explained, in which the author had remarked upon the intransitive uses of the Portuguese verb *descobrir* in connection with the arrival of da Gama's fleet in northern Kerala in 1498. I realised that I had already lost her attention at this early point in my explanation — and that she was looking over my shoulder for help. We were soon rescued by an older man, a colleague of hers, who, when I said we were discussing Vasco da Gama, regaled us with an unexpected piece of Anglo-Indian doggerel, which exposed the Portuguese explorer as an unlikely flasher:

Vasco da Gama
took off his pyjama

showed his banana
and paid a *zurmana*.[1]

We all laughed nervously, and they made their excuses. I stood there alone, sipping a mango juice, feeling a little embarrassed. I turned my wrist to look at my watch and, in Chaplin fashion, emptied half my juice onto the floor. I decided to leave early.

Later at home, I again flicked back through the pages of Sanjay Subrahmanyam's superb Vasco da Gama biography, reflecting on the career of possibly the most foul-tempered and unperceptive visitor to India of all time. I realised that what I had been trying to say to Pinky about Vasco went something like this: It is amusing, surely, even ironic, to think that all these years after Vasco da Gama landed in northern Kerala, this same strip of coastal India was still awaiting its discovery by foreigners. And how odd, Pinky, that this strangely hyperbolic secondary use of the verb 'to discover', or *descobrir* in Portuguese, has survived translation and several centuries, with only minor mutations. It is, after all, impossible to justify the claim, made at the time, that Vasco 'discovered' India — in the traditional primary sense of finding something for the first time. And yet the word discovery is sometimes used in a similar way today, by you, Pinky, and as generic travel-agent lingo ('discover the Chernobyl region'; www.discoverportugal2day.com) meaning little more than an invitation to visit places that, sometimes for good reasons, tourists don't normally explore.

As I dug deeper, I, well, discovered that the verb *descobrir* is used in early Portuguese texts, with and without an object, to

[1] A *zurmana* is a fine or a forfeit. Other versions of the verse have Gama rhyming with drama, Panama and Rama. There is also a popular children's cartoon character called Vasco Pyjama who has a very large nose and who explores the world in an amphibious armchair accompanied by his pet duck.

describe an activity which is praiseworthy in its own right, as well as for the benefits it might bring. And so it partly reflects the competitive spirit in which those Christian neighbours, the kings of Portugal and of Spain, sought to send their fleets to different parts of the globe before each other. In a boastful letter, written in 1499, to his fellow European kings, Manuel I of Portugal describes how he sent Vasco da Gama on a journey with four ships, and says that his purpose was simply to discover, *a descobrir*. He claims in the same letter that as a result of the journey, 'India and other neighbouring Kingdoms and Seigneuries have been found and discovered'. Others sneered[2] at this, pointing out that many Europeans had travelled to India before Vasco — and everyone knew where it was already. And, of course, Vasco da Gama did not discover India even in the sense in which Columbus may be said to have discovered America less than six years earlier. However, the partisans of Vasco are quick to take a different tack, and point out that since their hero and Columbus were both actually searching for a sea route to India, the former was indubitably the more successful of the two.

Vasco da Gama has largely been forgotten in India — even in those enclaves, principally Goa, which were ruled by Portugal from the early sixteenth century until 1961. His fellow viceroy Aphonso d'Albuquerque has been honourably immortalised in the name of India's most fragrant and most over-rated mango, the Alfonso; the missionary Francis Xavier has been canonised, and has schools, churches and babies named after him throughout India; while poor Vasco has been memorialised

---

[2] The Italian explorer Amerigo Vespucci, after whom America would be named, said of Vasco da Gama's journey that 'such a voyage as that I do not call discovery, but merely a going to discovered lands'. The Portuguese writer Diogo do Couto, an acolyte of Francisco da Gama (who was the great-grandson of Vasco and the sixteenth viceroy of Portuguese India), proposed that just as America had been named after Vespucci, so the parts of Asia 'discovered' by Vasco should be renamed Gama.

in verse for a fictional act of indecent exposure. But there are a few other Indian traces of Vasco da Gama. In Cochin, his gravestone, embedded in the floor of a side-aisle of the Church of St Francis, is roped off, protected from the feet of the faithful, though the bones that lay beneath were taken to Portugal long ago. The largest and least attractive town in Goa,[3] perhaps the only place in the

state 'undiscovered' by tourists, is still, despite some objections, named after him — as is Goa's fifth-best football team. And set into the Viceroy's Arch amid the ruins of Old Goa is a sweat-inducing over-dressed statue of Vasco da Gama, his banana well-hidden beneath several layers of clothing.

Three Portuguese ships, commanded by Vasco da Gama, left Lisbon in July 1497, rounded the Cape of Good Hope, nervously shadowed the eastern coast of Africa, and crossed the Indian Ocean — eventually anchoring in May 1498 at Kappad, near Calicut, in what is now northern Kerala. The traditional, but partly inaccurate, account of the Portuguese arrival in India tells how Vasco da Gama proclaimed to a crowd of Indians who had gathered on a beach, 'We seek Christians and spices'. The accurate part is that the Portuguese were indeed seeking both Christians and spices, and they would head for home three

---

[3] Antonio Tabucchi, in his 1984 novella, *Indian Nocturne,* describes Vasco da Gama as 'an exceptionally ugly, dark town with cows wandering about the streets and poor people wearing western clothes, an inheritance of the Portuguese period'.

VASCO - DA - GAMA
LANDED
HERE
KÁPPKADAVU
IN THE YEAR
1498

months later believing, mistakenly as it happens, that they had succeeded in both quests.

According to the original unnamed chronicler of the journey, those words about 'Christians and spices' were indeed uttered, but not by Vasco da Gama, and not to an audience of Indians. Vasco had sent — on arrival at Kappad — a single person ashore, a *degredado*, a Portuguese convict brought along for such occasions, when the captain wanted to dispatch someone whose life was of little consequence to him into a potentially dangerous situation. The Portuguese convict had no language in common with the Indians he met on the beach, and was taken to see two fellow foreigners who were staying nearby. They were Muslim traders from Tunis, who had travelled almost as far as the Portuguese to reach India, and who spoke some Italian and Spanish. And they asked him what had brought the Portuguese ships here, to which he gave the famous reply, 'We seek Christians and spices'. One of the North Africans then came on board, telling the crew about the 'many rubies, many emeralds' to be found in India and wishing them all *'buena ventura, buena ventura'*, good luck. He told them to 'give thanks to God for having brought you to a land where there are such riches'. He could even, to the amazement of the crew, understand some words of Portuguese. There's an evident sense of both relief and disappointment at discovering the presence of other foreigners, people from the western Mediterranean, after what must have felt like a journey to the end of the world.

It was another eight days before Vasco da Gama himself dared to set foot on land. He was carried by palanquin to the house of a local notable, where he was fed on rice and fish, and then taken to Calicut to meet the local ruler, a Hindu king known as the Zamorin.[4] The Zamorin is described in a way that would become an archetypal image of an eastern ruler. He was reclining on a couch covered with fine cloths and at his side were a gold pot used as a spittoon, a large gold basin and several silver vases;

[4] Zamorin is a European mishearing of *samudrathiri* — meaning 'the one who borders the sea'. The Zamorins in fact were very used to having foreign visitors — mainly Muslims. One of them was Abdur Razzaq of Herat, an ambassador of what was left of the Timurid Empire after the death of its founder. He complained a lot about the ugliness of the 'ill-proportioned black faces', about the lack of court etiquette and the near-nudity of the Hindus, including the Zamorin himself. He goes on to visit Vijayanagar (modern Hampi) which he finds much more impressive and to his taste.

while the couch was on a raised platform in a room containing many courtiers, and with a gilded roof. The meeting with the Zamorin was handicapped by the lack of a common language, and some Muslim traders helped translate from Arabic (spoken by some of the Portuguese) into the local language, Malayalam. This may help, in part, to explain the embarrassing mix-up that surrounds the start of the European colonial period in India. Vasco da Gama and his crew returned to Lisbon believing that the Zamorin was a Christian, and that the Hindu temples they were shown were in fact Christian churches. It's hard now to read the early chronicle without laughing at their folly.

The chronicler is careful with his description of what he thinks is a church, but it evidently does not occur to him that the building might be something else. Outside the 'church', he says, is a pillar with 'a cockerel' on top (presumably an idol of Garuda, the man-eagle mount of the Hindu god Vishnu). He refers to the white ash 'which the Christians of this land have the habit of putting on their foreheads', and says the religious ceremony was conducted by men wearing a thread across their upper bodies, while some of the 'saints' painted on the walls had 'four or five arms'. The chronicler describes how the Zamorin, 'as Christians are accustomed to do before God', folded his palms high in salutation. This is clearly an account of the traditional Hindu *namaskar* greeting.

Relations with the Zamorin rapidly deteriorated, mainly over the issue of presents, and the Portuguese were quick to blame a group of Muslims who played a key role at the Zamorin's court. Vasco da Gama had proudly shown these Muslims the gifts he was planning to give the Zamorin: 'some cloth, a dozen coats, six hats, six basins, some coral, a bale of sugar, and two barrels each of honey and of butter'. The Muslims laughed out loud at such paltry presents. But where is the gold, they asked him, saying that the poorest merchant gives better presents than these. They refused to take the gifts to the Zamorin. Vasco was humiliated, and became, according to the chronicle, 'melancholy'. However, he soon after became *apasionado*, or enraged, not for the last time, when his next meeting with the Zamorin, supposedly being organised by the Muslim traders, did not transpire. They said that they were too embarrassed by the Portuguese gifts to show them to the Zamorin.

Vasco da Gama did eventually get another audience — and the Zamorin asked why, if he really came from a rich kingdom, had he brought nothing of value with him? Vasco blustered that these were just his own gifts to the Zamorin, and next time he would bring something more fitting from the king of Portugal. They never met again. Vasco da Gama, increasingly paranoid, feared a trap and headed back to the safety of his ships — believing that some of his crew still on shore had become hostages. According to the chronicler, the Portuguese were bemused, wondering how a 'Christian king' like the Zamorin could behave in such an atrocious 'dog-like' manner. Vasco da Gama, furious, took some Indians hostage. Eventually a resolution was reached and the Portuguese fleet headed home.[5]

[5] There is a strange codicil to the journey, in the form of the extraordinary story of Gaspar da Gama (no relation). After leaving Calicut, the Portuguese fleet anchored further up the coast, near Goa, to prepare for the long journey home. A well-dressed man who spoke Venetian appeared from nowhere, and came on board. He claimed to be a Middle Eastern Christian who had been forcibly converted to Islam, but after being flogged he confessed to being a spy for the local Muslim Sultan. The Portuguese kept him on board and as the ships crawled slowly around Africa, he revealed himself to be a Polish Jew, whose parents had fled a pogrom in Poznan, and moved to Alexandria. He had spent many years in India at the court of the Sultan of Bijapur and had converted to Islam.

By the end of the journey to Portugal, he had converted to Christianity, was given the name Gaspar — after one of the Magi who, like him, had travelled from the east — and Vasco da Gama's surname. In Lisbon, Gaspar da Gama was introduced to King Manuel who was enormously impressed — 'a man of great discretion and ingenuity', and he became a court favourite. At first, he went along with the notion that the Zamorin was a Christian, and helped draw up a list of other Christian kings, but then privately began

Vasco da Gama would return to India in the early years of the new half-millennium, and many thousands of Europeans would make the same journey over the next decade — sailors, soldiers, administrators, fortune-seekers and missionaries. Some real Indian Christians were 'found' — though they weren't quite as pliable or as numerous as the Portuguese had hoped. The false Christians of Calicut were forgotten, a reminder today perhaps of India's almost unfailing ability to live up to, often in an illusory manner, the expectations of its visitors — whether they are seeking wealth or poverty, monsters or enlightenment, or even fellow believers. The other all-too-common travellers' trait shown by Vasco da Gama is less endearing. He, like a significant percentage of visitors to India ever since, became angry whenever anything went wrong.

On Vasco da Gama's second visit he lost his temper even more frequently than before. He was determined, at any cost, to consolidate the Portuguese presence on the west coast of India, and to take revenge for the death of more than forty of his countrymen who had been killed in Calicut two years earlier in a battle with Muslim traders. The consequences were chilling. When he arrived off the coast of India in September 1502, to the consternation of members of his own crew, he set fire to a ship called the *Miri*, full of Muslim pilgrims returning from Mecca — more than two hundred people, including many women and children, were killed.[6] Seventeen children survived, who were all

to admit that Vasco da Gama and his crew had been mistaken. He was later a member of the crew led by Cabral which 'discovered' Brazil. His son also converted to Christianity and, like his father, took the name of one of the Magi, Baltasar.

[6] The sinking of the *Miri* would have an unlikely twentieth-century consequence — in the story of the oddball French physician, who founded 'phosphenism', a movement which claimed to teach one how to transform light into mental energy. Francis Lefebure (1916–88) said his epiphany came when he realised, while reading a history book, that he was a reincarnation of Vasco da Gama. He said that because of the 'crime' Lefebure (as Vasco) had committed by sinking the *Miri*, he had been unable to overcome the

converted to Christianity and sent to a monastery in Lisbon. He then captured some Muslim sailors whom he strung up from the masts of his ships. Their severed heads, hands and feet were sent to the mainland with a letter demanding reparations for Portuguese losses. The new Zamorin (the old one had died) did not capitulate, and the Portuguese fleet headed further south to Cochin where they adopted less confrontational tactics, meeting some Christians and doing some trade. They returned home with a cargo of some pepper and cinnamon on behalf of Portugal and the king, and, according to contemporary gossip, some wonderfully valuable black pearls for Vasco da Gama's own pocket.

From the early sixteenth century there are suddenly dozens of travellers' narratives, reports and letters, as the Portuguese attempt to settle small enclaves along the western coast of India. Most tell stories that are not as bloody and piratical as Vasco da Gama's second coming — and they often deal with practical matters. The European newcomers, not all of them Portuguese, build trading posts, forts and, of course, churches — often with the consent of the locals — and explore other parts of the subcontinent. In this minor avalanche of testimonies, India begins to emerge as a land of risk and opportunity — where fortunes can be made, where the young can be powerful and where death can strike quickly. They display an unsophisticated combination of pre-imperial religious and economic motives for coming to India — a variation on the 'Christians and spices' theme associated with Vasco's first journey. India becomes also irredeemably a land of exotic rituals — though there is much less talk of monsters and miracles.

The most influential of these early accounts was written by an itinerant Italian, Ludovico di Varthema, who served briefly as

hurdles in his life. Now, he knew the 'truth' and could, in his words, 'cut open the abscess that poisoned the eternal being within myself'. Lefebure's guru was an unlikely Zoroastrian, Arthème Galip, a diplomat of Ukrainian origin who disappeared in South America in the 1930s.

the factor at the Portuguese trading post in Cochin in 1507. His *Itinerario* published in 1510 tells of his wanderings and amorous adventures in the Middle East, India and south-east Asia. It was translated into seven European languages and was as popular in the sixteenth century as Marco Polo and Mandeville. He visits Mecca disguised as a Muslim. And in southern Arabia he has an affair with the wife of a Sultan, who, he insists on telling us, stared at his body for hours and then prayed to God with these words: 'O Allah! Thou hast created this man white like the sun. Thou hast created me black. O Allah! O Prophet! My husband is black; my son is black; this man is white. Would that this man may become my husband! Would that I may bear a son like this man.' In India, he keeps his banana well hidden, but he does get very excited about the exotic practices he encounters.

The Sultan of Gujarat, Varthema assures us, has elephants that bow down to him, a moustache long enough to be tied over the top of his head, and poisonous saliva that will kill anyone he spits on. He has a harem of four thousand women from whom he chooses his companion for the night, a companion who is never still alive in the morning — the victim, presumably of a poisoned kiss of death. He does dispel any lingering doubts about whether the Zamorin is a Christian. 'The King of Calicut is a Pagan,' he assures us, 'and worships the devil,' though he tells us that he also worships God. Many of the early editions of Varthema's *Itinerario* have woodcut drawings based on his description of the devil as having 'three crowns, four horns and four teeth with a very large mouth, nose and most terrible eyes. The hands are made like those of a flesh-hook, and the feet like those of a cock.' This is not a recognisable Hindu god, and far closer to traditional European images of the devil. It seems likely that Varthema was not allowed to see inside the Zamorin's shrine, and relied on the tales of others and his own hyperactive imagination. But the four-horned devil would become a stock-in-trade image of a Hindu idol, while the notion of Indians as

openly worshipping the devil became established in the minds of many Europeans. The monsters of India had been transformed from living creatures into imagined objects of Hindu devotion.

In 1524, Vasco da Gama, as irascible as ever, returned to India — and died soon after, of malaria. In the same year, a poet was born who would ensure that Vasco da Gama's popular reputation was not destroyed by those mundane chronicles of brutality and piracy by which professional historians would later judge him. Instead, Vasco da Gama is semi-divine, superhuman — a new Alexander — and his object of conquest is India. The poet Camoes would himself travel to India, spending part of his time in a Portuguese jail in Goa, accused of embezzlement. His great epic, known in English as *The Lusiads*, is Portugal's national poem, and was once highly regarded as part of the canon of European literature — admired by Cervantes, Milton, Blake and Wordsworth. It's now, sadly, little known outside Portugal, and is often dismissed, unfairly, but almost understandably, as little more than a derivative piece of nationalistic propaganda — and, well, it is, undeniably, both derivative and nationalistic.

The Lusiads is derivative, overtly and amusingly so, of Virgil's *Aeneid* (and its Homeric forebears), in form and in content, complete with quarrelling Roman gods and strange sea-monsters. Bacchus, anciently described as the first king of India, reappears in this Indian avatar after one and a half millennia of literary silence, and is a malevolent, jealous god. He attempts to stop Vasco da Gama's journey to the east

> . . . well aware
> His own powers in India would cease
> If such men came there as the Portuguese.

He is opposed by the goddess Venus, 'lovely Venus', a sailor's wet-dream, who comes to Vasco's rescue, saving the Portuguese from shipwreck by leaning

> . . . her soft breasts against the hard timbers,
> Forcing the powerful warship back.

As one might predict, the bosom[7] of Venus prevails, and the

---

[7] Venus is portrayed in *The Lusiads* both as a sailor's fantasy and as an incestuous seductress. In one of the most memorable scenes in the poem, after Venus has saved the ships with her breasts, she goes crying to her father, Jupiter, with 'trembling nipples' and 'marble thighs', to beg him to protect the Portuguese.

> With sheerest silk she hid those parts
> Normally veiled by modesty
> Though not so demurely as to hide
> Or quite reveal her mount of lilies.

As for Jupiter,

> He dried her tears and kissed her face,
> Embracing her flawless bosom
> So fervently that had they been in private
> Another Cupid might have been arrived at.

Portuguese reach India,

> . . . to which they bring
> Faith in Christ, new customs and a new king.

The India described by Camoes is a place of 'strange names and startling customs', where people worship idols and animals. Their religion is described as 'a tissue of fables', their gods painted in 'colours as discordant as if the Devil had devised them'. But, he reassures his Portuguese readers, 'the unbroken Indian offers his neck to the yoke'. Indians, we are told, are not only ripe for conquest, but often complicit in it. And this is after all what the gods have ordained, and Portugal therefore has both the God-given right and the duty to rule India. *The Lusiads* is probably the most important literary text of early European imperialism. It describes the destiny and identity of a small, impoverished western European country in terms of its rule over another much larger, richer land. An unlikely tale, if it was fiction — and, of course, Portugal only ever ruled small parts of India. But a slightly larger, even more distant, western European nation would later control almost all of the subcontinent, and also claim that it was its destiny to do so.

There is a sting in the tale, so to speak. It is possible to make the case for an alternative reading of *The Lusiads,* as a subtly subversive text which undermines Portugal's great power pretensions, and questions its ability and competence to rule

And so, instead of having sex with his daughter, Jupiter declares

> I promise you, daughter, you will see
> The Greeks and Romans far outshone
> By what people of Portuguese descent
> Will accomplish throughout the Orient.

Portugal's conquest of India is, thereby, assured.

India. A wise old man appears in the middle of the poem, who seems to speak for Camoes himself, when he says, 'You ignore the enemy at the gate/ in the search for one so far away'. That enemy was Islam — and his warning was timely, but unheeded. Just six years after the publication of *The Lusiads*, a Portuguese force of more than eighteen thousand troops was obliterated by a Muslim army in nearby Morocco. The young Portuguese king, Sebastian, the 'Boy King' to whom Camoes had dedicated *The Lusiads*, was killed on the battlefield. It was a national disaster. Sebastian had no clear successor and the Spanish king claimed the throne of Portugal. According to legend, as the Spanish army advanced on Lisbon in 1580, Camoes[8] died of a broken heart, unable to bear the idea of a Spanish takeover. The date of Camoes' death, 10 June, is still marked as Portugal's national day. Portugal and Portuguese India would have a Spanish king for the next sixty years.

The early European colonial experience in southern India was deeply coloured by the presence of large numbers of Muslims who had got there long before the Europeans, and who were still coming. By the time of Vasco da Gama's appearance in the subcontinent in 1498, there had been large numbers of Muslims living in and visiting India for several hundred years. They came from many parts of the Muslim world and included

[8] In fact, Camoes died of the plague. His bones, like those of Vasco da Gama, are now in a nineteenth-century tomb in the church of the Jeronimos Monastery in Lisbon, close to the Belem Tower from where ships left Portugal for India. There are some doubts about whether Vasco da Gama's bones are really inside the tomb. The bones of several putative Vasco da Gamas were collected in the nineteenth century and sent to Lisbon, though some of his descendants insist that his bones are still buried in a secret location on his estate. The body of King Sebastian was never recovered, and a myth developed that he did not die, or was in some kind of suspended animation, the 'sleeping king' who would return to help Portugal in its hour of need.

Central Asians, Persians, Arabs and east Africans who often did not have a great deal in common beyond their faith. Even the most famous Chinese traveller to India of the period was a Muslim.[9] And most of these Muslims knew far more about India than the Europeans, often spoke local languages, made many converts, and many friends — and quite a few enemies; and they were well entrenched all along the coast, controlling much of the maritime trade. For many Europeans, Muslims — of any kind, anywhere — were the enemy. And they didn't have to be at the gate. Muslims, after all, had defeated the forces of Christian Europe in the Crusades, had captured Constantinople, the capital of eastern Christendom in 1453, and in the first half of the sixteenth century Muslim armies had reached deep into Europe, besieging Vienna and occupying Budapest.[10] In this context it is not entirely surprising that India could often only be seen through the prism of a wider competition between Islam and Christianity. And so, for many European travellers and spectators, India became a minor battlefield in what might

[9] Admiral Zheng He who visited India in the early fifteenth century was a Muslim — though it would be hard to claim that his religion was the most important thing about him. Zheng He (1371–1435), previously known in English as Cheng Ho, was castrated at the age of eleven, and entered into the service of the Ming dynasty — which employed large numbers of eunuchs on the basis that they could be relied on not to be distracted from their duties as civil servants by the temptations of building a dynasty. Zheng He's fleet sailed from China, via India, as far as the Middle East and eastern Africa. The amateur historian and former submarine commander Gavin Menzies has argued that Zheng He rounded Africa before Vasco da Gama, reached America before Columbus, circumnavigated the globe before Magellan, and later visited Florence and sparked off the Italian Renaissance. Menzies' theories have not been taken seriously by professional historians, but his writings have proved very popular with the wider public.

[10] For the Portuguese and the Spanish there were other scars; the last Muslim dynasty had been driven out of Spain in the 1490s, while southern Portugal had been ruled by Muslims until the mid-thirteenth century.

be categorised — in that blinkered binary shorthand of the modern era — as a 'clash of civilisations'. Then, as now, this helps to explain why so much local detail and difference and nuance were ignored. And it might help explain why — in spite of the excitement of 'discovering' India — there was so little intellectual, historical or religious interest in the great mass of Indians who were not Muslims, or for that matter, so little interest in the huge variety of Muslim experiences and practices in India.

Another long-lasting empire was established on Indian soil in the sixteenth century — one that survived more than three hundred years, not quite as long as the Portuguese — an empire that would at its acme control more of the country than at any time since Ashoka the Great. Its Muslim founders, like those of the Portuguese empire, were strangers to India, but unlike the Portuguese, this empire soon lost touch with the land from which its founders came. The Mughals battled their way onto the plains of northern India in 1526, led by a peripatetic warlord called Babur, a man who seemed to hate almost everything about India. In his memoirs, Babur provides a long list of all that is wrong with India. These are words that have not been forgotten — they were quoted to me recently, verbatim and with obvious pain, by a former Indian Foreign Secretary whom I encountered at a Delhi party. Babur declares that,

Hindustan is a place of little charm. There is no beauty in its people, no graceful social intercourse, no poetic talent or understanding, no etiquette, nobility or manliness. The arts and crafts have no harmony. There are no good horses, meat, grapes, melons, or other fruit. There is no ice, cold water, good food or bread in the markets . . . The one nice aspect of Hindustan is that it is a large country with lots of gold and money.

Babur, like Alberuni, came from modern-day Uzbekistan,[11] a princeling from the lush Fergana Valley, who succeeded his father as the local ruler at the age of twelve. He was descended from Genghis Khan, from whose line he was, in part at least, ethnically Mongol — a word that was then twisted into 'Mughal' in Central Asia. But Babur always described himself as a Timurid — and was a more proximate descendant of Timur, better known in the west as Tamerlane.[12] He also composed one of the world's earliest political autobiographies — the *Baburnama* — with little of the self-serving pomposity that tends to distinguish that genre. It's an extraordinary document, one that reaches out eloquently through the obstacles of translation, time and culture. Babur provides graphic pen-portraits of his contemporaries — his father, for instance, was short, fat, brave and a middling shot, fond of alcohol, gambling, poetry and backgammon, and had absolutely no dress sense; while others in his retinue told good jokes or were good at leapfrog. Babur is disarmingly honest about himself, telling us how shy he was with his first wife, how he fell in love with a young boy, how much he vomited after a drinking binge, and how he likes nothing more than a juicy melon — he doesn't even neglect to tell us the colour of his turds, 'pitch-black like burnt bile', after an attempt to poison him. And it is perhaps because he speaks so intimately to his readers that it is hard, despite his proclivity for violence, including a fondness for

[11] They came from opposite ends of modern Uzbekistan, and were born more than a thousand kilometres and five hundred years apart. Babur was born in Andijan in the far east of Uzbekistan, and Alberuni came from the town of Kath near Khiva in the west.

[12] Babur also claimed descent from Alexander the Great, through his maternal grandmother, who was the daughter of the Shah of Badakhshan. It is thought that Alexander has no descendants beyond the first generation. His legitimate son by Roxana, and a second putative illegitimate son by Barsine, were both murdered before adulthood.

creating pyramids of the decapitated heads of his enemies, and his dislike of India, not to feel some small sympathy for him.

While still a smooth-cheeked teenager (he tells us that he didn't need to shave until he was well into his twenties), Babur became a wandering warlord. He was accompanied by a small ragtag army, searching for new lands to rule and to plunder. Babur twice captured and lost Samarkand, once Timur's great capital. And it was in Samarkand that he saw a mural depicting his ancestor's invasion of India a century earlier, when Delhi was sacked and its rulers forced to accept Timur as their overlord. At twenty-one, Babur captured Kabul, and over the next two decades consolidated his rule over many parts of modern Afghanistan, with a number of forays in the direction of India — and demanded the restoration of the tributes once paid to Timur by the rulers of Delhi. And then in 1526, at the age of forty-three, Babur crossed the Indus and conquered the plains of Hindustan — that 'place of little charm'.

Babur's dislike of India reeks of homesickness and nostalgia — for a distant homeland, and, perhaps, a lost childhood. He tries, like many later empire-builders, to replicate the landscape of his past. Babur misses gardens most of all, especially the rectilinear walled garden known as the *charbagh* — divided into four parts by shallow water channels. And as he visits his newly-acquired territories, he lays out *charbagh*s and other gardens. 'Thus,' Babur explains, 'in unpleasant and unharmonious India, marvellously regular and geometric gardens were introduced. In every corner there were beautiful plots, and in every plot there were regularly laid-out arrangements of roses and narcissus.'

When not discussing horticulture, Babur can be appreciative of Indian landscapes, traditions and learning. As his army moved beyond the plains he found waterfalls, and precipices and hill-forts that delighted him. He wrote vivid passages about Indian wildlife and he was particularly intrigued, like many Europeans of the sixteenth century, by the rhinoceros. Although he complained repeatedly about India's poor melons, he reluctantly admits that there were some other fruits worth eating. 'When the mango is good, it is really good . . . There are two ways to eat it. One is mash it to a pulp, make a hole, and suck the juice out. The other is to peel it like

a peach and eat it.' In fact, buried in the text are more positive remarks about India — often forgotten in historical accounts of Babur, so many of which seek simplicity in trying to categorise the Mughal emperors. He described the Indian system of weights and measures as wonderful, he admires the skills of its craftsmen and its acrobats — and, as he spends more time in India, he even begins to show a little interest in Hindu beliefs. But ultimately, Babur makes it clear that if it weren't for the riches of India, he would much rather be somewhere else. He never left India. Like Vasco da Gama, he died far from home in a country he never loved. And like Vasco, his bones were disinterred and taken to the land he called home.

Babur's legacy is complex — and still a matter of strife. He was the founder of the Mughal Empire — a dynasty which would later be seen in the west as almost proverbially Indian. But as the first of the Mughal emperors he was always seen in India as a foreigner. Most of Babur's gardens no longer exist, and there are few buildings from the very early Mughal period. However, until late 1992, three small mosques built in his short reign survived — each referred to by the name Babri Masjid, or Babur's mosque. But by sunset on 6 December of that year, a date still remembered by many Indians, there were but two.[13]

Earlier in 1992, I had visited the Babri Masjid in the town of Ayodhya, reporting on attempts by some Hindus to have it demolished, and to replace it with a temple. They argued that it was built on the site of an ancient temple marking the precise spot where the Hindu god, Lord Ram, was born. The mosque was, by then, no longer a place of worship for Muslims, and Hindu idols had been installed inside — including one of Ram as a baby, which Vasco da Gama would, almost certainly, have mistaken for the baby Jesus.

At the BBC we struggled over the language we should use to report the dispute. The BBC as a foreign news organisation needed to explain the issue in simple terms to a distant audience, yet it was also the most trusted news broadcaster in India, with popular radio programmes in several Indian languages. Should we use the word 'mosque' to refer to a building which still looked like a mosque, but was used as a temple? Should we refer to historical uncertainty over the existence of Ram? Should we point out that other Hindus believe that Ram was born elsewhere? If we answered yes to any of those questions we would quickly be portrayed as having taken sides by those who wanted the mosque demolished. If we answered no, we would be failing to tell the story. We answered yes.

In Ayodhya, I went to interview Uma Bharti, a young Hindu leader who wore the saffron robes of a *sannyasini*. She was a famous firebrand — seen by more secular Indians as the unacceptable face of Hindu extremism, and for this reason, as a good agnostic, I approached her with some trepidation. She looked like an attractive elf — short-haired, snub-nosed, bright-

[13] The two surviving Babri Masjids are at Panipat, north of Delhi, close to the site of Babur's greatest military victory in India, over the ruling Lodi dynasty, and at Sambhal, east of Delhi.

eyed and diminutive. She charmed me immediately; smiling, giggling, offering me tea, and as I explained that I wanted to interview her in both Hindi and English, she did something quite unexpected. She looked into my eyes. It was not an ordinary glance, but a long, deep, intense stare that disturbed me. No one, except a lover — and that pretty rarely — had ever looked at me that way. I was half-smitten — perhaps three-quarters. And then she held my hand in hers, something no Indian woman apart from my wife had ever done, and told me how she'd been practising her English so that she could give interviews. She stumbled frequently in her English interview, but resorted to simple locutions with their own rhythm and internal logic. I have lost the recording, but I have gone over it so many times in my mind that I feel I can recall more than its drift.

'You are a foreigner,' she said, 'you are our guest. We make you welcome. And will you destroy temples?' I shook my head from side to side. 'You are a good foreigner. Babur was a foreigner. Babur destroyed the temple of Lord Ram. This is how a foreigner behaves? He was a bad foreigner.'

'What about Muslims in India?' I asked.

'They are welcome, but they must know that this is a Hindu country. If they do not — they can go.' She lifted and nodded her head as if to signal where they could go, to a neighbouring country, not to be mentioned by name.

'But they were born here,' I pointed out meekly, still in thrall to her eyes.

'Islam is a foreign religion.'

'And what about the mosque?'

'It is not a mosque, no.' And then she repeated a phrase that had clearly been schooled into her, 'It is a mosque-like structure. It is a temple now.' She continued, 'You have seen Ram Lalla — baby Lord Ram — inside. And soon we will build a new temple for Lord Ram.'

Bizarrely, I found myself burbling in agreement when I didn't really agree at all. It was probably the most ineffective, least interrogatory interview of my broadcasting career.

A few months later, watched by Uma Bharti,[14] the mosque was torn down by Hindus armed with hammers and ropes. They left behind a pile of rubble on which they constructed a makeshift shrine, with the idol of baby Ram inside. There were riots in many parts of the country and thousands of people, mainly Muslims, were killed. More than two decades later, the rubble of Babur's mosque is still there — one of the best-guarded building sites in the world — and Ayodhya is a sore that still weeps.

[14] Uma Bharti was charged with a series of criminal offences in relation to the destruction of the disputed structure. The court cases against her (and several others) were continuing in 2013, more than twenty years later. In this period, Uma Bharti has been a central government minister (including, briefly, the Minister of Tourism) as well as chief minister of her home state of Madhya Pradesh.

A Sixth Intermission

IN EARLY 1991, I moved to India, my wife's country. We were newly-weds in Delhi without jobs or a place to live, behaving like frontier-folk — heading off to a place we barely knew in the hope of excitement, opportunity and exceptional mangoes. We found a *barsati*, a small rooftop flat in Nizamuddin — a cricket ball throw from the magnificent tomb of the second Mughal emperor, Humayun. And we began to make our life in Delhi. We quickly acquired, in circumstances that seemed to involve no agency on our part, a member of staff, a thoughtful, taciturn man from the Himalayan foothills — even before either of us had a job that might pay his salary, or our rent. Shireen began teaching at a nursery school. I did a small amount of freelance journalism, and became anxious about my failure to find much work.

I had given up my London job as a radio producer, and began hanging around the BBC office in Delhi, hoping to become a foreign correspondent. I was told, after I had sent a radio dispatch to London which was not used, that I had the wrong kind of voice. Too posh and too 'sing-songy'. I wouldn't, I was informed, even make it to the short-list for such a job. A former colleague of mine took me in hand and schooled me, at a distance, down a phone line from London, in the art of presentation. He pointed out that I was imitating what I thought a BBC correspondent should sound like, and told me instead to speak as I normally spoke. I followed his advice. On the day of the interview for the job of Delhi correspondent, the Indian government collapsed — and Mark Tully, then the chief of bureau, was uncontactable, up in the hills, far from a phone, in that pre-mobile era. And so it was my news dispatch and my voice that led the world news that day.

I was appointed Delhi correspondent in March 1991 — and the months that followed were tumultuous. An election campaign was under way in India, and suddenly, to my William Boot-like consternation, I seemed to be one of the most popular people in the country. The BBC in those days had the status and reach of a domestic broadcaster — and, unlike the state-owned broadcaster, the BBC was seen as impartial. For my BBC colleagues in London I was a slightly incompetent tyro, with a lot to learn. And they were right. But in India, I could walk on water. I was, as a foreigner working for the best-known media organisation in the world, in an extraordinarily privileged position. I could wander into the prime minister's office and would be sought out by MPs and party leaders. I travelled widely during the campaign, and spent two days in late May 1991 in Bihar, eating an unusually large number of mangoes and litchis, and watching electoral malpractice at work. One candidate proudly took me around the city of Muzaffarpur in his jeep to show me how his workers 'captured' a polling station by simply marching inside, and ordering all the election staff to leave. His workers then stamped and placed crosses on thousands of voting slips, before stuffing them into the ballot box. A police officer turned up after an hour, fired his pistol once into the air, and the candidate and the ballot-stuffers all left, slightly grudgingly. The officer told me there was nothing he could do about the fake votes, but other candidates had captured polling stations elsewhere in Muzaffarpur, and that it all evened out in the long run. I returned exhausted to Delhi the following evening, and put myself to bed early. By 10pm I was fast asleep.

Fifteen minutes later the phone rang. Shireen came into the bedroom. 'It's Mark, Mark Tully. Something's happened.' I wrapped myself in a lungi, and struggled to the phone. 'Rajiv's been killed,' he told me. The former prime minister Rajiv Gandhi — a man whom I had interviewed (and on whom Shireen had a long-running crush) — had been assassinated by Sri Lankan Tamil separatists in southern India. I would barely sleep for the next week. With my colleague Satish Jacob, I was summoned to the prime minister's office in the morning — only the BBC had been called. We were given exclusive interviews, in English and Hindi, with the interim prime minister, who understood the importance of the BBC in addressing his own citizens, and in calming the public mood. Later I would travel by train, with Rajiv's family, and much of the leadership of the Congress Party, on a bizarre sleepless night-time journey to Allahabad. Huge crowds gathered at every station, peering through the windows of a freight carriage, draped with sheets, in which Rajiv's family sat with his ashes. We all then gathered at Rajiv's ancestral home, where his grandfather, Jawaharlal Nehru, India's first prime minister, was born in 1889 — before heading to the *sangam*, where the waters of the Ganges and the Yamuna meet, for the immersion of the ashes. Polling resumed soon after and the Congress Party won the election. A party loyalist was appointed prime minister in Rajiv's place, and India began liberalising its economy and opening up to the world.

Those were heady times for India, and busy pre-children years for the two of us. I was amazed to be in such demand, professionally and socially. The arrival of satellite TV in Delhi meant that I would occasionally be recognised on the streets. People would ask me for advice on how to become a foreign correspondent. But we were peripatetic troglodytes — attached to our one-bedroom *barsati*, and shunning diplomatic parties and society weddings. Shireen, who by then had begun to work for Save the Children, had an admirably unacquisitive quality, born perhaps of childhood affluence. Otherwise it might have all gone to my head.

There were sides to Delhi life that I detested. It was, as now, an aggressive city whose streets and buses teem with misogynists. It was also then a small-minded, uncultured, parochial city (and this is no longer true) dominated by politicians and the bureaucracy. Simple matters like getting a phone line or a gas connection took months. One of Shireen's relatives laughed at me. 'You know lots of MPs, they can get you a phone — like that,' and he snapped his fingers theatrically. I was even more uncomfortable with how my Britishness was interpreted, especially by the older generation. I had no colonial connection that I knew of, and yet I often felt typecast as a latter-day colonial. For me, my British heritage was entirely coincidental. My wife was Indian, and I had followed her here, and I had managed to get a job in Delhi in my chosen profession, journalism. And it was on those few sparse facts that I expected to be judged.

I was, of course, fooling myself. There were then still many alive who remembered the last days of empire. Imperial legacies, including the English language and the English legal system, as well as my own employer, the BBC, remained important. The game of cricket still seemed, in those days, more English than Indian. As a Brit, I was expected to be honest and arrogant, and I fear I sometimes lived up to the bad as well as the good

154

aspect of that stereotype. I was also expected to be impassive and unemotional. And that, I was not.

Our landlord, an elderly Sikh man who lived below us, was a tiresome character — some of whose most amusing habits (such as counting how many times our toilet was flushed in the course of a day) were immortalised in the book *City of Djinns* written by my friend William Dalrymple. Our landlord would 'steal' our electricity by running a wire into his flat from our fuse-box. I spotted this and asked him to remove the wire. He did so grumpily, but it came back the next day. I went purple, and shouted at him. 'You are not a true Englishman,' he told me. 'A true Englishman does not shout. I know, I worked for an English company.' We also rented a fridge from our landlord. One day it gave up the ghost, and failed to respond to the attentions of the local electrician. I asked the landlord to stop charging us for the fridge, and to take it back. He said no to this proposition, and argued that a broken fridge was still more effective for cooling than no fridge at all. At that point, I'm afraid, I threatened to throw the fridge off our balcony. Again he said, 'You are not an Englishman,' as if there were no greater insult. Shireen intervened. She spoke to the landlord and told me he'd agreed not to charge us any more so long as we kept it in our flat. We bought our own fridge. Much later she revealed her deceit. He was still charging us for his fridge, but she felt that forty rupees a month was a cheap way of keeping the peace between her husband and our landlord.

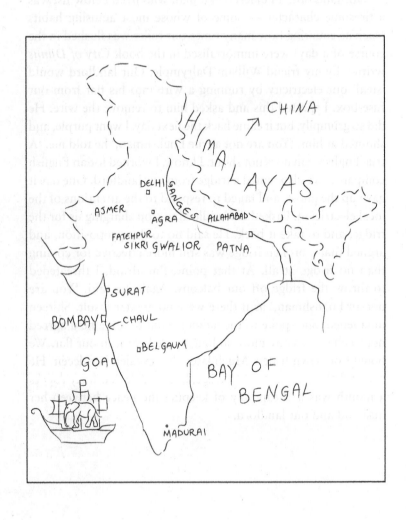

Chapter Seven: In which the Author investigates the testicular anatomy of the elephant, encounters the first of many pompous Englishmen, and admits to being a supporter of an obscure football team

IN FEBRUARY 1962, as I lay bawling in my cot in London, my first milk-tooth forcing its way through my lower gum, some Italian workmen were digging in one of the courtyards next to the Vatican Library, installing a new air-conditioning unit. In the soil under some old steps they came upon some pieces of bone and a broken tooth. They weren't particularly surprised. After all, in the pre-Christian era, Vatican Hill was a cemetery — and bones were always being dug up here; indeed, the Apostle St Peter, associate of St Thomas, and victim of an inverted crucifixion, was buried here in the first century AD. On closer inspection, though, the fragments found in the Library courtyard nineteen centuries after the death of Peter clearly belonged to an animal much larger than a human. They were provisionally identified as the remains of a dinosaur, or possibly of the extinct species *elephas antiquus*, a pachyderm that tramped around Europe fifty thousand years ago. The bones and the tooth were then squirrelled away in the Vatican Archive. In the 1990s, an Italian-American historian called Silvio Bedini rediscovered the remains and had them sent to palaeo-biologists working at the National Museum of Natural History in Washington. As a result the historian was convinced he had found the mortal remains of a famous young elephant who had journeyed from India to Rome in the early sixteenth century.

 We know more about Hanno the elephant, the beloved pet of Pope Leo X, than any of the hundreds of Indian *Homo sapiens* who travelled to Europe (mainly to Portugal) in the sixteenth century. Hanno's arrival in the outskirts of Rome on a rainy day in February 1514 would herald the resumption of a European obsession with the Indian elephant that dated back to Alexander and Megasthenes — and, arguably, lasts to this day. Hanno was just four years old when he arrived in Lisbon, having been sent as a gift by the king of Cochin to King Manuel I of Portugal, who then, in a tradition of circulatory gift-giving that I would later come to associate with my in-laws, decided to present the elephant, and lots of smaller exotic animals, to the Pope.

The ark containing Hanno and the other animals left Lisbon[1] and headed, through the Straits of Gibraltar, into the western Mediterranean. At each stop — Alicante, Ibiza, Majorca — huge crowds appeared on the dockside, and many rowed out to the ark in small boats, some of them even clambering on board to get a sight of Hanno. The captain feared that the boat might capsize, and decided not to stop anywhere else. And the boat made for

[1] Hanno, according to a story that became popular in Lisbon, refused to get on the boat for Rome, because his Indian keeper, who had fallen in love with a young girl in the Portuguese capital, had told the elephant that they were being sent to a barbarous and unhealthy country. King Manuel is then said to have intervened, threatening to cut off the keeper's head unless he got Hanno onto the boat. The keeper then tells Hanno that he had been misinformed and that they were actually going to a land where the prince ruled over all the other princes and kings, and that Hanno would become very rich. Hanno obliged. Hanno's name seems to have come from *aana*, the Malayalam word for elephant.

the harbour of Porto Ercole near Rome — from where, over a period of several weeks, usually surrounded by large numbers of excited locals, Hanno trudged his way for more than 120 kilometres through the winter rains to Rome. Several cardinals rode out on horseback from Rome to see the Indian elephant and, at one point, archers from the Pope's Swiss Guards had to be sent to protect the convoy from the crowds.

The menagerie was formally presented to Pope Leo X in a grand ceremony before the high clergy, ambassadors and other dignitaries on the First Sunday of Lent, 19 March 1514. Hanno had been dressed up in crimson velvet and gold brocade. On Hanno's back was placed a tall silver tower with turrets, and in each turret were religious objects to be given to the Pope — golden chalices and tabernacles, and vestments embroidered with pearls and rubies. Hanno was prodded into kneeling before the Pope. He then dipped his trunk in a trough of water, and, to great applause, sprayed the dignitaries. The following day, the Portuguese envoys kissed the Pope's feet, and one of them made an 'oration of obedience', during which, we are told, without additional information, 'India was placed at the feet of the Pontiff'. It was a celebration of how Christendom, under the temporal leadership of Portugal and the spiritual leadership of the Pope, was 'discovering' and conquering large parts of the globe. And the young elephant from India was the centre-piece of the occasion.

Leo X was later accused of cavorting with his elephant while the Roman Catholic Church burned. These were the early years of the Protestant Reformation, and Martin Luther even refers to the Pope's obsession with his elephant in a long essay about the tyranny and wickedness of the Papacy. Hanno died in June 1516, after ingesting a gold-based purgative prescribed by some of Rome's finest physicians as a cure for constipation. The Pope was bereft. Memorials were constructed for Hanno, including an elephant-sized mural by Raphael which no longer survives, and an epitaph written by the Pope himself:

Under this great hill I lie buried
Mighty elephant which the King Manuel
Having conquered the Orient
Sent as captive to Pope Leo X.[2]

In fact, King Manuel and Portugal had not even conquered a thousandth part of India's land mass, let alone the entire Orient — but such was the hyperbole of the times. The myth of conquest, and its beastly showpieces, enabled a small peripheral nation to take centre stage in Europe. And throughout the sixteenth century, elephants and, to a lesser extent, rhinoceroses, shipped from India, were used by Portugal as royal gifts and as symbols of its empire. But they almost became symbols of India, as a land of strange, exotic animals. The Portuguese brought at least twenty-two elephants and three rhinoceroses to Europe in the sixteenth century — though most of them did not survive long. The first Indian rhinoceros to reach Europe drowned during a storm in the Mediterranean en route to Rome. It was washed up near Marseilles, and its skin was stuffed with straw and sent to the Pope. It appears not to have been much of a comfort to Leo X, who was still grieving the death of Hanno a few months earlier. An elephant presented to the Archduke of Austria in 1552 survived for eighteen months in Vienna, and the city's mayor then used the animal's shoulder blades to make an armchair that can still be seen in the Kremsmünster Abbey

[2] Less reverentially, the great Renaissance satirist Pietro Aretino made his name with his 'Last Will and Testament of Hanno the Elephant', a ribald document in which the poor pachyderm donates his body parts to named clerics. His penis, for instance, is to be given to the Cardinal of Grassi, 'so that he can become more active in the incarnation of bastards with Madame Adriana', while Hanno's testicles are to go to the Cardinal of Senegaia, so that he will become 'more fruitful in progeny and in the merry procreation of the Antichrist with the Reverend Julia of the nuns of St Catherine'.

museum in central Austria.[3] Elephants became a common theme in European paintings, woodcuts, engravings and statuary — and were often used to symbolise India. And so did the less ubiquitous rhinoceros — 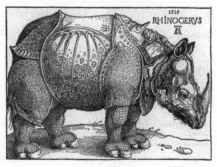 most famously through Dürer's woodcut, based on someone else's drawing of the rhino that drowned, and which Dürer provided with a little extra body-armour, and what look curiously like rivets.

Elephants also feature widely in early European travellers' accounts of India, though by the late sixteenth century their concern had become less exotic and more technical. There was some bemusement, for instance, at the lack of external testicles on the male of the species. It was even suggested that the swollen, tender lobes that distinguish the forehead of the Indian elephant were the source of its prodigious supply of semen — though in fact their bollocks are to be found internally, sensibly placed near the base of the penis, better protected than the testicles of other mammals. Elephants were often ascribed positive human qualities including sympathy, modesty and wisdom. According to one British traveller, the cleric Edward Terry, 'these brutes [i.e. elephants] will not endure any to behold them when they are coupling together', and he lamented that the same was not true of many humans. There were tales of elephants who used their trunks to rescue a fallen child from a stampede of humans — and how elephants were scared of ants and mice. But elephants could also terrify and be brutal, and there are several eye-witness

[3] This story was the inspiration for the 2008 novel *The Elephant's Journey* by the Nobel Prize-winning Portuguese writer Jose Saramago.

accounts of how they were used to torture and crush criminals and enemies at the court of the Mughals in northern India.[4]

Tall tales from the Mughal court begin to reach Europe in the late sixteenth century. These early stories were dominated by a single man, sometimes referred to as the Great Mughal, a third-generation migrant by the name of Akbar. He was the grandson of Babur the Indophobe, but became in western eyes the quintessential Indian ruler — generous, unpredictable, naive, whimsical, all-powerful and rich beyond imagination. The Jesuits of Portuguese Goa, who could also be pretty naive (but don't merit those other adjectives), were convinced that Akbar was willing to convert to Christianity, and in 1580 sent a mission to the Mughal court at Fatehpur Sikri near Agra. The Jesuits were the youngest of the major Catholic orders, children of the Counter-Reformation, attempting to renew the Roman Church after the decadent years of Leo X. One of the founders of the Jesuits, Francis Xavier,[5] made Goa his base — reputedly converting ten thousand Indians in just one month. Jesuits flocked to Goa in the belief that Indians, Hindu and Muslim, noble and commoner, were ripe for conversion. Several accounts of the first Jesuit mission survive, including references by contemporary Mughal historians. But the most important for understanding how early Christian missionaries saw India is the account by Father Antonio Monserrate of Vic, an undistinguished town north of Barcelona — best remembered for the ninth-century rule of Wilfred the Hairy, and as the venue for the heats of the

---

[4] In 1921, Winston Churchill told the British Secretary of State for India, Edwin Montagu, that he wanted Gandhi to be 'bound hand and foot at the gates of Delhi and then trampled on by an enormous elephant with the new Viceroy seated on its back'.

[5] Francis Xavier died in 1552 and most of his body still lies in Goa's main cathedral. Francis Xavier's right forearm is in Rome, while part of his upper arm is in Macao. One of his toes was bitten off by a Portuguese woman in Goa, and is now kept in a separate reliquary in the cathedral.

Roller Hockey tournament at the 1992 Summer Olympics.[6]

Monserrate was one of three Jesuits sent from Portuguese Goa to Akbar's court. He and his companions had some strange ideas of Indian history, believing — in a Renaissance mangling of the Prester John myth — that the ancient kings of Delhi, whose ruins they saw, were Christians. They also believed the great rock-cut images of Jain saviours at Gwalior were really Jesus and the apostles, while Monserrate's readers are informed that the ancient peoples of Kashmir were Jews. But as a contemporary record, Monserrate's chronicle of his stay at the court of Akbar is largely corroborated by Mughal histories from the same period. Monserrate is also one of the few early travellers to India who paused to think about how Indians might have seen him and his fellow Jesuits. 'Everyone stopped and stared,' he records, 'in great surprise and perplexity, wondering who these strange-looking, unarmed men might be with their long black robes, their curious caps, their shaven faces and their tonsured heads.'

Monserrate's descriptions of the earliest encounters between the Jesuits and the Mughal emperor have elements of touching, occasionally farcical, detail. When the Jesuits come to visit Akbar in private he tries to make them feel at home by putting on Portuguese clothes — a scarlet cloak with gold fastenings — and gets his sons to don Portuguese hats. Akbar kisses the Bible and then places it, for reasons that are not explained, on his head — the Jesuits are delighted. He has pictures of Christ, Mary, Moses and Muhammad in his dining room; and Christ, Monserrate

[6] Wilfred the Hairy, Count of Barcelona, who died in battle against Muslim forces in AD 897 has become an early hero for Catalan nationalists. He was almost certainly a descendant of Charlemagne (who had a pet Indian elephant), and is said to have, St George-like, killed a dragon. Wilfred is reputed to have had hair in places where it was to be found on no other man, probably the soles of his feet. Roller Hockey was an exhibition sport at the 1992 Summer Olympics in Barcelona. India suffered the worst-ever defeat at an international Roller Hockey match, beaten 56–0 by Switzerland at the 1980 World Championships in Chile.

proudly points out, has pride of place. They complain about the 'haughty pride' of Muhammad, and Akbar still listens attentively. They suffer a setback when Akbar supports a suggestion by a Muslim courtier of a competition between Islam and Christianity in the form of an ordeal by fire. Akbar says that a Muslim carrying the Koran and a Christian carrying the Bible both be burned on a pyre — arguing that God will save the true believer. The Muslims agree to take part, the Christians demur in a manner that smacks of panic and self-preservation. They quickly explain that they are all sinners, so God might not save them — and then gently accuse Akbar of siding with 'miracle-hunters'.

To the great relief of Monserrate, the ordeal by fire does not go ahead, and the Jesuits continue with their task of chivvying Akbar along the path towards Christianity. Monserrate says that Akbar told him, 'I will pretend that I wish to go on pilgrimage to Mecca, and will go to Goa to be baptized.' And Akbar does visit the Jesuits' chapel in Agra at Easter, prostrating himself 'in adoration of the Christ and his Mother', while one of his sons was handed over to the care of the Jesuits who then supervised his education. But ultimately the Jesuits were disappointed. Akbar did not convert. According to Monserrate, the mission failed because Akbar was spurred on not by 'any divine prompting, but by curiosity and too ardent an interest in hearing new things'. Ignorance of the Koran meant that many European missionaries did not realise that Jesus and Mary are both deeply revered figures in Islam.

The Jesuits were briefly able to assume a powerful position at the Mughal court — spending many hours alone with the emperor — and this became a matter of concern to some of Akbar's more orthodox Muslim courtiers. Akbar was genuinely interested in Christianity, as he was in other religions, and listened to the doctrinaire lectures of the Jesuits with politeness and an open mind. Monserrate notes the 'courtesy and kindliness' that Akbar showed to foreigners — a contrast with the way he treats his own countrymen and subordinates. Each of his nobles is treated as if he is 'not only a contemptible creature but as the very lowest and meanest of mankind'. Monserrate would not be the last foreign traveller to remark on the contrast between Indian xenophilia, and the appalling way some Indians would treat the people of their own country.

Monserrate's early twentieth-century translator, John Hoyland, refers to his religious bigotry, and felt it necessary to 'tone down . . . some of the bitter attacks upon Islam in his journal'. But, even in Hoyland's translation, there are many bilious passages directed against Muslim practices and ideas. Other religions are similarly disparaged. Even the normally inoffensive Parsis are 'wild and savage', and he asserts that Parsis cut off the noses of adulterous women, whom they then send to work as prostitutes — a practice that is not attested to elsewhere. Hindus are described as shameless and impudent. Monserrate is particularly incensed by the tales of the god Krishna, whom he describes as a petty thief and liar, largely because he is said to have stolen sixteen thousand wives 'by fraud and guile' from their husbands. Despite the negative picture that Monserrate gives of many social and religious practices that he encounters, he is awestruck by the wealth and splendour that he finds in India, particularly at the Mughal court. Hoyland the translator points out, 'If an observer so prejudiced and bigoted against the bases of that [Mughal] civilisation gives a picture so rosy-tinted, the reality must have been even more gorgeous than the picture.'

In the same month that the Jesuits returned to Portuguese-ruled Goa, having failed in their mission to convert Akbar, a flowery, sycophantic letter was written more than four thousand miles away, and stamped with the royal seal. This letter can be seen as the starting-point of a long and often difficult relationship between India and an even more distant European power. In February 1583, Queen Elizabeth of England placed her seal on a letter addressed to 'the most invincible and most mighty

Prince, Lord Zebaldin Echebar, King of Cambaia; Invincible Emperor, etc.', better known as Akbar. In that letter, which was handed to a merchant called John Newbery, Queen Elizabeth appealed for Newbery to be accorded whatever 'privileges' Akbar deemed appropriate and, foreshadowing many future discussions, referred to her hope for 'the mutual and friendly traffic of merchandise' between England and the Mughal Empire.

In the late sixteenth century, the English, as witnessed by the garbled address on the letter to Akbar, knew little of India. The references to India in English literature of the period are far less precise or knowledgeable than those in the languages of southern Europe. The ancient obsession with India's legendary affluence remains; most frequently as a land where precious jewels are ubiquitous. One of the greatest pre-Shakespearean English plays, Christopher Marlowe's *Tamburlaine*, written in about 1587, refers twice to India's great wealth, once in a passage in which the eponymous hero talks of 'a chair of gold enameled/ Enchas'd with diamonds, sapphires, rubies,/ And fairest pearl of wealthy India'. But there is no real attempt at geographical or historical accuracy in *Tamburlaine*, and at times Marlowe almost seems to advertise his ignorance of India, and of the real person on whom his impetuous, tyrannical hero was based. Because Tamburlaine is, of course, none other than Timur, who conquered northern India, and whose seventh-generation descendant, the Emperor Akbar, was proud to call himself a Timurid.

Shakespeare, meanwhile, has no Indian characters, except for the Indian boy in *A Midsummer Night's Dream*, who never appears on stage. But he mentions the word India, or a derivative, twenty-four times in his plays, almost always as a metaphor for fabulous wealth, most famously when Othello, having killed Desdemona, compares himself to a 'base Indian' who throws a pearl away not knowing its true value. Only in *The Merchant of Venice* does Shakespeare show any specific knowledge of India, when he mentions a 'beauteous scarf/ Veiling an Indian beauty', which can presumably be read as both a reference to purdah and to Indian textiles.

It's not known if Queen Elizabeth's letter to Akbar ever reached the Mughal court. Its bearer, John Newbery, did eventually get there — but lost most of his possessions while imprisoned by the Portuguese in Goa. He and his companions had been accused of espionage and heresy, at a time of great tension between Protestant England and the Catholic kingdoms of Spain and Portugal. The latter, rightly, saw England as a growing maritime threat, and the detention of the English merchants in Goa represents the start of a period of several centuries in which European rivalries would be fought out on Indian soil. The merchants were released after two weeks in jail, following the intervention of an unexpected intermediary — the Wiltshire-born Catholic, Thomas Stephens, usually described as the first Englishman in India.[7]

Newbery and his companions travelled on to the Mughal capital, Agra, where they would leave behind one of their group, a jeweller, whom Emperor Akbar provided with a home, five slaves, a horse and the equivalent of six shillings per day. Newbery died on his way back to England — but one of his companions, Ralph Fitch, eventually did return home in 1591, by which time the maritime balance of power had shifted — following the defeat of the Spanish Armada — towards England and the Dutch. By the time Fitch's travels were published in 1600 there was a new assertive spirit of mercantile exploration among the northern Europeans, for whom India had become a land of opportunity. These early years of the century saw the formation of rival East India Companies, one English and one

[7] Thomas Stephens, a Jesuit, arrived in Goa on 24 October 1579, four years before Newbery and his colleagues. He was known as Padre Estavao by the Portuguese. Other candidates for the first English person in India, included Sigehelm of Sherborne in the ninth century (see page 104) and two unidentified survivors of the siege of Diu in 1546.

Dutch, which would become the major players in maritime trade between Asia and Europe. Fitch was an early adviser to the East India Company in London and his travels were widely read,[8] as part of a compendium of travels that was enormously popular.

Parts of Fitch's account, written chronologically, as he travels through India and the Far East, read like a merchants' guide to the lip-smacking riches of the subcontinent. The Portuguese coastal settlement of Chaul, just south of modern Bombay, trades in 'spices, drugs, silk, sandals, elephants' teeth and China work', while Belgaum, inland from Goa, is a great market for diamonds, rubies and sapphires. Patna is best for gold, cotton, sugar and, he notices, opium — later to become the commodity most closely associated with the East India Company. Fitch is a pretty hard man to shock, but even he is rather astonished to find in Allahabad a naked man, a beggar, with fingernails two inches long, and who 'covered his privities' with the hair of his head. But mostly, he is keen — in a rather down-to-earth and often unprepossessing manner — on comparing places and people in India with what his readers might find more familiar. 'Agra and Fatepore [Fatehpur Sikri] are two very great cities,' he declares, 'either of them much greater than London and very popular,' while Brahmins 'are a kind of crafty people, worse than the Jews'. The English, in general, tended to show little interest in monsters and miracles, or in whether the 'natives' were ripe for conversion to Christianity. India had become a place to make money, where market knowledge and good contacts were critical to profitable

[8] Fitch's wanderings were included in the popular travel anthology produced by Richard Hakluyt, which may have been a source for Shakespeare's *Macbeth*. The First Witch refers to a woman, a 'rump-fed ronyon', whose 'husband's to Aleppo gone, master o' the Tiger'. The first page of Fitch's book described how he travelled to Aleppo on a ship called the *Tiger*. In fact neither Fitch nor Shakespeare's witch's ronyon's husband could have made the journey to Aleppo by ship, since the city is sixty miles from the sea. A ronyon is a word of contempt, used to refer to a mangy creature.

business, and where the main competition was from other European countries.

P. Robertus de Nobilibus Romanus Soc. Iesu apud Maduremses 45 annos ob Euangelij prædicationem commoratus Sanctæ obijt Meliapore 16 Ian. anno Sal: 1656. ætat: 80

Not every European wanted to make money, though — and throughout this story of foreign engagements with India there are those whose tales are strikingly different. One Italian Jesuit, Roberto de Nobili, moved to the southern city of Madurai, learning Tamil, dressing and behaving like a Hindu holy man — in order to win converts.[9] The English eccentric and court jester Thomas Coryate, famous for his unusually large head and for having introduced the fork to his homeland, decided to walk to India, where he delivered an oration to the Mughal emperor and was rewarded with one hundred rupees. He died soon after, of dysentery, and was buried at Suwali near Surat in western India, in 1617. Suwali, or Swalley as the English called it, is one of those places, long forgotten now, that was briefly famous: a symbol of English ambition and success. In the early years of the seventeenth century, the English East India Company had begun to jockey for position with the Portuguese and the Dutch along India's coastline — and had tried, and largely failed, to set up trading posts. There was a naval engagement in 1612, known

[9] Eighteen months after he started dressing as a Hindu holy man, Nobili had fifty converts. He later convinced the exiled ruler of a small Tamil principality to become a Christian — the first time a member of the ruling elite had converted — but no other princes followed his example. Nobili had made four thousand converts at the end of his thirty-nine years in Madurai — but they had, despite converting, retained their caste.

as the Battle of Swalley, at which a Portuguese flotilla of four boats was defeated by a similar number of English vessels. Surat would soon become England's first important settlement in India.

In 1615, at the request of the East India Company, and with its financial support, James I, Queen Elizabeth's successor, sent an ambassador to Akbar's son and heir, Jehangir. The envoy, Sir Thomas Roe, was a self-consciously pompous and conceited Member of Parliament — 'a man', as he pointed out to almost everyone he met, 'of quality'. He was attempting to build a special trading relationship with the Mughal Emperor — which became the obsession of the British for more than a century. On his arrival at Surat, he is appalled at his treatment by Mughal officials, so 'barbarous' that he cannot, in his egotistical, whinging memoirs, quite bring himself to describe what happened. He complains about this treatment repeatedly — and is gratified to hear that action will be taken against the culprits. Roe travels towards the Mughal court, encountering further disrespect to his office, and refusing to bow his head before a Mughal prince — the future emperor Shah Jahan. He eventually meets Emperor Jehangir at Ajmer in Rajasthan, a Muslim holy city that was temporarily the Mughal capital — where he becomes obsessed with protocol and being allowed to stand near the imperial throne. There is much exchanging of gifts, and inconclusive discussions about a *firman*, an imperial directive, which would give England the seventeenth-century equivalent of most-favoured-nation trading status.

Roe is too self-important to admit to being amazed by what he sees, but his long descriptions of the emperor's riches and rather unpredictable largesse (he tries to give Roe an elephant) indicate that he was not prepared for such affluence. But he does not like India, and feels free on his return home to say it was 'the dullest, basest place that ever I saw'. He dismisses the Mughal Empire as an 'overgrowne Eliphant', and refers to Indians as 'barbarous unjust people'. For Roe, Indians appear as an undifferentiated mass of 'faithless people'. His memoirs speak to his own countrymen. And for this reason, he can drop the pretence of ambassadorial civility which he had to assume for his three and a half years in India — just as the occasional western diplomat in modern Delhi, in his cups at an embassy party, has revealed to a fellow white man how much he hates India and Indians, and longs to go home, and expects, but does not receive, a sympathetic response.

Fortunately, for our understanding of the first official English mission to the Mughals, Roe was not alone, and his companions were not all angry foreigners. Roe's chaplain, Edward Terry, could be pretty blinkered on religious matters and was very critical of Emperor Jehangir and of Brahmins, but was interested enough in India and its people to open his eyes and ears, and write about what he saw and heard. And in his five-hundred-page-long *Voyage to East India*, he often described the same events as Roe but with far greater detail and understanding. He can sometimes be a little gullible. He believes that water from the Ganges weighs one ounce less per pint than any other water; bizarrely, he thinks the word Mughal means circumcised; and he claims, incorrectly, that the writing on the iron pillar near the Qutb Minar in Delhi is in Greek, and had been inscribed by Alexander the Great. But Terry is indefatigably excited and intrigued by India. And he was so dazzled by the wealth of the Mughal courts at Ajmer and Agra that he felt that Christians would need to revise their traditional descriptions of the riches of the kingdom of heaven — which seemed just a little basic in comparison.

Terry manages to capture the multicultural multi-religious flavour of India in a way that marks him out among early European visitors. There's a long digression about Parsis, for instance, who, he tells us approvingly, believe in 'but one God . . . and talk much of Lucifer', and he tells us how he admires India's 'heathens' for the greater care they show to 'base inferior creatures' than most Christians. Brahmins were once learned, he says, but are now 'a very silly, sottish and ignorant sort of people'. He admires the civility of most Indians, but declares them, on the whole, to be a cowardly people — another description which would resonate in more recent times. According to Terry, the people of north India, apart from the Rajputs, would 'rather eat than quarrel, and rather quarrel than fight'.

Terry was also an eater, not a fighter — and spent pages describing the breads, meat, fish and fowl that seem, in all ways, better than English food. Unlike Babur, ninety years earlier, Terry is in gluttonous raptures about Indian fruit — though the melons he so admires may have been first seeded by Babur's companions. Best of all are the pineapples, the bananas and, of course, the mango, for which he has a particular reverence — and uses a series of arboreal and fruity comparisons appropriate to his English audience. A 'most excellent fruit', that grows 'upon trees as big as our walnut trees', and 'in shape and colour like unto our apricots, but much bigger'. There is not a word of complaint against a single item of food he eats in India, and not a note of nostalgia for English cuisine.

But everything in India is not pleasing. He describes at some length the 'annoyances': beasts of prey, jackals that will dig a man up from his grave, crocodiles, scorpions, flies, mosquitoes, and rats which will bite your nose and fingers as you sleep. The pre-monsoon heat is so terrible that it can 'blister a man's face', and every day, Terry recalls, 'us English . . . would stew in our own moisture'. And then there was the shadow of death. Twenty out of Sir Thomas Roe's twenty-four English officers and servants died in India, or on the journey back. India would remain, for English people, a diseased and dangerous place, from where many would never return.

The centre-piece of Terry's tale, as with so many other western accounts of this period, was a description of the Mughal court, and the Emperor Jehangir — surrounded by courtiers, jugglers

and snake charmers. The word 'Mughal', usually written 'Mogul' in Terry's time (but sometimes 'Mogor' in the Portuguese style), was entering everyday English. Its most common use was in the description of the emperor as 'the Great Mogul', often said to have been a deliberate mimicking of the Ottoman emperor's epithet, 'the Grand Turk'. But Mughal or Mogul gradually came to mean much more, so that by the twentieth century it could be used to describe movie impresarios and business tycoons, a riff on those original English-language connotations of fabulous wealth and limitless power. Terry includes three drawings in his *Voyage to East India*: a full-length portrait of Jehangir, 'bedeck'd and adorn'd with jewels', a copy of the imperial seal whose inscription traces the emperor's descent from Timur, and the imperial standard showing a 'couchant lion shadowing the body of the sun'. Jehangir, in Terry's account, is absurdly swollen with pride; he 'feeds and feasts himself on this conceit, that he is Conqueror of the World'. When Sir Thomas Roe presents Jehangir with a copy of Mercator's world atlas, the emperor is briefly delighted — until, according to Terry, he turns over the pages and discovers maps of many places that he does not rule. With a slightly troubled look, he returns the gift to Roe.

Jehangir is portrayed by Terry as an archetypal oriental despot — much as Ibn Battuta had depicted Muhammad bin Tughlaq almost three hundred years earlier — as capricious, generous, brutal. Jehangir's 'disposition', he writes, 'seemed unto me to be composed of extremes; for sometimes he was barbarously cruel and at other times he would seem to be exceeding fair and gentle'. He describes how one of Jehangir's servants broke a china cup, and was punished by being sent to China to get a replacement. Terry has an almost visceral delight in describing the various ways of execution dreamed up by the emperor. A woman from Jehangir's harem was found kissing a eunuch — she was buried up to her neck in the ground, and died there after one and a half days; while the eunuch was cut up into pieces in front of her. A man who killed his mother was stripped naked, and had poisonous snakes placed all over his body. He survived for just half an hour. Death by elephant could take several forms — from simply being trampled on or crushed, or dragged by a chain around the countryside, to being sliced up by sickles attached to the legs of elephants.

Modern visitors to Jehangir's small fortified palace in Ajmer, where he received Sir Thomas Roe on 10 January 1616, are greeted by three separate signboards. Each recalls, with slight variations of language, an encounter that would, in the eyes of British historians, be laden with portent. For that date would later become, with the advantage of hindsight, the most often mentioned 'real' starting-point of a dysfunctional relationship between the Mughals and the British, with unimagined implications for India and Britain, which would end only with the death, in British-imposed exile, of the last Mughal emperor almost a quarter of a millennium later. In fact, there were far more visitors from the Middle East and Central Asia to Jehangir's court than Europeans, and the appearance of Roe in Ajmer was little more than a minor curiosity for the Mughals. The palace where they met is now a forgotten museum — newly renovated and devoid of tourists.

Ajmer itself is a city of many avatars, whose hills and lakeside are dotted with reminders of previous conquerors and travellers — a palimpsest of the last millennium. For Ajmer was one of

the capitals of Prithviraj Chauhan, the Hindu king defeated by the first Muslim ruler of north India, Muhammad of Ghor. And the latter's generals built one of India's earliest and grandest mosques,[10] whose wonderful crumbling ruins sit at the foot of the ancient hill-fortress of Taragarh. In the nineteenth century, Ajmer re-emerged as an island of British territory, from where the viceroy's representative supervised the nominally independent princely states of Rajputana, now known as Rajasthan — and where they set up the still-flourishing Mayo College, as an Eton for India, to provide a classical British education for local princelings.

Ajmer is today situated in the centre of modern Rajasthan, the state that is indubitably the best beloved of western tourists. But very few of them make it to Ajmer,[11] though it does receive huge numbers of other foreign visitors. Most of them

[10] The Arhai Din ka Jhompra Masjid built in 1200. Its name means, literally, 'two and a half days hut'.

[11] Western tourists do go in large numbers to Ajmer's alter ego, the Hindu temple town of Pushkar, just nine kilometres away. They travel there for, probably in this order, spirituality, drugs, sex and camels. The last three appear to be in shorter supply in Ajmer.

are pilgrims. This is because in the early thirteenth century, probably the most influential Sufi Muslim preacher of all time, an itinerant Persian called Moinuddin Chishti, came here, and preached, and died. And the presence of Chishti's tomb meant that for several of the Mughal emperors, Ajmer played the role of a spiritual capital, and Akbar and Jehangir, father and son, made the city one of their many homes. Indeed, Akbar, as a way of giving thanks for the arrival of the future emperor, Jehangir, his firstborn, walked every step of the way from Agra to Ajmer, a distance of more than two hundred miles. The tomb complex, or *dargah*, remains the most important Muslim pilgrimage site in the country, visited by Hindus and Sikhs and Christians and Parsis, as well as Muslims from India and elsewhere — particularly Pakistan. It has become the paramount symbol of syncretic India, a land where all religions are supposed to feel at home.

A friend of mine used to organise tours to Ajmer for foreign students. Christians from Africa tended to dislike it. 'Too Muslim,' they said — 'what are we doing at a mosque in India?' But many Muslim Arabs, she told me, often objected for what was almost the opposite reason. 'Too Hindu,' they would tell her. They were used to a more austere Islam, without the rituals, without the good-luck charms, the mantras, the rose petals, the incense, the mingling of men and women, the music and the poetry — all visible and audible at Ajmer. For many Pakistani Muslims, it is their holy place, not exactly holier than Mecca, but often more cherished; a place to which they belong, to which their forefathers could freely travel, and which has come to represent the softer, more lyrical side of Islam. I have several Indian and Pakistani friends and acquaintances who swear by Ajmer; disaffected semi-believers distrustful of organised religion, but who hope for minor miracles in their lives — a reprieve for an ailing parent or relationship, a nicer boss, or a more responsive willy. Some of them have reported progress after a visit to the *dargah*, and one of them pointed me to a website for those who can't actually make it to Ajmer. Believers can print off a '*taweez*' — or a small piece of paper with Arabic verses written on it which functions as a talisman (donations via Western Union or Moneygram). A 'barren woman . . . should take the Taweez on Thursday and read for 7 days, 11 times. On the 7th day mix the Taweez in milk and drink.' People with pot bellies, on the other hand, are advised to tie the *taweez* to their tummies, while sufferers from toothache should eat the *taweez* with rice.

I used to call myself an atheist, and though my beliefs have barely changed, my language has softened and I no longer proselytise. When I am asked in India about my religion, people really want to know about my religious heritage, and so I respond 'Christian'; and if I am asked about my beliefs I say I am an agnostic, which sounds less arrogant and adamant. I still enter shrines nervously, as if I am intruding into a world I do not really understand, and am always hoping to be allowed to be an observer, not a participant. I have a lingering dislike of joining in a ritual; of, for instance, having vermilion smeared on my forehead, of having to eat fudgey or popcorn-like substances deposited in my hand by a priest, or of putting my lips to an old stone — but I put up with it if I think it will please others. And normally it does please them, a large foreigner taking part in their rituals.

At the Ajmer *dargah*, the crowds were discombobulating but unaggressive. I found a place to sit on the ground near the main tomb, and began writing notes, and trying to map the progress of pilgrims through the *dargah*. A young woman seated near me looked over my shoulder to see what I was writing. Her younger sister pulled her back — talking to her in Hindi, telling her she was *besharam*, shameless. I intervened in Hindi, to their astonishment, telling them both that it was fine — and they could look at my scribbles. They stared aghast at each other and then looked at me, and burst into giggles. The older one then gave me a red piece of string. And she told me to tie it to a railing of the *dargah*, and make a wish — which she said would definitely come true. The two of them scampered off, their heads rocking with laughter.

I stood up holding the thread — and tried to think of something that I desired. I couldn't think of anything. I had quarrelled with my sister but we'd made up. My daughter had broken her ankle, but was recovering quickly. My father had cancer but was in remission. My first book was about to be published — I somehow couldn't bring myself to wish for anything so trivial as good reviews. My marriage, I thought, was strong. I was in good health. I could not think of anything to wish for. And I briefly considered how fortunate I was. And then I thought of something — a truly frivolous test of Moinuddin Chishti's power. The once-great football team that I supported as a child had sunk very low, into the third tier of the English League. I tied the thread and prayed for their promotion, and promised to become a believer if my wish came true.[12]

[12] I am not a supporter of Leeds United for reasons that relate to my family or where I grew up. At the time I first showed an interest in football (I was about seven years old), Leeds United were probably the best team in the country, and the possibility of associating myself with success was, slightly shamefully, my only reason for supporting them. They fell on hard times, and I, a fair-weather supporter at the best of times, showed little interest — until my son became a football fanatic. Then I ramped up my interest almost out of deference to his obsession. My Ajmer prayer did not help them that year, though the following year they were promoted into the second tier of the league — and have failed to return to the top tier each year since then.

A Seventh Intermission

WE RETURNED TO London in mid-1993, our embryonic son concealed about Shireen's person. It had been hard to leave, and both of us wanted to linger in India — but with a baby about we'd need a more sedentary life, and Delhi's charms had begun to pall. Moreover, my BBC contract had ended, and somehow — to me at least — the idea of parenthood seemed simpler in the UK. Shireen had barely lived in London, but seemed to adapt quickly to life in the defiantly multicultural North Kensington. As if by magic, a Nepali woman who lived on Millionaires' Row turned up to help give her daily succour, and all-body oil massages to Zubin, our newborn. She was a diplomat's wife who spoke no English and needed company. And so my son's first language was a strange mélange of Hindi and Nepali. And it was then I learned that those intimate words Shireen had taught me when we first met more than six years earlier — *susu, bagal, nunga-punga* — were not erotically charged crudités, but the traditional vocabulary of an Indian babyhood.

I became a junior apparatchik, head of the BBC Urdu Service which broadcast radio programmes to India and Pakistan. I learned to draw up rotas, balance budgets and conduct performance reviews. My Urdu language skills were poor — and my recurrent nightmare was that everyone in the Urdu team would fall ill, and I would have to go live on air, broadcasting to millions. My solution: a simple English-learning programme for Urdu speakers in which I would say things like '*Mera naam* Sam *hai*', 'My name is Sam,' in that special, dim-witted voice always used on language-teaching tapes. There was something uncomfortable about the fact that I was the only white person, and the only non-Urdu speaker in the Urdu Service — and I was in charge of it all. I tried not to think too hard about this, telling myself, in the words of my boss, that I was a man with a plan, that I was there to bring change: more news and less high-minded culture on the Urdu airwaves. But it did smack of the last of empire, a thirty-two-year-old Brit running an office of fifteen-odd Indians and Pakistanis, including my deputy, almost twice my age, and one of the most respected broadcasters in the subcontinent. I was treated with exquisite kindness. In retrospect I'm rather surprised that no one placed a dead rat in my briefcase.

My second defence against the suggestion that I was the last outpost of empire was to tell myself I was partly Indian, in spirit, by osmosis, by marriage and by loyalty. This was a harmless and useful lie. I did, however, in the mid-1990s, spend more time in India than my wife, and, as I pedantically teased her, I'd been to India more times than her. We both, then, in different ways, were able in our minds to remain partly in India.

And we did return. Every winter, just after Christmas, we went to India, immersing the children (our daughter, Roxy, appeared in 1995) in the humidity of Bombay, and introducing them to the affluent Parsi lifestyle that their mother knew as a youngster, and that I discovered on my first visit in 1987. It was all slightly Hellenic as well, with Tony Mango, or Tony Papou, as the children called him, indulging them with a second present-giving festivity to mark Christmas in the Eastern Orthodox calendar. In other ways, it was typically unorthodox: Tony's Christmas tree, for reasons that no one could explain, was hung from the ceiling, where it could swing in the ocean breeze; the household servants — none of them Christian — would queue up in the main room to receive their annual bonuses and a new shirt each; and we would lunch off taramasalata, *tiropita*, turkey and imported Christmas pudding. Jesus went unmentioned. As an Englishman, I was presumed to have superior Christmas pudding skills. And therefore Tony gave me the responsibility for what was always supposed to be the high point of the day: the ritual cremation of the pudding using large quantities of flaming brandy. One year, I managed to set the table on fire and was never trusted with the Christmas pudding again.

Every year, after our second Christmas, I would head off, family-less, into the hills and plains of coastal Maharashtra. This was my romantic escape into a rural India, peppered with wonderful hill-forts and deserted beaches, where I would never meet other foreigners. This was an India where I stood out, both because of my colour and my linguistic shortcomings, but where I was never hassled or ripped off. At the great tourist sites of northern India, I always felt that I was an object and victim of commodification, a minor source of income in a tourism-centred economy. But in rural Maharashtra, I now realise, I was probably, on balance, a bit of a nuisance. Someone who would pay the same as any Indian visitor to the region, but whose demands — for toilet paper, perhaps, or a hotel room with a window — were unpredictable and hard to comprehend.

This became, in my mind's eye, my secret, personal India — a place of peace and discovery, onto which I could project my own modest fantasy of the country that I had come to love. It was, of course, a false utopia. Rural poverty and corruption and violence abounded — and I both knew this and shut it out. Like so many others, I wanted to imagine my little piece of India that was unsullied by the outside world; a minuscule heaven on earth.

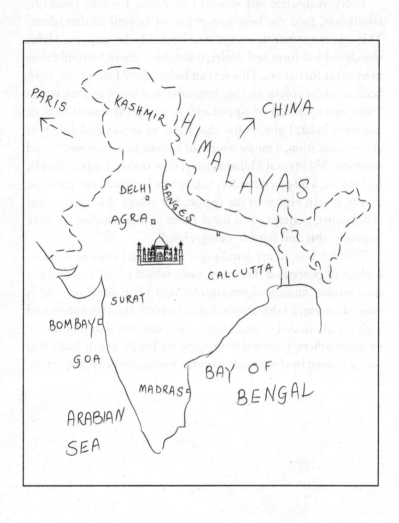

Chapter Eight: In which the Author is slightly rude about the Taj Mahal, considers the curative powers of cows' urine, and fails to take a nuanced view of sati

'AGRA IS A shithole,' Tim, a student from London, informed me, wrinkling his nose. I was conducting an informal ethnographic survey among independent foreign travellers visiting the former Mughal capital, now most closely associated with the building known as the Taj Mahal. His girlfriend, Louise, explained, 'First, he stepped in cow poo, then he bought some fake jewels, and then someone gave him a photocopied hundred-rupee note.' She smirked. 'That was the funniest. Who else in the world except my Tim would be fooled by a photocopied banknote? And it wasn't even a colour photocopy.' He gave me a sheepish look, as she cuffed him lovingly over the head. He had something more to tell me: '. . . but the Taj, it was wizard.' Louise swooned theatrically. 'It was quite wonderful,' she added.

Like Tim, I think Agra is a bit of a shithole. It is, of course, the city which every foreigner has to visit, usually within days of arriving in India. And its popularity among foreigners means that it has attracted more touts and rip-off merchants than any other Indian city — and I've never been hassled and prodded as I have in Agra. It is a continuing sadness for me that many foreigners judge India by this often dirty and uncouth city. And yet it does contain several wonderful buildings and gardens, and not just that monument to hyperbole, the Taj Mahal — Tagore's 'teardrop on the cheek of time'.

There's little new to the hype that surrounds the Taj Mahal — though Agra seems only to have been hated in recent times.

Edward Lear,[1] the English illustrator and poet, a master of the faux demotic and best known for writing nonsense, said after a trip to Agra in 1874, that the world could be divided into two groups of people — 'them as has seen the Taj Mahal; and them as hasn't'. The Taj was firmly on the tourist trail by then, and when, a year after Lear, the future Edward VII popped by, he pointed out, rather wisely, I think, that it was commonplace for every writer 'to set out with the admission that [the Taj Mahal] is indescribable, and then proceed to give some idea of it'. His view would be corroborated more than a century later by that former advertising executive Salman Rushdie when he said that the Taj is 'beyond the power of words to say it, a lovely thing, perhaps the loveliest of things'. The image of the Taj remains ubiquitous, replicated on boxes of tea and Indian restaurant signboards the world over.

The British writer and admirer of Hindu philosophy Aldous Huxley once complained that the Taj was a product of 'a poverty of the imagination', and was smacked down for trying 'to be original'. In another book, I described the Taj Mahal as 'a flashy jewel-encrusted latecomer', and some of my dearest ones objected, in tones that might normally be reserved for an unrepentant cannibal or for a desecrator of the tomb of Princess Diana. I am largely unrepentant, but have learned the wisdom of keeping silent on the subject. I still believe that Humayun's Tomb in Delhi, to which I'd compared the Taj, is a finer piece of architecture, though I do think that the instant when one

[1] Lear's limericks include Kashmir ('scroobious and queer'), Madras ('cream-coloured ass'), Calcutta ('bread and butter') but no Delhi — surely a gift to rhymesters — or Agra. Lear also wrote a nonsense verse called *The Cummerbund: An Indian Poem* in which he deliberately misuses every Anglo-Indian word he comes across. It ends 'Beware, ye Fair! Ye Fair, beware!/ Nor sit out late at night, —/ Less horrid Cummerbunds should come/ And swallow you outright.' A cummerbund is in fact a sash worn around one's middle, similar in some ways to the Virgin Mary's girdle (see page 104).

sees the Taj through the main gateway was as breathtaking on my last visit, my eleventh, as on my first.

The most interesting historical point, for me, about the Taj is that it is surely the world's greatest architectural success story. And it was always intended to be. It was built to be acclaimed as a wonder of the world. And it still is, almost universally. In the prescient words of Emperor Shah Jahan's court historian, Qazwini, the Taj Mahal would 'be a masterpiece for ages to come', and provide for 'the amazement of all humanity'. It was built to be visited and to be admired. It was, according to the Viennese art historian Ebba Koch, constructed 'with posterity in mind: we, the viewers, are part of its concept'. The Taj Mahal has been admired since it was created, and although it was undoubtedly a memorial to the love of Shah Jahan for one of his wives, Mumtaz Mahal, it was also a demonstration of the power, wealth and aesthetic values of the Mughal Empire.

The most informative foreign visitors to India of the second half of the seventeenth century were two Frenchmen — the physician François Bernier[2] and the jeweller-merchant

[2] In the early 1850s Karl Marx developed his theory of the Asiatic mode of production after reading Bernier's *Travels in the Mogol Empire*. He told Engels that 'Bernier rightly sees all the manifestations of the east — he mentions Turkey, Persia and Hindustan — as having a common basis, namely the absence of private landed property. This is the real key, even to the eastern heaven.' Marx was misled by Bernier, and was wrong to believe that private property in land did not exist in the east, but this view of the east became enormously influential. It is also possible to trace Bernier's influence on Montesquieu and on Hegel, particularly in forming the notion of 'Oriental despotism'.

Jean-Baptiste Tavernier, who both spent much time in Agra, some of it in each other's company. Both were convinced that the just-completed Taj Mahal was a quite remarkable building, and they each compared the dome of the tomb to that of the recently built Val de Grace church in Paris. The older Tavernier comes across as slightly more restrained, avoiding hyperbole, and pointing out how Shah Jahan had chosen the site carefully because it was in the part of Agra which every foreigner visited. While Bernier, twenty years his junior, is full of romantic admiration for Shah Jahan's devotion to Mumtaz, and describes the Taj Mahal as 'magnificent' and 'astonishing'. And he makes an important comparison in view of the Taj's rapid elevation as one of the greatest of buildings: 'I decidedly think that this monument deserves much more to be numbered among the wonders of the world than the pyramids of Egypt, those unshapen masses which, when I have seen them twice, have yielded me no satisfaction.' But, tellingly, Bernier feels the need for reassurance about his own views of Indian art and architecture, and the Taj Mahal in particular. He is worried that he had spent too long in the country, and had lost his European sense of judgement and aesthetics. Bernier explains how he visited the Taj with a French merchant (whom he does not name but was almost certainly Tavernier): 'I did not venture to express my opinions, fearing that my taste had become corrupted by so long residence in the Indies . . . It was quite a relief to my mind to hear him say that he had seen nothing in Europe so bold and majestic [as the Taj].' The fear which Bernier describes is one that would become commonplace among Europeans — the fear of being thought to have 'gone native'. This may mark the start of a particular attitude of mind in which foreigners could alternately, or even at the same time, be attracted and repulsed, besotted and disgusted, by their idea of India, and by what they felt India did to them.

The 'going native' trope appears particularly early in Goa, where Portuguese men often married local women, and began to follow local traditions, such as wearing local clothes, joining in Hindu festivals, eating with their hands and washing more frequently than was common in Europe of that period. But it also would come to imply a loss of artistic judgement, sexual morality and of the capacity for rational thought. And the history of this and later periods is replete with double-edged tales of how eastern ways have fuddled western brains. One European traveller in the 1690s notes with horror how, in one Portuguese settlement, a girl with fever was being treated by having her head covered in pepper, rather than the time-honoured (but much more dangerous) European practice of bleeding with leeches. Tavernier blames local influences for falling standards in Goa's main hospital, where only Europeans were treated. He was shocked that after patients have been bled, they are prescribed a glass of 'pissat de vache', or cow's urine, three times a day, for twelve days, before they are allowed to go home. This 'disagreeable . . . remedy,' Tavernier complains, 'has been learnt from the idolators'.

By the late seventeenth century, the occidental interest in Indian fauna had partly switched from the exoticised elephant

to the common cow.[3] It had, of course, been noted by previous travellers that a bull, known as Nandi, was a minor deity, and some had claimed, misleadingly, that cows were worshipped in India. But Tavernier had a particular obsession with bovine by-products. He tells two stories, neither of which I have been able to corroborate, and which seem aimed at deliberately and gleefully exciting feelings of squeamishness and disgust among European readers. First, he says that some Hindu widows take a vow to eat nothing but what they find, undigested, in the 'droppings' of cows. Second — and be warned, Tavernier's Victorian translator refused to render this passage into English on the grounds that it was 'too disgusting' — he says that in some places along the eastern coast of India, there is a tradition of taking a dying man out of his home, and placing him beneath the largest cow that can be found. The cow is then encouraged to urinate on the face of the dying man. This will not cure him, but is considered, Tavernier insists, a sign of good fortune. One can only presume that he confused this with the accidental outcome of a tradition still practised in parts of India, when a dying person touches the tail of a cow.

The subject that obsesses seventeenth-century travellers far more even than the Indian cow is the Indian woman. The surviving accounts are all by men — and few European women

[3] The cow in European writings of this period is frequently described as 'sacred', though the English-language metaphor 'sacred cow', used to refer, often subversively, to something that is apparently immune from criticism, dates from the late nineteenth century.

travelled to India in this period. These very male accounts have an ogling quality, born presumably of sexual excitement and frustration, and the desire to titillate audiences back home. These tall tales often sowed a great deal of confusion — though it is hard to know whether they were simply the creations of a fevered imagination or stories that were mischievously told to European visitors. These tales tended to create a binary world — in which Muslim women were usually seen as chaste, and Hindu women as promiscuous — though some travellers reversed this equation.[4] Sometimes the 'chaste' Muslim women of the Mughal harem were represented as so sexually frustrated that any vegetables shaped like a phallus had to be kept away from them.[5]

For Hindu women, the imagined object of penetration was the temple idol — and there's a long description in Sir Thomas Herbert's *Travels*, in which a just-married virgin is forced to have sex with a 'bodkin made of gold or silver' attached to 'the privy parts' of a statue. She is then returned to her husband and, Herbert says, if she becomes pregnant within a year, her progeny is seen as the child of God. Elsewhere Herbert describes how young girls are handed over to temple priests and become prostitutes. One of the most controversial and successful English novels of the period, Richard Head's *The English Rogue*,[6]

---

[4] One seventeenth-century French traveller, Jean de Thévenot, referred to Muslim women in India as wanton, and Hindu women as chaste. These differing views on female sexuality in different communities seem largely to have been a result of assuming that all women of the same religion behave in a similar manner.

[5] This might seem ridiculous, but note that in 2011 a news story saying that an Islamic preacher had ordered that women should stay away from bananas and cucumbers in case they caused sexual arousal was published all over the world. The website which carried the earliest English-language version of the story later apologised saying the piece should never have been published and was not properly sourced.

[6] It was originally turned down for publication for being 'too much smutty', according to his obituarist William Winstanley, and Head had to 'refine' his text before it was eventually published in 1666.

borrows from and builds on Herbert's account, which is allowed to pickle and ferment in Head's paedophiliac imagination. So that when his eponymous rogue reaches India, Head refers to 'little young girles, who for devotion sake, prostitute themselves freely to the heat of any libidinous spectator'. And by young, he means very young — girls of seven who are, Head claims, 'extremely salacious and leacherous as fit, nay, as prone to enjoy man at that age as Europeans at fourteen'.

The second major theme of western descriptions of Indian women in this period is less sexually charged (though there is a twist to this tale): suttee, or the supposedly voluntary immolation of widows — now known as *sati* in its modern transliteration. Traditionally, *sati* had been described by many early western travellers in admiring tones, as the ultimate act of devotion and bravery by a grieving widow who would cast herself, of her own volition, on her husband's funeral pyre — a tragic old-fashioned heroine of a kind recognisable to western audiences. The best-known account of a heroic *sati* from the seventeenth century is entirely fictional, in John Dryden's play *Aureng-zebe*, which is based on Bernier's account of the Mughal court in

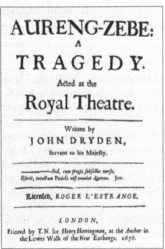

the final years of Emperor Shah Jahan. The heroine is the long-suffering Melisinda, the invented wife of Prince Murad, one of the quarrelling sons of Shah Jahan. She is devoted to the fickle, womanising Murad, and after his death in battle, she appears on stage dressed in white at the back of a procession of slaves and priests. She is announcing her intention to join Murad on the funeral pyre. There is a mild attempt to dissuade her from doing so, when another princess, Indamora, points out, 'You have no right to die; he was not kind.' This is dismissed by Melisinda, with an appropriate analogy, as irrelevant:

> My love was such, it needed no return;
> But could, though he suppli'd no fuel, burn.
> Rich in itself, like Elemental fire,

And then as Melisinda begins to walk off the stage towards the unseen pyre, and the corpse of her husband, she declares:

> For I will die: die is too base a word;
> I'll seek his breast, and kindling by his side,
> Adorn'd with flames, I'll mount a glorious Bride.

Dryden's description of the women of India is deliberately derivative, in a way that introduces an equivalence with what was then the best-known other 'pagan' civilisation — ancient Rome. And Dryden makes the comparison overt, saying of Melisinda:

> Her chains with Roman constancy she bore
> But that, perhaps, an Indian wife's is more.

And, in response to the criticism of 'fair ladies' in his audience, Dryden declared his own position on *sati*, firmly and uncomfortably astride a fence. In the preface to the first published edition of *Aureng-zebe* he explains that he 'dare' not support *sati*, nor would he 'wholly condemn' it. And he declares, 'Indian wives are loving fools . . . [who] keep company with the Arrias and Portias of old Rome.'[7]

[7] Arria was the wife of the rebel leader Paetus. The Emperor Claudius ordered him to kill himself, and he refused. Arria took the knife, and stabbed herself, telling him as she did, '*Paete non dolet*' or 'Paetus, it doesn't hurt'. Portia (or Porcia) was the wife of Julius Caesar's assassin,

Dryden seems never to have travelled outside Britain, and the burning of Melisinda, which forms the climax of his play, showcases his ignorance in a way which would have made any Indian laugh. For Melisinda, the wife of a Mughal prince, is not a Hindu, but a Muslim — and therefore not a possible victim, willing or otherwise, of *sati*. And Dryden's romantic idea of *sati* as self-sacrifice and heroic suicide is rarely supported by travellers' texts of the period. And, in fact, by the late seventeenth century, several much more nuanced accounts had been published which look at issues of coercion and desolation in the context of *sati*.[8]

Both Bernier and Tavernier witnessed several *sati*s and provide a series of more complex explanations of what they saw. Bernier describes how, when a Hindu friend of his dies, his widow plans to commit *sati*. Bernier finds the 'infatuated creature' sitting at the feet of her dead husband, 'her hair was dishevelled and her visage pale', and a group of 'hags' and Brahmins were there too, egging her on. Bernier asks her not to throw herself on the pyre, to which she responds, 'Well, if I am prevented from burning myself, I will dash my brains out against a wall.' Bernier responds with 'undissembled anger' and some speechifying. 'Let it be so then, but first take your children, wretched and unnatural mother! Cut their throats, and consume them on the same pyre; otherwise you will leave them to die of famine.' Bernier's heroic tirade, according to his own account, restores the woman to her senses, and her husband's corpse is burned alone.

Elsewhere, *sati* is sometimes clearly described as an act of murder. Bernier records how 'diabolical executioners' with long

Brutus. She is said to have committed suicide by swallowing hot coals. In Shakespeare's version of the story she 'fell distract,/ And her attendants absent, swallow'd fire'.

[8] One eighteenth-century account, by Luke Scrafton, includes the suggestion that *sati* is really a way of stopping women from poisoning their husbands, because if their husbands die, so too will they.

poles poked and pushed the widow so that she could not flee the flames of the funeral pyre, while other widows were tied up or drugged. Tavernier also describes the drugging of a widow by Brahmin priests who 'give her a certain Beverage to stupefy and disorder the senses'. And their motive, says Tavernier, is greed. They want the jewellery worn by the widows — gold and silver bracelets, pendants and rings which they wear on the pyre — and, 'all of these belong to the Brahmins, who search for them among the ashes when the party is burned'.

There's an unexpectedly romantic and imperial twist to the story of *sati*, a narrative which would percolate into western consciousness as an oriental fairy tale. There are many versions — in the works of later writers as varied as MM Kaye and Jules Verne — but in principle it's a simple story of derring-do, in which a gallant foreigner, usually an Englishman, snatches a beautiful widow, often a princess, from the funeral pyre of her husband. And they run off together, fall in love and live happily ever after.

The earliest version of this fairy tale is based on a real story. It's part of the complex mythology that surrounds the best-known and most intriguing of the early British settlers in India — Job Charnock, usually referred to as the founder of Calcutta. Charnock, according to a story only written down twenty-five years after his death, went with some soldiers to see the burning of a young widow, 'but he was so smitten with the Widow's Beauty, that he sent his Guards to take her by Force from her Executioners and conducted her to his own Lodgings. They lived together lovingly many Years and had several Children . . .' The author of this story, a sailor called Alexander Hamilton, did not see Charnock as a romantic hero. He knew and disliked Charnock, and thought him morose and brutal; and in that context it can be noted that Hamilton refers to the failed *sati* more as a kidnap than a rescue, and that Charnock was 'smitten' rather than outraged by what was happening. And when he says that Charnock lived lovingly with the widow, he is describing a man whom he considered to have gone native. 'Instead of converting her to Christianity,' Hamilton complains, 'she made him a Proselyte to Paganism,' and, after she died, 'he kept the anniversary Day of her Death by sacrificing a Cock on her Tomb, after the Pagan Manner.' Hamilton is so concerned that no one will believe this story (perhaps understandably given that Hindus aren't buried and cock-sacrifice is not exactly *de rigueur* in Hinduism) that he adds: 'I have been credibly informed, both by Christians and Pagans, who lived at Calcutta under his Agency, that the Story was really true Matter of Fact.'[9]

In fact, Charnock came to be admired, as Hamilton's story took wing and soared. Grumpy old Job became a romantic hero. Later versions have the widow, who has been provided with the name Lila, running through the Bengali countryside chased by a group of Brahmins who wish to burn her. In these versions, Charnock appears on horseback with a gun, and scares off the cowardly Brahmins by shooting in the air. Lila and Job get married, Lila becomes Lily — and they have several daughters who get married to important Englishmen. Some of all this is true — such as the Anglo-Indian daughters who married well — but it has also got conflated with later stories about *sati* (in which, according to the literary critic and Derridologist Gayatri Spivak, 'white men save brown women from brown men') and with the larger myth of Charnock as the founder not just of Calcutta, but of an embryonic British Empire in India.

There were, of course, older British settlements in India,

[9] It is not always easy to trust Hamilton, who clearly liked to titillate his readers. In his *New Account of the East Indies* (1727) Hamilton describes meeting a naked yogi, seven foot tall, with an enormous penis, 'like an ass'. A gold ring had been inserted through a 'hole bored through his prepuce'. And, he continues, 'This Fellow was much revered by Numbers of young married Women, who prostrating themselves before the living *Priapus* and taking him devoutly in their Hands, kissed him, while his bawdy Owner stroked their silly Heads, muttering some filthy Prayers for their Prolification.'

at Surat and Madras. And, in fact, the British Empire in India could be said to have begun, more formally, in 1661, when a small piece of coastal territory, known as Bombay, was pledged to Charles II (along with Ibn Battuta's home town of Tangiers) as part of the dowry when he married the Portuguese princess Catherine of Braganza. There was little pride or excitement about the acquisition of Bombay, no presentiment of empire, and Charles is said to have seen it as a burden. He would later rent out Bombay to the East India Company, for ten pounds payable 'in gold, on the 30th day of September, yearly, for ever'. However, the founding of Calcutta in 1690, by Job Charnock, would, for the historians of Victorian Britain, become retrospectively the most important event of the late seventeenth century in India.

People like Charnock were in India to make money, and not to acquire territory, or found cities. But to make money they needed trading posts, which, bitter experience had shown, needed to be defended, both against local rulers and against fellow Europeans. The British soon adopted the maxim, 'A fort is better than an ambassador'. Charnock had tried to build a British trading post in three other places in Bengal. Calcutta would be his final attempt. And in 1690, on 24 August, a date later celebrated as Calcutta's birthday, Charnock entered a subdued note in his logbook: 'it is RESOLVED that such places be built as necessity requires and as cheap as possible.' This was followed by a list of buildings that should be constructed: 'a warehouse, a dining room, a room to sort Cloth in, a Cookroom with its conveniences, an apartment for the Company's Servants, the Guard House'. A year later, he wrote, everyone was still living in 'only tents, hutts and boats'. Charnock's choice of Calcutta would be greatly romanticised by later historians, and he was sometimes portrayed as a visionary, sitting beneath a tree beside the river, and imagining a great city around him. In one famous piece of Victorian purple prose, Charnock was described by the Scottish historian Sir William Hunter:

> . . . as a block of rough hewn British manhood. Not a beautiful personage perhaps, for the founders of England's greatness in India were not such as wear soft raiment and dwell in kings' houses; but a man who had a great and hard task to do, and who did it — did it with small thought of self, and with a resolute courage which no danger could daunt nor any difficulties turn aside.

The fact that so little is known about Charnock made it possible to invent a range of possible Charnocks — a visionary, a businessman, an imperialist, a frontiersman, an impetuous lover, an uxorious husband, a curmudgeon and a foreigner who went native — that could be dragged out for the telling of a particular story about the British abroad, usually set against a lush and largely welcoming Indian backdrop, without fear of interruption by discordant Indian voices.

The discord came quite recently and gives the Charnock story an important postscript. I first travelled to Calcutta, in 1989, near the start of the year-long tercentenary celebrations. As I interviewed people for a radio programme, I came across just one dissident voice; an amateur historian and proud Bengali nationalist who said that the celebrations were a nonsense, and Calcutta was much more than three hundred years old. His comments seemed so contrary at the time that they were not included in my programme. This was an error on my part. In 2001, as part of a spate of late-in-the-day post-colonial renaming, Calcutta underwent a modest transformation and became Kolkata (much closer to the Bengali pronunciation of the word) — less dramatically than Bombay and Madras changing to Mumbai and Chennai. Soon after, the Calcutta High Court was petitioned with the demand that Job Charnock be relieved of his official status as the city's founder. The petitioners were led by members of a family, the Sabarna Roy Choudhurys, who owned large tracts of land on which the city was built. The High Court appointed a committee of experts, five historians, to consider the issue and they decided that Calcutta, or rather Kolkata, existed before Charnock, and therefore had neither a founder nor a birthday. The High Court ordered the state government to delete all reference to Charnock as the founder of Calcutta from official documents, websites and school text-books — and this was dutifully done. Job Charnock is now just another early settler.

An Eighth Intermission

UNTIL MY MOTHER set foot on the tarmac of Bombay airport, two years before me, no direct ancestor of mine — at least not since prehistory — seems to have travelled to India. I took some pleasure from that pointless factoid when I lived in India in the 1990s. It somehow helped to absolve me of any responsibility for the empire; and it encouraged me to imagine myself as somehow stateless and global, a world citizen who belonged to everywhere and nowhere. While others of my country-folk scoured the great imperial graveyards, pored over passenger lists, and dug out ancient letters from the India Office Library — I imagined myself smiling and saying, 'Nothing to do with me.' The 1980s had been a time of Raj nostalgia — and I would have nothing to do with it. My British nationality seemed an irrelevance. My determinedly scatterbrained grandmother was the only one who brought me back to earth. 'Why do you keep going to India?' she would say (forgetting that I was married to an Indian). 'Is it still ours?' she'd continue, 'I thought we'd given it up.'

However, as my grandfather lay dying in London, he and my mother began discussing their family, and she would relay these conversations to me in India. It emerged that there were unexpected Indian connections. In the early eighteenth century, a brother of my direct ancestor and namesake, Samuel Collet, had been the governor of Madras. Just before my return to London I found a book about old Madras with a gently equivocal tale[1] about Joseph Collet, the governor, and showed it to my grandfather.

In 1993, in the summer of his death, the summer of my return from India, I climbed up a step-ladder and entered the unlit attic of my grandparents' home. There was no floor to the attic, though sheets of plywood had been roughly laid across some of the joists, and resting on them were dozens of cardboard and tin boxes, and several suitcases. I slipped almost immediately, my trailing leg causing a great crack and bulge in the ceiling of the room below, a studio where my grandmother painted. Gradually, I brought the boxes downstairs, and began to skim and dip through their contents. I had come across an extraordinary treasure trove. It was a collection of family letters and documents that went back to the early eighteenth century — mainly little-known people with a lot to say for themselves, but also some letters from, among others, Karl Marx and George Gissing. My grandmother seemed a little put out by my discoveries and my disruptive influence, and wanted to get back to her painting, and perhaps was unhappy with all this fuss over something that had been sitting in her attic for decades. And so my mother attempted to distract her mother, and I hurriedly carried the boxes out to the car — and off to my home. We thought she hadn't noticed, but a few months later I spotted a recent painting of hers that

[1] The story told how Governor Collet was angry with one of his Indian assistants, who was always late because he visited his favourite temple. The governor asked him to prove his closeness to his god by describing what he was doing at the moment. The assistant described how the god was being pulled through the streets in a chariot but had got stuck in the mud. This, on investigation, turned out to be true. Collet was very impressed. He gave instructions for a new temple to be built, nearer his assistant's place of work, and had it lavishly endowed. The temple still stands in a part of Madras called Kaladipet, once known as Colletpetta.

showed me sheepishly sneaking out of the house carrying a large green box.

I spent many evenings and weekends going through the family papers. I was slightly relieved to find no secret relatives, no embarrassing colonial connection with India — and happily surprised to find a different kind of link. There were some writings of Joseph Collet from his time in Madras, by which time he had become a bewigged bore, uninterested in the country he lived in — while his earlier writings from the small British colony of Bencoolen on Sumatra had been full of lyricism and gentle amazement. The surprise was a woman, my grandfather's great-aunt Sophia Dobson Collet, an Indophile who never left

the British Isles, born with a damaged spine that left her a life-long invalid. As a ten-year-old living in London, she was taken to hear the Indian reformer Rammohun Roy, sometimes accorded the soubriquet, 'the father of modern India', not long before his death in 1833. She was captivated for the rest of her long life. Many decades later, in a biography that was only published after her death in 1894, she described him as 'a majestic looking man, nearly six feet in height, and remarkable for his dignity of bearing and grace of manner, as well as for his handsome countenance and speaking eyes'. I imagine my aunt as a devotee of Roy, who admired his spirit and his flesh — and whom she always referred to as Rammohun, as if they were intimate friends.

Roy remains a complex figure, still revered in India, but accused at the time, and, sometimes since, of being just a bit too much of an Anglophile. He was the leading figure in attempts to reform Hinduism, by eradicating what he saw as its corrupted customs and theology, and returning it to its supposed origins. The schismatic movement which he fathered, known as the Brahmo Samaj, was opposed to polytheism, to the worship of idols and to the caste system — which in many western accounts had come to define Hinduism. In 1831, Roy came to Britain, and helped to reshape how Hinduism was viewed in the west. His ideas were welcomed by nonconformist Christians, who saw his belief in just one god, without avatars, as similar to theirs. My ancient aunt, despite her devotion to Roy, remained a Unitarian Christian, but developed her own ideas about Brahmoism as a means by which Hindus could become Christians in all but name. This was, for her, the dawning of a new universal religion. Roy's final writings, she claimed, held up a rather striking five-fold prospect:

India speaking English
India Christian
India socially Anglicised
India possibly independent
India the Enlightener of Asia

This is an ambitious and unlikely list. Most of Roy's modern-day admirers would argue that my aunt had traduced their hero — particularly in those first three 'prospects'. Or perhaps, to give her the benefit of the doubt, that she had read into one tiny part of Roy's corpus of writing what she had hoped to find there. Just as visitors to India have usually been able to find, somewhere, somehow, whatever it is in India that they were expecting to find.

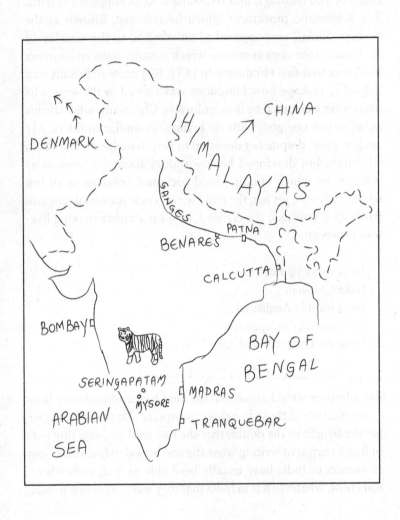

Chapter Nine: In which the Author is exposed to the secrets of ozone therapy, recalls a childhood encounter with a tiger, and considers the symbolic meaning of circumcision

THERE IS A small, forgotten corner of southern India that is for ever Denmark. Indeed, the coastal village of Tranquebar is the most recognisably European of the former colonial settlements built by five nations: the British, the French, the Portuguese, the Dutch and the Danes. It is, in those words beloved of tourist literature, 'unspoilt'. Unspoilt, presumably, by modernity, and perhaps, by India — though Tranquebar was spoilt, or even decimated, in the true sense of that term, by the great tsunami of 2004 which tore away its seafront and swallowed up half of the town's main temple.

'I have come here for the ozone,' blonde Barbara barked at me. When I saw her sauntering along the Tranquebar beach in her blue bikini, undeterred by ogling males, I hoped that she would be Danish, and provide me with a neat tale that could connect her to her country's past. But she was from Germany. I tried not to look crestfallen. She smiled broadly at me, as if we shared more than our colour. I became a slightly nervous flirt, and found myself winking back, as if in collusion. And then, a little later, conversation under way, I mentioned that Tranquebar was once part of Denmark. She laughed, with an uncontrollable, sneering guffaw. 'Denmark?' she squealed back at me, in a voice several octaves higher than normal. And she showed little interest when I pointed out the beachside Fort Dansborg, like a giant sandcastle, with strange conical protrusions. She explained to me that she had come to Tranquebar for its 'ozone beach'. She turned out to be something of an alternative-therapy junkie, though she had nothing much obviously wrong with her — and her almost naked body did seem like a testament to Teutonic well-being. She firmly believed that exposure to ozone was good for her health — and Tranquebar, she solemnly informed me, was full of ozone. I was in no position to contradict her, and wandered off.

As I explored tiny Tranquebar, with its handsome Danish churches and whitewashed colonial buildings, I encountered not a single Dane; nor, as I had foolishly hoped, any bacon or Danish pastries for sale. But I did re-encounter bountiful Barbara, now fully-clad, striding down what was once Kongensgade or King's Street. She slowed for me and we strolled up to a towering golden statue erected in 2006, amidst its own rock garden, of a long-dead German preacher bearing the name Ziegenbalg — one of the most important figures of the early colonial period in India. Barbara, still wittering on about ozone, showed no interest in her golden countryman, and almost as little in me. Our brief relationship was going nowhere. I strode on alone, slightly regretful that Barbara found my conversation so boring — and I stopped here and there to talk to local people. To my surprise, as I interrogated them in that popular Indian language best described as 'simple and empathetic English with hand gestures', I heard several confusing accounts of Tranquebar's mysterious ozone surplus. Buxom Barbara was clearly on to something. I should have engaged her on the subject of ozone, then — not the history of Tranquebar, or German missionary activity in India in the early eighteenth century. What a fool I had been. I rushed about Tranquebar looking for her, using a new range of hand gestures to describe my missing German. But she had gone.

I do not now regret having no further intercourse with Barbara. And ozone therapy, I would later learn, has a long and undistinguished history. It has been described both as a cure and a cause of cancer — and the proponents of the former position still provide ozone therapy to fee-paying believers. In London, for instance, I learned that it is possible to pay a very large sum of money to be locked naked in a very small cabinet, with your head sticking out of the top, and have ozone wafted over your enclosed body. But on Tranquebar beach the ozone contained in the local air is said to be more concentrated than elsewhere in the world and comes for free.[1] An influx of both alternative-therapy seekers and aficionados of Danish history is seen as providing a potential (if rather niche) boost for the local tourism industry.

As I continued to wander the Barbara-less back-streets of Tranquebar, I encountered a second, smaller memorial to Ziegenbalg, even more delightfully strange than the first. It took

the form of a silver-painted bust of a plump-cheeked man with a curly periwig. The bust was protected from the elements, but not the ozone, by an umbrella that had miniature bells hanging from its rim, and under the fulcrum of the umbrella was a light-bulb dangling over Ziegenbalg's bewigged frontal fontanelle. There

[1] The notion that Tranquebar has higher than normal concentrations of ozone appears to be a myth based on a series of scientific investigations into a slightly different phenomenon — the large daily and seasonal fluctuations in ozone level in Tranquebar. See SB Debaje, S Johnson Jeyakumar, K Ganesan, DB Jadhava and P Seetaramayyaa: 'Surface ozone measurements at tropical rural coastal station Tranquebar, India' (*Journal of Atmospheric Environment*, November 2003), and LM David and PR Nair: 'Diurnal and seasonal variability of surface ozone and NO_x at a tropical coastal site: Association with mesoscale and synoptic meteorological conditions' (*Journal of Geophysical Research*, May 2011).

are no less than four statues of Ziegenbalg in the village of Tranquebar, all erected as part of the 2006 celebrations marking the arrival of India's first Protestant missionary three hundred years earlier. India today has more than five million Protestants, a tiny percentage of Indians, but approximately equivalent to the population of modern Denmark.

It is not only as a missionary that Ziegenbalg is remembered in this small corner of India. On a large signboard in Tranquebar, there's a long list (numbered one to twenty-four) of Ziegenbalg's achievements, under the unlikely tagline 'Be Always The First — Ziegenbalg Was': the aspirational invention, presumably, of a local marketing firm. In fact, the list is full of inaccuracies: Ziegenbalg did not, for instance, introduce the printing press to India, and he was definitely not the first to organise inter-religious dialogues.[2] But he did re-establish printing in the subcontinent and showed a more-than-energetic interest in the language and culture of the Tamil-speaking south. No foreigner since Alberuni had shown such a scholarly commitment to understanding Indian belief systems. And, in the wake of the great Orientalist debate at the end of the last millennium, stirred up by Edward Said, Ziegenbalg has sometimes been typified as a proto-Orientalist, an Orientalist *avant la lettre* — in which case Alberuni should probably be burdened with the same monicker.

Ziegenbalg describes how he learned the Tamil script in the traditional way, shaping the curvilinear letters by tracing them with a stick in the sand. He set himself a rigorous daily timetable.

---

[2] There was something of a false start to the Indian printing industry. The Portuguese brought the first press to Goa in the sixteenth century, and a number of mainly religious texts were printed over the next hundred years. However, prior to the arrival of Ziegenbalg's press, there is no record of any book having been printed in India for more than thirty years, and it is thought that there was no extant printing press. And as for inter-religious dialogues, those presided over by Emperor Akbar preceded Ziegenbalg's by more than a century.

From seven to eight o'clock each morning he would repeat words and phrases that he had previously learned and written down. From eight o'clock to noon, he would read Tamil-language books, in the presence of a poet who would help explain the text, and put what he had read into more colloquial language. Even while eating lunch, he had someone read to him, followed by a little nap. From three to five in the afternoon, he would read some more Tamil books, and from seven to eight in the evening someone would read to him from Tamil literature in order to avoid strain on his eyes. After three years, he wrote home that 'their tongue . . . is as easy to me as my mother tongue' and he was able to read, write and preach in Tamil. He translated and printed the entire New Testament in Tamil, and he was almost one-third of the way through translating the Old one, having completed the Octateuch, from Genesis to Ruth, when he died in Tranquebar, in 1719, at the age of thirty-seven.

Ziegenbalg's *The Genealogy of the South Indian Gods* was the first serious attempt by a foreigner to study and explain what the author called 'heathenism' and what we now refer to as 'Hinduism', a word — and, arguably, an idea — that was not in use in Ziegenbalg's time, in any language. The preface to the genealogy begins with the traditional German invocation *Geneigter Leser!* (or 'Gentle Reader!'), and continues, in epistolary mode . . .

As we have hitherto, from year to year, communicated to dear Europe various particulars concerning the nature of Indian heathenism, we reflected also this year how we might do more, and rejoice our patrons and friends by some further news. To this end we arranged, in our leisure hours, the chief facts regarding the gods of these heathens in a table, and enlarged them . . . so that herewith a complete Genealogy of their gods is presented to the reader.

And so, for the first time, thanks to a German cleric heading a Danish mission in southern India, the Hindu gods were tabulated and correlated, ranked and compartmentalised, pigeon-holed and labelled — eight pages of tables, 250 pages of explanation. Ziegenbalg's account is both precise and inquiring, full of lists and detail in which he seeks, like so many later Orientalists, to bring order to confusion. His modern admirers have pointed out that he is far less trusting of upper-caste priestly Brahminical sources than most later Orientalists.[3] He not only reads Tamil texts, and discusses their finer points with learned men, but he talks to ordinary believers — and records himself telling a local physician, 'I look upon you as wise, ingenious people of very easy and agreeable conversation.' He seems genuinely interested in Indian belief systems. He even attempts to reassure his European audiences by arguing that Hindus are essentially and ultimately monotheistic, despite the proliferation of deities that he lists in almost interminable detail.

Notwithstanding the open, critical manner in which he carried out his inquiries, Ziegenbalg was, quite openly, a religious zealot, and comes across to the modern reader as deeply bigoted. He declares in his preface that it 'was with reluctance, that we spent our time in the inquiry into their foolish heathenism, more especially because there occur many indecent and offensive stories; but as no one before us ever did this thoroughly . . . we were content to do the work'. He calls upon Jesus to 'destroy and annihilate' their 'false gods'. He also shows some of the prurience which would infect later Orientalists: 'the linga,' he declares, '[is] a figure by which the genitals of both sexes are represented — contrary to nature which teaches us to conceal them . . . We might here also mention several stories that are

---

[3] And some modern Indian Protestants portray him as a supporter of what were once known as 'untouchables', and are now known as Dalits, from which group many Christian converts have come.

related of the Linga, but we will rather forbear, inasmuch as they contain such very absurd things'.

In another influential work, *Thirty Four Conferences between the Danish Missionaries and the Malabarian Brahmans*, which was published in English in 1719, the year of Ziegenbalg's death, the author and a fellow missionary debate religious issues with a wide range of interlocutors, including Hindu and Muslim clerics, fishermen and local women. Here, Ziegenbalg is at his most anti-Brahminical, savaging the caste system; denouncing Brahmin priests as proud and vain; calling female temple servants 'great whores' and claiming that the temples themselves are 'promoters of all uncleanness and filthy lusts'. He accuses 'idle, lazy' Brahmins of insulting 'poor industrious men who get their living by the Sweat of their brows' and here he refers specifically to a caste he calls Bareyers, now known in India as Periyars, and whose nineteenth-century mis-spelling gave us the modern English word 'pariah'.[4] Ziegenbalg's anti-Brahminism takes a less revolutionary, almost joyously convoluted, form when he attacks Brahmins for being vegetarian. 'Living creatures are made to serve man,'

---

[4] Percy Bysshe Shelley was one of the first to use the word 'pariah' in its more general sense, meaning 'outcast', by which time he'd already used it in its more specific Indian sense in his 1810 poem *The Solitary*, where he refers to 'the swart Pariah in some Indian grove,/ Lone, lean and hunted by his brother's fate'. In his 1819 letter to Thomas Love Peacock, Shelley refers to himself as 'an exile and a Pariah', asking to be remembered to a mutual friend who was 'an acknowledged member of the community of mankind'. Peacock, a poet and novelist, was by this time a London-based employee of the East India Company, and later wrote *A Day at the India Office* about being utterly bored in a bureaucratic job:

> From ten to eleven — have breakfast for seven
> From eleven to noon — think you've come too soon;
> From twelve to one — think what's to be done;
> From one to two — find nothing to do;
> From two to three — think it will be
> A very great bore to stay until four.

he explains, carnivorously, 'and many of them are incapable of doing us any service except by furnishing our Tables with wholesome food.'[5]

Ziegenbalg's primary purpose in being in Tranquebar was not to discourage vegetarianism, learn Tamil, or study Hinduism. Rather it was his mission to win 'heathen' converts to his particular Protestant version of Christianity — which had arrived with him in India. The main competition was, in a way that often baffled the local population, from other Europeans: Roman Catholics who had been operating out of the older Portuguese enclaves for two centuries, and among whom the Jesuits were the most active. For Ziegenbalg, a staunch Lutheran, Catholicism was anyway a diseased form of Christianity, but in India it was even worse. It had degenerated into a version of heathenism. Some of the Portuguese are, he says, 'scandalously corrupted in their manner — and [there is] little or no difference between a Portuguese church and a heathen temple with regard to all outward rites and ceremonies and the idolatrous worship of images'.

Ziegenbalg was concerned that this gave Catholics a head start among the heathens. However, he argued that Catholics (the 'Romish persuasion') were failing to take advantage of this, and of their long presence in India. He pointed out that 'few of the missionaries learn the Indian languages but content themselves with reading the Mass in the Latin tongue and trust the natives with the important office of teaching, who . . . know nothing else but to repeat the Ten Commandments, the Lord's Prayer and Ave Maria and to sign themselves with the cross'.

So for Ziegenbalg and his Lutheran latecomers, the road to conversion was through language, not ritual, through the power of prayer and persuasion, not the creation of a Hinduised version

[5] He goes on to defend his bibulousness in similarly unconvincing terms: 'and as for our drinking strong liquors, the coldness of the northern region requires it: for the continual drinking of water as you do in these warmer climates would kill us in the colder climates of Europe.'

of Christianity. The Jesuits, on the other hand, went out of their way to link Hinduism and Christianity — pointing in particular to the 'trinity' of gods, Brahma, Shiva and Vishnu, as a parallel with the Christian Trinity.[6]

It is at this period that there is the first sustained identification of India as a land of great poverty, rather than of great wealth — and it is largely transmitted through the writings of missionaries. There were telling reasons for this — ones which don't relate, at this stage, to any significant change in the economic circumstances of either Europe or India. Both Protestants and Catholic missionaries won most of their 'new Christians' from the poorest of the poor, usually members of socially excluded groups — such as the lowest castes. These were easy converts, won over by promises of jobs and status, as well as the promise of, at the instant of death, entry into the kingdom of heaven. And they showed little interest in the fratricidal and nationalistic divisions within western Christianity, or the theological niceties that sustained those divisions.

These converts would later be derided by some European missionaries as 'Rice Christians', people who had changed their religion for economic reasons, and would therefore be condemned to hellfire anyway. However, in the early eighteenth century there was such an emphasis, driven by sectarian competition, on creating an embryonic Christian community, a Christian foothold in India, that neither Protestants nor Catholics were very fussy about the reasons why Indians converted.

Missionaries would send letters back to Europe begging for money to support the new converts, whom they described as living in great poverty. These letters were collected as books, which were widely read, and played a key role in the eighteenth

---

[6] Indeed one Jesuit cleric, Père Bouchet, believed that early Jewish and Christian travellers had influenced Hinduism — and that Brahma was really Abraham, while Krishna was Moses, and Rama was Samson.

century in informing Europeans about India, although their prime purpose was fund-raising. The Jesuits published, over seventy-four years, the thirty-four-volume *Lettres Edifiantes et Curieuses,* which are full of heart-rending accounts of how the lives of the poor of India (and elsewhere) had been saved by the generosity of Europeans. One lady, we are told, '*une Dame de distinction*' heard of the 'nudity and hunger' (*'la nudité et la faim'*) of the new converts and sent a two-string pearl necklace to relieve their misery and buy them some clothes. One writer talks of how 'we must do all we can to pull our poor converts out of the extreme misery to which they have been reduced because of the constancy in practising the Gospel'. Orphans and new converts would often be named after a European donor. One benefactor, a nun, is informed that 'by this means your name is known and revered as far away as these barbarous lands'. Her name was Hyacinthe, not a name that ever caught on in India.

As Europeans competed against each other for new converts, they also competed for control over progressively larger swathes of Indian territory. Parts of India became a European battlefield, and by the middle of the eighteenth century European wars were being fought on Indian soil. What began as the War of the Austrian Succession, fought over the issue of whether a woman could succeed to the Austrian throne, became what might, with a little imagination, be described as the First World War. Two of the outlying protagonists, Britain and France, carried the dispute well beyond the bounds of central Europe. To Scotland and to north America, and even to India,[7] where the French, under their hero-

[7] In Scotland, it took the form of the rebellion known as 'the '45', after the year in which it was fought. The rebellion was a French-backed uprising led by Bonnie Prince Charlie, the son of the pretender to the British throne. His rebellion was crushed by the army of his third cousin, the Duke of Cumberland, remembered as 'Butcher Cumberland'. And in North America, in what was known as King George's War, the French and the British, who each had local 'Indian' allies, skirmished and raided for

commander Dupleix, with some under-acknowledged assistance from their local Indian allies, captured the city of Madras from the British. Under the treaty that eventually ended the War of the Austrian Succession, Louisbourg (in Canada) and Madras, colonial outposts more than twelve thousand kilometres apart, were exchanged — and Madras would remain in British hands until 1947. Indian territory was a tradable commodity, something that could be swapped as if it were a child's toy.

Among those captured by the French in Madras was a junior clerk named Robert Clive, who then escaped by blacking his face and dressing up in the clothes of his servant. He would later be known as 'Clive of India', the man who transformed the British East India Company from a trading organisation with a few coastal settlements into a colonial power and, in doing so, destroyed French hopes of dominating the subcontinent. By the mid-eighteenth century, for many later writers, India had become a zone of Franco-British rivalry, most famously between Dupleix and Clive,[8] where the locals were often little more than innumerable extras. In many western eyes, Indians were, by turns, barbarous (as at the Black Hole of Calcutta) or timorous (in the face of an advancing European army), often bewitched by the almost magical power of the Europeans, particularly Clive of India. It's a tradition of exaggerated importance that continues. There's even a winsome website called 'Cliveless World', whose central conceit is that a suicide attempt by

more than two years. The British captured the fort of Louisbourg from the French, and returned it to France under the 1748 treaty of Aix-la-Chapelle which ended the War of the Austrian Succession.

[8] In fact, Dupleix and Clive are from different generations. Dupleix was born in 1697, Clive in 1725 — and though their paths did cross, Clive was a much more junior figure.

Clive in 1744, when his pistol jammed, was instead successful — thereby creating a counterfactual world in which France, not Britain, came to rule India.[9] Contemporary descriptions of Clive, in particular, do often portray him as if he were superhuman. A fellow Company official Luke Scrafton describes how, when Clive's army marched on Patna, almost two thousand years after Megasthenes, the more numerous defenders of the city simply capitulated. Clive's reputation went before him and 'these eastern people', says Scrafton, look upon 'fighting against a fortunate man, as contending with GOD HIMSELF'.

Back home, Clive's reputation was less exalted, though he was much envied. He was not the first Englishman to make a fortune in India, but the wealth he accrued was astonishing to his contemporaries. When he returned he was one of the richest men in the country. And his story transformed the British idea of India into a place where those of a modest background could become very rich and powerful, extremely quickly. This was the era of the 'nabob', a mis-hearing of the Indian princely title, Nawab,[10] which entered popular English usage in the second half of the eighteenth century. It was a word used by the ruling elite to describe the *nouveaux riches*, and carried with it connotations of vulgarity and greed. The nabobs found it easy, in those pre-democratic times, to buy their way into Parliament, and by the early 1770s Clive, now settled in Britain, had a caucus of eight MPs, consisting of himself, his father,

[9] See http://www.clockworksky.net/cliveless_world/ah_cliveless_top.html. In this imagined world, the French came to rule much of India — and the history of the entire globe changes. There was no French Revolution, no United States of America, and the Ottoman and Russian empires survived into the twenty-first century. The same website also has an imagined world in which Dara Shikoh, not Aurangzeb, succeeded Shah Jahan as Mughal emperor — and the Mughal Empire survives to this day. Indeed the world is dominated by India, and many Europeans are considered 'untouchables'.

[10] In fact, the word 'Nawab' comes originally from the plural of the Arabic word *na'ib* meaning deputy or representative.

other relatives and close friends.[11] The returning nabobs were seen as a threat to the existing social order. Some of the old gentry responded by attempting to co-opt them into the elite. But others wished to exclude them from society as parvenus and plunderers, while happy to sequester their ill-gotten wealth.

The return of the nabobs to the UK created a series of conflicting new perceptions of India, which for the first time was having a direct impact on the day-to-day internal politics of a European nation. These perceptions often had little to do with reality, but reflected a very British political debate. The voluble opponents of the nabobs used any means they could, including parliamentary debates, the theatre and anonymous pamphleteering, to argue that India was either a nation of innocents, immorally stripped of their dignity and their wealth by the nabobs, or that it was a licentious nation, a cesspool of sin and sodomy, which had seduced the future nabobs into a world of chicanery and thieving. In Parliament, Clive defended his fellow nabobs as pragmatists, who accepted that 'Indostan was always an absolute despotic government' and that 'from time immemorial it has been the custom of that country, for an inferior never to come into the presence of a superior without a present'. They had, Clive insisted, simply adapted their moral code to the situation, which meant that they had no choice but to accept each and every gift that was offered to them.

In June 1772, just four months after Clive's speech, the one-legged satirist Samuel Foote staged his new play, *The Nabob*, at

[11] By the late 1780s there were more than fifty nabobs in Parliament. William Cowper wrote in his 1775 poem *The Task*, 'thieves at home must hang; but he that puts/ Into his overgorged and bloated purse/ The wealth of Indian provinces, escapes.' Later in the same poem Cowper asks, 'Is India free? And does she wear her plumed/ and jeweled turban with a smile of peace,/ or do we grind her still?'

the Haymarket Theatre in London.[12] The villain of the title, a nabob called Matthew Mite, was loosely based on Clive. Recently returned from 'the Indies', Mite desperately wants to be accepted into the gentry. And so he threatens an impoverished baronet with bankruptcy if he doesn't hand over his daughter in marriage. Mite is accused 'of scattering the spoils of ruined provinces', of 'voluptuously rioting in pleasures that derive their source from the ruin of others'. And he uses 'strange jargon', Indian words newly entered into the English language, such as *lakh* and *jagir*.[13] Lady Oldham, the wife of the baronet, declares that 'with the wealth of the East, we have too imported the worst of its vices'. And later in the play, Mite tries to set up a seraglio, and proposes to bring 'three blacks from Bengal' to oversee his harem. The audience is asked to believe that Indians are both innocent and immoral — as if, perhaps, they were all the descendants of Eve.

In 1774, at the age of forty-nine, Clive killed himself,[14] cutting his throat with a penknife. The mantle of chief nabob passed to Warren Hastings, whose actions in India divided Britain's political elite more deeply, and even more theatrically, than

[12] In fact, the play was a direct response to Clive's speech, which included a personal challenge to Samuel Foote. Clive said in his speech that since 'there has not yet been one character found amongst them [the nabobs] sufficiently flagitious for Mr Foote to exhibit on the theatre in the Haymarket, may we not conclude, that if they have erred, it has been because they were men, placed in situations subject to little or no control?'

[13] He actually spells these words 'lacks' and 'jagghire'. A *lakh* is one hundred thousand, while a *jagir* is a grant of land.

[14] Clive's family tried to cover up the cause of his death. This was his second suicide attempt and he was a depressive. He may also have been suffering from a painful disease at the time — possibly gallstones or porphyria. There have been other theories about his death. According to one early biographer, he actually died of an overdose of opium, and the suggestion of suicide by penknife was a 'contemptible slander'. And it has even been proposed, without evidence, but with possible motivation, that he was killed by an Indian patriot, or even by his own wife, or by a young woman staying in his house.

Clive's. In 1788, Hastings, the first British governor-general of India, was brought to trial in the Houses of Parliament, in what was one of the greatest set-pieces in British history. The contemporary record of the trial describes how 'by 8 o'clock in the morning the avenues leading to . . . [Westminster] Hall were filled with ladies and gentlemen of the most respectable appearances, many of them Peeresses in full dress, who stood in the street for upwards of an hour before the gates were opened'.

Hastings' accusers included the playwright Richard Sheridan, and the greatest orator of the day, Edmund Burke, who charged Hastings with having 'wasted the country [India], destroyed the landed interest, cruelly harassed the peasants, burned their houses, seized their crops, tortured and degraded their persons, and destroyed the honour of the whole female race of that country'. It was a bravura performance, so dramatic and shocking that when he described the torture of Indian women ('they put the nipples of the women into the cleft notches of sharp bamboos and tore them from their bodies'), several women in the public gallery were said to have fainted.

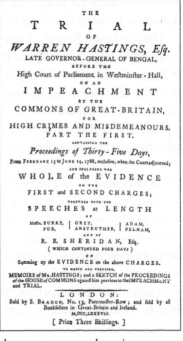

THE

T R I A L

OF

WARREN HASTINGS, Esq.

LATE GOVERNOR - GENERAL OF BENGAL,

BEFORE THE

High Court of Parliament in Westminster - Hall,

ON AN

IMPEACHMENT

BY THE

COMMONS OF GREAT-BRITAIN,

FOR

HIGH CRIMES AND MISDEMEANOURS.

PART THE FIRST.

CONTAINING THE

Proceedings of Thirty - Five Days,

From FEBRUARY 13 to JUNE 14, 1788, inclusive, when the Court adjourned;

AND INCLUDING THE

WHOLE of the EVIDENCE

ON THE

FIRST and SECOND CHARGES;

TOGETHER WITH THE

SPEECHES at LENGTH

OF

Messrs. BURKE,   GREY,   ADAM,
FOX,   ANSTRUTHER,   PELHAM,

AND OF

R. B. SHERIDAN, Esq.

(WHICH CONTINUED FOUR DAYS)

ON

Summing up the EVIDENCE on the above CHARGES.

TO WHICH ARE PREFIXED,

MEMOIRS of MR. HASTINGS; and a SKETCH of the PROCEEDINGS of the HOUSE of COMMONS against him previous to the IMPEACHMENT and TRIAL.

L O N D O N:

Sold by S. BLADON, No. 13, Paternoster-Row; and sold by all Booksellers in Great-Britain and Ireland.
M,DCC,LXXXVIII.

[Price Three Shillings.]

The trial, officially an impeachment, staggered on, in staccato fashion, for seven years, and Hastings was eventually acquitted. The impeachment was, of course, a political trial, as well as a conflict over competing philosophies and economies of empire. It was also, arguably, a reflection of how the British political elite managed to deal with change through a bloodless excess of verbosity (at a time when, on the other side of the channel, the guillotine became the most popular way of settling political disputes). The impeachment also focused attention — in a way that had a direct impact on public opinion — on the rights and responsibilities of a colonial power. Officially, the East India Company was a private trading firm, but it was now understood, in a way that was not yet articulated in an overt fashion, that Britain would be judged by the actions of its citizens in India. And for the first time, individual Indians became household names, their lives allegedly ruined by Hastings, their sorry stories of victimhood widely discussed in the popular press.[15]

The complex British domestic reactions to the growing entanglement with India have been referred to as 'the anxieties of Empire', and there is little doubt that tales from India, true or false, or something in between, were leaving their mark on the British psyche. India had become a land of dreams, a place where less affluent British males could live out their fantasies — the old English lament 'Alas and Alack-a-day' was transformed into the swaggering toast 'A lass and a lakh a day'. But it was also a land of perils and horrors. The Black Hole of Calcutta,[16] and its powerful mythologies, had established India as land of nightmares, as well as dreams. Towards the end of the century, still more nightmarish tales of incarceration began to emerge from the dungeons of Tipu Sultan, the Muslim ruler who controlled large tracts of southern India from the river island of Seringapatam, near the city of Mysore. For the British, Tipu became a new, seemingly invincible, bogeyman

[15] People such as the dispossessed Raja Chait Singh of Benares, or the Begums of Oudh (who according to Burke, were 'bereaved even of their jewels: their toilets, these altars of beauty, were sacrilegiously invaded, and the very ornaments of the sex foully purloined') were among the first Indians whose names became well known in a western country.
[16] See page 74.

whose reputation for brutality would concentrate many minds.

'Terribly alarmed this morning for our foreskins,' wrote Colonel Cromwell Massey in his Seringapatam prison diary. His alarm was understandable — though it is easy to argue that there are many fates worse than circumcision. In the 1780s and 1790s, more than three hundred British prisoners of Tipu Sultan were bound, drugged and their genital regions shaved. The prison barber then severed their foreskins. By doing so he was ritually converting them to Islam; they were 'Mohammedanized',[17] as one outraged and prepuce-less prisoner put it. Accounts of the circumcisions were widely published in books and newspapers in Britain — including several by those who had themselves been at the sharp end of the barber's knife. The circumcisions are described almost as if they were castrations — and as if nothing more inhuman could have been done to the prisoners. And the accompanying stories of slavery, of torture, of starvation, of disfigurings and mutilations, of poisonings, of protracted, painful deaths, are told in an almost jaunty fashion, as if they were just the everyday collaterals of warfare.

Circumcision, however, seemed to do more damage to the mind than the body — it became a symbol of humiliation and

[17] All the earliest Christians, born as Jews, were, of course, circumcised. As many as eighteen different churches in Europe have claimed that they have the genuine Holy Prepuce, Jesus' own foreskin. The foreskin relic which the Vatican views most favourably — having been presented by the Emperor Charlemagne to Pope Leo III — spent several centuries in a church in the town of Calcata, north of Rome. It was stolen in 1983 from a shoebox kept in the home of a priest living in Calcata. This particular Holy Prepuce has not been seen since. The issue of circumcision has long troubled Christians. It was one of the main subjects at the Council of Jerusalem in AD 50, and again at the Council of Florence in 1442. The recently retired Pope Benedict XVI reaffirmed (in spite of the words of Genesis that the uncircumcised should be 'cut off from his people') that the 'Apostles had decided to discontinue the practice of circumcision so that it was no longer a feature of the Christian identity'. Many Christians, including some Roman Catholics, continue to practise male circumcision.

emasculation, as well as a loss of Britishness. And for all this there seemed to be no redress. One group of prisoners found some strange solace by capturing stray dogs, and circumcising them in front of the jailers: 'this operation never failed to exasperate them, particularly as the dog is held a very impure animal.'

Among the other anxieties exacerbated by the success of Tipu Sultan, who had become an almost archetypal Anglophobe, was one related to a much older enemy. For Tipu courted the French, who reciprocated, both under the *ancien régime* and during the revolutionary period. In 1797, more than fifty French soldiers stationed at Seringapatam formed a Jacobin Club, and proclaimed the Rights of Man. They received an audience from Tipu Sultan, whom they hailed as '*Citoyen* Tippoo', and before whom they planted a tree of liberty, on which they placed a cap of equality. One of the Frenchmen then stood up and demanded of his compatriots,

'Do you swear hatred to all Kings, except Tippoo Sultaun, the Victorious, the Ally of the French Republic? War against Tyrants, and love towards your Country and that of Citizen Tippoo!!!!!'
'Yes! We swear to live free or die,' they replied in unison.

But it was not the fear of revolutionary ideology spreading across India that made the British so anxious; rather, it was a diminutive twenty-eight-year-old Corsican called Bonaparte, who had just invaded Egypt. The British had managed to intercept a letter from Napoleon, written in Cairo, which was addressed 'To the most magnificent Sultan, our greatest friend Tippoo Saib'. It declared, chillingly for the British, 'You have already been informed of my arrival on the borders of the Red Sea, with an innumerable and invincible army, full of the desire of delivering you from the iron yoke of England.' The fear of a European power interposing itself between Britain and its Indian colonies would play a central role in British foreign policy for the next 150 years — and India was seen once again, by both France and Britain, through the prism of an ancient rivalry. But this particular anxiety attack was short-lived. At the Battle of the Nile in 1798, the British under Admiral Nelson defeated Napoleon's navy, though Napoleon himself was elsewhere and survived to fight again, and again — and to command his forces in the wars that are named after him. However, less than a year after the Battle of the Nile, the British also defeated Tipu Sultan at the Battle of Seringapatam. Tipu, shot twice through the head, did not survive.

Tipu's legend lived on, vicariously and in decidedly different forms. In the years immediately after his death Tipu continued to be demonised, particularly by the British, as the archetypal oriental despot — a foreskin-cutter, an impaler, a severer of noses and ears — who could also be absurdly generous. But the British authorities, still officially the East India Company, attempted to demonstrate its own generosity once it had deported Tipu Sultan's children to Calcutta, by setting them up as Anglicised princelings, dispossessed of their patrimony but the recipients of mini-pensions. Tipu's fourteenth son, Ghulam

Mohammed, became a venerable supporter of the British Empire in India, a Justice of the Peace, and a KCSI,[18] a Knight Commander of the Order of the Star of India, entitled to use the title 'Sir', while Tipu's grandson travelled to London to be formally received by Queen Victoria. The story of Tipu's defeat came to be used as a just-deserts morality tale which would later be used to demonstrate the inevitability of British victory.

But there were always alternative readings of Tipu's life and death. Some of the British plunderers of his Seringapatam palace seemed almost embarrassed by the size of Tipu's personal library, the high quality of the jewelled inlay work on his furniture, the superb craftsmanship of his weaponry. The idea that this patron of the arts was really no more than an uncivilised bigot became harder to sustain. Tipu's death was also turned into an act of Romantic courage. Sir Walter Scott,[19] commenting on Napoleon's temporary abdication in 1814, said, 'I did think he might have shown the same resolve and dogged spirit of resolution which induced Tippoo Saib to die manfully upon the breach of his capital city with his sabre clenched in his hand.'

In modern India, Tipu re-emerged controversially as a putative national hero and an early freedom-fighter, thanks to the sixty-part TV series, *The Sword of Tipu Sultan*, which had huge audiences when I first lived in Delhi in the early 1990s,[20] and had some of the campest, most flamboyant over-acting ever

[18] The last KCSI, the former Maharajah of Alwar, a princely state in eastern Rajasthan, died as recently as 2009.

[19] Walter Scott's 1827 novella, *The Surgeon's Daughter*, is about Menie Gray, a Scottish girl who leaves her village to find her childhood sweetheart in India. The sweetheart has gone to the bad and is in league with 'Tippoo Saib' who wants Menie for his harem. She is saved from Tipu's clutches, and the former sweetheart is crushed to death by an elephant.

[20] Some Hindus objected to the near-deification of a man they considered a Hindu-killer and as a result of a court case, a multilingual statement appeared at the start of each episode declaring, 'This serial is a fiction and has nothing either to do with the life or rule of Tipu Sultan'.

witnessed on a TV screen. This was soon followed by an even more hagiographic Pakistani drama series about Tipu, with a similar commitment to the grandiose hand gesture, and the never-ending death scene. The two countries seemed to be competing over Tipu's legacy.

But the most powerful memorial to Tipu is a bizarre artefact kept in London's Victoria and Albert Museum. One rainy day when I was a child, my grandparents took me and my brother to the V&A, just five minutes by bus from the London house in which I was born and raised. I remember my grandfather pointing out an extraordinary exhibit, like a three-dimensional cartoon, a near life-size image of a skinny white man dressed in red and black being eaten by a tiger, its teeth near his neck. 'Is he dead?' I asked. And then my brother laughed at me, and my grandfather joined in. 'He's made of wood,' my brother snorted. I wanted to say, 'That's not what I meant.' But the moment had passed. I wanted to know whether the prostrate wooden man, with a tiger at his throat, was supposed to be a corpse or a dying man. I later discovered that my question was a good one — and that the man lay permanently in the borderlands between life and death.

Tipu's mechanical tiger is an automaton, a wooden sculpture with moving parts. Inside, there is an organ that can be played with a crankshaft, or on a sharp-less keyboard concealed beneath a hinged flap on the side of the tiger. Tipu's Tiger was brought back to London from Seringapatam as a curiosity, and installed in the East India Company museum, and later the V&A. It has always been loved by visitors — among the earliest was John Keats, who made it the subject of one of his least convincing rhymes:

> . . . that little buzzing noise
> Whate'er your palmistry may make of it,
> Comes from a play-thing of the Emperor's choice,
> From a Man-Tiger-Organ, prettiest of his toys.[21]

For the Anglophobe French poet Auguste Barbier writing in the 1830s, the victim is clearly English:

> It is in the heart of London, in one of its museums
> An object which often occupies my thoughts
> It is a wooden tiger, whose claws tear at
> The red mannequin of an English soldier.

Later in the poem he imagines Tipu referring to England as 'a little pile of shite',[22] and has him declaiming that he would never let his enemies capture him alive. And so for Barbier, there is a delightful irony to Tipu's Tiger finding its resting place in a London museum.

[21] From the unfinished Spenserian burlesque poem, *Caps and Bell* (1819). My wife's grandfather, a merchant seaman from Bombay, was a great admirer of Keats. On his death, as a memorial, his brother had two chairs copied from an old painting showing Keats at work in his study, and presented them to Keats House in London, where they can still be seen.

[22] Thanks to Nathan Steele for suggesting 'shite' as the best translation, in this context, for the French word 'fange'.

He kept his word; a king fallen on the field.
He died, but left the instrument of his hatred
As his memorial among his conquerors

The wooden tiger should be seen both as a wild animal and as Tipu himself, the Tiger of Mysore, teaching the British a lesson. In Keats' day, members of the public could wind the crankshaft on the body of the tiger, and the tiger would roar, while the man would wail plaintively and raise his hand in vain protest. He was permanently in his death-throes, but never quite dead.[23] Visitors to the V&A can no longer operate the organ; only experts are now allowed to touch Tipu's Tiger — but both the roar and the wail can be heard on the museum's website.

Tipu's Tiger has been much mimicked in recent times. The Colombian artist Carlos Zapata created a tiny working model of the tiger, almost identical to Tipu's original, except that the animal licks the face of his victim, while Wisconsin-based Bill Reid, best known for his fantasy toilet-paper holders, has created at least two painted metal homages to Tipu's Tiger — one of an astronaut and another of an

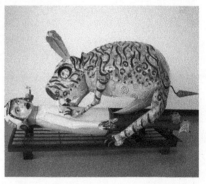

---

[23] In the twentieth century, the American poet Marianne Moore took the mechanical approach in *Tipu's Tiger*:

... a vast toy, a curious automaton
a man killed by a tiger; with organ pipes inside
from which blood-curdling cries merged with inhuman groans.
The tiger moved its tail as the man moved his arm.

Ms Moore was slightly misled — the tiger's tail never moved. Most recently, the award-winning British Indian poet Daljit Nagra called his second collection *Tippoo Sultan's Incredible White Man Eating Tiger Toy Machine!!!* which was published in 2011 to much acclaim.

astrologer: each of them being eaten by a giant rabbit. The V&A, meanwhile, has developed a 'fun, interactive' iPad application called 'Tipu's iTiger' which you can download for free, and which allows you to, virtually, 'play the organ within the tiger's body to create your own terrifying masterpieces, with a choice of three different groups of keyboards and sounds'. Bizarrely, the only pre-installed tune on the iTiger could hardly be less appropriate for an object whose real-life avatar belonged to Tipu Sultan — the eighteenth-century dirge currently known as *God Save the Queen*. Or perhaps it's just a laborious post-colonial joke.

A Ninth Intermission

AN INDIAN PhD student in the German town of Tübingen e-mailed me after reading my last book. She asked me, *inter alia*, if my work might be seen as part of the 'colonial endeavour'. I think the question must have rankled, and my answer was a spluttering mess. I've since begun to articulate a better, though rather long-winded, response.

I am of the Left, tribally and by personal commitment. As my hair has begun to grey, I have become less evangelical, and less engaged, but have not, as have many of my contemporaries, moved to the Right. I once, as a teenager, hectored belligerently on behalf of the British Labour Party; now I seek to subvert those who are certain that they know the truth. Living in India has been part of that transformation.

As a student of politics, I admired Hegel and the early Marx, progressing later to Gramsci and Lukács, then Foucault and Kuhn, and temporarily found a home in the work of post-colonial writers. Edward Said upended the Orientalist in a way that gave me pleasure, even if there was a frisson of masochism in that pleasure. He was almost a hero to me. I knew Said slightly. He was a friend of my parents; and when he came to tea at my family home, I would always find an excuse to be there. I wanted him to talk about India, about how the subcontinent fitted into his thesis. But he never did — and I felt unable to press him.

Tintin discovers Edward Said.

He discussed Mozart and Joseph Conrad with my parents, with modest meanderings into other territories — the Palestinian diaspora and feminist theory. As a BBC producer I would call him occasionally and invite him to appear on radio programmes; he was always warm and agreeable, with the distinctive timbre, in my playful imagination, of a Brooklyn Jew. His health had begun to dissolve when I last saw him, and I could only entice him to admit he knew little about India.[1] I still defend Said against his more intemperate detractors, but recognise, as do others of his admirers, that his greatest achievement was to have undermined orthodoxies rather than to have provided answers.

Said's *Orientalism* unnerved many western readers, particularly those who made a living from studying the east. They, rather than their objects of study, were suddenly in sharper focus. And the great names of eighteenth- and nineteenth-century oriental scholarship were not heroic *hommes de lettres*, or eremitic eccentrics, but complicit in colonial conquest. Other writers would extend and adapt Said's work to India — though the country's size and variety, and complex experience of European colonialism, meant that the more determinist Saidians struggled with their theses, as the easy generalisations eluded them.

It is possible, I think, to understand the colonist's experience of India as, at the same time, both infinitely varied, by character and motive, and yet as unavoidably part of a definable colonial endeavour. There is an essential tension between the two, but not a contradiction. And do I, then, belong to that colonial endeavour? Of course not, I instinctively protest. The sun has long set on the European empires, after all — and I feel unimplicated in colonialism. And yet I am a white British man in Delhi, and if people think I am implicated, then I cannot gainsay them.

[1] He does, I later discovered, talk at some length and with some sophistication, about India in his introduction to the Penguin Classics edition of *Kim*.

Indeed for most Indians, I am just another white person; and my Britishness consigns me to a subset of former rulers famed for their arrogance and their organisational skills. And so I seek quickly to establish my distinctiveness. I open my mouth, and speak my creaky Hindi, or express my opinion on a new Hindi movie — and the category to which I am deemed to belong narrows slightly. But here again is the tension. My individuality is imperilled by the dregs of empire; my complex ideological history is of little interest; my leftist leanings irrelevant. And although this sometimes makes me bristle, it is no more than an inconvenience, a minor peril of whiteness — and it may even be good for me.

Because, for me, India has been about unlearning — though others, including Kuhn, also helped with this. My cherished certainties have been eroded, my intellectual arrogance has been tamed (though not entirely subdued). I delight in the nuance, the fractal, in the exception that doesn't prove the rule. I now respond to newness with excitement, not with some desperate desire to locate a place for it in my existing world-view. Perhaps, then, this is one way in which I differ from the Orientalists of old, and is at least a partial answer to the Tübingen question.

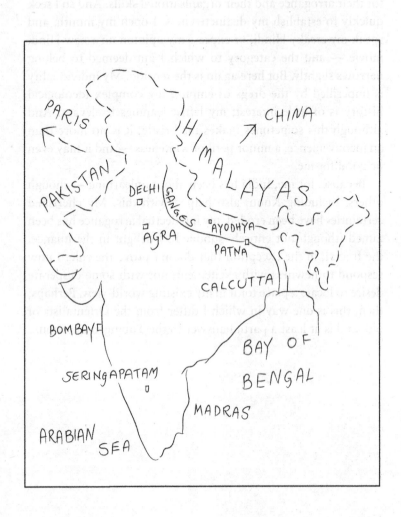

Chapter Ten: In which the Author uncovers the truth about killer pineapples, learns about the washing habits of Indian concubines, and is baffled by Macaulay's mangophobia

I AM AN aficionado of cemeteries and of tombs. I can think of no more romantic location for an urban wander than the hillside cemetery of Père Lachaise in Paris; and of no necropolis that is more memorable and unsettling than Cairo's City of the Dead — with its grand Muslim mausolea occupied by the living poor. London's Brompton Cemetery, five minutes' walk from *Sam Janambhoomi*,[1] my childhood home, is inhabited by a wonderful medley of Gothic and neo-Classical funerary architecture. And it's a place to which I venture every time I return, a grown-up guest, but really the ghost of a child, to that same family home. Brompton Cemetery has also become a good place for spotting body parts. Bobbing buttocks and tumescent members pop up between the tombstones and sepulchres in the under-visited outer reaches of the cemetery; as if outdoor sex were a competitive sporting activity, even in winter. In many Indian parks, body parts — rarely buttocks, but often penises half-disguised by a *pallu* or a *dupatta* — are on demi-display largely because lovers have nowhere else to go. But never, in my long experience of such things, in an Indian cemetery. Many Indians, I've found, are scared of cemeteries — except when they house the tombs of

[1] I can't remember which of my friends first made this very silly joke. It was possibly Karuna Nundy. It's a piece of bilingual paronomasia. Ram Janambhoomi literally means the birthplace of Ram, and is the name given by some Hindus to the old mosque, the Babri Masjid, that was torn down in Ayodhya in 1992 (see page 148).

ancient emperors and their consorts. They often find my desire to visit graveyards a little strange, as if I were a necrophile or had a perverse desire to disturb the ghosts of the dead. Delhi, my adopted home, is full of remarkable cemeteries, Muslim and Christian — and indeed a huge swathe of south Delhi is really a necropolis, with smart residential 'colonies' built around the tombs of medieval Muslim rulers and courtiers. But Calcutta has the pride of cemeteries, on Park Street: a dank Gothic jungle of trees and creepers, urns and columns, cenotaphs and crucifixes,

where British denizens of the city at the turn of the nineteenth century were interred. And at a minor junction of walkways between the clusters of tombs is a carved obelisk, covered in moss, placed above the remains of a famous English teenager who died of 'a surfeit of pineapples' on the 2nd of March, 1800.

Rose Aylmer was the subject and title of one of the most anthologised poems[2] of the nineteenth

[2] Ah what avails the sceptred race,
    Ah what the form divine!
What every virtue, every grace!
    Rose Aylmer, all were thine.

Rose Aylmer, whom these wakeful eyes
    May weep, but never see,
A night of memories and of sighs
    I consecrate to thee.

century, a Romantic paean to necrophilia, or, at a bare minimum, unconsummated love. It was written by the famously ill-tempered Walter Savage Landor, who had fallen for seventeen-year-old Rose while she was on a visit to Wales. In 1799, not long after meeting Landor, she travelled out to India, as a marriageable, well-connected beauty — searching for a suitable boy.[3] Calcutta had by this time become a very British outpost, in which many of the social conventions of Georgian London had been replicated in a much younger city eight thousand miles away. That replication was not always easy — the heat, the rain, the tiny number of western women, the insects and reptiles, and the local inhabitants were all a bit of a shock to the British colonists. But they strove on regardless — with their Christmas balls and harpsichord concerts, their dinner parties and amateur theatricals. The diarist

Shortly before his death Landor wrote one more poem about Rose:

The grave is open; soon to close
   On him who sang the charms of Rose,
   Her pensive brow, her placid eye,
   Her smile, angelic purity,
Her voice so sweet, her speech so sage,
It checked wild Youth and cheered dull Age,
Her truth when others were untrue,
And vows forgotten.
Friends, adieu!
The grave is open . . . O how far
From under that bright morning star.

[3] Vikram Seth, in his 1993 novel, *A Suitable Boy*, devotes a large part of a chapter to a very chaste and rainy perambulation through Park Street Cemetery by the book's heroine, Lata, and one of her suitors, Amit. They visit the tomb of Rose Aylmer, and recite Landor's poem, though pedantic Amit corrects Lata at several points. When Amit informs her that she died not from the sorrow of parting from Landor, as Lata had hoped, but from 'a surfeit of pineapples', it is as if the spell in their own relationship has been broken, and Amit makes things worse by comparing the tomb to an upside-down ice-cream cone. I think it actually looks more like a pineapple, peeled whole and in a spiral, in the Indian fashion.

William Hickey, whose river boat was commandeered to bring Rose Aylmer and her companions on shore, described her as 'charming and lovely' and that she 'soon had several professed admirers'. However,

> she was attacked with a most severe bowel complaint, brought on entirely by indulging too much with that mischievous and dangerous fruit, the pineapple, against eating so much of which I had frequently cautioned her, but instead of my remonstrances being attended to they only excited her mirth ... At the end of a few days this lovely young girl fell a martyr to the obstinacy of the malady.

Hickey records how her death provoked different reactions in her two main admirers. Henry Russell became 'truly miserable', while 'her other lover, Mr Ricketts . . . sought comfort for himself in the arms of a vulgar, huge, coarse Irish slammerkin [called] Miss Prendergast'. In fact, Henry Russell also soon found comfort in the arms of another, an Indian mistress, a *bibi*, who bore his child.

There were very few British women in Calcutta. According to the first proper guidebook for travellers to India, the *East India Vade-Mecum*[4] by Captain Thomas Williamson, 'respectable' European men outnumbered European women (respectable or otherwise) by sixteen to one, which would explain some of the excitement at Rose Aylmer's arrival, and the disappointment at her dramatic pineapple-induced demise. The *Vade-Mecum*, first published in 1810, is a remarkable book, full of practical advice for 'gentlemen' planning to live in India. There is not only much detail on household servants, on the religions and castes

[4] The full title was *The East India Vade-Mecum or Complete Guide to Gentlemen Intended for the Civil, Military or Naval Service of the Hon. East India Company* by Captain Thomas Williamson (1810). *Vade mecum* literally means 'go with me' in Latin.

of India, on agricultural methods, insects and reptiles, fruit[5] and the climate — but it also provides a matter-of-fact account of how the British lived, and how they saw themselves.

The *Vade-Mecum* carries a long section about Indian women 'domiciliated' by British men, many of whom had one or more live-in mistresses. India is represented as a place where it is possible, if you are a man, to have lots of sex with multiple Indian partners — a male sexual paradise. Williamson tells, with amusement and some envy, the story of one old major who had a harem of sixteen mistresses, 'of all sorts and sizes'. Captain Williamson calculates the cost of 'concubinage in the East' — sixty pounds per mistress per annum, 'which must certainly be considered no great price for a bosom friend when compared with the sums laid out upon *some* British damsels'. The reader learns, as if this were some bizarre custom, that 'native women' like to wash themselves after each time they have sex; and that they tend to be over-fond of jewellery. Williamson exclaims that 'the attachment of many European gentlemen to their native mistresses is not to be described! And infatuation, beyond all comparison, often prevails, causing every confidence, of whatever description to be reposed in the sable queen of the harem!'

William Hickey describes in some detail his relationship with his beloved Jemdanee, whom he first met as the mistress of a friend who was moving back to Britain, and whom he then invited to be 'an intimate' with him. She eventually died in labour, which Hickey describes in heart-breaking terms — and tells us how his friends and colleagues accepted her in life and mourned her death. Others, such as James Kirkpatrick, married their paramours, in his case a Muslim princess, and had himself converted to Islam and circumcised in the process. The prepuce-less jailbirds of Seringapatam would have been baffled.

[5] He advises strongly against too many coconuts and jackfruit, but does not discuss the dangers of pineapples.

General Charles Stuart chose a different faith, and became widely known as Hindoo Stuart. He visited temples as a worshipper, kept Hindu idols at his home, and refused to eat beef. He also became a devotee of Hindu women: 'the majority of Hindoo women are comparatively small, yet there is much voluptuousness of appearance — a fullness that delights the eye; a sleekness and purity of skin . . . I already begin to think the dazzling brightness of a copper-coloured face infinitely preferable to the pallid and sickly hue of the European fair.' Unlike Hickey or Kirkpatrick, he was seen as slightly eccentric, having stepped beyond the normal bounds of British behaviour (he was actually Irish) in India. But he was still respectable enough to remain a very senior officer in the British army. He, like Rose Aylmer, was interred in Park Street Cemetery, in a mausoleum that resembles a Hindu temple, his soubriquet, 'Hindoo Stuart', carved in stone.

By the time of Stuart's death in 1828, a new edition of the *Vade-Mecum* had been published — and a new era of what might almost be termed apartheid had begun. The days of open, accepted, enduring sexual liaisons between British men and Indian women were over. The long passages in the first edition of the *Vade-Mecum* devoted to 'native mistresses' had been excised, and tales of British men adopting eastern ways had also been removed. And the guide was no longer aimed just at male travellers. There's a new appendix on 'necessaries for a lady proceeding to India'. On this long list of necessaries are

APPENDIX.

Nᵒ I.

ARTICLES REQUIRED IN AN OUT-FIT.

(See p. 12.)

NECESSARIES FOR A LADY PROCEEDING TO INDIA.

72 Chemises.
36 Night Gowns.
36 Night Caps.
 3 Flannel Petticoats.
12 Middle ditto, without bodies.
12 Slips.
36 Pr. Cotton Stockings.
24 Pr. Silk ditto.
 2 Pr. Black Silk ditto.
18 White Dresses.
 6 Coloured ditto.
 6 Evening ditto.
60 Pocket Handkerchiefs.
 4 Dressing Gowns.
   Silk Pelisse.
 3 Bonnets.
12 Morning Caps.
24 Pr. Long Gloves.
24 Pr. Short Gloves.

thirty-six night caps, twenty-four pairs of long gloves, twenty-four pairs of short gloves and four corsets. There's an extra section on musical instruments with lots of useful advice: 'ladies partial to music should be particularly careful that the piano-fortes they bring with them be so constructed as to exempt them from those wondrous effects produced by the climate of India . . . experience has fully proved that the pianos most appropriate for hot climates were made by Clementi, Kirkman and Tomkinson.'[6] Not only were women being shipped out[7] to India to prevent British men from straying into the arms of local women, but they were expected to lead the way in the re-Anglicisation of the rapidly growing British community, and this included matters of taste and fashion, and of general social and sexual behaviour.

Just as most of the early foreign travellers to India were men, so, universally, were those who wrote about their experiences. There are occasional glimpses of women arriving in India, usually unwillingly, concealed in the interstices of history — the putative Greek daughter-in-law of Chandragupta in about 300 BC, the slave-girls Ibn Battuta brought with him to Delhi in 1334, and of course, Rose Aylmer — but they are never given much of a voice. But from the late eighteenth century British female travellers, normally accompanying their husbands, did begin to record their journeys. Unlike their menfolk who were active participants in Indian society, as businessmen, rulers and lovers, British women often behaved more like observers, and were frequently uncomfortable, and occasionally pleased, with

---

[6] There is advice for male musicians too. 'Gentlemen who perform on stringed instruments should be careful to provide an ample supply of strings, firsts and fourths especially; they being not only very dear and perhaps damaged when procurable, but at times not procurable in any part of India, for love or money!'

[7] The large number of unmarried young women from Britain in search of a husband who would later turn up each year in India was known as the 'fishing fleet', while those who went home unwed were known as 'returned empties'.

the world they had stumbled into. They were also often more willing than their male companions to admit to ambivalent, uncertain responses to what they were seeing.

Jemima Kindersley, who arrived in India in 1765 as the wife of an artillery officer, recorded that the first view she had of India

> rather surprised than pleased me, I could not be reconciled to the vast numbers of black people who flocked to the shore on my first arrival; although I must acknowledge that they were so far from being terrible in their appearance, that at first I believed them all to be women, from the effeminacy both of their persons and dress, the long white jemmers [pyjamas] and turbands [turbans] appear so truly feminine to strangers.

Fifteen years later, Eliza Fay[8] is confronted by the people of Madras. 'On your arrival you are pestered with . . . servants of all kinds who crouch to you as if they were already your slaves, but who will cheat you in every possible way . . . I wish these people would not vex one by their tricks; for there is something in the mild countenances and gentle manners of the Hindoos that interests me exceedingly.'

The supposed effeminacy of Indian men would remain a theme of European writing about India into the twentieth century, as would the roguishness of servants. The 'servant problem' was an obsession for Eliza Fay, who settled in Calcutta:

[8] Eliza Fay's writings found an unexpected champion in the 1920s when EM Forster persuaded Virginia and Leonard Woolf to republish her *Original Letters from India*. Forster wrote an introduction and notes to the book. Eliza accompanied her feckless lawyer husband, Anthony Fay, to India in 1779, where they were almost immediately captured by Hyder Ali, Tipu Sultan's father. They spent fifteen weeks in captivity, but not in Seringapatam — and therefore, as Forster points out delicately, Mr Fay avoided being circumcised. The Fays move to Calcutta, and Eliza leaves her husband after he fathers a child by his Indian mistress.

'I am happy to say that our house is a very comfortable one, but we are surrounded by a set of thieves. In England, if servants are dishonest we punish them, or turn them away in disgrace, and their fate proves, it may be hoped, a warning to others; but these wretches have no sense of shame.' She describes how one of her servants has left: 'he says poor servants have no profit by staying with *me*; at other gentlemen's houses he always made a rupee a day at least! besides his wages.'

These early writings of British women are full of homesickness and nostalgia for the land they have left. Most are letters home, and so it's unsurprising that everything is to be compared to Britain. They are full of descriptions of their attempts to create a Little Britain in their three main settlements at Bombay, Madras and Calcutta. Anne Elwood arrives in Bombay in the mid-1820s: 'After so long *roughing* it among turbaned Turks and semi-civilised Arabs, the well-dressed, *hatted* gentry on the wall of the Fort of Bombay . . . and the cheerful appearance of several good-looking white houses, promising English comforts and accommodations were, to such weary weather-beaten wanderers, really most agreeable objects.' She is amused to notice that some Indian goods that she had seen being sold as eastern exotica in London, were everyday objects: 'Indian mats, which are thought so much of in England . . . are here used for the commonest purposes.' The reverse was also true: 'it is laughable to see how much store is set by raspberry and strawberry jam; but the difficulty of obtaining an article, and the distance whence it comes, wonderfully enhance its worth.' The same, she says is true of tongues, hams and cheeses.

There are many dozens of foreigners' accounts from this period, an exponential growth in scribbling, most of them written by British male servants of the East India Company and their wives. And so, quite suddenly, in this story of mine, there is no shortage of primary sources; almost, one might say, a surfeit. These diarists and letter writers told a wide range of wondrous

239

and tawdry tales, Indophobe and Indophile, reflecting as much their preconceptions and biases and fantasies as their actual experiences, let alone the views of the Indians they encounter. And all of them were circumscribed, in one way or another, by what had become, by stealth, a colonial endeavour — with little pretence any longer that the British presence was just some kind of trading outpost. And these travellers, as they attempted to replicate British society, searched hard for the language and metaphors with which to describe their time in India to those who had never been there. Landscapes are shrunken, belittled. The Himalayas became Alpine at best, or failing that, were likened to the Scottish Highlands or Snowdonia. Rivers were measured against the Thames at Chelsea; ruins, such as Tipu's palaces, were compared to Tintern Abbey. A new vocabulary entered circulation — spreading slowly back to what would become known as Blighty.[9] Words like 'jungle', 'bungalow', 'verandah', 'juggernaut' and 'pyjamas' were mangled as they crossed the racial divide and the oceans and then entrenched themselves permanently, as hybrids, half-castes, in the English language. It seemed almost to mimic the discovery of a deeper, more significant connection between the languages of the west and of India.

The best maintained of all the graves in Calcutta's Park Street Cemetery takes the form of a stone obelisk, with urns in

[9] Blighty as a synonym for Britain, is derived from *bilayati* or *vilayati*, used in Hindustani to mean foreign. *Hobson Jobson: The Anglo-Indian Dictionary* refers to *bilayati pani* to mean foreign water, i.e. soda water, and to *bilayati baigan* meaning foreign aubergine and used to describe the tomato, which is not native to India. *Vilayati* is, in turn, derived from the Arabic word *wilaya* meaning province or governorate, i.e. place ruled by a *wali*, or governor. Blighty seems only to have been used in Britain from the First World War, having been brought back from India by the soldiers. A number of music-hall songs used the word, including most famously, 'Take me back to dear old Blighty!/ Put me on the train for London town!', best known in the version sung by Florrie Forde. This version was sampled for The Smiths' 1986 hit record, *The Queen is Dead*.

high relief, erected above the bones of a polymath and polyglot,[10] who died in 1794 and who was, and remains, the most influential of the British Orientalists. Sir William Jones is generally, to this day, given a good press, that of a man who took India more than seriously, the Alberuni of his age. No one questions his enthusiasm and his genius, as the founder of the Asiatic Society, as

the translator of Sanskrit classics, as the man who began to tell the west about the glories of India's past. He helped make the critical discoveries that allowed the integration of Indian and Classical Greek timelines; he identified the Palibothra of Megasthenes both with the Pataliputra of old Sanskrit texts and with modern Patna; and he realised that the King Sandrocottus who ruled Pataliputra when Megasthenes visited was the same person as Chandragupta who founded the Mauryan dynasty. It was Jones who popularised the idea of a common linguistic ancestry, of a prehistoric cousinhood between Sanskrit and Greek (and Latin); and his writings are imbued with the notion that Indian civilisation should be considered alongside those of ancient Greece and Rome.[11] He would write hyperbolically

---

[10] Jones is said to have joked to Louis XVI that he knew almost every language except his own — Welsh.

[11] The correspondence between Sandrocottus and Chandragupta had been spotted earlier, in the 1770s by the French Orientalist Joseph de Guignes. Another early French Orientalist, Abraham-Hyacinthe Anquetil-Duperron,

of almost all things Indian: from the beauty of its languages to the transmigration of souls. Sanskrit, he said, 'is of a wonderful structure; more perfect than the *Greek*, more copious than the *Latin*, and more exquisitely refined than either'; while he declared: 'I am no Hindu; but I hold the doctrine of the Hindus concerning a future state to be incomparably more rational, more pious and more likely to deter men from vice than the horrid opinion inculcated by Christians on punishment without end.' These remarks did not endear him to everyone back home.

India, for Jones, became something to be incorporated into his world-view, a world which, disconcertingly, appeared to be expanding even faster than its inhabitants' imaginations. And the similarity to, and imagined connections with, ancient Greece and Rome became his central conceit. Jones claimed to 'live among the adorers of those very deities, who were worshipped under different names in Old Greece and Italy'. He refers to Krishna as the Indian Apollo; he argues that it is not possible to read the Vedas 'without believing that Pythagoras and Plato derived their sublime theories from the same fountain with the sages of India'.

Anne Elwood, an over-enthusiastic follower of Jones, argues, in a passage which reads like a pastiche, that the Roman and Hindu gods of love, Cupid and Kama, are the same. Part of her evidence is that Cupid, spelled backwards, is Dipuc (presumably an unusual spelling of Deepak), which she claims as one of the names of Kama. She repeats the older notion of a Biblical connection with Hinduism, demonstrated by a 'curious similarity in their names', that Abraham is really Brahma, and his wife, Sarah, is Saraswati — while Jones suggested that Rama was the same person as Raamah, the great-grandson of Noah. And

was a strong advocate of treating ancient India on a par with the great Classical civilisations of Europe. 'Let us study the Indians as we do the Greeks and the Romans; when we understand them well, it will be permissible for us, if we are better than they, to criticise their course, but without arrogance, without rancour, and without ridicule.'

he strays even further afield in his search for those strangely similar names, known to linguists as false friends. He refers to 'the Peruvians, whose Incas . . . styled their greatest festival Ramasitoa; whence we may suppose, that South America was peopled by the same race, who imported into the farthest parts of Asia the rites and fabulous history of Rama'. And he goes on to invent a world of 'immemorial affinity' between the Hindus of India and a long list of disparate nationalities, including Persians, Ethiopians, Egyptians, Phoenicians, Greeks, Scythians, Goths, Celts, Chinese, Japanese and Peruvians. It's an appealingly deracinated view of our planet, stripped of ideas about purity of language and culture. And it's hard not to admire his instincts, even when his facts seem a little wayward.[12]

It was on mainland Europe that Jones' influence was most profound, in circumstances which he could scarcely have predicted, and in ways which helped form a new Romantic idea of India. His rendering into English[13] of the Sanskrit drama, *Shakuntala*, itself adapted from a tale in the *Mahabharata*, was in turn quickly translated into German — and it was this translation of a translation of an adaptation, originally written in the early centuries of the first millennium, that became a European

[12] There were limits even to Jones' gullibility. He scoffed at his friend, the amateur philologist General Charles Vallancey, who insisted that the ancient Irish were really Persians. Jones wrote to another friend, Earl Spencer, that Vallancey's book was 'very stupid', and added 'Do you wish to laugh? Skim the book over. Do you wish to sleep? Read it regularly.' According to Vallancey, the Sanskrit word *suvarna-kuta*, meaning 'golden peak', used in ancient Hindu texts, became, by contraction, Skuta, then Scotia, and then Scotland; while *pitrsthana*, meaning abode of the ancestors, was really (St) Patrick's land, or Ireland.

[13] According to his biographer Michael J Franklin, Jones de-eroticises Shakuntala in translation. Her lover, King Dushyanta, presses only her feet rather than her 'beautiful tapering thighs', balm is spread across her 'bosom' rather than specifically on her breasts, and where Kalidasa refers to her breasts no longer being firm — Jones simply removes the reference. And Jones never allows her to sweat.

best-seller. In Germany it went, to use the modern demotic, viral. It was the start of what would later become known as the Second or Oriental Renaissance (though its foremost twentieth-century scholar, Raymond Schwab, dates this back, not to Jones, but earlier, to Anquetil-Duperron). The poet Novalis nicknamed his teenage girlfriend Shakuntala after the play's sexy, naive heroine — who became an archetype of Indian womanhood. Goethe was moved to write a quatrain which ended with the lines: 'If you want to encompass Heaven and Earth with one name/ Then I name you, Shakuntala, and all is said.' He would later speak of 'the incomparable Jones', and at the same time be rather rude about Hindu gods.

The philosopher Herder, who wrote an ecstatic preface to the second edition of *Shakuntala*, was the most rapturously hyperbolic; he said he had found in this ancient drama, 'the mistress of his heart'. And India became his new *Morgenland*, the morning-land from which human civilisation emerged many aeons ago. *Shakuntala* revealed 'an earlier age of innocence, where gods and men live together'. Herder, in turn, was enormously influential — and in the early decades of the nineteenth century, an unlikely strain of Indomania entered German intellectual and academic life. At its heart was this *Morgenland* — an imagined ancient India, the cradle of mankind, the source of all religion and all language. And some of them even came to identify Germany — under Napoleonic rule for several years — with India under British rule. For Friedrich Schlegel the connections were far more ancient. He echoed William Jones on the subject of the common origins of Indian and European languages, but argued that the earliest route of transmission was by migrants from India who settled in northern Germany and Scandinavia. Schlegel was the first of many German Sanskritists, and to this day no other European country, including the UK, has such a strong tradition in Sanskrit studies.[14] None of the important early German Indophiles actually travelled to India — and Friedrich Schlegel's brother August went so far as to suggest that this gave them greater objectivity than the British, whose scholarship, he went on to argue, had been subordinated to the country's political interests in India.

In modern times, even William Jones has come under attack for being complicit in the colonial endeavour. One recent British historian argues that Jones, 'continues to function as a reassuring vindication of British rule' in India. And his modern critics point to the fact that, according to his own account, Jones went to India to make a fortune, and that his original purpose in learning local languages was to ensure that Indian agents and lawyers didn't cheat him. He was, of course, a man of his times, who gave little space to contemporary Indians as tellers of their own stories. But by appointing himself as the great interpreter, who would bring the best of India to the west, he was able to stand apart, and there are still moments when his voice cuts through the centuries, as when he implored westerners to take a more sophisticated view of India. 'In Europe,' he said, 'you see India through a glass darkly; here we are in a strong light; and a thousand little nuances are perceptible to us, which are not visible through your best telescopes, and which could not be explained without writing volumes.'

Those 'thousand little nuances' were ignored by many who came after Jones, notably by those people who were reformers

[14] Friedrich Schlegel learned Sanskrit under unlikely circumstances. He was visiting France when he met his Sanskrit teacher, Alexander Hamilton, a British prisoner-of-war briefly interned in Paris during the Napoleonic Wars. Hamilton had studied Sanskrit in Calcutta. This Hamilton was the first cousin of the American statesman of the same name. It is not known if they were related to Alexander Hamilton, the sailor, who wrote so scathingly about Job Charnock (see page 193). In Germany (mainly Prussia), six professorial chairs were established in Sanskrit and related studies between 1818 and 1840, and a further seven before the First World War.

by instinct and ideology. As a student of British history, men like William Wilberforce, James Mill and Thomas Macaulay were early heroes of mine, articulate and outspoken, and key figures in the abolition of slavery, and in broadening the electoral franchise. And yet, on the subject of India, they appear at best to have had closed minds, or to show contempt at worst. Wilberforce, usually remembered for his campaign to abolish slavery, was an evangelical Christian who described the Hindu gods as 'monsters of lust', and implored Indians to exchange their 'dark and bloody superstitions for the genial influence of Christian light and truth'. James Mill, in his immensely popular *History of British India*, first published in 1818, made many dozens of scathing references to Jones, whom he accused of being both pompous and rather too imaginative. Mill himself never travelled to India, and saw no need to do so. Distance, he felt, would make him more objective. He scoured the newly-translated Indian classics for proof that India was uncivilised. He quotes Jones' translation of the Laws of Manu as if it were *the* canonical Hindu text,[15] and relishes its ancient peccadilloes, scoffing away at Jones and at Hindus, cherry-picking those passages which would make westerners either guffaw or recoil with disgust, or both. He informs his readers, for instance, as if it were an everyday event in early nineteenth-century India, that any high-caste man who has committed the sin of drinking alcohol made from rice must 'drink boiling hot, until he die, the urine of a cow, or pure water, or milk, or clarified butter, or juice expressed from cow-dung'. While the 'penances for venereal sin', Mill teases ominously, 'are unfit to be transcribed'.[16]

[15] There is, of course, no canonical text.

[16] Among the more serious penances for sexual misbehaviour that Mill is too coy to mention, but which is translated without comment by Jones, is that the sinner, 'having himself amputated his penis and scrotum, and holding them in his fingers, he may walk in a direct path towards the south-west . . . until he fall dead on the ground'.

In modern India, Thomas Macaulay remains, on balance, the most infamous colonial ruler of the nineteenth century — more so than anyone, for instance, who took part in crushing the 1857 Uprising, and despite the fact that he was only in the country for three years, and was only a relatively junior member of the ruling Council of India. His modern infamy largely relates to a single eighteen-word clause in a memorandum submitted in 1835 to the British governor-general. In Macaulay's 'Minute on Education', he stated that 'a single shelf of a good European library was worth the whole native literature of India and Arabia'. It is an assertion that has become almost the epitome of British colonial arrogance, a supercilious sneering statement from a man who was often deceived by his own eloquence, and who knew no eastern languages.[17] But for all his sneers, Macaulay was not exactly a bigot, except on the subject of Indian fruit, which he found 'wretched' (apart from, strangely enough, the pineapple). It was Macaulay who first drafted a uniform penal code for India, and he demanded that 'no native of our Indian empire shall, by reason of his colour, his descent, or his religion, be incapable of holding office', something that made him very unpopular with many of his countrymen.

Macaulay's 'single shelf' remark needs to be seen in the context of a long-running debate about Britain's view of India and its culture, between Orientalists such as William Jones, who believed, in brief, that the west had much to learn from the country they were colonising, and the Anglicists, like Wilberforce, Mill and Macaulay, who didn't. Their positions reflected very different imaginings of India. The Orientalist

---

[17] According to Pavan Varma in his 2010 book, *Becoming Indian,* Macaulay 'in one rhetorical flourish rubbished the entire civilizational heritage of all Indians'. On that matter that is almost as serious — Indian fruit — Macaulay said: 'All the tropical fruits together are not worth any of our commonest English productions — cherry, strawberry, currant, apple, pear, peach.' He declares that mangoes taste of 'honey and turpentine'.

image of India was born of its pre-colonial past, an ancient civilisation waiting to be discovered, its artefacts collected and categorised; while the Anglicist image of India was born of the present, and of an anxiety about the future of British India. For the Anglicists, the land they were conquering became a test-bed, a potential palimpsest that could be scraped clean of its past, and where they could experiment with their ideas about Christianity, progress and education. In many ways, the Orientalist–Anglicist debate said more about Britain than it did about India, and about different ideas within the British ruling elite about what constituted progress.

Macaulay's 'single shelf' statement was also, more specifically, part of a debate about the language in which the Indian elite should be educated — an argument that has profound repercussions to this day. Macaulay wanted to abolish financial support for schools and colleges in India which taught Sanskrit and Arabic, and he wanted English to be the language of education. His aim was what would now be called social engineering. He wanted to create a class of people who would be 'interpreters between us and the millions whom we govern — a class of persons Indian in blood and colour, but English in tastes, in opinions, in morals and in intellect'. And so it was that the elite of India were introduced to an English liberal education — at a time when such a thing barely existed in the UK. Its many guinea pigs would later be scornfully represented as 'Macaulay's children', rootless Anglophones who could quote Milton and Wordsworth, but knew little of their own culture and language. They attracted a number of disparaging epithets — coconuts (brown outside, white inside) and brown sahibs — words that have been used to describe a wide range of occidentalised Indians from opera-lovers, collectors of British royal memorabilia, devotees of Tennyson, English grammar pedants, to the admirers of colonial cuisine.

In the early years of the twenty-first century, Macaulay made an unexpected and unlikely comeback in India. Some Dalits, members of the caste which the British knew as 'untouchables', led by a journalist called Chandrabhan Prasad,[18] declared Macaulay a hero. That decision to use English as the language of education, Prasad claimed, provided an opportunity to break the upper-caste stranglehold on education. The English language became a means of emancipation for the lowest castes. Prasad announced that Macaulay's birthday would henceforth be marked as 'The English Day'. In 2009, he sent out an ecstatic invitation for a celebration to be held at the august and slightly snooty India International Centre in Delhi:

The English Day
October 25, the Birth Day of Lord Macaulay,
to be the English Day
The Foundation Day Ceremony & Dinner

Dear gym goers, organic-food eaters, late-night daters, cattle-class enthusiasts, also fatalists, naysayers and Luddites, listen please, I have this call for you: Shilly-shally not, and come. Join the company of Day Makers. To be commemorated every year globally, October 25 will be instituted as the English Day — a la Father's Day, Mother's Day, and the Valentine's Day.

A large crowd of Delhi-ites gathered, in obedience to the command of 'shilly-shally not', and Chandrabhan Prasad handed out bronzed statuettes of a woman to six dignitaries. The woman was modelled on the Statue of Liberty, but with a floppy hat instead of a crown, a pen in place of a torch, and was mounted on a plinth constructed in the shape of a desktop

[18] Prasad has gained the reputation of a contrarian and gadfly. Most famously, he once said, 'The British came too late and left too early.' At a Delhi book launch, he once got up and asked, 'How many Dalits are there here?' There were none.

computer. The woman, Prasad explained, was the Goddess English. And there was even a birthday cake (with 'Happy Birthday M' written in icing on its surface) beneath a framed portrait of Macaulay, which had been inscribed with the words 'The Father of Indian Modernity'. It's all now posted on his website, chandrabhanprasad.com, including a photo of a rather embarrassed British Council official receiving his statuette. Thomas Macaulay would be delighted, William Jones would be bemused.

A Tenth Intermission

TWO HOARY FAMILY tales, now, from the end of the last millennium; tales that linger with me, and which made me think again about racism and the politics of identity in the context of south Asia.

London racism story No. 1: Once upon a time, when we were struggling through the streets of west London, with a double-buggy containing our infants, a young, white Englishman, discommoded by the way our caravanserai blocked the pavement, became agitated and threatening. He shouted, 'Fuck off, Paki!' at Shireen. She responded, instinctively and volubly, 'I'm not a Paki, I'm Indian.' I was too befuddled by this exchange to say or do anything — and the young man ran off. I was later, quite justifiably, carpeted over my failure to intervene, verbally or physically. It got worse. My unwise response was to suggest that Shireen might have shown greater solidarity with the people of Pakistan — rather than have attempted to differentiate herself to a white racist, in a way that would have meant nothing to him. Soon afterward, I saw a television documentary about Bangladeshi street gangs in Somerstown, near King's Cross, who were laughing at the ignorance of the white gangs who called them Pakis. 'It's like us calling white kids "Nazis",' one of them said.

London racism story No. 2: Once upon a time, Shireen was chatting with three Pakistani women outside the gates of our children's primary school in London. They were quite new to Britain. She had met them before, and they had struck up a polite friendship. They, Shireen told me, were delighted to find someone who could speak their language, who was well informed about their new country and who, they presumed from her name, was, like them, a Muslim. She didn't disabuse them. One of them asked her, on this occasion, about her husband;

that is, about me. 'Was he,' they asked, 'a British Indian — or did he come from India?' 'No,' she said, 'he's British.' And partly then in order to fill the confused silence, she added, 'He's white.' They were stunned, and one of them burst out, spontaneously, with that very subcontinental ejaculation of disgust, 'Chee-chee cheeee.' They then became embarrassed and apologetic — but the friendship shrivelled away. At the time, it was a story that I liked to tell, for reasons that now seem trivial — I felt it gave me some brief insight into what it was like to be the victim of racism. But today on reflection it serves, like the 'Paki' story, more as a reminder of the complications of defining 'foreign-ness' in the south Asian context.

Historically, the nuances of identity in India, and that larger place that was also known as India until the partition of 1947, have been lost on many foreigners. Many of us have sought out that archetypal Indian, one whom we first met in storybooks or sit-coms, and India has enough inhabitants for examples of almost any 'archetype' to be identified. For those who know India better, including many Indians, the search is slightly more sophisticated, for more localised archetypes — the typical Parsi (sometimes depicted, for instance, as having a large nose, and a love of the British royal family[1]), or a typical Bengali (a piscivorous intellectual), or a typical Tamil Brahmin (vegetarian and fastidious). The deeper we dig, the more incomplete and misleading these stereotypes become.

In the last years of the old millennium, and the earliest years of the new one, my work at the BBC pulled me back to the subcontinent several times a year. I spent much time visiting India's south Asian neighbours, particularly Pakistan. I would hop back and forth between India and Pakistan, in a way that

[1] Neither of these is true of the Parsi family into which I married, who are mostly small-nosed admirers of America. One of Shireen's aunts did have a fine collection of Coronation crockery.

252

no citizen of those countries can; an undeserved privilege for me, and one denied to those who need it most. The similarities between north India and Pakistan were far more striking to me than the differences (and much more alike than south India and north India). I could use the same language, eat the same food; people wore similar clothes, they had similar cultural references. Sometimes I would forget which country I was in. But for some of those I told this to, in India and in Pakistan, I was a gullible fool who had failed to realise, either that Pakistanis were India-hating fundamentalists or that Indians were Pakistan-hating zealots. A fearful reciprocated hatred had become part of their own identity, of the way they defined themselves, and became part of the way the world came to see the two countries — a hyphenated India-Pakistan, united only by enmity.

Much mistrust remains. But since 9/11 India and Pakistan, once coupled together as if they were disruptive Siamese twins, have been separated, dehyphenated. Af-Pak is the new hyphenated disturber of the western status quo, and India stands on its own, an emerging economy, with dreams of world leadership — and sought as a friend by most countries around the world. India's reputation has risen, as Pakistan's has crumbled. India, for all that ails it, is far more popular than its neighbour.

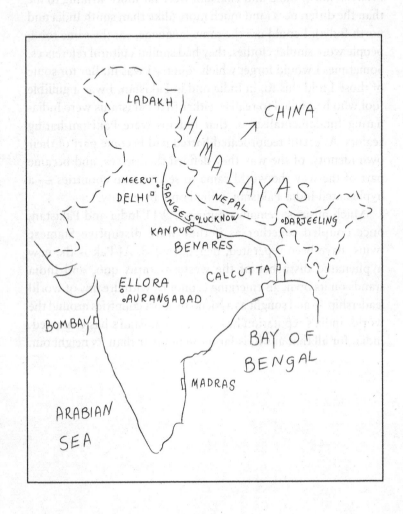

Chapter Eleven: In which the Author discovers the true meaning of the acronym 'BBC', gets caught up in the 'Mutiny' of 1857, and reveals the Indian identity of Captain Nemo

ON THAT FIRST trip to India, more than a quarter of a century ago, my future mother-in-law drew up my travel itinerary. She sent me, *tout seul*, on a long, daytime train journey — where I was repeatedly asked by fellow passengers about my marital status and my income — to the city of Aurangabad and the nearby Ellora Caves. I did not, at the time, believe in guidebooks, and had a Romantic dream, as others had had before me, of experiencing India in an unmediated manner. And so, one chill morning in early 1988, soon after dawn, I wandered into the Kailash Temple at Ellora, quite unprepared for what I was about to see. It appeared to be a large stone temple built against the side of a hill, with a high outer wall, a courtyard around the temple, and, everywhere, rock-cut friezes with hundreds of carvings of writhing and flamboyant gods. And then I realised that I was

seeing a mirage of sorts. The temple was not a building at all. It was what had been left behind by an excavation. Huge quantities of rock had been removed, but not a single bit of stone had been

255

brought in. Each carving was a part of the same single enormous rock, as was each roof finial, each balustrade, even the stone bridge that linked the gateway to the main shrine. Just as Michelangelo had imagined his David in a block of marble, so the architects of Ellora had imagined a great temple in a rocky hillside. I struggled for words to describe something quite as discombobulating as the Kailash Temple. Twenty years on, I revisited Ellora to write, of all things, a guidebook; and managed to crush every hyperbolic cliché — stunning, unbelievable, extraordinary, remarkable — into a few sentences. Perhaps I should just have admitted that I was lost for words.

The Ellora Caves were first mentioned in the writings of a foreign visitor in the seventeenth century, and by the second half of the eighteenth century, were becoming, among the European cognoscenti, 'a wonder of the East', an essential destination for those who had time to travel to the Indian interior. Anquetil-Duperron, the foremost of the early French Orientalists, went there and compared the friezes to the medieval reliefs at Notre Dame in Paris. The French botanist Pierre Sonnerat raised the comparative stakes higher, declaring in the 1780s that the pyramids of Egypt 'are very feeble monuments' compared to the temples of Ellora.[1] Soon images of Ellora would become well known in the west, through the publication of the sixth volume of *Oriental Scenery*, the influential India engravings of the uncle–nephew team of artists, Thomas and William Daniell, who actually never made it to the caves but relied on drawings by a dead friend. India's first British royal visitor, George FitzClarence, the illegitimate son of King William IV, turned up in 1818. He repeatedly described the caves as 'stupendous', compared their

[1] Sonnerat calculated that the caves took more than a thousand years to excavate, and date back almost five thousand years. In fact, the Kailash Temple was excavated in less than a century, and completed in the ninth century AD. More than 200,000 tons of rock were removed to create the temple.

architecture to that of ancient Greece, and sat down to eat 'a few slices of a round of beef' inside the main shrine. The taste, he explained with an unmistakable sneer, 'suffered nothing from the idea of feasting on the flesh of the most sacred and venerated animal of the Hindus, in their most singular temple'.[2]

In 1820, Ellora was the subject of the first in-depth study of a major Indian historical site, compiled by the British soldier John Seely, who compared it to the Parthenon, St Paul's in London, St Peter's and the Pantheon in Rome, as well as Fonthill Abbey — and rounded it all off by saying that Ellora was better than anything in Egypt. Seely turned his Ellora monograph into a discursive travelogue, pronouncing on numerous controversial subjects — 'there is no fruit in the world equal to the Alphonso mango'; Hindu women 'are small but exquisitely proportioned', and, unlike so many British women, they bathe daily; and 'prostitutes', he points out, are so much better treated in India than in his homeland. At the Kailash Temple, Seely is only slightly more sensitive to Hindu tradition than FitzClarence. He gives a Brahmin priest three bags of rice, as a payment for clearing all devotees out of the temple, and has his bed made up in the main chamber of the shrine. He has a signed agreement with the Brahmin in which he has promised not to cook meat inside the temple, but it says nothing about pre-cooked meat and so he takes his salt beef into the inner sanctuary.

On other matters, Seely is a prude. Of the lingam, he says 'whatever enthusiasts may say to the contrary, this symbol is

[2] George FitzClarence was the eldest son of William IV, and, if legitimate, would have succeeded to the throne instead of Queen Victoria. In 1842, in what the newspapers called 'a fit of insanity', FitzClarence committed suicide by shooting himself in the head with a pistol presented to him by his uncle, George IV. He is said to have been depressed by news of the recent British defeats in Afghanistan. FitzClarence's parents — the actress Dorothea Jordan and King William — had at least ten children. Among their descendants is a great-great-great-great-greatgrandson called David Cameron, currently the British prime minister.

grossly indecent, and abhorrent to every moral feeling', while after spotting some rather mild erotica on the outer wall of the Kailash Temple, he says, 'there is nothing too depraved or lascivious for the Hindoo mind to contemplate and describe.' But Seely does undoubtedly adore the Kailash Temple, asking without embarrassment: 'Reader, is not this entire temple wonderful?' And he invents, with another rhetorical question, and without any evidence, an ancient and romantic tradition for the caves. 'Where now is the whole mechanism of Elora's former splendour — the mystic dance, the beautiful priestesses, the innumerable midnight lamps . . . the solemn supplications of the graceful-looking Brahman of the "olden day", clothed in long white vestments? All are fled.'

In fact, in the Britain of the 1820s, when Seely was writing, the William Jones-inspired romantic image of ancient India was a minority view, one that appeared almost eccentric. The practicalities of colonial rule had intervened, Mill and Macaulay were about to have their day, and the Oriental Renaissance would only have an ephemeral existence in Britain. But in the rest of Europe, a kind of Indomania, kindled by Jones, fanned by the romantic Orientalisms of Herder and Schlegel, spread like wildfire, and became increasingly detached from the realities of modern India. Schlegel got particularly carried away, declaring in a moment of unscholarly over-excitement that 'everything without exception has its origin in India'.

The German linguist Friedrich Creuzer[3] took the Roman idea that the Greek god Dionysus travelled to India, and reversed the flow of influence, so that the gods of ancient Greece came

[3] Creuzer's interest appears to have been sparked by the influence of his India-obsessed girlfriend, Karoline von Günderrode, who in 1805 wrote a play called *Udohla* about sibling incest set in Delhi. She also wrote a poem, *Die Malabarische Witwen*, which romanticised *sati*. Günderrode committed suicide by stabbing herself in the heart, when she realised that Creuzer would not divorce his wife.

originally from India. He was obsessed by some of the more esoteric religious rites of Greece and Rome, the 'mysteries' as they were known. And he found their roots in the worship of Shiva which he described as a 'wild orgiastic religion', the *Phallusdienst* (or Phallic cult), which he claimed then spread through Egypt to Greece, Rome and the rest of the ancient world.[4] For the lyric poet Heine, India was a dreamland, a place to which he'd flee with his beloved, in famous words, later set to music by Mendelssohn:

Auf Flügeln des Gesanges,	On wings of song,
Herzliebchen, trag ich dich fort,	Love of my heart, I'll carry you away,
Fort nach den Fluren des Ganges,	Away to the fields of the Ganges
Dort weiß ich den schönsten Ort	Where I know the most beautiful place

The poet-revolutionary Lamartine,[5] who briefly ruled France during the 1848 revolution, declared, in less heady times, 'Indian philosophy eclipses all others; it is the ocean, and we are only clouds.' After reading the Vedas, he took to kneeling down and praying to the rising sun.

Not everyone joined in. The philosopher Hegel was less easily swayed by Indomania, though he wrote at some length about

---

[4] The eponymous hero of Balzac's semi-autobiographical early novel, *Louis Lambert*, published in 1832, had similar views. 'He thought that the mythology of the Greeks was borrowed both from the Hebrew Scriptures and from the sacred Books of India, adapted after their own fashion by the beauty-loving Hellenes.'

[5] Alphonse de Lamartine was effectively the French head of state for six weeks in May and June during the 1848 revolution. He came fifth (out of six) in the presidential election later that year, receiving less than twenty thousand votes, compared to the more than five million votes received by the future Emperor Napoleon III.

India, and admired its ancient literature. He declared quite categorically that India has 'no history', but is instead a 'petrified' society, frozen in time by the caste system, where no sense of the concept of freedom had ever developed. Karl Marx would, in an 1853 newspaper article, echo Hegel's words: 'India has no history at all, at least no known history. What we call its history, is but the history of the successive intruders who founded their empires on the passive basis of that unresisting and unchanging society.' Hegel's great rival, Schopenhauer, meanwhile, praised the detachment that was central to early Hindu and Buddhist philosophy, and said of his translated version of the Upanishads, 'It has been the solace of my life, it will be the solace of my death.'

None of these wiseacres actually made it to India. Nor did the vast majority of Europe's burgeoning legions of Sanskrit scholars. The first professor of Sanskrit was appointed at the Collège de France in Paris in 1814 — but it was in Germany that Indological and Sanskrit research flourished, and between 1818 and 1852, no less than ten German universities created chairs for the proliferating professors of ancient Indian studies; at least twelve other European cities from Helsinki to Turin all followed suit in the same period. Their main interests were literary and philological, and they were no more interested in modern India than Classicists were in modern Greece. India had become, in much of continental Europe, a symbol of ancientness, of the dawn of civilisation, and a source of ancient spiritual wisdom.

There were, of course, European visitors and settlers in India during this period — many of them on a personal and often eccentric quest. The Transylvanian traveller and philologist Alexander Csoma de Kőrös walked and hitched his way from Europe to the Himalayas, to seek the origins of his mother tongue, Hungarian, among the Tibetans of Ladakh. He died in Darjeeling in 1842 after compiling the first Tibetan–English dictionary. The Greek merchant Demetrius Galanos lived in India for forty-seven years — almost as long as Tony Mango. He

EIΣ ΜΝΗΜΗΝ ΔΗΜΗΤΡΙΌ
ΓΑΛΑΝΟΥ ΤΟ ΥΑΘΗΝΑΙΟΥ.

To the Memory of DEMETRIUS GALANOS an Athenian,
Who died at Benares the 3ᵈ of May 1833 Aged 72 Years.

stayed in Benares for most of that time, dressing as a Brahmin and, like Csoma de Kőrös, becoming a freelance lexicographer, compiling the first Greek–Sanskrit dictionary. The former Russian diplomat Prince Alexei Saltykov travelled through India in the 1840s, publishing a book of letters and drawings in French and Russian, and became known back home by the nickname, 'the Indian'.

British officials, under-employed in their day jobs, would pootle away in their free time — as amateur archaeologists, numismaticians and riddle-solvers. They took to deciphering forgotten languages and imagery, in a way that would gradually reveal the importance of Buddhism in Indian history and culture. Although Buddhism itself was all but dead as a faith in nineteenth-century India, the notion of India as the land of the Buddha took hold. James Prinsep, whose real job was to mint coins for the East India Company, became obsessed with the inscriptions of ancient India, and managed painstakingly to understand the Brahmi script, in which many of Ashoka's edicts had been written more than two thousand years earlier. He was astonished to discover that the Graeco-Egyptian king, Ptolemy, was referred to in one of the edicts, as were three other Greek rulers of the third century BC. His younger friend Alexander Cunningham,[6] an army engineer, began digging up old mounds of earth in search of Buddhist artefacts. After receiving French translations of ancient Chinese texts he became a little more methodical, identifying the places referred to by Buddhist pilgrims, including my own dear Tripitaka, more than a millennium earlier. In this way several major Buddhist sites were identified and excavated. Ancient India suddenly appeared much closer, in time and in space. Contemporary India seemed, in contrast, to have been largely forgotten, or seemed unnoticed by scholars. Thugs apart, that is.

The word 'thug' entered the English language during the 1830s and contributed to a quite different image of India, one of exotic criminality. Taken from the Hindi *thag*, or ठग, pronounced with a strongly aspirated and retroflex 't', and meaning swindler or cheat, the word was used to describe bands of murderous highwaymen who patrolled central India, drugging and strangling their victims. They would become a leitmotiv of English-language descriptions of India, resurrected for twentieth-century audiences in films like *Gunga Din* starring Cary Grant, and *Indiana Jones and the Temple of Doom* with Harrison Ford. The motivation of the Thugs, or Thuggee, remains the subject of academic controversy to this day — but in the popular telling of the story they are part of a Hindu cult, providing human sacrifices to the goddess Kali. The 1839 novel *Confessions of a Thug* written by the East Indian Company official Philip Meadows Taylor was enormously popular in Britain. Queen Victoria was

---

[6] Alexander Cunningham later founded the Archaeological Survey of India. In spite of his deep and genuine interest in Indian architecture, he continued to judge it with a very European perspective. He wrote that the 'architectural remains of Kashmir are perhaps the most remarkable of the existing monuments of India, as they exhibit undoubted traces of Grecian art'. He went on to describe the Hindu temple as an 'architectural pasty, a huge collection of ornamental fritters'.

a pre-publication reader, given unbound proofs as they came off the press. The narrator is himself a Thug — providing a rare early example of a western writer imagining the life of an Indian. And the account is unexpectedly sympathetic. Based on a real Thug whom Meadows Taylor interviewed in jail in India, Ameer Ali is portrayed as a charming and intelligent man, a Muslim who respected Hindu gods, a seducer of women, a man with a complex moral code of his own, but nonetheless a brutal murderer. The meaning of the word 'thug', like 'juggernaut' earlier and 'shampoo' a little later, would soon be Anglicised and turned to new uses. And by the end of 1839, the Scottish historian and essayist Thomas Carlyle had used it to describe the activities of some of his own countrymen, violent trade-unionists, who had indulged themselves in what he termed 'Glasgow Thuggery'.

Thugs apart, then, British accounts of the 1840s and early 1850s represent India as a quieter, less frenetically exotic place than it used to be. The battles for British supremacy had switched away from the Indian heartland to the frontiers, to Afghanistan in particular — and a strange somnolescence had settled over British rule in the subcontinent. In 1853, William Makepeace Thackeray began writing *The Newcomes*, a novel set in England and in Europe, but which was steeped in the British experience of India. It is full of people who are referred to as 'Indians' but who are actually white — that is, British people who have returned from India. They have strange food preferences ('curry and rice'), an endless supply of Indian fabric and bric-à-brac ('ivory chessmen, scented sandalwood workboxes and kincob scarfs'), and some interminable stories about the east ('tiger-hunting, palanquins, Juggernaut, elephants, the burning of widows—all passed before us in . . . splendid oration'). The only real Indian in the book is also a fake — Rummun Loll, who pretends to be an Indian prince ('How the girls crowd round him!'), and runs off with everyone's money. His dodgy bank, known as the BBC, or the Bundelcand Banking Company, goes bust. Thackeray, who was born in Calcutta, knows he is playing with clichés, and even interpolates his own narrative with a rant against those who stereotype the nabob as a symbol of rapacity and vulgarity.

He is neither as wealthy nor as wicked as the jaundiced monster of romances and comedies, who purchases the estates of broken-down English gentlemen, with rupees tortured out of bleeding rajahs, who smokes a hookah in public, and in private carries about a guilty conscience, diamonds of untold value, and a diseased liver; who has a vulgar wife, with a retinue of black servants whom she maltreats, and a gentle son and daughter with good impulses and an imperfect education.

And so on the eve of 1857, the year that marked the traumatic events that would bear many names, the predominant British image of India was not of Indians, but of the British themselves. And it was an image in which India seemed in British eyes to have become a place of lesser evils, where *sati* and Thuggee were things of the past, where a Pax Britannica appeared to reign and where local rajahs and ranis seemed, in an often annoyingly sullen manner, to accept British hegemony.

The events of 1857 changed all that — and mark a watershed of sorts, where British and European imaginings of India are seen quite clearly to diverge. The Uprising of 1857, which began as a mutiny, was a brutal affair on all sides. But it was not quite as brutal as the British public were led to believe, or as they conjured up in their fevered fantasies. A skim through the newspapers of the time shows just how wild the imaginative faculties of some individuals had become. The Earl of Shaftesbury, a great reformer[7] in Britain, stomped around public meetings spreading

[7] The seventh Earl of Shaftesbury was the best-known social reformer of his day, leading campaigns to stop the use of boys as chimney sweeps, to improve conditions in lunatic asylums and to regulate child labour. He was also an early supporter of a mass Jewish migration to Palestine. The statue

untruths. He told one audience that mutinous Indian soldiers had 'cruelly and anatomically' tortured British children in front of their parents — before killing them. Another meeting was told by Shaftesbury that European women had been seen 'stripped stark naked, lying on their backs, fastened by the arms and legs, exposed to a burning sun; others, again, had been actually hacked to pieces, and so recently, that the blood which streamed from their mangled bodies was still warm'. None of this happened. One historian of 1857 describes this as a period of trauma[8] in Britain when many people became quite deeply disturbed by reports from India — which often arrived more than two months after the events they described had taken place. They were so psychotically disturbed, that they took to imagining that even worse things were happening — gruesome hallucinatory imagery of, for instance, the amputated feet of British women and children arranged neatly in rows, of children being force-fed raw flesh that had been cut from the bodies of their just-alive parents. The priest-novelist Charles Kingsley was able to articulate this trauma: 'My brain is filled with images fresh out of hell' and 'I can think of nothing but these Indian massacres. The moral problems they involve make me half wild. Night and day the heaven seems black to me.'

These tall tales from India led other famous people to articulate genocidal thoughts that, to this day, to me at least,

known as Eros in London's Piccadilly Circus is officially the Shaftesbury Memorial, set up to commemorate his philanthropic works. His great-granddaughter, Edwina, would travel to India as the last vicereine, Lady Mountbatten, and be best remembered in India as the real or imagined lover of Jawaharlal Nehru.

[8] Christopher Herbert in *War of No Pity: The Indian Mutiny and Victorian Trauma* also speaks of 'the Victorian culture of retribution', and of a punishment complex which many novelists portrayed 'as a defining susceptibility of their age, a moral and psychological disorder to which the English were constitutionally prone'. He gives the example of Tom Tulliver in George Eliot's *Mill on the Floss*, and the schoolteachers in *David Copperfield*. He might have added Mr Brocklehurst in *Jane Eyre*.

seem deeply shocking — although I have also heard people I once thought wise talk like this about the people of Afghanistan, after that first great trauma of the third millennium, remembered as 9/11. Suddenly, in 1857, everyone in Britain seemed to have a view about India. The essayist and rhetorician Thomas De Quincey, best known for eating opium, wrote publicly, with purple passion, demanding that in response to the Mutiny, Britain should destroy Delhi and eradicate Hinduism: 'Thou, therefore, England, when Delhi is swept by the ploughshare and sown with salt, build a solitary monument to us; and on its base inscribe that the last and worst of the murderous idolatries which plagued and persecuted the generations of men was by us abolished.' Charles Dickens declared in a private letter to his friend, Britain's richest woman, Angela Burdett Coutts: 'I wish I were Commander in Chief in India . . .' he told her, 'I should do my utmost . . . to exterminate the Race upon whom the stain of the late cruelties rested.' These are hateful thoughts, and the British retaliation would also be hateful,[9] in the literal sense of that word. And though the language would later be tempered, and others — often old India hands — would point out that many reports of Indian cruelty were fabrications, the horrors of 1857 would leave deep scars.

The garrison town of Cawnpore, now the large industrial city of Kanpur, was the scene of the most brutal anti-colonial violence — though still nothing like the horror-fantasies dreamed up by the British. And the name Cawnpore, like the Black Hole of Calcutta, exactly a century earlier, would come to denote all that was most terrifying and most treacherous about India. At the heart of the story of Cawnpore was a dispossessed Indian

[9] In Cawnpore, alleged mutineers were forced to lick the floor clean of British blood spilled in the killings, before being executed. Elsewhere, many were killed by being strapped to the muzzle of a cannon, which was then fired, scattering their body parts far and wide.

prince, Nana Sahib,[10] who would become in the eyes of many in Britain, the devil incarnate. The earliest English-language novel to deal with the events of 1857 was written by a British soldier called Edward Money — and ends dramatically in Cawnpore with the British being terrorised by Nana Sahib. It's a strangely telling document. *The Wife and the Ward* is the story of a Captain Edgington who is posted in Patna and falls for a coldly calculating Collector's daughter. But Edgington is also the guardian of a teenage English rose called Marion Paris whom he secretly adores. All of the main characters in the first half of the book are British, waited on by silent, obsequious, opinion-less Indians. And no Indian says much more than one word until page 216, when a white-bearded Muslim servant who sees Marion for the first time is allowed to speak this sentence: 'The English girls are many of them angels, but I've never seen such perfection as this before.'

The first half of *The Wife and the Ward* is almost a parody of British life in the colonies: regimental dinners, a day at the races, morning horse-rides, boar-hunting and ballroom dances with quadrilles, waltzes and polkas — and a parade of 'dusky attendants'. The second half is shockingly different. The novel and the main characters move to Cawnpore and 'the bachelor's ball', where a bejewelled Nana Sahib first appears, casting his 'coal-black eyes' in the direction of Marion. Her first reaction is dismissive: 'Such great ugly thick lips, and such a savage face altogether.' He tries to talk to her and she becomes silent. He pays her a courtesy call, and his gaze 'sends the blood back

[10] Nana Sahib, born Dhondu Pant, was the adopted son of the last Peshwa, hereditary leader of the Maratha confederacy. The last Peshwa, Baji Rao II, defeated by the British in 1818, was exiled to Bithur, twenty kilometres from Kanpur — where he died in 1851. In 1827, he adopted the three-year-old Nana Sahib as his son. On Baji Rao's death, the British would not allow Nana Sahib, as an adopted son, to receive his pension — and this is often seen as the start of his difficult relationship with the British.

cold to her heart'. Soon the Mutiny takes place, the British are trapped — and betrayed by Nana Sahib. They almost all die, women and children included — murdered by the mutineers.

Nana Sahib and Marion do not meet again, except in Marion's nightmares, until the final dramatic scene in the book, on the Ganges, where Nana Sahib sees Marion on a boat and tells his soldiers to bring her to him: 'There is the prize — the girl in white.' Captain Edgington, seated next to Marion, plants a 'long and ardent kiss' on her lips, takes out a pistol (at her request) and holds it to her head. There is no happy ending, as the author describes how 'the brains of Marion Paris bespattered the chest of her guardian'. But it could have been worse, we are made to feel. She has, after all, avoided the ravishing cliché, that 'fate worse than death' — of being raped, and of becoming Nana Sahib's concubine. In an earlier scene, with slight comic undertones which the author surely cannot have intended, Marion is told by the wife of a British officer, 'I, as a married woman, can assure you that death is not nearly as bad as our fate would be in sepoy hands.' Marion's response to this piece of information is to blush.

In fact, there is no evidence at all that Nana Sahib coveted any of the British women, who, by the end of the siege, were in a pitiable state. According to Captain Mowbray Thomson, one of just two British soldiers who survived, 'when the siege had terminated, such was the loathsome condition into which, from long destitution and exposure, the fairest and youngest of our women had sunk, that not a sepoy would have polluted himself with their touch'. But Nana Sahib's

The "Nana Sahib."

carnality, and that of other 'rebels', soon became part of the myth of the Mutiny. The truth is far more complex. Nana Sahib's right-hand man, Azimoolah Khan, had travelled to England in 1854, and was reported to have had affairs with more than one young Englishwoman; a well-known piece of gossip of the time. Captain Thomson even asks rhetorically, in his account of Cawnpore, 'Will Azimoolah . . . ever again be seen in London drawing-rooms, or cantering on Brighton Downs, the centre of an admiring bevy of English damsels?' And, Thomson continues, offering some sharp advice to the louche British elite, 'Let us point the moral, by warning Belgravia to be careful ere she adorns the drawing-room with Asiatic guests.' Even if he acquits Nana Sahib of lechery, his message is clear: beware of Indian men — they will seduce your women and betray you all.

In fact, one of the Englishwomen besieged at Cawnpore appears to have had an enduring consensual relationship with a mutineer called Ali Khan. Margaret, the eighteen-year-old daughter of the British commanding officer at Cawnpore, General Wheeler, disappeared at the end of the siege, and was presumed or imagined to have been killed. In fact, she survived into the twentieth century, having lived in purdah in Cawnpore for many years. A British visitor to Cawnpore who discovered her secret urged her to inform her family — but she said she was too ashamed and did not want to risk the life of Ali Khan.

The story of Nana Sahib soon became a legend. The slightly dull, portly, clean-shaven princeling who barely spoke English and rarely attended British functions had already been transformed by the time of *The Wife and the Ward* into a satanic, sinewy, bearded, Anglophone habitué of bachelor balls. Edward Money's demonisation of Nana Sahib was explicit and exclamatory:

Nana Sahib! Are they not almost household words in English mouths? Are they not the personification of all we conceive terrible and to be hated in human nature? Does not the name call up the idea of a perfect devil in man's shape, — a being full of treachery, cruelty, cowardice and every despicable vice — void of compassion, void of any heavenly-born attribute, gloating over the hellish torments he inflicts; in whose ears the manly shriek of anguish, the supplicating voice of woman, the cry of childhood finds no response — a being execrated by the whole civilized world, and calling up a blush in every honest man's cheek, that such an incarnate fiend should wear his own shape.

As the British reclaimed control of northern India, Nana Sahib evaded them and disappeared — never to be found. He became, in absentia, the subject of a sarcastic poem in *Punch* magazine, which demanded stronger retaliation against the rebels by British forces in India.

First catch your NANA SAHIB; then, though you may speak your mind to him,
Oh! Pray do not harsh language use, or be at all unkind to him,
Point out how naughty 'twas of him with cruelty to slaughter
The mother and her little boy, and helpless infant daughter:
But there stop
Don't doom your brother NANA SAHIB to the drop.

He also ended up, multifariously, as a waxwork in the Madame Tussauds' Chamber of Horrors, an evanescent hermit said to be living in a cave in central India, and the hero or villain of several more novels. His relatives claim he lived, like Margaret Wheeler, into the twentieth century, having, as a legendary master of disguises, evaded the British for some fifty years.[11] Nana Sahib

[11] It may never be known for sure when Nana Sahib died. There were reported sightings of him, often dressed as a Hindu ascetic, from across India and as far afield as Bhutan and Constantinople, until the early years of the twentieth century. It seems most likely that he died in Nepal in the early 1860s. However, a blog written by Professor Colonel Dr K Prabhakar

lived on in nightmares and in rhetoric, in the inventive minds of writers, as an object of fascination and dread across Europe. He would become a generic symbol of Anglophobia and an exemplar of the otherness of India.

Nana Sahib made the first of many bizarre fictional appearances in 1858 in a baroque novel named after him. *Nena Sahib or the Uprising in India* was written by a German whose Anglophobia didn't stop him adopting the very English pseudonym of Sir John Retcliffe. His real name was Hermann Goedsche, a former postal clerk, now best remembered as having written an anti-Semitic story that inspired the *Protocols of the Elders of Zion*.[12] Goedsche's novel was 1400 pages long and fabulously popular in Germany. It was never, despite Goedsche's Anglicised alias, translated into English — and it's easy to see why. The book is an open attack on British colonialism, completely inverting the British telling of 1857, and with enough Indian clichés to make the most turgid of travel writers shrink — with parades of dancing girls, snake charmers, sacrificial orgies, Thugs and suttees. The main narrative follows the breathlessly convoluted and entangled story of several individuals from a range of countries — Ireland, Holland, France, Greece, Germany

Rao quotes an old diary indicating that Nana Sahib died in 1926 at the age of 102. Dr Rao laments that, 'Thus we find that a mystery surrounds the death of Nana sahib . . . Let us hope some day truth would prevail. Sadly Indian youth have no time to dwell on past history and are very busy in keeping themselves involved on face books, twitters, running after film actors and their new born grand children, drinking, gossiping and shaking their groins at pubs and in IT craze.' Dr Rao's many wisdoms can be accessed at kuntamukkalaprabhakar.blogspot.in.

[12] The anti-Semitic hoax known as the *Protocols of the Elders of Zion* was first published in Russian in 1903, and drew on the work of the French satirist Maurice Joly, and on Hermann Goedsche's novel, *Biarritz*. The notion of a conspiracy of Jews that was hatched in the Jewish cemetery in Prague came directly from Goedsche. Umberto Eco used the story of Goedsche and the Protocols for his 2010 novel, *The Prague Cemetery*.

and India[13] — who all have reason to hate Britain.

The central character is not quite the Nana Sahib of history, or of British demonology. He is provided with a new back-story, to explain how he became so vengeful. Goedsche invents for him an Irish wife, Margaret O'Sullivan, a woman he loves deeply. She is kidnapped and then dies, insane in the harem of a British officer. Nana Sahib is now eaten up with hatred for the British, and becomes, slightly anachronistically, a leader of the Thugs. Towards the end of the novel, the brutality of Cawnpore is played out on all sides, with a few romantic death scenes thrown in. Nana Sahib has been turned into a tiger-like monster — with 'an ugly, evil sneer, an expression of cruel greed which raised the upper lip and let his sharp white teeth show through like the fangs of a predator'. Many of the protagonists die but Nana Sahib escapes, and disappears — only to re-emerge briefly in a later Goedsche novel as a 'Gul',[14] a Gollum-like wraith who has one of the three rings which give their owner the power to rule the world.

One of the most successful writers of all time[15] also showed

[13] Representatives of each country meet at the empty grave of Napoleon on St Helena, under the leadership of a disgraced Irish colonel called Ochterlony, and they all agree to 'join forces in a holy union of vengeance against England'.

[14] Nana Sahib is also in league with the Jesuits, in a manner that appears to combine key elements from those as yet unwritten fantasies, *The Lord of the Rings* and *The Da Vinci Code*.

[15] See UNESCO's *Index Translationum* whose top five translated non-anonymous writers are 1. Agatha Christie 2. Jules Verne 3. William Shakespeare 4. Enid Blyton 5. Lenin. There are nine India-born authors in the top thousand. Two of them turn up side by side in the mid-40s: Osho at 44, Rudyard Kipling at 45. Tagore appears at 139; Deepak Chopra at 165; J Krishnamurti at 169; Salman Rushdie at 312; (VS Naipaul is at 400); Sathya Sai Baba at 640; Aurobindo at 752; with Mahatma Gandhi bringing up the rear at 921.

Verne has been particularly badly served by his many translators, and towards the end of his life lamented this fact to someone who complained about how poor an Italian translation had been: 'I'm not surprised that a certain phantasmagorical obsession with Nana Sahib. Jules Verne, who like Goedsche never made it to India, wrote a novella in 1880 called *The Demon of Cawnpore*, starring Nana Sahib as the 'demon'. Verne was less anti-British than Goedsche, and to a modern reader comes across as relatively even-handed in his treatment of 1857 (though several English translations of his work omit or distort key passages which would have been seen as Anglophobic). Verne's story begins ten years after the Cawnpore massacre, in the city of Aurangabad, with a mysterious and murderous fakir, who carefully tears off the name 'Nana Sahib' from a British 'Wanted' poster — offering a two-thousand-pound reward for the capture, dead or alive, of the leader of the 'Sepoy revolt'. The fakir is, of course, Nana Sahib himself. His hiding-place is in the Ellora Caves, where he glided into a deep crevice, concealed behind a stone elephant. His pursuer is Colonel Munro, the invented husband of an invented victim of Cawnpore, who travels through India in an imaginary machine, known as the Steam House, which is a cross between a train, a house and an elephant. Munro is ambushed, and it is Nana Sahib who leads Munro to a cannon. 'You are to be bound to its mouth; and tomorrow morning, when the sun rises, the cannon's roar shall announce that the vengeance of Nana Sahib is at last complete.' Munro escapes, freed by his wife, who isn't dead after all, but has gone mad. Nana Sahib is then captured. He's tied to the neck of the elephant-shaped Steam House, which crashes and explodes. But his body is not found — and so, Verne explains, 'there being no certain proof of the death of Nana Sahib, a legend sprang up among the population of Central India. To them their unseen nabob was still living; they regarded him as an immortal being.'

the translations you've been speaking to me about are bad. That is not particular to Italy; in other countries they are no better. But we can do nothing about it, absolutely nothing.'

The shadow of Nana Sahib then reappears as an inspiration for Verne's most famous character, Captain Nemo, the submarine commander who on his deathbed reveals his true identity. He is a hero of 1857, on the losing side, and the imagined relative of another legendary opponent of British rule in India. 'Captain Nemo,' Verne informs us, 'was an Indian, Prince Dakkar, son of a rajah of the then independent territory of Bundelkund and a nephew of the Indian hero, Tipu Sultan (as Tippo Saib). His father . . . provided him with a complete education with the secret intention that he would fight one day with equal arms against those whom he considered to be the oppressors of his country.'[16] And then, the passage that makes clear that Nemo, aka Prince Dakkar, is modelled on Nana Sahib: 'In 1857, the great Sepoy revolt erupted. Prince Dakkar was its soul. He organized the immense uprising. He put his talents and his riches to the service of this cause. He sacrificed himself.' Soon after revealing all this, Nemo breathes for the last time. And for once Nana Sahib, or his fictional avatar, is well and truly dead. His submarine, the *Nautilus*, becomes his coffin and sinks to the bottom of the ocean.

The 150th anniversary of the 1857 Uprising was marked with a slew of books, by British and Indian authors, most of which took issue with the traditional British view of those events. But no one in India seemed quite able to work out whether the events of 1857 should be lamented as a defeat, or celebrated as the First War of Independence. There was an official event

[16] Nemo, of course, means 'no one' in Latin. In Verne's first draft Captain Nemo was Polish. Nemo first appears in *Twenty Thousand Leagues Under the Sea* (1870), and is then revealed as an Indian in its sequel, *The Mysterious Island* (1874). The best-known English translation omits any mention of Tipu, the reference to the British 'oppressors', and other passages that relate to British imperialism. Captain Nemo reappears in the comic book series *League of Extraordinary Gentlemen* (1999) as a turban-wearing, maniacal 'Hindu mariner' still in command of the *Nautilus*, and still loathing the British. He has an estranged daughter called Janni Dakkar with whom he converses, for reasons that are not explained, in Punjabi.

outside the Red Fort in Delhi involving a speech by the prime minister, and a song-and-dance show in which Great Britain was represented by an enormous grey balloon the size of a house, shaped and painted like a ghoul, with a Union Jack on its chest. A government-organised march from Meerut, where the Uprising started, to Delhi, was briefly disrupted when some of the marchers rioted, complaining about the poor quality of the food they were given. But overall, the commemorations were low-key and good-humoured, apart from the series of incidents which were quickly christened the 'Indian Mutiny of 2007'.

A tour group from Britain had come out to visit sites connected with the Uprising. Some of the visitors were descendants of those who had fought in 1857, others were former British members of a regiment which had played a key role in the early fighting in Meerut. The latter wished to commemorate their dead by placing a plaque in a Meerut church, which an Indian historian described as 'inappropriate and objectionable'. The trip quickly became a media event. A crowd gathered outside the visitors' Agra hotel chanting '*Angrez hatao*' (Down with the English!) and '*Mangal Pandey ki jai*' (Long live Mangal Pandey! [17]) as word spread that the real purpose of the British visit was to celebrate their victory in 1857. Riot police were called in. Empty mineral water bottles were thrown at the tour group in Lucknow, as were pats of dried animal shit. A minor politician then said that the visitors should all be 'hanged from a tree and [their] bodies put on the first flight out of India'. They never made it to Kanpur, where an old woman with a bottle of kerosene had threatened to set herself on fire if they came close to the old mutiny entrenchments. They cut short their tour. The British were rather incredulous, and the *Daily Mail* ran a story under

[17] Mangal Pandey, hanged by the British as a mutineer, is probably these days the most well-known Indian hero of the 1857 Uprising. He was introduced to a new generation of admirers as the leading character, played by Aamir Khan, in the popular 2005 Hindi movie *Mangal Pandey: The Rising*.

the headline 'Death threats and a terrifying hotel siege'. One of the tourists, the great-great-grandson of Henry Havelock[18] was quoted as expressing his 'enormous admiration for what . . . all the Brits who fought and lived here did'. To which a Bangalore blogger responded, 'these Britons . . . are unwilling or unable to come to terms with their gruesome past and the reality that the British Empire was like any other empire in history. It was an enterprise of loot, pillage and oppression.' Whatever one makes of either statement, it's a reminder of how important history is in creating modern identities and stereotypes. The British Empire in India is long dead, but is not entirely forgotten, nor fully forgiven.

[18] Major-General Sir Henry Havelock helped capture many of Nana Sahib's supporters in the aftermath of the siege of Cawnpore. In November 1857, he died of dysentery contracted during the second siege of Lucknow. The plinth in the south-east corner of Trafalgar Square is occupied by a large bronze Havelock, thought to be the first statue to be based on a photographic image.

An Eleventh Intermission

MY RETURN TO India at the end of 2002 feels like a fortuitous accident. I was sent to Delhi, rather unwillingly, by the BBC, for just six months. More than a decade later I am still living here. My bosses had panicked over the decline of the BBC's radio audiences in India, and I was given the more-than-difficult task of getting them to rise again. And so, family in tow, I was posted, almost literally, to a spacious south Delhi flat in an area popular with foreigners.

I had disliked Delhi when I first lived there in the early 1990s. It had seemed parochial and mean-spirited compared to Calcutta and Bombay. And so it was with some trepidation that I returned. I had become a bit of an India know-all, one of those old India hands with more experience than wisdom, scoffing at the frailties of newcomers, and keen to show off to Indians how much he knows about their country. But I was in for a surprise. It was the closest I have ever come to an epiphany. I was older now, a father at home, a boss at work — and was far less interested in chasing politicians and disasters around the subcontinent, and perhaps a little more mature of judgement. And this unloved city had grown and flourished in my absence.

Within weeks, Delhi, the city I'd hated, became my siren — and the cause of a new-found humility. I began to wander around Delhi, to walk its streets, and found myself obsessed with the city I had scorned, and I began to realise how little I understood even of the neighbourhood in which we lived. And when we were faced with returning to the UK, we baulked. Shireen was devoting herself to Save the Children, while our own children seemed gloriously enthralled by their new school and new life. I decided Delhi was a place where I could be happy, and escape the dystopian routine of a mid-level apparatchik's daily commute on

London's Central Line, and escape, most of all, the sunlessness of another British winter. I joined the ranks of the self-employed, working from home, a chore-less house-husband spending more time with my children, living out an idyll. I had found in India, almost by chance, the life of my dreams.

It was not always idyllic, of course — and Delhi had, and still has, its many drawbacks. But I had made my peace with the city. And I began to explore its interstices; and by doing so reconstructed my knowledge of the city that had become, to my surprise, my home again. I began to write, for myself and others, about Delhi and about the people I met on its streets. And I began to unlearn. As a journalist, I had been taught to be neutral, a questioning observer. And I still questioned, and rarely took sides — but I am a white man in a country that had been colonised by white people. And, whatever modern post-colonial spin I put on that fact, it is part of the prism through which many Indians see me. And so, to make sense of the world around me, I had to make sense of the way I was seen in this world. I could never just be an observer — however much energy and shoe-leather I put into the business of observing.

I also realised that however long I lived in India, however

much I improved my Hindi, however much I knew about my adopted country, however much I feel it is my home — for most people here I remain a foreigner. And there are advantages. I can eavesdrop on conversations about me, I am given latitude for minor transgressions, I am pushed to the front of queues. But more than that, being different can be a wonderful release. I no longer feel the need to measure myself against my contemporaries. I can be eccentric — indeed it is almost expected that I will be; and Delhi has become large and accommodating enough for me to find many friends who, thankfully, aren't just like me.

I've been drawn to people who also don't quite fit. Most marriages in India are arranged — and most couples belong to the same linguistic, regional, caste and religious grouping. But I realised recently that that's not true of my friends. Bizarrely, the only exception I can think of among my friends who live in India are a Scottish couple, long-term residents of Delhi, both of them descended from long lines of Catholic gentry. My friends are almost all in, or children of, what may loosely be called mixed marriages. I have decided I am at home among people who are not at home; who are wandering, literally or figuratively — and whose lives would be too dull, too meaningless if they did everything society expected of them. And I sometimes find myself becoming evangelical on the subject of mixed marriages, in a way that can make people snigger. But I don't mind, any more. I do believe, for instance, that miscegenation can contribute to world peace, that the mixing of the races is a force for good. And, since we're all out of Africa originally, we're completing the circle, perhaps fulfilling our destiny, by ending the tyranny of bloodlines.

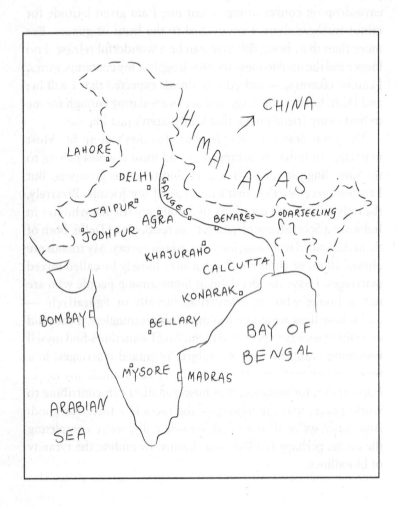

Chapter Twelve: In which the Author rewrites the history of Mowgli, deconstructs late nineteenth-century western views of Indian female sexuality, and finds two words that rhyme with 'Hindu'

EVERY WEEKEND FOR several years in the late 1990s, Zubin, my firstborn, would sit down in our London home to watch a video of *The Jungle Book*. He remembers it as his first film. And he can still, more than a decade later, recall the intensity of the moment of fear and anticipation that would always send him running out of the room — as the man-cub, Mowgli, and Baloo the bear, do battle with that most superior tiger, Shere Khan. Zubin would peer round the door, waiting until Baloo, apparently clawed to death by the tiger, re-opened his eyes. He could then return safely to the sofa, and watch, with uninterruptible interest, the end of the film, in which Mowgli turns his back on Baloo and the jungle, and enters a man-village. For Mowgli leaves Baloo behind, and perhaps his childhood as well, because he has fallen for a flirtatious pig-tailed little girl with a red dot, a *bindi*, on her forehead and golden rings in her ears.

That ending is the most obviously Indian part of the Disney version of *The Jungle Book* — which has been shorn of both the Indian and the imperial context of Rudyard Kipling's original tales. When I began reading the original Kipling version with my man-cub, he objected fiercely, 'This isn't the real *Jungle Book*,' he insisted. And for many children brought up in the west, the 1967 cartoon version — Walt Disney's own last film — is their introduction to India, a land of jolly jungle animals, lost cities and a boy who runs around in a loincloth. There have been multiple screen versions of *The Jungle Book* with a variety of perspectives on India — and little sense of loyalty to the original text or to the time it was written. These versions include an unaccountably addictive Japanese fifty-two-part animated TV series[1] that became a cult hit in Europe in the 1990s, just as *Monkey Magic* was going out of fashion. It seems to depict India in the dying years of British rule, with evil white men called Nigel and Dickie, seaplanes and soft-top trucks, and sari-wearing local women with a pox-like profusion of *bindi*s on their foreheads. And then there's a second 'live-action' Disney version from 1994, with real people and real animals, partly shot in the city of Jodhpur. It has a distinctly late nineteenth-century setting, a land which Kipling would have recognised, but is anti-imperial in tone, and comes complete with snake charmers, firewalkers, rope tricks and all the paraphernalia of exoticised India. Mowgli, played by an actor of Hawaiian–Chinese origin, is for the first time allowed to fall for a white woman — the nominally feline Kitty — and they even get to share a kiss at the end.

But most memorable of all is the earliest screen version, from 1942, filmed in Technicolor, with rubber snakes and cardboard crocodiles, in the hills and lakes of southern California, more than eight thousand miles from the jungles of central India. And for my family, this was another minor cinematic landmark, one which joins the generations. For, half a century before my son was born, this *Jungle Book* was my mother's first-remembered film, when she was dazzled by the lights of a north London cinema during wartime, and watched, awestruck, the adventures

[1] Transliterated from Japanese, the title of the series was *Janguru Bukku Shōnen Mōguri*. *Shōnen* means boy and it's not hard to guess the meaning of the other words if they are spoken out loud. The series was dubbed into eighteen languages.

of handsome Mowgli, 'brown and shiny' in the jungle.[2] It's the only time Mowgli has been, in fact, played by an Indian actor. At the time, Sabu, an elephant keeper's son from Mysore, and already, at the age of  eighteen, a veteran of four Hollywood movies, was arguably the world's most famous Indian, or perhaps level with Mahatma Gandhi. A decade earlier, if one could find a reason to include people who were born in the subcontinent, then Rudyard Kipling, who died in 1936, would have been the world's most famous Indian. And Kipling probably did more than almost anyone to shape international perceptions of the land of his birth during the period of British rule, and after.

Rudyard Kipling was always a controversial figure. Mowgli and his friends are still adored by generations of children, while *If*, Kipling's paean to the stiff upper lip is, if opinion polls are to be believed, Britain's best-loved poem. Kipling's political views, particularly about the empire, however, seem outdated, and draw little sympathy even from those who admire his writings. He is remembered as the man who invented the phrase, 'the White Man's Burden', which became a shorthand excuse for

[2] There was just one non-Indian character in the film: a ride-on part for an Englishwoman on a horse. And only one Indian actor: Sabu. All the other characters were played by American actors, most of whom blacked up. An exception was the rather pale Patricia deCamp, playing Mowgli's mother, who would later be the screen mother of, among others, Ronald Reagan, Doris Day and Buck Rogers. The film was directed by the Hungarian-born Zoltan Korda, and produced by his older brother, Alexander — who was married to the Anglo-Indian film star Merle Oberon.

empire, and who spoke of the colonised as '. . . new-caught, sullen peoples,/ half-devil and half-child'.[3] Kipling was, in the famous words of another India-born writer, George Orwell, 'a gutter patriot' and a 'vulgar flagwaver'.

Kipling, who was born in 1865 in a hut in the grounds of Bombay's JJ School of Art, where his father worked, would spend less than one-sixth of his life in India. But his best-remembered prose works — *Kim*, *The Jungle Book*, and his early short stories — are all set there. His relationship with India was complex. He romanticised it as the idyllic land of his early childhood, from which he had been untimely ripped at the age of five — to be sent to school and a hated foster home in Britain. He returned to India at the age of sixteen as a journalist living mainly in Lahore, and travelling around large parts of northern India, visiting as many seedy locations as he could find. His dark complexion meant that many British believed him to be 'eight annas to the rupee', the contemporary euphemism for mixed race, or 'half-caste' as Kipling might have said. His genuine interest in ordinary Indians sets him apart from most of his British contemporaries, giving a democratic undertone to the overpowering rhythms of his British Empire. But he was deeply opposed to even minor measures of self-rule, and could be disparaging and vicious towards those who disagreed with him.

[3] In fact, the 'sullen peoples' referred to in the poem, are not, as is often supposed, Indians, but Filipinos. And the original version of the poem *White Man's Burden* bore the subtitle 'The United States and the Philippine Islands'. Another of Kipling's poems that is frequently misread and misquoted is *The Ballad of East and West*, whose first two lines appear to stand for a kind of East–West perpetual apartheid, 'Oh, East is East, and West is West, and never the twain shall meet,/ Till Earth and Sky stand presently at God's great Judgment Seat'; but this statement is immediately and defiantly reversed in a tribute to cross-cultural male camaraderie in the next two lines, 'But there is neither East nor West, Border, nor Breed, nor Birth/ When two strong men stand face to face, tho' they come from the ends of the earth!'

An impressive case can be made for Kipling as a writer who invented the idea of India as a land of childhood, a place of innocence and wonder. Mowgli and Kim are both inquisitive, parentless, good-natured boys, running free in a very masculine world that they don't quite understand but which does, in the end, take care of them. But it's often forgotten that the first Mowgli story written by Kipling, but omitted from most *Jungle Book* collections, has him as a young man, not a boy, in a very imperial setting. He has earned the admiration of a British forest officer called Gisborne, because of his way with animals and he becomes a forest ranger and employee of the British administration. And, in a twist that has never made it to the silver screen, Mowgli converts to Islam in order to marry the daughter of Gisborne's Muslim servant. Elsewhere, there are several admiring references in Kipling's *Jungle Book* to British rule. When Baldeo, the village villain, threatens to burn Mowgli's adopted parents, he is told that 'The English . . . were a perfectly mad people, who would not let honest farmers kill witches in peace.' Kipling never visited the jungles of central India, and the idyll he invented there was borrowed from other writers. The Jungle Books abound with metaphors, deliberate and unintended. The key message of the 'Jungle Law', as enunciated by Baloo the bear (and presumably translated from the ursine by Mowgli), is this . . .

> Now these are the Laws of the Jungle, and many and mighty are they;
> But the head and the hoof of the Law and the haunch and the hump is — Obey!

. . . which has, understandably, been interpreted as Kipling's defence of authoritarian British rule. The 'Lost City', meanwhile, which appears in every version of *The Jungle Book*, is a metropolis in ruins, a memorial to human hubris. But it can also be read as a reminder of India's proverbial ancientness, perhaps

Herder's *Morgenland*; and of the view of so many westerners that Indian civilisation had been in decline ever since.

The novel *Kim* has probably survived the years less well[4] than *The Jungle Book,* but it is still one of the most influential books about India ever written in English. And for Kipling obsessives, who still seem to abound in southern England, it is his masterpiece. Its characters are very much of their time — and the imperial and geo-political context is overt. But India is portrayed in several different ways — and Kipling is wise enough to allow his readers to choose their own India from among them, or not to choose at all. For instance, India is represented as the playing-field of 'the Great Game',[5] one of those many cliché-metaphors which Kipling invented or popularised, a half-imaginary battle for Asiatic supremacy between Britain and Russia. Another India that he depicts is a land of orientals who are different in character, in a defining way, from Europeans. The novel has many of those Orientalist tropes that can make Kipling's most earnest admirers recoil — including the lines that 'Kim could lie like an Oriental'; or that 'all hours of the twenty-four are alike to Orientals'; or a reference to the 'huckster instinct of the East'. But there's a third India here as well: the land of the Buddha, and it is possible to see *Kim* as a tale of spiritual awakening, the quest of a Buddhist lama, a late nineteenth-century Tripitaka, for enlightenment — and we are left uncertain at the end of the novel whether Kim will be drawn into the Great Game, as a junior spy, or if he

---

[4] *Kim* still has plenty of admirers. My children's unread copy bears the inscription from their other grandmother, my mother-in-law, a mildly Anglophobe Indian who was born under British rule: 'Darling Zubin & Roxy — If you love India, you'll love Kim.' Edward Said is another unlikely fan — he calls *Kim* a work of 'great aesthetic merit'.

[5] The phrase 'the Great Game' is mentioned seventeen times in *Kim*, but its history appears to date back at least sixty years earlier to when the British intelligence officer Captain Arthur Conolly used it in relation to the rivalry between Russia and Britain in Central Asia. Conolly was defeated early in the game, beheaded in Bokhara in 1842.

will stay with the lama and become a Buddhist pilgrim.[6]

And, of course, *Kim* is, most obviously, a detailed and positive portrayal of northern India under British rule, the rule of the Sahibs — and parts of the novel read like a guide to the complex and minute hierarchies that separated people by race and colour and religion and caste and class. For instance, Kipling makes it clear that only the most vulgar of British people use the word 'nigger'[7] to refer to those whom the more refined called 'natives' — and, they are never, not once in the book, referred to as Indians. The story of Kim the boy, rather than *Kim* the novel, is the story of a search for identity. Kim, we are told on page one, was white — 'a poor white of the very poorest'. His father was a drunken Irishman who 'died as poor whites died in India', his mother, a nursemaid who died of cholera, his foster mother, a half-caste, and Kim himself was 'burned black as any native'. But he is ultimately, and whatever else happens, a Sahib — because both his parents were white. The word 'Sahib', used by Kipling more than three hundred times in the novel, is both an honorific, an equivalent of 'Sir', but also a group noun, used to describe white men and their white offspring, and just occasionally those who imitate them. Kim is obsessed with his own identity, asking himself,

> Who is Kim? He considered his own identity, a thing he had never done before, till his head swam. He was one insignificant person in all this roaring whirl of India.

[6] In a two-volume sequel to *Kim* published in the 1980s, the Indian novelist TN Murari imagines that Kim becomes a grown-up spy, but later regrets this and is transformed into an admirer of Gandhi and an opponent of British rule. He falls in love with a married Indian woman, a revolutionary who bears him a daughter. Kim is then killed by the British at Jallianwala Bagh.

[7] The future Edward VII, visiting India in 1875–76, objected to the 'rude and rough manners' of many of the British that he encountered, and was appalled that some of them referred to Indians, 'many of them sprung from great races, as "niggers"'.

A little later he protests, 'I do not want to be a Sahib.' He is sent to a school where he is taught that, 'One must never forget that one is a Sahib, and that some day, when examinations are passed, one will command natives.' And this was indeed the destiny of most Sahibs, to rule India and Indians. For the British at least, India had become the pride of the empire, a land turned cartographically pink, and, famously, in Disraeli's words, 'the brightest jewel in the crown'.

But the British ruled India nervously. The events of 1857 were not forgotten, and though they are little more than a shadow in Kipling's writings, for other authors, who were almost as popular — such as Flora Annie Steel and GA Henty — they remained the most important story to be told and retold about India. And the key lesson learned was that the British needed to understand India far better than they had before. And so for the British, Indians became both a subject race and an object of study and scrutiny. Photography, for instance, introduced to India during the 1840s, became a new way of bringing India to the rest of the world, and of cataloguing and archiving India for its rulers. The Venetian Felice Beato travelled to India in 1858 and produced a remarkable series of 'Mutiny photographs' that were later exhibited in London to great acclaim. At the Paris Exhibition of 1867, the Scottish architectural historian James Fergusson curated a display of more than five hundred photographs of Indian buildings. A year later, the first of eight volumes of *The People of India* was published — containing many dozens of annotated photos of Indians from different castes, tribes and religions. The project was conceived before 1857 as a photographic souvenir of India for a British governor-general, and then, after what the authors refer to as 'the great convulsion' of 1857, was refashioned into a major, early anthropological study, formally commissioned by the government, which felt previous administrations had not done enough to understand the people they ruled.

The sepia photos depict 'natives', usually portraits of unsmiling and often cowering men or women — though there are some group photographs as well — and later volumes have portraits and biographies of Indian princes and  dignitaries. The textual commentary for each photograph is an attempt to define and classify a particular caste or tribe, and in some ways they resemble, with less generosity of spirit, the descriptions of Tripitaka (or Xuanzang) more than 1300 years earlier. The Sonthals of Bihar, we are told, are 'quiet, inoffensive, cheerful, intelligent and obliging . . . and do not refuse to eat even snakes, ants, frogs and field rats'. Others fare less well, for it is a work full of vapid racial stereotypes. One Assamese tribe is described as 'wild and barbarous in manners and habits, and their persons filthy and squalid'; a sub-caste in northern India 'are a despised race, very ignorant, and extremely expert as thieves'; while the members of one 'wandering tribe . . . are repulsively mean and wretched; the features of the women, in particular, being very ugly and of a strong aboriginal type'.

There is an interest in the marriage customs and sexual habits of Indians that comes across today as both prurient and prudish. The men of one north-eastern tribe 'keep four or five wives, and when a man grows old his wives are distributed among his sons', while in a Himalayan sub-caste 'fornication in either sex is punished by a fine, sacrifice and consequent fasting'. For one tribal group in Bihar, 'Marriages take place mostly once a year, in January: for six days all the candidates for matrimony live in promiscuous

concubinage, after which the whole party are supposed to have paired off as man and wife'; while in the north-east, 'Infidelity on the part of either husband or wife is punished by the fine of a cow or a hog.'

Western interest in Indian sexuality was largely pushed underground during this period, but there was no shortage of such interest. Kipling hints at the issue in some of his short stories — where Indian women, and those of mixed European and Indian ancestry, are portrayed as almost embarrassingly loyal and passionate. But he was more concerned with the adulterous ways of 'grass widows', British women sent to the hill stations during the hot season while their husbands toiled on the plains. He was preceded in this concern, both in its literary and its real-life form, by an old India hand called Captain Edward Sellon — a pioneer pornographer whose posthumously published and unfinished autobiographical work of ambulant erotica, *The Ups and Downs of Life*,[8] describes how he had sex

[8] *The Ups and Downs of Life* was first published in 1867, the year after Edward Sellon committed suicide in a Piccadilly hotel. The book was published by the pornographer William Dugdale for whom Sellon had written, translated or illustrated several previous erotic works, including the sauciest of Martial's epigrams, and previously suppressed passages from Boccaccio's *Decameron*. Sellon was also a self-taught expert on the cult of the phallus. *The Ups and Downs of Life* was republished in 1892 under the title *The Amorous Prowess of a Jolly Fellow or His Adventures with Lovely Girls Related by Himself*. My 1987 edition is part of the 'Wordsworth Classic Erotica' collection and has a sepia photograph of a woman baring one of her breasts, with the word 'Unexpurgated' at the bottom. It contains copies of Sellon's original erotic drawings, one of which I would like to print here, but then this book would probably be banned by the Indian censors.

with a wide range of women while he served with the British army. There is much frigging and gamahuching and thrusting and licking as he makes his way around southern India. He was particularly keen to seduce the wives of his fellow officers, and they — by his account — put up little resistance. But after he pays to have sex with a 'half-caste' virgin in Madras, his tastes change: 'I now commenced a regular course of fucking with native women,' he earnestly informs his exhausted readers. An ordinary prostitute costs two rupees, he says. But for just five rupees 'you may have the handsomest Mohammedan girls and any of the high-caste women who follow the trade of courtesan'. And he points out, they 'are a very different set of people from their frail sisterhood in European countries; they do not drink, they are scrupulously cleanly in their persons, they are sumptuously dressed . . . they understand in perfection all the arts and wiles of love, are capable of gratifying any tastes, and in face and figure they are unsurpassed by any women in the world'.

Two decades later, Charles Devereaux wrote about spending 'five happy years in Hindustan', in *Venus in India,* describing the 'all but naked' graceful charms of native girls carrying water pots that he saw on his arrival at Bombay. He seems on the whole more interested in 'burying' his 'Johnnie'

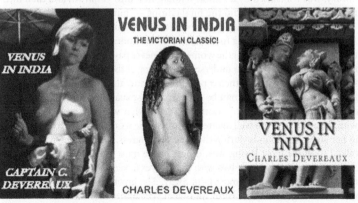

in the 'cavern' of a succession of wives and daughters of his fellow officers, than in the charms of Indian women. But his ultimately successful attempt to have consensual sex with three teenage English sisters is aided by an Indian woman, a maid, who teaches the girls the art of love, by means of a series of activities involving a peacock feather, a banana and a cucumber.

These and other works of what may be termed imperial pornography have been largely forgotten, consigned to the top shelf with other Victorian erotica. But printed in the same period, also by a pornographic publisher, was a far more serious work about Indian sexuality, which would become world famous, not always for the best reasons, in the 1960s — and editions of which, including a plastic-wrapped pop-up version, currently occupy two shelves of the bookshop at Delhi airport. And it's a book, along with the erotic carvings at Khajuraho and Konarak, and the teachings of a few New Age gurus, which continues to circumscribe western ideas of Indian sexuality. The *Kama Sutra*, probably written in the third century AD, was retrieved from anonymity[9] by the English explorer, linguist and footnote-lover[10]

[9] The Sanskrit version of the text, copied from a manuscript in a Benares library, was translated by a Hindu scholar, first into Gujarati, and then into English. Richard Burton did the final editing — but not the translation.

[10] Burton's edition has seventy-seven footnotes, including six on one page. Among his more interesting footnotes are these: Footnote 36 — 'So many men utterly ignore the feelings of the women, and never pay the slightest attention to the passion of the latter. To understand the subject thoroughly, it is absolutely necessary to study it, and then a person will know that, as dough is prepared for baking, so must a woman be prepared for sexual intercourse, if she is to derive satisfaction from it.' Footnote 38 — 'Men who are well acquainted with the art of love are well aware how often one woman differs from another in her sighs and sounds during the time of congress. Some women like to be talked to in the most loving way, others in the most abusive way, and so on. Some women enjoy themselves with closed eyes in silence, others make a great noise over it, and some almost faint away. The great art is to ascertain what gives them the greatest pleasure, and what specialities they like best.'

Richard Burton and his Bombay-based friend 'Bunny' Arbuthnot.

The first edition was published in 1883 with the message on the front 'For Private Circulation Only'. The translators, editors and publishers were unmentioned, for fear of prosecution under British obscenity laws (that future Indophile Annie Besant[11] was found guilty of obscenity in 1875 for having published a family-planning booklet which was described in court as 'filthy, bawdy and obscene'). Burton and Arbuthnot both had a long-standing interest in Indian erotica, though Arbuthnot saw the *Kama Sutra* more as a philosophic and spiritual work, with what he described as a lot of 'padding'. Burton was more interested in the practical details, not only for the usual reasons, but also because it provided evidence against the commonly held belief that women in the east were more oppressed than those in the west. And the *Kama Sutra* undoubtedly takes female sexual pleasure seriously.[12] Despite its small and clandestine early circulation, the *Kama Sutra* added to the belief that Indian women were unusually interested in sex.

Among those who did read the *Kama Sutra*, and quoted freely

[11] See page 297. Annie Besant and her lover, Charles Bradlaugh, published *The Fruits of Philosophy, or the Private Companion of Young Married People* by the American writer Charles Knowlton. They were found guilty of an 'obscene libel' and sentenced to six months in prison. This was overturned on a technicality — but Besant lost the custody of her children. Bradlaugh went on to become the most famous radical of the time — an atheist who was repeatedly elected as an MP but refused admission to the House of Commons. Gandhi, in his autobiography, records how he, 'like every Indian residing in London', travelled to Woking for Bradlaugh's funeral in 1891.

[12] Though, arguably, not quite as seriously as male sexual pleasure. The clitoris, for instance, is not mentioned once in the *Kama Sutra*. Burton lamented how little sex education there was for women in the west, and one of his favourite stories was of an Englishman finding his new wife unconscious on the marital bed, having chloroformed herself. She had pinned a note on her nightdress which read: 'Mama says you're to do what you like.'

from it, were the early sexologists Iwan Bloch and Havelock Ellis — both active from the 1890s onwards. They were each portrayers of India as a land of unusual sexuality and masters of the unverifiable generalisation. According to Bloch, 'the Indian regards a certain variation and artificiality in sex as highly beneficial to health and good in the eyes of the gods', and says that there are no less than forty-eight coital positions considered 'eminently proper' in India, while even the Italians only have thirty-three. Ellis declares that 'among the higher races in India the sexual instinct is very highly developed' and refers to the 'eastern style of coitus' as one in which the primary purpose is the pleasure of one's partner, not oneself. He relies both on ancient texts and on several unreliable informants in turn-of-the-century India. Ellis advises his readers that 'in India, I am told that *fellatio* is almost universal in households, and regarded as a natural duty towards the paterfamilias'. Again, the sexuality of Indian women is emphasised, and there are long passages on female masturbation and lesbianism, including one in which a jail superintendent writes to tell him of his discovery of 'a number of phalli in the females' enclosure; they were made of clay and sun-dried and bore marks of use'.

Others such as the German Sanskritist Richard Schmidt, who translated the *Kama Sutra* into German (though he rendered the more obscene passages into Latin), was one of the first to use that modern trope of India as 'a land of opposites' or contrasts, a place

> where the human temperament oscillates between the sublime and the vile, the gracious and the monstrous, the beautiful and the hideous, and desire bounds from the most atrocious asceticism to the maddest debauchery.

And he went on to provide an unforgettable meteorological and floral rationale for his *Kama Sutra*-influenced idea of Indian sexuality.

The blast-furnace heat of the Indian sun, the faerie splendour of the vegetation, the enchanting poesy of the moonlight nights permeated with the fragrance of the lotus flower, finally — and by no means least — the peculiar role the Indian people have played from time immemorial, the role of world-forsaking dreamers, philosophers, impractical enthusiasts all unite to make the Indian a true virtuoso in love.

India had long been seen as a land of magic, of miracles and of trickery — and that theme could take on a more tangible and complex form in the nineteenth century. Indian magicians began to travel to the west. One of them, Ramo Samee, a juggler and sword-swallower, settled in London, became a stalwart of the British stage, and his name would be used as a kind of shorthand for the archetypal oriental magician. Western conjurors began to dress up as Indians, adopt Indian names, and such feats as the Indian basket trick and the Hindoo cup trick became part of a generic repertoire.[13] Charles Dickens, who fancied himself as an amateur magician, chose what he intended to be an Indian alias, Rhia Rhama Rhoos, for a charity performance he gave on the Isle of Wight. And in *The Moonstone* by Wilkie Collins, three Brahmins, 'mahogany-coloured Indians', appear on the Yorkshire moors in order to reclaim a jewel taken from Tipu Sultan at the Battle of Seringapatam; but they disguise themselves as Indian jugglers in order not to arouse suspicion.[14]

[13] The Indian rope trick, perhaps the most famous piece of magic connected with India, was in fact the 1890 invention of a Chicago journalist, John Wilkie, using the carefully chosen pseudonym Fred S Ellmore. And his tall tale of an Indian boy disappearing up a rope did indeed help the *Chicago Daily Tribune* sell more copies. Wilkie later became head of the US Secret Service in 1898, charged with the safety of President McKinley, who was shot and killed by an anarchist in 1901.

[14] In *The Moonstone*, the jewel, not in fact a moonstone but a yellow diamond, was said to have been originally taken from the temple in Somnath to Benares to escape the army of Mahmud of Ghazni (see page 81). It was

Despite this close identification of India with magic, not everyone was impressed by India's conjurors. A fiercely competitive American magician, Harry Kellar, toured India in the 1870s, performing himself, and seeking out Indian magicians wherever he went. He declared that 'apart from their skill as snake charmers, in the basket trick, and one or two other illusions, the ability of the entire fraternity of Indian jugglers is beneath contempt'. He proclaimed that clairvoyance was a sham, and said he could copy any 'trick' performed by a magician or a spirit medium, and would hand over two hundred dollars or two thousand rupees if he failed. At the time, there was a western rage for spiritualism, and for clairvoyant mediums who held séances, talked to the dead, and got objects to float in the air — and the spiritualists, under attack from a wide range of smirking opponents, looked to India and its ancient magical traditions for support and succour.

It was from this shadowy world between magic and religion that a new syncretic faith emerged, largely in India, which would, at times, claim millions of followers, but which today feels like a forgotten sect. The founder of the Theosophical Society was Madame Blavatsky, a world-wandering Russian from what is now the Ukraine, who became, depending on your point of view, the arch-priestess of dottiness, an unprincipled fraudster or the philosopher-prophet of a new world. She believed in the curative and spiritual powers of Indian magic, and was convinced that those fellow Europeans who had been to India, and denied this, were simply liars. 'As for the wonderful powers of prediction and clairvoyance possessed by certain Brahmans, they are well known

then stolen from Benares by one of Emperor Aurangzeb's officers, and fell into Tipu's hands a century later. At the end of the novel the diamond is restored to its place in the head of the statue of the four-armed 'god of the Moon' in the temple in Somnath. Wilkie Collins was the godson of (and named after) the Scottish artist David Wilkie who was responsible for the famous painting of Tipu Sultan's death at Seringapatam.

to every European resident of India. If these upon their return to "civilized" countries, laugh at such stories, and sometimes even deny them outright, they only impugn their good faith, not the fact.' She declared that 'India was the Alma Mater, not only of the civilization, arts, and sciences, but also of all the great religions of antiquity; Judaism, and hence Christianity, included'.

Madame Blavatsky[15] helped build a new faith, known as Theosophy, from the Greek for divine wisdom, with its roots in eastern religions, particularly Buddhism, with strong elements from Jewish and Christian esoteric traditions. She travelled to India several times, settling for a while on the outskirts of southern Madras overlooking the Adyar river, not far from the site of St Thomas' supposed murder 1800 years earlier. The site became, and still is, the Theosophists' international headquarters. Blavatsky attracted an eclectic group of international followers, several of whom came to live in Madras, such as Colonel Henry Olcott, an American Civil War veteran whom she had met at a séance in Vermont, a pederast ex-priest from Lancashire called Charles Leadbeater, and the former socialist and atheist Annie Besant, who had become a celebrity in Britain for her outspoken views on family planning and her role in labour disputes during the 1880s. The Theosophists often took a stance that was at least mildly opposed to British rule in India — and during the First World War, Annie Besant would become the first female president of the Congress Party, which eventually led India to independence in 1947.[16]

In the western imagination, and in real life, India had become a

[15] Madame Blavatsky's continued popularity in the inter-war years is reflected in Louis MacNeice's 1937 poem *Bagpipe Music* about changing cultural values in Scotland's Western Isles: 'It's no go the Yogi-Man, it's no go Blavatsky/ All we want is a bank balance and a bit of skirt in a taxi.'

[16] The Indian National Congress has had several non-Indian presidents, and a non-Indian founder, Allan Octavian Hume. The current president of the party is Sonia Gandhi, born in Italy but now an Indian citizen.

less distant place. The Suez Canal, the steamship and the railways had all made the world a little smaller — and international travel was faster, safer and more affordable. Foreigners of very different types descended on India from the west — grand tourists, Maharajahs' mistresses, pilgrims, artists, fortune-seekers — quite apart from the large number of soldiers and civilians on whom British rule in India depended. And Indians began to travel abroad in greater numbers. Many people living in large western cities would have encountered occasional Indians by the late nineteenth century. These would range from the bejewelled Maharajahs who attended Queen Victoria's Golden Jubilee in 1887, and whose daily activities in London were covered in detail in the British press, to the poor Hindu crossing-sweeper immortalised in a much reproduced print of 1883.

A shy law student called Mohandas Gandhi, not yet a Mahatma, turned up in London in 1888, and found a thriving community of Indian students, and a serious lack of prandial opportunities for vegetarians. In his autobiography he describes how he takes dancing lessons, visits Brighton, the Isle of Wight and Paris, and meets Madame Blavatsky, Annie Besant and Dadabhai Naoroji. The latter was a Parsi from Bombay who was soon to be elected with a three-vote majority to Parliament as a Liberal MP for Finsbury Central. Gandhi becomes, almost by default, part of a group of vaguely radical people connected with India and living in London.

In the USA in the 1890s, there was a remarkable growth of interest in India. Earlier in the century, America's leading intellectual figures of the period, Ralph Waldo Emerson and Henry David Thoreau, had been heavily influenced by early Hinduism. Thoreau called the philosophy of the Bhagavad Gita 'stupendous', and said it made modern literature seem 'puny and trivial'. Emerson spoke of ancient Indian texts as 'pure and sublime', and 'the best gymnastics of the mind'. His 1856 poem *Brahma* was described by his fellow Bostonian poet Oliver Wendell

Holmes[17] as a 'vacuum of intelligibility', and indeed it is a little easier to make sense of if one has read some Indian philosophy. And the god Brahma, 'old occult Brahma interminably far back', reappears in Walt Whitman's poem *Passage to India* (from which EM Forster would take the title of his novel). Whitman portrays India as a symbol of ancientness, recently 'connected by network' to the world, by those 'modern wonders' — the Suez Canal and railroads and underwater telegraph cable.[18] Another unidentified north American 'poet' of the late nineteenth century takes a rather unsophisticated view of Hinduism:

> The poor benighted Hindu;
> He does the best he kindu;
> He sticks to caste
> From first to last;
> For pants he makes his skindu.

But in all of this there was very little sense of modern India, until a charismatic thirty-year-old English-speaking Hindu monk dressed in yellow robes and a red turban turned up at the World Fair in Chicago in 1893, and spoke several times at one of the events: the Parliament of the World's Religions.

Accounts of Swami Vivekananda's first speech in Chicago make him sound like a nineteenth-century rock star.[19] Unknown

[17] Oliver Wendell Holmes invented the phrase 'Boston Brahmin' to describe people like Emerson and himself, members of what Holmes called the 'harmless, inoffensive, untitled aristocracy'.

[18] Though Whitman also name-checks Alexander the Great, Marco Polo, Ibn Battuta and Vasco da Gama as those who have attempted to connect India with the world in the past.

[19] Some modern historians have suggested that Swami Vivekananda was not quite the star of Chicago that his followers have suggested. The much-quoted statement attributed to the *New York Herald* that 'Vivekananda is undoubtedly the greatest figure in the Parliament of Religions. After hearing him we feel how foolish it is to send missionaries to this learned nation' did not appear in that newspaper, and has not been found in any other.

outside India, and a last-minute addition to the list of speakers, he was repeatedly interrupted by applause, and attracted a large female fan club that followed him around Chicago. Annie Besant was a fellow delegate, representing Theosophy, and she described how the audience was 'enraptured; the huge multitude hung upon his words'. He then gave a series of lectures at Harvard, and was lionised by the elites of New York and

London, preaching the message that each soul has the potential to be divine, and advocating meditation and yoga as a means to bring one closer to divinity. This should be seen as the start of the spread of yoga in the west, though it was many years before it took the hyperactive and sweat-inducing form now encountered in thousands of gymnasiums around the world.

Vivekananda spent more than three years in the west, making many converts and friends, and signing lots of photographs to give out to admirers. In Britain, he met the world's leading Sanskritist Max Müller, a German, and author of *India: What Can It Teach Us?*, and they declared their great admiration for each other. Some of the converts followed Vivekananda to India, including Margaret Noble, an Irish schoolteacher whom he met in London. She became, as Sister Nivedita, one of his disciples, working, in a way that prefigured Mother Teresa, among the Calcutta poor. Vivekananda died at the age of thirty-nine in 1902, but not before he had returned to the USA, where his American disciples had set up Vedanta societies in San Francisco and New York; and a Californian devotee granted him land in the San Antonio Valley for building the Shanti Ashram, which remains a retreat for Vedantists. In 1905, the first Hindu temple in the west was built in San Francisco by Vivekananda's American followers, a startling three-storey building, with several varieties of oriental domes, and a crenellated turret that could have been stolen from a Crusader castle.[20]

In 1896, Mark Twain became a hyperbolic admirer of India, a kind of anti-Babur. It was, he wrote in his memoirs a decade later, 'the only foreign land I ever daydream about or deeply long to see again'. He was the first important American writer to visit India, a superstar on a world tour. It was a trip that had been inspired partly by Rudyard Kipling, but even more so by Twain's desperate need to pay off his debts. Seven years earlier, Kipling visited America for the first time, landing at San Francisco, and then headed eastwards to New York State where he turned up uninvited at Mark Twain's remote farmhouse. Twain had no idea who he was, but liked the man — and so did his seventeen-year-old daughter, Susy. He describes how Susy kept Kipling's business card with its address in Allahabad, India, 'and treasured it as an interesting possession'. Twain writes of how for Susy, 'India had been to her an imaginary land up to this time, a fairyland, a dreamland, a land made out of poetry and moonlight . . . and doubtless Kipling's flesh and blood and modern clothes realized it to her for the first time, and solidified it'. Bankruptcy forced Twain to embark on a round-the-world lecture tour in 1895, and as he prepared to leave he wrote Kipling a playful note, declaring his ignorance of India, by deliberately misusing words of Indian origin.

Dear Kipling . . . Years ago you came from India to Elmira [in New York State] to visit me, as you said at the time. It has

[20] The Old Vedanta Temple (for there is a new one — three blocks away) still stands on the corner of Webster and Filbert streets in the affluent area of the city, near the Bay, known as Cow Hollow. The main priest or swami of the temple has normally been from India, but the vast majority of the congregation has always been from the local, non-Indian community — mainly former Christians.

always been my purpose to return that visit and that great compliment some day. I shall arrive next January and you must be ready. I shall come riding my ayah with his tusks adorned with silver bells and ribbons and escorted by a troop of native howdahs richly clad and mounted upon a herd of wild bungalows; and you must be on hand with a few bottles of ghee, for I shall be thirsty.[21]

In the event, Kipling was not there, but Twain had the time of his life, and he would later describe how he would re-read *Kim* every year, 'and in this way I go back to India, without fatigue'. It was a tiring two months for Twain, who had just turned sixty, and who gave twenty-seven lectures in fifteen locations across the north of the country. But his account of his travels, published as *Following the Equator*, rhapsodises India. He is as quotable as Kipling, and his prose is brimming with breathless excitement

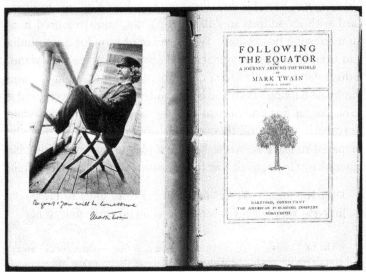

[21] An *ayah* is a maid or a nanny; a *howdah* is like a small carriage placed on an elephant's back forming both a saddle and a canopy; a bungalow is not to be confused with a buffalo; and *ghee* is clarified butter.

about the newness of it all, and uses phrases so smoothly seductive that they would become travel-writing clichés. In one portentously purple passage, spilling over with antonyms and hyperbole, he refers to India as:

> the land of dreams and romance, of fabulous wealth and fabulous poverty, of splendor and rags, of palaces and hovels, of famine and pestilence, of genii and giants and Aladdin lamps, of tigers and elephants, the cobra and the jungle, the country of a thousand nations and a hundred tongues, of a thousand religions and two million gods, cradle of the human race, birthplace of human speech, mother of history, grandmother of legend, great-grandmother of tradition . . .

Twain first went to Bombay: 'A bewitching place, a bewildering place, an enchanting place.' And he begins by fervently admiring most things he sees and hears: he talks of the 'picturesque natives of both sexes'; he declares that 'nearly all black and brown skins are beautiful, but a beautiful white skin is rare'. He admires the noisy Indian crow and its 'sublime march to ultimate perfection'; he adores the titles of India's princes — 'how good they taste in the mouth'; and as for the Parsis — well they are 'remarkable'. He relates that Indians know little of America, beyond the name of George Washington, and 'the Holy City — Chicago'. The latter, he explains, is an 'erroneous impression' on the part of Hindus who had learned about the rapturous reception of Swami Vivekananda at the 'Congress of Religion' in Chicago three years earlier.

But there are several subplots in Twain's telling of his Indian wanderings. And all is not rapture. There is an unexpected defence by Twain, who tended to dislike imperialism, of British rule in the subcontinent — and acclaim for the victors in what he calls 'the Great Mutiny'. And there are long digressions on 'Thuggee', swindlers, 'suttee', female infanticide, famine, and —

particularly in the section on Benares — naked holy men and filth.

The city of Benares, now Varanasi, overhanging the Ganges, has attracted visitors, alive and dead, for many hundreds of years — and is not to everyone's taste. Tripitaka visited in the 630s, and found thousands of Shiva devotees, some of whom 'go naked, without clothes; they cover their bodies with ashes and . . . practise all sorts of austerities'. These may have been the ash-covered sadhus known as Aghoris who to this day inhabit some cremation grounds, and who are best known for occasionally eating human flesh. Others tried to explain away the strangeness that is Benares with a soubriquet: the 'Athens of India' according to Bernier; the 'Oxford and Canterbury of India in one' according to Edwin Arnold, whose epic paean to the Buddha, *The Light of Asia*, was a best-seller in the 1880s. James Kennedy, a disconsolate and unsuccessful missionary who lived there for more than twenty years, called Benares 'wild, grotesque, unnatural, forbidding, utterly wanting in verisimilitude and refinement, with nothing to purify and raise the people, with everything fitted to pervert their taste and lower their character'. Kipling referred to Benares as the city 'of two Thousand Temples, and twice two thousand stenches'.[22]

Twain gives over twenty-two pages to the city. The buildings along the river, best seen from a boat, are 'a splendid jumble of massive and picturesque masonry, a bewildering and beautiful

[22] In the story 'The Bride's Progress', Kipling describes an irritating young Englishwoman in Benares who says at the end of her visit to the city: 'Oh! You horrid people! Shouldn't I like to wash you.' Kipling also invents a false etymology for Benares — '*be*' meaning 'without' in Urdu, and '*nares*' meaning 'nostrils' in Latin. It's not only foreigners who have complained about the dirtiness of Benares. Gandhi, in one of his first political speeches, at Benares in 1916, upbraided the city for its filthiness, and later in his autobiography declared that the 'swarming flies and the noise made by the shopkeepers and pilgrims were perfectly insufferable. Where one expected an atmosphere of meditation and communion, it was conspicuous by its absence.'

confusion of stone platforms, temples, stair flights, rich and stately palaces'; Twain reworks his own 'great-grandmother of tradition' *bon mot* about India's antiquity, to tell us that Benares is 'older than history, older than tradition, older than legend, and looks twice as old as all of them put together' — which, again, is to be found in almost every modern India guidebook. But for Twain, usually so upbeat an Indophile, Benares is just too shocking — and his desire to be positive about all he sees crumples in the face of so much filth. The city is 'as insanitary as it is sacred' and he is appalled to find stagnant pools of sewage, 'filthy with the washings of rotten lepers' (he later refers to them as 'puddles of leper-pus'), and then to see a group of men, women and 'comely young maidens' waist-deep in the Ganges, scooping up the water with their hands, and drinking it, while a human corpse floated nearby.

Varanasi continues to divide visitors, as a quick trawl of any online travel forum will reveal. There are many tales of hotel scams, of thieving rickshaw drivers, of floating corpses and upset stomachs — and of moments of wonderment and spiritual awakening, and of some discomfort at being one of many goggle-eyed westerners watching the cremations along the banks of the Ganges. Victoria from Swansea called it 'the Marmite City — you either love it or you hate it'. For the north American blogger Mark Jacobs, the city was the 'Shithole of the Gods' — and he refused to apologise for this headline to his Varanasi travelogue, when readers commented adversely. Varanasi, he went on to argue, is 'a garbage dump masquerading as a city'. Dave Lewicki from California tells his readers, 'I'm not religious, new-age or whatever, but there's definitely an energy here that's hard not to feel'; while Naomi from Australia, on the Lonely Planet travel forum, declares that she had visited other cities in India 'and nothing felt as authentic and haunting as Varanasi'.

The issue of authenticity comes up repeatedly with visitors to India. One Scandinavian acquaintance, Pernille, on her first trip to the subcontinent, informed me authoritatively that Varanasi was the 'real India'. And when questioned, she explained that this was the real India because it was 'natural' and unspoiled by western influences. I bit my tongue. It was, she continued, the land she had heard about from her friends who had visited the country before her. 'The original India,' she insisted. For her, the naked sadhus, smeared in ash, were more Indian than those who commute on the Delhi metro. It was as if there could only be one 'real India' and it was as if Pernille wanted India to remain frozen in antiquity.

A Twelfth Intermission

WHEN MY WIFE'S stepfather, Tony Mango, died in 2008, I was more bereft than I had anticipated. He was ninety-two, after all — and had been ill for some time. But I felt I had failed him, and myself. I had been caught napping. It had been my plan to interview him at length, on video or tape, about his seventy years in India. I was always intrigued by his description of how, when he arrived in the 1930s, he belonged neither to the rulers nor the ruled. He was a European, born in Ottoman Constantinople to a Greek family, educated in French, fluent in English, but in British-ruled India he was still not quite 'clubbable', as he put it. He would later say, partly for these reasons, that he found independent India far preferable to British rule. And yet for Indians he was and always remained a foreigner. Indeed, once most of the Greeks of Constantinople had left what became Istanbul, he was a foreigner everywhere in the world. And he had made his home in India, first in small towns in the centre of the country, then Madras and then Bombay, where he became the doyen of honorary consuls, a part-time unpaid Greek diplomat for more than forty years. And then he was gone, and so were his memories.

He had told me he was writing his autobiography, but I had never seen a word he had written. A few months later my mother-in-law turned up in Delhi with a plastic folder containing a typescript and with a note across the top, in bold, that read: 'A story of my life written for my family so they can't say I left them with nothing.' The first chapter begins with a further explanation from Tony of why he was writing, an explanation that had me answering Tony out loud, as if he was still sitting in my Delhi study. He wrote:

I was coming to the end of a bout of reminiscences. There was silence . . . 'You should write a book!' someone said ['*Was it me?*' *I wondered out loud*]. Not for the first time. I am never sure what to think when somebody says this. Is it genuine interest or a 'sign off'? This time it sounded sincere.

He goes on to say that:

the sound of Marvell's 'winged' chariot is getting louder by the day [*Did Tony know that the same poem talks of finding rubies by the side of the Indian Ganges? He must have, making it his first, albeit oblique, reference in his memoirs to India*[1]], and since I have nothing else to bequeath to my loved ones let me, while there is perhaps still time, try at least to leave them with the story of my life and times, unadorned, I hope, except where discretion calls for a veil of mystery.

Sadly, the manuscript was far from complete; it stops, dead, in 1932, six years before he came to India. There are little scraps of information about India, buried in descriptions of his early years.[2] He refers to how he went on an abortive tiger shoot and came back with just one dead peacock, and he speaks of a wartime visit to Cawnpore, in which he had a very 'gay time', but doesn't mention Nana Sahib or the Mutiny. I have spoken

[1] Andrew Marvell's most famous poem, *To His Coy Mistress* (c. 1651) compares the Ganges to the Humber, the river on which his home town, Hull, sits. 'Had we but world enough, and time,/ This coyness, lady, were no crime./ We would sit down and think which way/ To walk, and pass our long love's day;/ Thou by the Indian Ganges' side/ Shouldst rubies find; I by the tide/ Of Humber would complain.'

[2] He described how the only advice his first boss in India gave him was to 'keep your bowels open'. He took lots of cholera belts with him. These were flannel sashes or girdles worn round the abdomen that were thought, erroneously, to ward off cholera.

to those who knew him best, including my mother-in-law, but there is still so much that is missing.

I cannot answer the simple question, 'What did Tony Mango think about India before he travelled there?' I have some clues, though. There was a significant Greek community in India in the British period,[3] and some of his relatives had been based here — from them he had heard stories about the land that would become his home. But the best clue comes from an action adventure story of the 1860s. Tony used to tell me that as a teenager he had loved a book called *Captain Corcoran*, whose eponymous hero, a Frenchman, married a beautiful Indian woman with lotus eyes. And he would joke that both our fates had been decided by Captain Corcoran, whose adventures had inspired him to marry an Indian woman, and that he, Tony, had in turn inspired me to do the same.

After Tony's death, I tracked down a copy of this book, first published in 1867, on eBay. And I now have my own copy of the eighth edition of *Aventures merveilleuses mais authentiques du Capitaine Corcoran*, by Alfred Assollant, bound in red.

Le capitaine Corcoran.

The book, never translated into English, possibly because it is so Anglophobic, is set during and just after the 1857 Uprising, and tells the story of a Breton sea-captain and

[3] The largest community was in Calcutta where there is still a Greek church and a Greek graveyard. The fine neo-Classical Greek Orthodox Church near Kalighat was built in 1925, while the graveyard in eastern Calcutta has tombs that date back to the late eighteenth century.

his pet Javanese tiger, Louison, who travel from France to India in search of an ancient Hindu text. Corcoran, tiger at his side, and with some help from the supporters of Nana Sahib, fights against the British, and he wins the hand of 'la belle Sita', with her lotus eyes, the daughter of a Maharajah. It's a wonderfully romantic and entertaining piece of boyish adventure writing, full of elephants and rhinoceroses, fortresses and palaces — and beautiful women. And it's easy to understand why Tony might have been rather keen to come to India. The book was typical of a swashbuckling genre, of which Verne was a master, and which was hugely popular in late nineteenth- and early twentieth-century continental Europe, but notably less so in Britain. The Italian journalist Emilio Salgari was the creator of the enormously successful *Sandokan* series,[4] full of charismatic and well-meaning pirates, and set in Malaysia and India. Much of the action again happens at the time of the Mutiny, one of the protagonists has a pet tiger, and the women of India are depicted, not entirely misleadingly, as exceptionally beautiful.

Not long after Tony died, my life began to change. My first book was published, the product of my Delhi wanderings. And I was already wandering around the rest of India — travelling every other week — as I began work on a guidebook which took me to almost every part of the country (and which began to take its toll on our marriage). For the first time I went to little-visited Bellary, where Tony had spent his earliest years in India as an agent for Rallis, the Greek-owned trading firm — and had dozens of questions that Tony would never now be able to answer. I forced myself back to places I had disliked or despaired of: Agra and Jaipur, for instance, so beloved of newcomers to India, and found new, hidden things to admire. There were places I had

---

[4] *Sandokan* reappears as a film, and an immensely popular TV series, which made the Indian actor Kabir Bedi a superstar in Italy and Spain in the 1970s.

failed to make much sense of before — Hampi and Mandu, for instance, both quite dazzling in scale — where I could now happily spend many days exploring.

It all made me realise how little I knew of the land that had become my home. It's a cyclical feeling, I find: one that I can now anticipate. It's that temporary, misleading belief that I have acquired great knowledge of India or of just one small part of it, followed by the dawning of a realisation that I am still skimming the surface. And, in honesty, I have been just one more victim of that modern and ancient travellers' fallacy, in which countries are somehow thought to be knowable. India is much larger than Europe in population; and few people would pretend to know Europe. And I have also long ago given up the search for the 'real India' — and tried to persuade others to do so as well. For the reason that, wherever one goes, the real India is everywhere — in the nightclubs and slums of Bombay, in towns like Bellary, and in the remotest villages. They are all — and so is everywhere in between — the 'real India'.

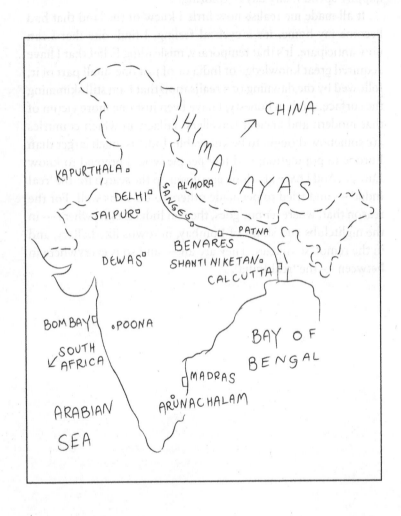

HIMALAYAS

CHINA

KAPURTHALA

DELHI

JAIPUR

AL'MORA

SANGES

DEWAS

PATNA

BENARES

SHANTI NIKETAN

CALCUTTA

BOMBAY

POONA

SOUTH
AFRICA

BAY OF
BENGAL

MADRAS

ARUNACHALAM

ARABIAN

SEA

Chapter Thirteen: In which the Author finds a connection between Gandhi and Mary Poppins, reflects on the potentially debilitating effects of early fornication, and has mixed feelings about the Jaipur Literature Festival

IN THE EARLY days of 1983, a slightly cynical college boy, who had never been to India, struggled through the rainy streets of Cambridge to see *Gandhi*. I went because so many of my British friends seemed unaccountably obsessed with India, and because so many of them had adored the film. It was, I decided, with the decisiveness and arrogance of youth, a triumph of middlebrow film-making — and a few months later was amused when *Gandhi*'s conventionality was rewarded with no less than eight Oscars, in what might otherwise have been the year of *ET* or *Tootsie*. But, and I admitted this to no one, *Gandhi* was also mildly inspirational, although not quite in the way that it was intended to be.

I had little time for what I saw as Gandhi's suffocating saintliness (though I have since come to realise that he was a much more complex and interesting character than the one portrayed in the film). The scenery in *Gandhi* was often spectacular, and long parts of the movie seemed like a romanticised tribute to the steam train and the Indian countryside. There was that slightly pleasurable frisson, that shudder of recognition, as I played 'spot-the-actor', as legions of Britain's most famous thespians made cameo appearances (and watching it again thirty years later I found myself playing exactly the same game with the Indian actors). And then there was the invisible make-up artist, who was nominated for an Oscar but didn't get one, and who did a sterling job in ageing several of the actors by at least fifty years over the course of a three-hour movie.

But it wasn't all this that sparked my interest back in 1983. Rather it was the glorious role that the media seemed to play in the political events depicted in *Gandhi* that seduced me gently into considering journalism as a calling after college. Throughout the movie, reporters and photo-journalists were depicted as playing a central role in Gandhi's struggles against injustice — first in South Africa, and then in India. Gandhi and his friends call in the media, local and international, at every opportunity, as their way of embarrassing the authorities. In the humble scribbles and snaps of journalists there seemed to be a source of secret power, of persuasive leverage, even, possibly, a way of changing the world. Much of this is over-played in *Gandhi*, predictably. The *New York Times* journalist Vince Walker, played by Martin Sheen, who appears at several decisive moments in the film, over more than forty years, was a fabrication, presumably inserted to give American audiences a character to whom they could relate.

Gandhi the person is, today, I would venture, best known around the world through the prism of *Gandhi* the film. It is hagiography with a smile; he is allowed, at least, to have a sense of humour. Gandhi is not faultless — but almost so. His sexual, hygiene and dietary peccadilloes are underplayed, and so too is his unpredictability and his inconsistency.[1] But *Gandhi* the film is far from hegemonic, and it's possible to encounter an extraordinary diversity of global views about Gandhi the man. His undying fame means that about two-thirds of a century after his assassination, he remains the world's most celebrated Indian. And that celebrity has not always exactly been used in a fashion that fits Gandhi's vision for the world. His image has been used

[1] Gandhi quoted Ralph Waldo Emerson on this subject in 1930, 'I must admit my many inconsistencies. But since I am called "Mahatma", I might well endorse Emerson's saying that "foolish consistency is the hobgoblin of little minds". There is, I fancy, a method in my inconsistencies.'

in this millennium to advertise Italian and Swiss mobile phone companies, Apple computers and $25,000-Mont Blanc pens. He has also been the subject of a very large number of poor jokes[2] and inappropriately alcoholic rhymes.

> You're the top!
> You're Mahatma Gandhi.
> You're the top!
> You're Napoleon Brandy

From the 1934 Broadway musical 'Anything Goes'.
Words by Cole Porter.

> There once was an old man called Gandhi,
> Who went into a bar for a shandy
> With his great loincloth
> He wiped off the froth,
> And the barman said 'Blimey, that's handy!'

British limerick from the 1970s attributed to the
Indian-born comedian Spike Milligan

---

[2] My favourite poor joke about Gandhi, which will appeal to sesquipedalians everywhere and to fans of *Mary Poppins*, is this: Mahatma Gandhi was an unusual person. He walked barefoot everywhere, to the point that his feet became quite thick and hard. He often went on hunger strikes, and even when he wasn't on a hunger strike, he did not eat much and became quite thin and frail. He also was a very spiritual person. Finally, because he didn't eat much and when he did his diet was peculiar, he developed very bad breath. He became known as a super-calloused fragile mystic hexed by halitosis.

The earliest Gandhi-related verse that I can find is recorded by Gandhi himself in his autobiography. He describes how he was beaten up by a group of whites in South Africa who wanted Indian migrants to be sent home. They then sang 'Hang old Gandhi/ on the sour apple tree', lines based on a verse from the American Civil War song *John Brown's Body* which refers to hanging the US Confederate leader Jefferson Davis from a 'sour apple tree'.

315

Gandhi is a favourite for fancy-dress parties the world over. A bald wig, pebble glasses and a white sheet are all that is needed to transform anyone, of any size, shape, colour or age into an immediately recognisable Mahatma.

His lookalikes turn up at sporting events, knowing that it is a sure way of getting at least ten seconds of camera fame. One turned up recently at a San Francisco Giants Baseball match,[3] bearing a placard announcing that 'Gandhi's back'.

Gandhi's distinctiveness makes him a gift both to cartoonists and satirists. The spoof trailer for the imaginary sequel *Gandhi II* has the Mahatma return as a gun-toting hoodlum ('No more Mr Passive Resistance — he's out to kick some butt') who goes into a restaurant, and says, 'Give me a steak — medium rare.' There's even a YouTube recording of a computer-game wrestling

match between a cartoon Gandhi and that proto-Mughal, Genghis Khan — in which the latter knocks Gandhi out cold with a kick to the head. Perhaps Gandhi's legendary sense of humour — and he certainly had one — makes

[3] There is an unlikely Gandhi connection with baseball, in the form of a spoof *New Yorker* article which describes how in 1933 the Mahatma visited a New York Yankees game, and asked if he could have a go. He hit a home run. The story then became the basis for the award-winning 2006 short film *Gandhi at the Bat* which took the form of a fictional newsreel of Gandhi's moment as a pinch-hitter for the Yankees.

him fair game for satire. But there are sometimes limits to what can be said without causing offence. Hillary Clinton went too far in 2004, when she joked about Gandhi running a petrol station in St Louis and was accused of pandering to racial stereotypes. She appeared on television to apologise, saying, 'It was a lame attempt at humour, and I am very sorry.' In 2011, a book about Gandhi by the American writer Joseph Lelyveld was banned in Gandhi's home state of Gujarat for suggesting that he might, just possibly, have had a homosexual relationship with his close friend Hermann Kallenbach.

Gandhi did not burst fully formed onto the international stage. His first coming was in the 1890s as a leader of South Africa's Indian community, when he was a suited lawyer with a good head of hair. He soon attracted followers and admirers, several of them white Christians. The first biography of Gandhi was by a Baptist preacher from Devon called Joseph Doke, who saw him as a saintly, even Christ-like figure who 'lives on a higher plane than most men do'. Doke's *M.K. Gandhi: An Indian Patriot in South Africa* appeared in 1909, with an introduction by Lord Ampthill, who had briefly served as viceroy of India.[4] Doke's book was not destined to be a best-seller, and Gandhi bought up most of the first edition to avoid what he referred to as a publishing 'fiasco', and distributed it through his network of acquaintances. In 1924, a book about Gandhi was published that did become a best-seller, by the Nobel Prize-winning French essayist and novelist Romain Rolland, who had previously written biographies of Beethoven, Michelangelo and Tolstoy. The biography was subtitled 'The man who became one with the universal being', and in the text Rolland directly compared Gandhi to Jesus — 'the only thing lacking,' he intoned, 'is the

---

[4] Better known as a founder-member of the International Olympic Committee, and one of the great rowers of the Victorian age. In 1904, in Lord Curzon's absence, he was acting viceroy of India for seven months.

Cross'. And Gandhi would attract many followers in the west who remained Christians. The most famous of them were the Anglican priest CF Andrews, and the Englishwoman Madeleine Slade, the daughter of an admiral, who learned of Gandhi through Rolland's biography. In *Gandhi,* the film, both Andrews and Slade are depicted playing an even larger role than they did in real life.

Western admirers were so comfortable with their simplified versions of the teachings of Gandhi, partly because he was easier to assimilate to western traditions, than, say, Swami Vivekananda or others from a more mainstream Hindu tradition. Gandhi's own early ideas had been heavily influenced by his readings of the American Transcendentalists Emerson and Thoreau of the Theosophists Madame Blavatsky and Annie Besant (both of whom he knew), by the British aesthete-reformer Ruskin, and by Leo Tolstoy, with whom he corresponded. By the late nineteenth century, there was a lively intercontinental merry-go-round of western and eastern ideas and influences — and Gandhi happily participated.

In his autobiography Gandhi explains, with a slight note of embarrassment, that he first read the Bhagavad Gita, which would later become his key Hindu text, while he was living in the UK. And the version he read was in English, a stylised translation composed by Edwin Arnold, a fellow evangelical vegetarian[5] whom Gandhi got to know slightly in London. Similarly, many of Gandhi's ideas about Buddhism were derived from Arnold's

[5] Gandhi formed a vegetarian society in the Bayswater area of London, where he then lived, and became its secretary. Edwin Arnold was the vice-president. Arnold had been president of Poona's Sanskrit College in the late 1850s, and later became editor of the *Daily Telegraph* in the UK. But he was best known as an Orientalist. His third wife was Japanese, and he spent most of the last years of his life in Japan. *The Light of Asia* was enormously successful in the USA, with eighty-three editions, and selling more than half a million copies.

most famous work, the epic poem *The Light of Asia*, and Gandhi would only later read original works from the Buddhist canon.

Gandhi's facility in English, his ability to see the world through western and Indian prisms, his accessibility (especially to the media) and his gentleness helped him attract an extraordinarily wide collection of foreign admirers: from pacifists and deists, to vegetarians, coitophobes, anti-imperialists, utopians, pedestrians, spinners and weavers, hip-bath manufacturers, honey-lovers, anarchists, neo-Luddites, city-haters and teetotallers. Not everyone loved him, of course, particularly diehard defenders of British rule, but he was hard to ignore, hard to forget, and was undoubtedly, by the mid-1920s, one of the most famous people in the world.

But Gandhi was not the first Indian superstar of the twentieth century. The poet-polymath Rabindranath Tagore is less remembered in the west these days, but from 1913 until the mid-1920s he was undoubtedly the world's best-known living Indian; and, outside the west, would remain better known than Gandhi for considerably longer, particularly in China and Japan. Like Gandhi, Tagore had come to England as a young man — and was not particularly impressed. His family was well travelled and his grandfather, Dwarkanath Tagore,[6] who visited Europe

[6] Dwarkanath famously upbraided the German Orientalist Max Müller who complained to him about some Indian music that he thought rather discordant. 'You are all alike; if anything seems strange to you and does not please you at once, you turn away. When I first heard Italian music, it was no music to me at all; but I went on and on, till I began to like it, or what you call understand it. It is the same with everything else. You may say our religion is no religion, our poetry is no poetry, our philosophy is no philosophy. We try to understand and appreciate whatever Europe has produced, but do not imagine that therefore we despise what India has produced. If you studied our music as we do yours, you would find that there is melody, rhythm and harmony in it, quite as much as in yours. And if you would study our poetry, our religion, and our philosophy, you would find that we are not what you call heathens or miscreants, but know as much of the Unknowable as you do, and have seen perhaps even deeper than you have.'

in the 1840s, was presented to Queen Victoria, and dined with Dickens and Thackeray.

Like Gandhi, Tagore's appearance was distinctive. His handsome face, long beard and flowing robes, often described as Christ-like, made him unforgettable. The English poet Frances Cornford, a granddaughter of Darwin, remarked after meeting him, 'I can now imagine a powerful and gentle Christ, which I never could before.' The German publisher Kurt Wolff wrote that Tagore, 'with his long grayish-white beard and dignity . . . presented a most impressive figure, so that it seemed a completely natural error when my three-year-old daughter assumed God was paying us a visit, and settled contentedly in the lap of the Lord'. His friend Harriet Monroe, the American poetry impresario, described how she felt she 'was sitting at the feet of the Buddha', while the seventeen-year-old Japanese schoolboy Yasunari Kawabata, who would more than fifty years later become the second Asian to win the Nobel Prize for Literature, recalled in 1968 that 'I remember even now the features and appearance of this sage-like poet, with his long, bushy hair, long moustaches and beard, standing tall in loose flowing Indian garments, and with deep, piercing eyes . . . he gave an impression, to the boy I was then of some ancient Oriental wizard'. Gandhi nicknamed Tagore *gurudev*, literally teacher-god, and in much of the world Tagore's appearance came to personify the image of what an oriental guru might look like.

Tagore came to London in 1912, bearing with him the English translation of the poetry collection *Gitanjali*[7] and was introduced to the Anglo-Irish poet WB Yeats, who suggested a few amendments to the poems, and became Tagore's most

[7] He immediately left the only copy of the manuscript on the London Underground, while travelling, presumably on the Northern Line, from his Charing Cross hotel to his publishers in Bloomsbury. Fortunately, he was able to retrieve it sometime later from the Left Luggage Office.

prominent admirer. *Gitanjali* was published in England in early 1913, with an introduction by Yeats in which he referred to the poems as the 'work of a supreme culture'. Yeats went on to declare, rather over-enthusiastically, of Tagore's imaginative faculties that 'a whole civilization, immeasurably strange to us, seems to have been taken up into this imagination, and yet we are not moved because of its strangeness, but because we have met our own image'. That idea of the sudden shock of finding one's own image in otherness probably remains the best explanation of the quite phenomenal immediate success of *Gitanjali*. Ezra Pound compared Tagore to Dante, and Paul Nash compared *Gitanjali* to the Bible. The book went through no less than ten UK editions between March and November 1913, when Tagore was awarded the Nobel Prize for Literature, at which point sales became stratospheric.[8]

Tagore soon became an international celebrity, touring the world to meet his adoring fans, giving well-paid lectures to support his educational community at Shantiniketan. Large crowds turned out for his 1916 US tour, and he told Harriet Monroe that 'I am like a show lion in a circus now . . . However, I shall try to look cheerful and go on dancing to the tune of your American dollars.' From his accounts and those of others, it is clear that the crowds were more interested in seeing him,

---

[8] He was the first Indian, but the third person born in India, to receive a Nobel Prize, which was first awarded in 1901. The first Indian-born winner was Ronald Ross, who won the prize for medicine in 1902 for his discovery that malaria was transmitted by mosquitoes. Ross was also a better than average poet, whose poem *India* begins, 'Here from my lonely watch-tower of the East/ An ancient race outworn I see/ With dread, my own dear distant Country, lest/ The same fate fall on thee.' The second Indian-born winner was Rudyard Kipling who won the literature prize in 1907. Of Tagore's award, the *New York Times* pointed out that this was the first time a non-white person had got a Nobel Prize, and then muddied the waters, and threw in an inelegant typo, by informing its readers that 'Babindranath Tagore, if not exactly one of us, is, as an Aryan, a distant relative of all white folk'.

and in having been at one of his lectures, than in what he had to say. In America at least, he became an archetypal oriental, wisely obscure and exotically ancient — and occasionally, when he was accused of supporting an Indian nationalist conspiracy  in San Francisco, just a little bit dangerous. He made repeated visits to the USA, and as late as 1931, he was able to fill the Carnegie Hall to its capacity of four thousand — and thousands more had to be turned away. He had a private meeting with President Hoover, and a much more public one with Albert Einstein, at a meeting of, as the *New York Times* captioned its photograph, 'a mathematician and a mystic'.

Tagore travelled widely throughout the 1920s and early 1930s and not just to the great capital cities of the west. He visited Egypt, Russia, Argentina and Iraq — and he made five separate trips to Japan between 1916 and 1929, and one to China in 1924. His east Asian odysseys provide some insight into the ways India was imagined in Japan and China. Tagore's own tangled Japan connection dates back to the early twentieth century, long before he was a global celebrity.

The Anglophone Japanese art historian Okakura Kakuzo had come to India in 1901 to meet the dying Swami Vivekananda. In Calcutta, Okakura stayed with the Tagore family, and worked there on his most influential book, *The Ideals of the East*, which begins with the words, 'Asia is one'. The book, written in English, is often described as a pan-Asianist manifesto, though it is essentially a work of cultural history.[9] Okakura has a rosily romantic image of an Asia that includes Japan, China and India and many other smaller nations. He insists that 'not even the snowy barriers [of the Himalayas] can interrupt for one moment that broad expanse of love for the Ultimate and Universal, which is the common thought-inheritance of every Asiatic race'. The most important pan-Asian cultural connection for Okakura is through Buddhism — 'that great ocean of idealism, in which merge all the river-systems of Eastern Asiatic thought'. Buddhism is allowed its Indian origins, but it is 'not coloured only with the pure water of the Ganges'. He recounts how Buddhism had been brought from India to other parts of Asia by pilgrims and travellers, and the 'genius' of other Asian nations brought 'new symbolism, new organisation, new powers of devotion, to add to the treasures of the Faith'.

Okakura was dead by the time Tagore visited Japan, but Tagore openly warmed to Okakura's pan-Asian philosophy. On that first visit in 1916, about twenty thousand people gathered at Tokyo's main railway station to greet him, and the prime minister held a reception in his honour. His Okakura-like pan-Asian vision gave him an immediate popularity, but Tagore's attacks on materialism and nationalism, and his aversion to the idea of Japanese leadership in Asia, meant that on subsequent visits he was given a less than ecstatic welcome. The Japanese philosopher Inoue Tetsujiro would dismiss Tagore's voice as 'like the song of a ruined country'; and the image of India as a defeated nation,

[9] The book, which was published in 1903, has an introduction by Swami Vivekananda's Anglo-Irish disciple, Margaret Noble, better known as Sister Nivedita. All Okakura's main books were written in English. Okakura had been sent to Vivekananda by another of his earliest disciples, Josephine MacLeod of New York, who had been visiting Japan. MacLeod in her writings admits that she was at first more interested in Vivekananda's good looks than in anything he said.

one which had succumbed to western imperialism, played an important role in how India was seen in both Japan and China.[10]

Tagore only went to China once, in 1924, and it was not an easy visit. He had admirers, certainly, including the poet Xu Zhimo,[11] who acted as his interpreter, and in the course of one long sentence compared Tagore to Whitman, Tolstoy, Michelangelo, Socrates, Lao Tzu, Goethe, and, of course, Jesus Christ. His lectures attracted large crowds, but there were also demonstrations by those who saw him as a conservative looking backwards to an imagined time when there was a great friendship between India and China. The Chinese scholar Wu Chih-hui wrote of Tagore as 'a petrified fossil of India's national past, [who] has retreated into the tearful eyes and dripping noses of the slave people of a conquered country, seeking happiness in a future life, squeaking like the hub of a wagon wheel that needs oil'. One leaflet distributed outside a lecture hall in Peking, later translated and reprinted in a Calcutta newspaper, attacked Tagore as someone who supported the 'useless and dead aspects of our civilisation' and accused him of wishing to have 'nationality and

[10] Japan, in particular, would give sanctuary to those who preached violent opposition to British rule — including two rather unTagorean Bengalis, Rash Behari Bose who fled there during World War I, and Subhas Chandra Bose who took over the leadership of the Indian National Army from the older Bose in Tokyo in 1943.

[11] The poet Xu Zhimo, an Anglophile admirer of Keats and Shelley, declared breathlessly of Tagore, 'His unlimited imagination and broad sympathy makes us think of Whitman; his gospel of universal love and zeal for spreading his ideas remind us of Tolstoy; his unbending will and artistic genius remind us of Michelangelo, the sculptor of Moses; his sense of humor and wisdom makes us think of Socrates and Lao-tzu; the tranquillity and beauty of his personality remind us of Goethe in his old age; the touch of his compassion and pure love, his tireless efforts in the cause of humanitarianism, his great and all-embracing message sometimes make us recall the Saviour of mankind.' Xu Zhimo is best remembered today for his poem *On Saying Goodbye to Cambridge Again* — a romantic paean to the punts and to the willows of the River Cam.

politics abolished, replacing them with the consolation of one's soul'. The youth of China tended to seek inspiration from the west and from Bolshevik Russia, rather than from Tagore or Gandhi.[12] India, when it was imagined at all, was seen as the ancient source of Buddhism, and as a country ruled by foreigners.

Tagore's star would also fade, rather more gently, in the west. He continued to attract large crowds, and be received by heads of state. But the intellectual elite began to turn against him and his admirers. Graham Greene said of Tagore, in a laudatory introduction to a novel by the young Indian writer RK Narayan, 'I cannot believe anyone but Mr Yeats can still take his poems very seriously.' And Auden also taunted Yeats, referring to the 'deplorable spectacle of a grown man occupied with the mumbo-jumbo of magic and the nonsense of India'. Tagore had become a celebrity sage, a wise man of the east; for the less discerning, he was an archetypal Indian mystic; and a source, for his harshest critics, of mumbo-jumbo. And his writings and his paintings were largely neglected, except in his homeland of Bengal.

Gandhi and Tagore were both subject to international veneration and occasional derision, and both came to symbolise, and even embody, the country in which they were born. This was something new. No Indians before or since have played such a central role in how India was imagined abroad. All the same, during the inter-war period there were many other competing ideas of India swirling around the globe. Now largely forgotten, the American journalist Katherine Mayo was a well-known and controversial figure in India and in the west. Her book *Mother India* contributed to an image of India as a poverty-stricken land of strange and debilitating sexual mores. *Mother India* was translated into thirteen languages, sold more than 400,000 copies

[12] An opinion poll taken on the campus of Peking University in the winter of 1923–24, ranked Lenin, Woodrow Wilson and Bertrand Russell well ahead of Tagore as the greatest non-Chinese men in the world.

in America, and was read by, among others, George V and the British Prime Minister (and cousin of Kipling) Stanley Baldwin. A copy of the book was sent to every British MP. *Mother India* even inspired a (not very successful) Broadway play, whose main characters were a fifty-two-year-old Indian man, and his twelve-year-old wife. The book aims to educate Americans, and the rest of the world, about India. Mayo asks rhetorically, 'What does the average American actually know about India? That Mr Gandhi lives there; also tigers.' Mayo describes her book as a health survey — for which she travelled throughout India, visiting hospitals, meeting doctors, politicians, princes, religious leaders, ordinary people and, of course, Mr Gandhi.

There is much that is commonplace, and true, in Mayo's book, but there is much that is speculative and even absurd — particularly when she discusses the sexual habits of Indians. She is obsessed with the adverse effects of early sexual activity. And she finds, from somewhere — she doesn't say where, and she seems to have made it up — plenty of evidence of pre-pubescent sexuality among Indian children. She tells her readers, for instance, that Indian mothers, 'high caste or low', regularly masturbate their children, and goes on to explain the reasons: 'the girl "to make her sleep well", the boy "to make him manly", an abuse which the boy, at least, is apt to continue daily for the rest of his life'. It is normal in many parts of the country, she adds, for little boys 'if physically attractive, to be drafted for the satisfaction of grown men or be regularly attached to a temple, in the capacity of prostitute'. Because Hindus, Mayo declares, have sex too early and so freely that their sexual powers dissipate, between seven and eight out of every ten Hindu males aged twenty-five to thirty are impotent. Only one part of her book deals with sexuality — but Mayo argues that much of what is wrong with India and Indians stems from this. And what is wrong? Her list is lengthy: 'Inertia, helplessness, lack of initiative and originality, lack of staying power and sustained loyalties, sterility of enthusiasm, weakness of life-vigour itself . . .' And for all this, she declares, Britain is blameless. It is the fault of Hinduism, and this made India unfit for self-government.

Predictably, *Mother India* caused an outcry. But the response was also complex. Many of the points Mayo made about the ill-treatment of women were accurate; and some of those who hated the book had been campaigning on exactly the issues raised by Mayo, such as child marriage. The India-based Irish feminist Margaret Cousins[13] said that many of her own experiences had corroborated 'a large number of facts and illustrations' used by Mayo, but that the 'total impression [that *Mother India*] conveys to any reader, either inside or outside India, is cruelly and wickedly untrue'. Gandhi wrote a combative 3500-word review of *Mother India*, in his own weekly English-language journal, *Young India*, under the headline 'Drain Inspector's Report':

The book is cleverly and powerfully written. The carefully chosen quotations give it the appearance of a truthful book.

[13] Margaret Cousins was an Irish suffragette, briefly imprisoned before World War I for throwing stones at 10 Downing Street. She became a Theosophist, and during the war moved with her husband, James Cousins, to Madras — and they became friends of Annie Besant, Tagore and Gandhi. She was a vegetarian, a Theosophist and a coitophobe: 'Something in me revolted then, and has ever since protested against, certain of the techniques of nature connected with sex. Nor will I . . . be satisfied, purified, or redeemed, life after life, until the evolution of humanity has substituted some more artistic form of continuance of the race.' She is best remembered as a founder-member of the All India Women's Conference in 1926. James Cousins was a mystic poet, who used the pseudonym Jayaram, and who asked Gandhi to recommend him for the Nobel Prize for Literature. Gandhi said he was not qualified to do so. James Joyce was also a friend and house guest back in Ireland. He fled their house because he couldn't stand any more vegetarian food, and complained of indigestion caused by a 'typhoid turnip'. Joyce later wrote, in the voice of his own publisher, about one of James Cousins' books, 'I printed mystical books in dozens:/ I printed the table-book of Cousins/ Though (asking your pardon) as for the verse/ 'Twould give you a heartburn on your arse:'

But the impression it leaves on my mind is, that it is the report of a drain inspector sent out with the one purpose of opening and examining the drains of the country to be reported upon, or to give a graphic description of the stench exuded by the opened drains. If Miss Mayo had confessed that she had gone to India merely to open out and examine the drains of India, there would perhaps be little to complain about her compilation. But she says in effect with a certain amount of triumph, 'The drains are India'.

Much of the review is a rather unGandhi-like rant. He feels personally traduced by her account of their meeting, which he describes as 'libellous',[14] and states that Mayo has 'violated all sense of propriety' by misquoting Tagore, 'the Poet', as Gandhi calls him, on the subject of child marriage. Gandhi was openly concerned that *Mother India* might shape western ideas of India. 'I warn Americans and Englishmen against copying Miss Mayo,' he declares. 'She came not with an open mind as she claims, but with her preconceived notions and prejudices which she betrays on every page.'

What followed was the first sustained attempt by Indians to challenge a foreigner's account of India. Dozens of books were written in response to *Mother India*. The most successful was KL Gauba's *Uncle Sham,* published in 1929, a *tu quoque* account of modern America, in which child sexual abuse, syphilis, prostitution and the Ku Klux Klan all feature prominently. CF Andrews, the Anglican priest who had long been a friend of both Tagore and Gandhi, wrote a rebuttal called *The True*

[14] Elsewhere, he used even stronger language — 'untruthful', 'scurrilous', 'unscrupulous' and 'insolent'. Mayo had sent him a copy of the book, and he replied to her, addressing her as 'Dear Friend', and going on to say 'I am sorry to have to inform you that the book did not leave on my mind at all a nice impression'.

India and travelled to the United States on a lecture tour. Sarojini Naidu, the poet-nationalist, was encouraged by Gandhi to go to America, and addressed anti-Mayo meetings across the country. She made a particular point of addressing African-American clubs and organisations, and there emerged at this time a growing interest in encouraging co-operation between the nascent black rights movement, and the anti-colonial struggle in India.

WEB Du Bois, the most important black leader of the inter-war years, and an early admirer of Gandhi, was among those who gave their support to the anti-Mayo campaign. He was also a close friend of the Indian nationalist Lala Lajpat Rai, who lived in America for several years and wrote *Unhappy India* as a rebuttal to Mayo's book. Like several of these rebuttals, Rai's suggested that if one followed Mayo's logic the number of lynchings in the United States would surely prove that America was not fit for self-government. Du Bois (and Rai) also intervened in a dispute over the legal status of the relatively small number of Indian migrants in the US. Some of the migrants had tried to get themselves identified as Aryans and Caucasians, who would therefore be considered legally white and entitled to citizenship. But in 1923 the Supreme Court ruled that Indians were not white. Du Bois encouraged them to identify themselves with what he called the 'darker peoples'.

Du Bois' 1928 novel, *Dark Princess*,[15] published at the height of the Mayo controversy, has as its central female character Princess Kautilya, rather predictably a Maharajah's daughter, a sensual and wise Indian woman, with golden brown skin, who 'was slim and lithe, gracefully curved'. Kautilya becomes a revolutionary, trying to bring together the 'darker' peoples of the world to unite against white supremacy. She travels

[15] Du Bois was heavily influenced by Hegelian ideas and by the writings of the real Kautilya, who was a contemporary of Alexander the Great and the chief adviser to the first Mauryan emperor, Chandragupta — the grandfather of Ashoka the Great.

the world, working at one point as a domestic servant in America, and ends up living with, and getting pregnant by, a black American doctor. They have a child, Madhu, who will not only be the next Maharajah of Bwodpur but is also destined to become the mixed-race 'Messiah to all the Darker Worlds'. It was as if Du Bois was offering India the leadership of the oppressed peoples of the world. And India itself, which he describes, elsewhere, under the influence of ideas that he had encountered as a student, as the 'birthplace' and the 'black womb' of the ancient world, might become a sort of holy land.

India was certainly becoming a place of pilgrimage for foreigners, attracted largely by Hindu holy men. Theosophy continued to flourish, somewhat schismatically, in and out of India, creating and nourished by a whirlwind of esoterica. J Krishnamurti, for instance, an Indian schoolboy chosen by Annie Besant as the 'vehicle of the World Teacher', broke away from Theosophy, moved to California and developed an eclectic international following that included Emily and Mary Lutyens (the wife and daughter of the architect of New Delhi), the novelist Aldous Huxley and the modernist painter Jackson Pollock.

The British mystic Paul Brunton, a master at covering his own tracks and identity,[16] wandered around India in the early 1930s as a self-appointed guru-detective and yogi talent-spotter,

[16] It's not absolutely clear what Paul Brunton's real name was. He was at various stages Hermann Hirsh, Raphael Hurst, Raphael Meriden, Raphael Delmonte and Brunton Paul, before settling on Paul Brunton. He would always refer to himself as PB. He later moved to Switzerland and attracted disciples from all over the world. Among them were the parents of the controversial psychoanalyst Jeffrey Masson, who, in his biography of his father, gives a less than flattering portrayal of Brunton. In *My Father's Guru*, Brunton comes across as a tyrannical coitophobe, who banned the Massons from having sex, lied about his proficiency in Sanskrit and, *inter alia*, performed a fraudulent act of levitation.

quickly dismissing the frauds, and drawing up a short-list of the wisest of the wise. He would write several influential books; rare examples of clear, accessible and occasionally waspish (and always opinionated) writing about Indian spirituality. Like so many Orientalists, he believed that the east was somehow in his soul. He claimed 'an inborn attraction towards things oriental . . . the East, before my first visit, threw out vast tentacles that gripped my soul'. He also believed he was unique — because, on the one hand, he did not have that 'cataract of credulity which covers so many Eastern eyes', but, on the other hand, unlike most Englishmen, he was 'prepared to prostrate himself before a brown, half-naked figure in some lonely cave or in a disciple-filled room'.

On Brunton's first journey through India he quickly found a large number of 'well-intentioned fools, scriptural slaves, venerable know-nothings, money-seeking conjurers, jugglers with a few tricks, and pious frauds'. One of them stuck skewers through his own cheeks, and then pulled out his eyeballs so that they hung down over his face. Brunton was not impressed. Neither was he by the bearded ascetic who rolled over and over in the dust for four hundred miles in order to get to Benares, or by a man who held one arm up in the air for so many years, that it had become withered, 'the flesh like parchment'. Mortification of the spirit intrigued him more. He visited Meher Baba, the 'Parsee Messiah', twice. Meher Baba had taken a vow of silence[17] and communicated via an alphabet board — Brunton decided that he was a good man who is 'suffering from colossal delusions

[17] Meher Baba's vow of silence lasted from July 1925 until his death in 1969. He visited the USA many times, and developed an elite following there. The actresses Mary Pickford and Tallulah Bankhead were among his fans. The rock musician Pete Townshend of The Who also became an admirer, referring to him in the title of the 1971 song *Baba O'Riley*, often known as, because of its famous chorus, *Teenage Wasteland*.

about his own greatness'.[18]

Eventually, having travelled throughout the country, Brunton selected the doe-eyed and unassuming Ramana Maharshi of Arunachalam in southern India as his chosen one. And Ramana's slightly dubious prize for winning this unusual competition was that Brunton becomes one of his disciples. The often truculent Ramana, by Brunton's own account, didn't seem best pleased. The key moment had taken place when Ramana responded to a series of earnest and self-preening Brunton questions, with his own question, 'You say "I". "*I* want to know." Tell me, who is that *I*?' This response marked Brunton's epiphany. He now understood how he might find the Truth — by trying to answer the question 'Who Am I?' And he described how, when he was in Ramana's presence, he sensed an 'ineffable tranquillity' and could feel 'benign radiations which steadily percolate into my brain'. This was the story that Brunton told, to popular acclaim, in *A Search in Secret India*, published in 1935. Almost immediately, Ramana Maharshi's ashram began to attract a steady stream of foreign visitors and devotees. Among them was the British novelist Somerset Maugham, who had read Brunton's account.

Maugham's novel of 1944, *The Razor's Edge*, was partly set in India, with an American hero who, with the help of a Ramana-like guru, finds both himself and the Infinite. When he returns to the west his friends ask him what he was doing in India, and their questions can be seen to symbolise older foreign views of India. 'Shoot any tigers?'; 'What about the Rope Trick? Did you see that?', they ask. The answer is 'No'. The hero is then a little reluctant to divulge exactly what he did do, and his new beliefs,

[18] Brunton described Meher Baba with a cod-Shakespearean quote, which would become a cliché later in the twentieth century. He says of Meher Baba, quoting Malvolio, that 'Some men are born great, some achieve greatness and others appoint a press agent. Meher seems to favour the latter course.' It could be argued that Ramana Maharshi had greatness thrust upon him, by, among others, Paul Brunton.

fearing perhaps that he will be mocked or misunderstood. But in a heavily theological penultimate chapter he reveals what the guru revealed to him — that 'only the Infinite gives enduring happiness'.

Two years later, *The Razor's Edge* was a Hollywood film, starring Tyrone Power, and in which Ramana is still recognisable, although he has been stripped of his name, translocated to a studio version of the Himalayas, and made to look like Rabindranath Tagore, with a long, white beard and flowing robes — the real Ramana wore next to nothing, and had cropped hair and a trimmed beard. In the movie, he helps Tyrone Power become one with God, but his portrayal is entirely and unusually uncynical. And India emerges as a land of spiritual wisdom.[19]

In the inter-war period an extraordinarily disparate group of foreigners voyaged to and lived in India — quite apart from the soldiers and civilians who were there to rule the country. Travel had become cheaper and quicker. It was possible to see India as a place in which to have a holiday, or to follow an obsession, or to get married or to build a career. Tony Mango — whom I met on my first day in Bombay in 1987 — came to India in 1938 as a trader for a Greek company. The anthropologist Verrier Elwin came to India as a missionary in 1927, married a tribal woman, and stayed on after independence. The Hungarian student Fori Nehru travelled to India as a young bride in 1934, and lives here still, as I write, having celebrated her 105th birthday in 2013. The British composer John Foulds moved to India, obsessed by its folk music traditions — and died in Calcutta in 1939. His wife, the Irish violinist Maud McCarthy, stayed on, becoming a guru under the name Swami Omananda Puri. The Danish

---

[19] In 1984, a new Hollywood version of *The Razor's Edge* appeared, with Bill Murray, best known as a comedy actor, as the American hero. The guru was no longer Hindu — but a Tibetan Buddhist monk. It was billed as 'The Story of One Man's Search — for Himself'. The film was a critical and commercial failure.

horticulturalist Alfred Sorensen came to India in the 1930s, after meeting Tagore in England, and became a cave-dwelling mystic under the name Sunyata, or 'Nothingness'.[20] The Polish engineer Maurice Frydman[21] became a Gandhian, invented a new machine for spinning cotton, and then became a Hindu, settling in India under the name Bharatananda. His close friend Wanda Dynowska, a Polish noblewoman and translator, moved to India in the mid-1930s, and also became a Hindu, Uma Devi, staying on in India until her death in 1971. There were many more. India was large and varied enough to attract visitors and migrants who came for a startlingly wide range of reasons.

When EM Forster left for India in March 1921, Virginia Woolf wrote in her diary, 'He will become a mystic, sit by the roadside and forget Europe . . . we shan't see him again.' She was quite mistaken. He was back in England within a year, after a few madcap months as the private secretary to a minor Maharajah. He had taken with him the first chapters of a new novel, based on a previous, pre-war trip he'd made to India. But Forster writes that once these chapters 'were confronted with the country they purported to describe, they seemed to wilt and go dead . . . the gap between India remembered and India experienced was too wide'. For Forster, India was never unchanging. The novel, which he finished on his return to the UK, was *A Passage to India* — a title he borrowed from Whitman's poem — and published in 1924. It's a text that is very much of

[20] Sorensen met Tagore at Dartington Hall in Devon in 1929, where the former was working as a gardener. Tagore invited him to India, and he stayed on. He lived for a while in a tree on a small island in the Ganges. He became a follower of Ramana Maharshi after reading Brunton's book. Ramana later declared Sorensen a 'rare-born mystic'. Sorensen went on to live in a cave on what became known as Crank's Ridge near Almora (where he was a neighbour of Lama Govinda — see page 364) in the Himalayan foothills before moving to California when he was in his eighties.

[21] Allen Ginsberg later dedicated his *Indian Journals* 'to Maurice Frydman who said stop going around looking for gurus'.

its time, but also one that gives a rare sense, from a foreigner, of an India that is in transition. And, in retrospect, it seems to foreshadow the end of the colonial period in the ways it describes the deeply dysfunctional nature of British rule.

Forster says that when he began to write A Passage to India he thought of it as 'a little bridge of sympathy between East and West, but this conception has had to go, my sense of truth forbids anything so comfortable. I think that most Indians, like most English people, are shits.' And many old India hands objected strongly to the portrayal of the British in A Passage to India as — on the whole — nasty, racist shits. While some Indians were unhappy with the rather clown-like rendering of the only important Hindu character in the novel, Professor Godbole, and with the depiction of Dr Aziz, the main Indian protagonist as something of a libertine, who has opinions on the optimal shape of women's breasts (mango-shaped), and on Post-Impressionism.

But Forster is not seeking to please, and mocks most of his characters. Including the small-breasted and awkward Adela Quested, fresh from England, who keeps insisting, 'I want to see the *real* India,' as so many modern tourists do. She ends up in a cave with a real Indian, Aziz, who she imagines has assaulted her. A trial follows at which most of the British characters unthinkingly presume the guilt of Aziz. One of them, a senior police officer, declares that the Mutiny records rather than the Bhagavad Gita are the best guide to understanding Indians, who, he says, are all criminals at heart. And Forster's British characters do have some pretty odd ideas of the country they have settled in. Most of them behave as if they were residents of a small English market town in the late nineteenth century rather than a twentieth-century Indian city. And they tend to discuss Indians as if they were a temporary infestation of insects, rather than the object of some supposed civilising impulse, let alone the rightful rulers of the land over which the British claimed sovereignty.

A Passage to India was Forster's most successful novel, and

was particularly popular in America where it sold thirty thousand copies in its first month. Forster was forty-five, halfway through his long life, and would never write another novel. A diary entry from 1964, written the day before his eighty-sixth birthday, gives a partial explanation, 'I should have been a more famous writer if I had written or rather published more, but sex has prevented the latter.'[22] Sex came late for Forster. He was still a virgin in

his mid-thirties (until a tryst with a British soldier on an Egyptian beach) and he was a nervous neophyte by the time he arrived in India in 1921. He later wrote *The Hill of Devi*, a non-fiction account of his time as secretary to the Maharajah of Dewas Senior, in which he describes his flirtations with several male palace servants. His diaries would later reveal these were more than flirtations — and that he had an affair with a palace barber, encouraged and partly arranged by the Maharajah.[23]

[22] One more Forster novel would be published, but only after his death. *Maurice*, his most openly homosexual novel, was originally written before the First World War, but revised by Forster in the 1930s and 1960s. His fellow novelist Simon Raven said sex was not the only reason that Forster did not write another novel. He was also, Raven says, 'bone idle'.

[23] These revelations, after Forster's death, would lead to a spectacular VS Naipaul outburst in which he referred to Forster as 'a nasty homosexual', who tried to seduce 'garden boys' in India. He also described *A Passage to India* as 'utter rubbish', which suggests Naipaul may have had something larger than an axe to grind with Forster. They were, of course, fellow non-Indians who wandered around India trying to make sense of the place. Naipaul, born in Trinidad, complained that his Indian origins meant that he was no longer distinctive. Forster had no such problem.

Forster recommended his friend Joe Ackerley, who — unlike Forster — was openly homosexual, as private secretary to another minor Maharajah. Ackerley admitted that he knew nothing about India except 'that there had been a mutiny there . . . and that it looked rather like an inverted Matterhorn on the map, pink because we governed it'. His journal *Hindoo Holiday*, published in 1932, was very racy for its time,[24] full of homosexual assignations, lots of dressing up and a wonderfully camp Maharajah — who sits around with Ackerley ogling the young men of the court. For Ackerley, always less self-conscious than Forster, it was all a quite wonderful laugh — and a chance to indulge himself. Princely India,[25] in direct contrast both to inter-war Britain and British-ruled India, had a comparatively relaxed attitude to homosexuality — and this made the tiny, obscure principalities where Forster and Ackerley stayed seem much more welcoming than anywhere closer to home.

[24] The 1952 edition, revised by Ackerley, was racier still, with lots of cuts restored, and full of sexual liaisons involving the Maharajah. The publishers no longer feared libel since the Maharajah was dead. But they still omitted a passage describing the Maharajah forcing the Maharani to have sex with *his* lover, given that it brought into question the paternity of the Maharajah's heir who was still alive. Ackerley's invented name for the state of Chhatarpur was Chhokrapur — meaning 'city of boys'. Ackerley wrote several memoirs including one about his dog, whom he loved above all humans. He later declared that 'I would have immolated myself as a suttee when Queenie died. For no human would I have done such a thing, but by my love for Queenie I would have been irresistibly compelled.' Ackerley died of natural causes in 1967. A 2009 animated film called *Tulip and I* was made about Ackerley's relationship with his dog. The voice of the dog's vet was provided by Isabella Rossellini, the daughter of Roberto Rossellini and Ingrid Bergman (see Chapter 14).

[25] The princely states were also places where showgirls could become princesses. Kapurthala was particularly striking in this way. A Spanish flamenco dancer, Anita Delgado, married the seventh Maharajah, while among the wives of the eighth Maharajah was Alice Villiers, a Kent-born cabaret dancer also known as 'Stella of Mudge'.

Forster returned to India for a final time after the war, in late 1945, to witness some of the dying days of the empire. Once again he wrote about how fast the country was changing, but also about the depth of the personal connection he felt with India. He referred in a radio broadcast to 'the love and respect which comes over me when I have been in India, or thinking about it — an emotion which may have no objective value, still I cling to it, because it proceeds from the heart, and this is an age when the heart speaks too seldom, and too shyly'. He told one friend, 'I have this romantic fantasy that I shall never come back [to Britain]'; and to another he declared that 'I feel like a sponge which has dropped back into an ocean whose existence it had forgotten.'

Forster was very famous by then, a well-known BBC broadcaster, as well as a writer, and he felt much more comfortable with celebrity, and with being fussed over, in India than in Britain. He was flown to India in grand style by the British Council — a two-day journey via France, Sicily and Egypt — to be the star turn at an international writers' conference in the city of Jaipur. He shared a platform with Sarojini Naidu, the poet sent by Gandhi to America during the *Mother India* controversy, and Forster described her in his diary 'as the loveliest of toads'.[26] He gave a talk on 'Literature between the Two World Wars', and was mobbed by autograph hunters. 'If this is fame, I can bear it,' he wrote.

Literary festivals still happen in Jaipur. There's been one every year since 2007 — held each January in a minor palace in the centre of the city. The Jaipur Literature Festival is enormously popular — and free, and one can get to meet writers just as famous as Forster. It's been billed as a place where cultures meet — mainly those of India and the west, but Pakistani authors have

[26] Sarojini Naidu described herself to the journalist CR Mandy as looking like 'a genial frog'. Her best-known soubriquet, 'the nightingale of India', referred to her voice, not her looks.

been conspicuous by their presence in recent times. The festival seems to attract controversy. The 2012 festival was disrupted by the Rushdie affair, in which threats against Salman Rushdie led him to cancel his visit, and prompted several authors to read out, apparently illegally, sections from *The Satanic Verses*. The year before, there had been a spectacular dust-up in the media between the Indian journalist Hartosh Singh Bal who described one of the organisers, the Scottish writer William Dalrymple, as, *inter alia*, 'the pompous arbiter of literary merit in India' and argued, a little tendentiously, that the festival was a success because of a 'romantic association that stretches back to the Raj'. All this did not go down well, and Dalrymple declared his love of India, *à la* Forster, and responded scatologically, describing Bal's piece as racist, and as being 'the literary equivalent of pouring shit through an immigrant's letterbox'. Bal then accused Dalrymple of mocking 'the experience of racism'. The debate generated more heat than light, but still raised complex issues about the legacy of British colonialism and of racism.

Reader, I have now attended two Jaipur Literature Festivals. I went in 2009 at the time of the publication of my first book, about my Delhi wanderings. I had not been to a literature festival before, rather priggishly contending that books were meant for reading, and that meeting my favourite writers could prove a terrible disappointment. I arrived shyly, with trepidation in fact, carrying a copy of my book, with its bright green cover under my arm, as if this was what a new writer did — like a doctor with a shiny new stethoscope, or a judge with a freshly dry-cleaned wig. I circled around, peeping into the tents and the durbar hall where writers were performing, often theatrically, in front of huge audiences. I was due to speak about travel writing as part of a panel with people who were well-known authors. And I couldn't think of much to say about travel writing. Despite years of broadcasting as a journalist, I felt nervous; I had no BBC veil to hide behind. In the end, it was fine. I read out a little bit from my book, and people laughed — and at first I thought they were laughing for some other reason, maybe someone had fallen over, but actually it turned out they were laughing because they thought what I had written was funny.

Afterwards I went outside, and found a quiet place to sit in the shadow of a tree. I was alone again, with my funny green book — that suddenly didn't seem to belong to me any more. And then after five minutes, a young Indian boy in school uniform came up to me. 'Are you a writer?' he asked. I looked at him with surprise, and then a smile. 'Yes,' I said, 'I suppose so,' the words catching in my throat. And he thrust his notepad at me, and asked for my autograph. I complied, and he called his friends over, more than twenty of them, and I began signing each of their notebooks. I could, of course, have signed myself EM Forster or Thomas Macaulay and they wouldn't have minded, or been able to read my scrawl. And then I began to giggle at the absurdity of the situation, and then felt embarrassed that I was letting the boys down by not living up to their expectations of a foreign writer. So I stiffened my upper lip — and studiously got down to the serious business of signing autographs.

A Thirteenth Intermission

DURING THAT FIRST visit to the Jaipur Literature Festival in 2009, there was a special screening, just for 'us' writers, of a new film. A film that had not yet been released in India, that had not yet received eight Oscars and that had not yet been described as 'poverty porn'. *Slumdog Millionaire*, set in modern Mumbai, is a memorable movie, distinguished by some fine child acting and some infantile adult over-acting, superb camerawork, great music and lots of clever references to old Bollywood and Hollywood movies. But it was also a troubling film, and one that would receive a mixed, sometimes chilly, reception in India. Some patriots praised the film, as if its international success was a reflection on the country rather than on the almost entirely Indian cast and largely foreign crew of the film. It was based on a novel, *Q&A*, by an Indian diplomat, a slight acquaintance, who was silently and smilingly diplomatic when I told him that I liked his book more than the film. The name of the lead character was changed from the deliberately multi-faith Ram Mohammad Thomas to Jamal Malik, a Muslim. He was then portrayed as being orphaned when Hindu mobs killed his mother, to the irritation of some Hindu chauvinists. Other amateur critics rightly mocked the accent of the lead actor, a British Asian, who struggled to pronounce his own name in the movie. And the film had an all too predictable series of almost cartoon-like stereotypes as cricket, call centres, Bollywood song-and-dance routines and the Taj Mahal played prominent roles in the film. But it was the name of the film, and its portrayal of poverty, and of cruelty, that drew the sharpest criticism.

Bombay slum dwellers demonstrated outside the house of one of the actors bearing signs saying 'I am not a dog', while slum dwellers in Patna ransacked a cinema in anger at the use

of the word 'slumdog'. Others objected to a shocking scene in which a small boy is blinded so that he can raise more money as a beggar on the streets of Mumbai. But the accusation that the movie was 'poverty porn' drew more extensive debate. The issues are complex and emotive — and partly veiled by a mist of nationalism. It's almost as if it is rude for a foreigner to point out poverty in India, especially if they do so in a way that suggests that they think it is the distinguishing feature of the country. The director of the movie, Danny Boyle, was accused of wallowing in India's poverty, and an early scene, intended as comedy, in which a small boy jumps into an open-air latrine in order to get a film star's autograph, was described as offensive and disrespectful. And undoubtedly, as with Allen Ginsberg,[1] there is often a certain *nostalgie de la boue*, a primeval delight in filth, which marks western accounts of Indian poverty.

[1] See page 362.

There was an attempt in recent years to portray India as 'shining', as a place where poverty was becoming a thing of the past. It was a new nationalist imagining of India in which both foreigners and Indians were complicit. It was almost as if poverty could be spirited away by the power of concentration, or the repeating of a mantra. Many Indians have undoubtedly benefited greatly from high levels of economic growth in recent years. But if one actually lives in India, one has to have quite exceptional powers of self-deception to believe that poverty is a thing of the past. I have occasionally met such people, who do not often stray beyond their air-conditioned homes, cars and offices. A dysfunctional economy often encourages self-deception: for instance, real-estate prices in central Delhi and south Bombay are similar to those in New York or Tokyo. In 2013, India had sixty-four dollar billionaires — that's significantly more than Britain. And it has a space programme and nuclear weapons. Foreigners, even more than Indians, are taken in by such facts, as if they on their own can encapsulate a nation of more than 1.25 billion people — and, in some way, magically cancel out the chronic child malnutrition still seen in several parts of the country. Poverty has not vanished from India.

I have met travellers at the end of a trip to India who said they had a good time, but they just couldn't deal with the poverty. Maybe they were saying that they were troubled by poverty, but I think that form of words actually means something else. They couldn't deal with being faced with poverty, with the reality of this unequal world. I worry that this shows a failure of both sympathy and imagination — as if people don't exist when you can't see them. Perhaps this is a little unfair, and too sweeping; and it may be a positive sign that they were upset, rather than unmoved, by the sight of poverty. But then I remember the words of my former BBC colleague Mark Tully, who when asked how he copes with poverty in India, replied that he doesn't — the poor do.

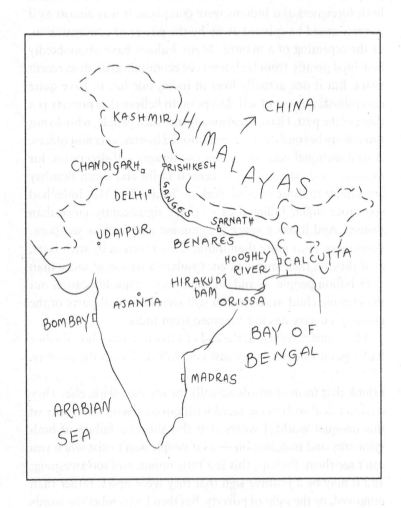

Chapter Fourteen: In which the Author quizzes his neighbours, gets a vague idea of the dimensions of Roberto Rossellini's penis, and watches far too many movies

I HAVE LIVED for the last nine years in three different homes in an area of south Delhi known as Panchsheel Park. It's a friendly, compact place, an upmarket residential sliver of the city, built in the 1960s, sandwiched between the glorious crumbling fourteenth-century ruins of Siri Fort and the slightly less picturesque Outer Ring Road. I love to wander around Panchsheel Park, talking to local people — a few of whom have become friends. And now, almost every evening, I walk from the house where Shireen lives, with our peripatetic children, to the flat, less than ten minutes' walk away, where I have stayed since 2011. And recently I've been in irritating flaneur-quizmaster mode, a pest on the streets, conducting a straw poll of neighbours, finding out if they know what the word *panchsheel* means, and why so many places in Delhi bear that name (at least a dozen localities,

 roads or institutions in the city are called Panchsheel). And the older neighbours smile, sometimes wistfully, and can tell me at least part of the story; while the younger ones tend to look at me blankly.

It's a name and a word (or two, since it is

often spelled '*panch shila*') that can be used to tell many stories, from the most ancient of times to the near future, from the global to the parochial; stories of Indo-European cousinhood, of Buddhist philosophy, and, rather unexpectedly, of the rise of independent Indonesia.[1] But the story that concerns me here relates to the world-vision and eventual sadness of one man, Jawaharlal Nehru, in whose honour 'Panchsheel' became a place-name in modern Delhi. In the 1950s, Nehru came to symbolise India to the outside world in the same way that Gandhi had done in previous decades. For most of that world, especially those in Africa and Asia who were attempting to throw off European colonial rule, that image of Nehru was strongly positive, even heroic. In Europe he was seen, and usually admired, as a great statesman; and for many westerners he cut a familiar figure — a westernised oriental gentleman, the clubbable product of Harrow, Cambridge and the Inner Temple. But he had left some of that behind, taken on the British, and led India through the transition to independence. And, after independence, he refused to let his country be pressured into joining either the American or the Soviet bloc. He became, in many ways, a personification of the Non-Aligned Movement, and *panchsheel* was the Sanskrit name Nehru would give, in 1955, to his 'five principles' of non-alignment: respect,

---

[1] *Panchsheel* is best translated as 'five virtues' or 'five precepts', and is derived from two Sanskrit words, *panch* and *shila*; and *panch*, in turn, comes from the same prehistoric Indo-European root as the Greek πέντε or *pente*, that has filtered through into modern English in such words as 'pentagon' and 'pentathlon'. Tripitaka (aka Xuanzang) talks of the five rules, known in Buddhism as the '*panchsheel*', which all Buddhists are enjoined to respect: no killing, no stealing, no adultery, no lying, no alcohol. It's a word that survived the disappearance of Buddhism in Java to become *pancasila*, the five-point state philosophy of Indonesia under Sukarno. In India, by Nehru's time *panchsheel* was normally translated as five principles.

non-aggression, non-interference, equality and co-existence.[2]

Nehru had first used the word *panchsheel*, and these five principles, verbatim, a year earlier, when India and China agreed on a closer relationship, under what became known in India as the Panchsheel Treaty. That India–China *panchsheel* would go through a number of stages, and had an unhappy ending. But it began well, and included a state visit in 1956 by the Chinese premier Chou En Lai, accompanied by the twenty-one-year-old Dalai Lama, who brought with him a fragment of the skull of my favourite deceased monk, Tripitaka or Xuanzang. It was a gift

[2] As early as 1946, Nehru — in a radio broadcast — said, 'We propose, as far as possible to keep away from the power politics of groups, aligned against one another, which have led in the past to world wars, and which may again lead to disasters on an even vaster scale.' Nehru is usually listed with four other 'fathers of non-alignment': Sukarno of Indonesia, Nasser of Egypt, Nkrumah of Ghana and Tito of Yugoslavia. The movement was formally founded in Belgrade in 1961.

to the Indian people, to celebrate the 2500th birth anniversary
of the Buddha. Three years later, the Dalai Lama fled to India;
and in 1962, India was defeated by China in a short border war.
According to popular mythology, Nehru was a broken man.

Over a period of fourteen months in the mid-1950s, the
Boston-based historian Harold Isaacs[3] interviewed 181 influential
Americans (he calls them 'leadership types') on the subject of
their opinions and prejudices about both China and India; the
first time ever, as far as I can tell, that such a study of national
stereotyping had been carried out.[4] His book, *Scratches on Our
Minds*, gives an in-depth picture of the startlingly wide range
of views, often ill-informed and sometimes racist, sometimes
ludicrously dismissive, and occasionally full of over-the-top
admiration, held by Americans, all of them anonymous, about
the two most populous nations on earth. Nehru, predictably,
and human hair, a little surprisingly, feature widely in the views
of those who have strong feelings about Indians (there are a few
who don't). A 'distinguished' journalist owns up to having been
turned off by all Indians thirty years earlier when a hirsute Sikh
gentleman came to stay and failed to clean the hairs from the
bath-tub. A State Department official told Isaacs that he'd met
Indians who were rather too friendly to his wife simply because
she was blonde, and 'this intensified my prejudice against these
buzzards'. A 'great' intellectual, meanwhile, told Isaacs that 'I

[3] Isaacs had once been a ship-hand, a bellhop, a journalist and was an old
China hand, a former Communist and a friend both of Leon Trotsky and of
Ho Chi Minh, whose room bill at the Shanghai YMCA he helped to pay in
1932. He later became a professor of political science at the Massachusetts
Institute of Technology. He is often mentioned in conspiracy theories about a
CIA plot behind the Kennedy assassination, partly because of his friendship
with Lee Harvey Oswald's cousin, Marilyn Dorothy Murret.

[4] Unfortunately, no such exercise was carried out in other countries. It
would be interesting, for instance, to know the extent to which the British
people were aware of the horrors of Partition or of the role that Indian
forces played in the Second World War.

feel a certain effeminateness about Indians that bothers me . . . I am irritated by Indians as a physical type, and it has to do with color and a certain oiliness.'

Much of what Isaacs records does not reflect terribly well on the American intelligentsia. There are the predictable stereotypes: Maharajahs and rope tricks; tigers and diamonds; snake charmers and the Taj Mahal. Isaacs builds long lists of responses, word associations really, to his promptings about India. Here he gathers those that relate to the supposed servility of Indians: 'like slaves, inert, whipped cur, hopeless . . . starving to death without lifting a finger, beaten down, no spark of gumption.' And then, on poverty and its victims: 'emaciated people, diseases, ribs showing, shriveled bellies, corpses, children with fly-encircled eyes, with swollen stomachs, children dying in the streets, rivers choked with bodies . . . a mass of semi-aboriginal humanity.'

Rudyard Kipling and Katherine Mayo are still, according to Isaacs, the main literary sources of information about India in 1950s' America; and Kipling is quoted on servility and Mayo on poverty. The majority of his interviewees, Isaacs finds, are anti-Indian. He doesn't claim that his sampling methods are scientific, and there are lots of fence-sitters, often with sophisticated views, and a few who are wide-eyed about everything Indian. One female Indophile who had actually visited India told Isaacs, 'I loved them very much, intelligent, stimulating, love to talk, very articulate, love to argue . . . Friendly, wonderful interesting people . . . Indian art is beautiful. Indian religion is a liberal kind of thing, not at all dogmatic.' And Isaacs provides lists of positive words taken from responses concerning Indian attitudes towards religion: 'deep, contemplative, tranquil, profound, full of wisdom about life and its meaning . . . the mystical quality in Indian religion; a great radiant faith; the capacity to depersonalize, to identify with animal life'.

Apart from Kipling and Mayo, the main sources of information about India related to the foreign-policy issues of the day. India under Nehru played a more important role in international diplomacy than at any time before or since; his skills as a speaker and writer were Churchillian, and he served as his own foreign minister during his seventeen years in office. It was on the subject of Nehru and his foreign policy that Isaacs' wiseacres were most divided and most vocal — at a time when the notion of non-alignment was seen as a threat by many in the American political establishment. Once again, there was an extraordinary divergence of views, with some who thought he could walk on water: 'superb mind, able, astute, self-giving, one of the ablest men in the world, one of the few morally incorruptible statesmen'; while others, a slightly larger group, who couldn't stand him: 'he is an arrogant, anti-American, pro-Communist, high class, aristocratic, stiff-necked Hindu'. And flowing from this came a cascade of chippiness directed against Nehru, and also against Indians in general: 'the claim of moral, cultural, spiritual superiority is infuriating; holier than thou; full of offensive moral pretence . . . Indians take a free ride on the absurd western image of the soul-like character of Indians.' It's unsurprising then that there was some slightly spiteful serves-you-right pleasure at India's defeat by China, and a few how-the-mighty-have-fallen jibes at Nehru's request for food and arms from America.

Foreigners were welcome in independent India, as visitors and sometimes as residents, particularly if they showed no obvious inclination to behave as if they ruled the country.[5] Many

[5] One post-independence British settler in India was the evolutionary biologist JBS Haldane. He left Britain partly because, as a socialist, he admired Nehru, and he opposed the British role in the Suez crisis. He also wanted to live somewhere warm ('one does not need,' he said, 'a fire, glass windows or socks'), and where he could observe the stars. He dressed in Indian clothes, became a vegetarian and declared himself a 'Hindu agnostic'. He spoke of his pride in 'being a citizen of India, which is a lot more diverse than Europe, let alone the USA, USSR or China, and thus a possible model for a world organisation'.

thousands of former rulers and their associates — British officials, tea-planters, teachers, journalists and business people — stayed on after independence, though the vast majority left.[6] And Nehru and his government deliberately courted professionals and intellectuals from the rest of the world. So, for instance, dozens of western architects worked in India during the 1950s. These included Le Corbusier, who was already one of the most famous architects in the world and who led the design and building of an entire new Indian city, Chandigarh, and Joseph Stein, who was the architect of several of Delhi's best-known modern buildings, and who would stay and live in India for almost fifty years. According to his son, Stein saw India as 'a new beacon for the world', a place where architects could 'do things they had never done before'. India felt like the new frontier; there was an excitement about a young country where it was possible to experiment with modern ideas about architecture and town planning.[7]

A large number of film-makers also passed through India, and they were also keen to experiment. While the architects were getting excited about a futuristic India, the French director

---

[6] According to Hugh Purcell, author of *After the Raj*, in 1947 about 55,000 British civilians went home. In 1951, there were still 28,000 British residents in India, 14,000 in 1961, and 6500 in 1971. The numbers declined partly through attrition rather than migration. Old India hands remember 6 June 1966, or 6/6/66, when the rupee was devalued, as an apocalyptic day, when the value of their rupee savings was slashed. Lots of Europeans opted to remain in India. Tony Mango would become one of the longest stayers-on — more than sixty years after independence. Those who tended to stay on longest, predictably, were the spouses of Indians.

[7] Le Corbusier was chosen as a replacement for the original architects, Albert Mayer and Maciej Nowicki, after Nowicki was killed in a plane crash while returning to the USA from India. Le Corbusier's team included the British architects Maxwell Fry and Jane Drew. Other foreign architects working in India in the 1950s included the German Otto Koenigsberger who laid out modern Bhubaneswar, and the Austrian Karl Heinz, still remembered in Delhi for his domestic architecture.

Jean Renoir set *The River*, his first colour film, released in 1951, in an unflappably unchanging land which appeared unaffected by modernity or political upheaval. The main characters are all foreign, American or British; most of the actors were amateurs and their performances were almost engagingly wooden. The camerawork, though, was superb, and the setting, on the banks of the Hooghly river, was stunningly lush. The producer of *The River* was a florist from California, who had served in India during the Second World War, and had somehow raised money for the film from Indian princelings. The florist-producer

repeatedly asked Renoir to include elephants and tiger hunts, or even some shots of the Taj Mahal, but Renoir refused — though there are some snake charmers and Indian dancers in the film. Renoir described himself as an 'anti-tourist', who hated famous places and so sat in a Delhi restaurant all day, while the crew visited the Taj Mahal. He did admire India's 'exotic dances and garments', 'the graceful bearing of the women in their saris', but, he said, 'what particularly delighted me as a film-maker were the Indian colours, which afford me a marvellous chance of putting my theories about the use of colour photography into practice'.[8] He came away from India full of fine stories of funeral pyres and

[8] Satyajit Ray and his future cinematographer Subrata Mitra both worked, uncredited, on the film. Renoir tried to get Marlon Brando to play the one-legged hero, Captain John, but ended up with Thomas Breen, who actually only had one leg — making it all a little easier to carry off.

friendship, and about how his visit had cured him of nationalism.

Other directors would show more interest in economic growth and in India's future. India was portrayed, again, as frontier territory, making brave leaps into modernity. In the mid-1950s, the Soviet director Roman Karmen, and the German refugee Paul Zils, made acclaimed documentaries about industrialisation, the latter in a series winningly called 'Great Industries of India'. But it was Roberto Rossellini, the Italian neo-realist director — slightly more famous in the Anglophone world as the husband of Ingrid Bergman — who set out in 1957 to make a more comprehensive cinematic assessment of India, ten years after independence. It was a grand project, born of Rossellini's desire to experiment and his disgust with the film industry in the west, 'where the producers don't want to let me work any more'. He complained that 'What I have to say no longer interests them. This is why I have accepted an offer from India. I've been given carte blanche.'

In 1955, Rossellini had met Nehru in London, and decided he was 'a saint . . . [whose] whole personality breathed spirituality, harmony, and intelligence at peace with the world'.[9] Nehru, in lesser measure, reciprocated — and gave official support to Rossellini's plans to make a film about India. Rossellini told his Iranian researcher, Fareydoun Hoveyda,[10] that he was interested in 'the actual and real India, not in exoticism and western-invented myths such as "spiritualism" and other tourist attractions — "yoga, serpent charmers, rope climbers"'. He said that he intended to debunk all the clichés and platitudes about India. He believed in demystification. But the great neo-realist

[9] He used similar hyperbole about Gandhi whom he met in Rome in 1931, calling him 'the only completely wise human being in our time of history'.

[10] Fareydoun Hoveyda later became Iranian ambassador to the UN. His brother was Amir-Abbas Hoveyda, who was prime minister for twelve years under the Shah of Iran, and was executed in 1979 at the start of the Iranian revolution.

soon told his cameraman that, 'We're going to a wonderland', and, once there, Rossellini became as obsessed with elephants as Megasthenes, more than two thousand years earlier, and many other foreigners in between. He would later suggest that he went to India because he felt his marriage to Ingrid Bergman was over.

Rossellini's trip to India was memorable for several reasons, and not just for the film and television programmes that he made. There were some eccentricities. He carried with him one hundred kilogrammes of spaghetti; he was appalled by the lack of good cheese, and disliked Indian food in general. He later claimed to have lost more weight in India than he did during the Nazi occupation of Rome. Like Jean Renoir, with whom he discussed his trip in advance, he was an anti-tourist. He looked the other way when he passed the Taj Mahal; he refused to get out of the car at the Ajanta caves. He had an argument with a truck driver in south India, who stunned Rossellini by returning his curses in chaste Italian; they embraced each other, and Rossellini learned that the trucker had been with the British army in Italy during the war. He visited a palm reader who told him, ominously, that in India he would find the greatest love of his life. He boasted about the enormous size of his penis to the painter MF Husain, who became one of his closest friends. And he rather mystified people, wherever he went, by informing them that India was like 'a stomach'. He later explained what he meant in an interview with a French journalist, in which he answered the grandiose question, 'What is India?', with 'India is a stomach, an enormous stomach with a huge digestive capacity. That is what India is. It has digested all religions and made them its own . . .'

Rossellini was given extraordinary access. One day in early 1957 he had breakfast with Nehru, who immediately invited him on a tour of north and east India — flying to Hirakud in Orissa to witness the inauguration of what was then the longest dam in the world. And he was in Bihar when the Dalai Lama and Chou En Lai handed over the relics of Tripitaka to Nehru. While he was doing all this he also found time to make a film, and to fall in love. The love affair curtailed the film schedule — and made Rossellini turn to Nehru for help. It all began when Jean Renoir told Rossellini to call on a film-maker, Hari Dasgupta, who had been his assistant on *The River*. They met, and Rossellini and Dasgupta's wife, Sonali, fell — secretly at first — into each other's arms. She moved into his hotel room as the story leaked out to the Indian and international media. Eventually Rossellini left India early, and Nehru intervened to make sure he got his reels of exposed film, and a passport for Sonali.

Rossellini's completed film *India: Matri Bhumi*, or *India: Motherland*, released at Cannes in 1959, is a little unconventional. It does, however, clearly belong to the neo-realist corpus, with its emphasis on the lives and tragedies of the poor. In form, it's a series of dramatised vignettes, connected by documentary accounts of how much, and how little, India is changing. The film is bookended by shots of teeming Bombay; a cow resting, ruminating, in the middle of the street; pedestrians in a variety of costumes and headgear — all, except possibly the cow, unaware of the camera. There's an eighteen-minute sequence about the building of the Hirakud dam, and about one of its workers, a sequence that would later become — separated from the rest of the film — a specimen of neo-realist cinema, much debated on film studies courses. Then there are large segments of the film which are devoted to a strange conflation ('bestial neo-realism' perhaps) of Disney-like anthropomorphism and socialist progressivism — with animals who are given particular human-like qualities, as if they were members of the Indian proletariat. There's a twenty-four-minute sequence involving elephants and a mahout, another starring a monkey orphaned when his human owner dies and who eventually finds his way in the world. And there is, of course, a tiger, with whom a brave cigarette-smoking villager forms a silent *panchsheel* pact of mutual respect and non-interference.

The film achieved some critical success, but it failed commercially. It was not put on general release in France, much to the irritation of Rossellini, who claimed the film was being ignored because it did not resemble 'the prattle of the Indian tourist guide regurgitating things about the country meant for western ears'. Of course, Rossellini himself does go on a lot about elephants[11] and tigers, perhaps in the vain hope that this would make it a less 'difficult' film in the eyes of the distributors and cinema-hall owners. And, to give Rossellini his due, *India: Matri Bhumi* does represent a genuine and unusual attempt to capture something of the variety and nuance of independent India.[12]

No such argument can be made about two movies released by another of Europe's great directors in the same year, 1959. Fritz Lang's *The Tiger of Eschnapur*,[13] and its sequel, *The Indian*

---

[11] Rossellini would later ask that after his death, his ashes be scattered in the elephants' cemetery near where the pachyderm sequence was filmed. There was no such place, and elephants don't have cemeteries.

[12] There is a growing Italian interest in India at this point. The journalist Carlo Levi, best known for *Christ Stopped at Eboli*, was in India at the same time as Rossellini, and wrote a series of thoughtful articles in *La Stampa* that was later published as *Essays on India*. In 1961, the film director Pier Paolo Pasolini and the husband-and-wife novelists Alberto Moravia and Elsa Morante travelled together to India — and both Pasolini and Moravia wrote books about their travels. Pasolini returned in 1968 to make a documentary film about India.

[13] There have been three German films called *The Tiger of Eschnapur*, based on the novel of the same name written by Fritz Lang's second wife, Thea von Harbou. Both Lang and von Harbou were obsessive Indophiles. They collaborated on the screenplay of the first version, which was released in 1921. Their marriage ended after Lang found von Harbou in bed with a man seventeen years her junior — the Indian journalist and Gandhian Ayi Tendulkar, whom she then married. The second version of *The Tiger of Eschnapur*, filmed, like the third, in Udaipur, appeared in 1939. The two films, released in 1959, were combined for Anglophone audiences as *Journey to the Lost City*, and later repackaged as *Fritz Lang's Indian Epic*. Debra Paget is now best remembered for her role as Elvis Presley's wife, Cathy Reno, in his first film, *Love Me Tender*. Her dance scenes in the Fritz Lang films were considered too salacious for late 1950s' America and were edited out.

Tomb, were pure, absurdist fantasy, wonderfully inauthentic, but not everyone seems to have realised this. To this day, Indians will occasionally get asked in Germany whether they have been to Eschnapur, an entirely imaginary place — but one imprinted on the minds of many Germans, because the films have become staples of German Christmas TV schedules. The films were shot amid the palaces and lakes of Udaipur, with a full cast of German actors, and one minor Hollywood starlet — the buxom and diminutive Debra Paget, later a born-again TV preacher — who played a temple dancer called Seetha. Her

most famous scene consists of a near-naked snake dance, her nipples hidden, just about, by two stick-on leaves of silver sequins, and in which she performs a wide range of pelvic floor exercises. The dance, which ends  with the snake being crushed to death, has become a YouTube mainstay — with more than sixteen million hits since it was first posted in 2006.

Paget struggles throughout both films with her patent unfamiliarity with the simple sari, which has a way of trailing along the ground, or getting pushed down beneath her breasts as if it were some post-modern fashion accessory. For the scene where she almost married the nasty Maharajah, she has a special fusion sari with a white bridal train — and wears a tiara and silver stilettos. Her defiantly unIndian appearance, and unIndian dance moves, are explained away by the slightly baffling revelation that she has an Irish father called

Joe.[14] She falls in love with an impetuous German architect called Harold, who saves her life many times over, and who himself survives attempts on his life by a tiger, a crocodile and several human beings. At the end of the film, we are led to believe that they will live happily ever after somewhere as far away from India as possible.

All the characters speak High German, which certainly makes communication easier — but which makes it even harder than usual to suspend one's disbelief. Most of the actors are blacked up to look Indian, but the precise shade of black or brown varies noticeably as the films progress. Every cliché is there. The Indian rope trick is performed by a fakir, whose head is then chopped off, put in a bag and presented to the Maharajah. There are very hungry crocodiles lounging about in every lake or puddle. There's even an army of angry lepers who have been forced to live in an underground cave. There are scores of camels and elephants, and a toothpaste-stealing monkey. And there are tigers almost everywhere — and diamonds and emeralds galore. It's an entertaining romp, really, through almost every imaginable India stereotype.

By the 1950s, film had become the key medium through which ideas and images and stereotypes and fantasies of India were conveyed around the globe. But very few countries had a Renoir or a Rossellini or a Fritz Lang who could serve as the self-appointed (and sometimes Nehru-supported) intermediary. They would rely therefore on home-grown Indian films, with home-grown stereotypes that were often a little closer to the truth. Hindi movies, dubbed or with subtitles, became enormously popular

[14] It is not explained how she came to have an Irish father, and her mother's identity is not referred to. She says she was orphaned, and was adopted by priests. She is also a devotee of a goddess called Shiva, when of course the Hindu god Shiva is male. He does have a half-male half-female form, known as Ardhanarishwara, who is unmentioned in either film.

in the Soviet bloc, and in Greece, Turkey, China and east Africa. The first of these films to do well was the melodramatic *Awara*, 'The Vagabond', in which Raj Kapoor plays the title role. It's a tale, like so many of these tales, of a good man forced by poverty into a life of petty crime. It's hard, sixty years later, and whichever country you come from, not to be moved by *Awara*, and by its final courtroom scenes, in which Raj Kapoor declares, 'I did not inherit crime from my parents. From that gutter full of filth that flows beside my shanty I picked up crime. That gutter is still flowing over. And the virus still breeds. And countless children who live in those slums are falling prey to the virus every day.'

Most of the internationally popular Hindi movies had a socially relevant, leftist flavour that left an impression of India as a land of great poverty and inequality. But they are also remarkable for their use of absurdly contrived coincidences and plotlines, for their song-and-dance sequences, and their end-of-film redemptive optimism. It is hard to overstate their popularity, or that of the mythology that surrounds them, in India, or almost everywhere except in the west. *Awara* was said to be Mao Tse Tung's favourite film, and sometimes even Stalin's. When Raj Kapoor, and his best-known leading lady, Nargis, turned up in Moscow in 1954 (and again in 1956) they were greeted as superstars. *Awara*'s scriptwriter, KA Abbas, also visited the Soviet Union, and found 'bands and orchestras were playing tunes from this film, Russian and Ukrainian and Georgian teenagers were singing the *Awara* songs in chorus and one met people who boasted that they had seen the film twenty or thirty times'. The film was adapted into Turkish as *Avare*, starring the leading actor Sadri Alışık; and was no less popular in Greece where Hindi movies drew enormous audiences in the working class districts of the main cities. Hindi songs were reversioned in Greece, often with entirely new lyrics, in a genre that was called *indoprepi* or Indian-style, and no less than four songs from *Awara* received this treatment.

Nowhere has *Awara* been more enduring than in China. When Vikram Seth visited north-west China in the early 1980s, he heard songs from *Awara* being hummed in the marketplaces, and he charmed the locals with his own rendition of the one song from the film they all know, *Awara Hoon* (I'm a Vagabond). The 2001 feature film *Platform*, directed by Jia Zhangke, has a scene set in small-town China in the early 1980s in which youngsters gather to watch *Awara* at their local cinema. And when in 2007 the Indian journalist Pallavi Aiyar met one of China's most powerful industrialists, he sang to her a 'full-throated, word-perfect rendition' of the same song. Beijing taxi drivers would do the same, and Aiyar was also asked repeatedly whether all Indian women can sing and dance like they do in the movies.[15]

In the spring of 1962, two of the most influential writers of the latter half of the twentieth century arrived in India. They were both born in the Americas; both misfits in the land of their birth; each of them now on a year-long voyage of discovery — a pilgrimage of sorts. But in other ways they could hardly have been more different. The Beat poet Allen Ginsberg — gay, Jewish, a hero of the burgeoning counter-culture; and the young novelist VS Naipaul — obsessive, judgemental, a Trinidadian of Indian descent. Ginsberg would have a wild old time in India, hanging

[15] The 'vagabond' character played by Raj Kapoor in a series of films was openly based on 'The Tramp' character created by Charlie Chaplin. Both of them were cheeky and good-hearted and always dressed in ill-fitting suits (Chaplin's were too large, Kapoor's too small). Raj Kapoor (1924–88) was the most famous member of India's foremost acting family (his father and brother had important roles in *Awara*, and his grandfather played a minor character). And the fifth generation of acting Kapoors still star in Hindi movies, and have intermarried with several other acting families. Raj Kapoor remains a famous actor among eastern Europeans of a certain age. See the IMDB website (imdb.com) on *Awara* for accounts by a Bulgarian and a Romanian who grew up considering that *Awara* was one of the great films of the world, and that Raj Kapoor was one of the greatest actors of all time. VS Naipaul, in Greece in early 1962, notes all the film posters showing Nargis, 'a favourite, I was told, of Greek audiences'.

out happily with burning corpses and sadhus at cremation grounds, while a nauseated Naipaul appears to have spent most of his year in India trying to avoid any encounters with human faecal matter.

It was fairly predictable that Naipaul would not take to his ancestral homeland. As a seventeen-year-old, in 1949, living in Trinidad, he had written to his sister — then studying in Benares — about what he called those 'damned inefficient scheming Indians'. And, he continued, 'I am planning to write a book about these damned people and the wretched country of theirs, exposing their detestable traits.' And this is what he did, with a travelogue called *An Area of Darkness*, published fifteen years after that letter — to much acclaim. It is an angry book, with telling contradictions. In the preface he wrote: 'My India was full of pain. Sixty years or so before my ancestors had made the very long journey to the Caribbean from India . . . So, writer though I was, I wasn't travelling to Forster's India or Kipling's.' But actually Kipling, perhaps crossed with Katherine Mayo (who is not mentioned by Naipaul), is Naipaul's intellectual forebear — on the subject of India, at least. He even declares, towards the end of *An Area of Darkness*, 'It was all there in Kipling, barring the epilogue of the India inheritance. A journey to India was not really necessary. No writer was more honest or accurate.' He had similar views to Kipling's about Indian servility, but Naipaul strikes out on his own in his obsession with the subject of shit. He spends many pages discussing what he primly refers to as defecation, including one remarkable passage that has a Churchillian cadence. 'Indians,' he intones, 'defecate everywhere. They defecate, mostly, beside the railway tracks. But they also defecate on the beaches; they defecate on the river banks; they defecate on the streets; they never look for cover.'

Naipaul admires Gandhi, but his greatest 'failure' was that he didn't reform defecation. And there's much more from this high priest of scatology. All India's woes, from inefficiency to colonialism, can be blamed on what Naipaul terms 'casual defecation', which causes the problem of sanitation, and 'sanitation was linked to caste, caste to callousness, inefficiency and a hopelessly divided country, division to weakness, weakness to foreign rule'. And so shit is at the heart of all that ails Naipaul's India. In a letter to an Indian friend, he declares, after spotting a particularly filthy toilet at Delhi airport, 'I wonder, wonder if the shitting habits of Indians are not the key to all their attitudes. I wonder if the country will be spiritually regenerated if people were only made to adopt the standards of other nations in this business of shitting.' Unsurprisingly, many Indian readers of *An Area of Darkness* were appalled by the book; as they would be by Allen Ginsberg's poetry and diaries, which depict his journey into a malodorous underworld unfamiliar to most English-speaking Indians and visitors.

Allen Ginsberg's purposes in coming to India were very different from Naipaul's. He was certainly more open-minded, some would say too open-minded, and his expectations of India read almost like satire — a manifesto of the first hippie, perhaps. He told an Indian acquaintance in New York, a short while before his departure, that he wanted to touch real poverty, he wanted to find a guru and he wanted to experiment with drugs. And then, as an afterthought, that he wanted a 'gay guru', one whom he could love. He travelled through much of north India and certainly saw lots of poverty, searching for it in many places; and he took a wide range of drugs, some of which were sent by post from the USA. His search for a gay guru was inconclusive.

Ginsberg's *Indian Journals*, eventually published in 1970, contains poems, dreams, notes, drawings and very little traditional narrative. He is an aficionado of the interior monologue, of the hyphen — and barely uses the full stop. There are long, detailed notes about how human corpses burn at the cremation ghats of Calcutta and Benares; diary entries about having oral sex with his travelling companion, and about their various gastro-intestinal illnesses; breathless morphine-influenced dream sequences, and poems about leprous beggars; and a scribbled drawing of the Taj Mahal. There are photographs, some of them of crippled beggars lying in the street with the author standing nearby; others show a disembodied hand and 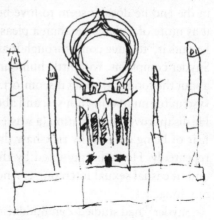 foot spotted near the railway line. Ginsberg's journals are not for the weak of stomach.

The India that Ginsberg loved was largely the one that Naipaul hated — and neither searched hard for other Indias.[16] For much of the sixties and seventies it was a toned-down version of Ginsberg's India that attracted young travellers from around the world. Many of them came not to find India, but to find themselves and other like-minded travellers. Perhaps more typical than Ginsberg was a fellow Beat poet, Gary Snyder, who journeyed through India at the same time, sometimes travelling together with Ginsberg. Snyder was keen on Buddhism, free love, yoga, meditation and peace. And, he would recall forty-five years later, 'we learned to love the street life of India, maddening and illuminating, as we paced along the lanes with our backpacks and tattered maps'. He venerates the music, dance and sculpture of India — and the ancientness and variety of its culture. But

[16] Naipaul returned many times, and his views softened slightly, and he became less obsessed with Indian ways of shitting. Ginsberg also returned, in 1971, during the Bangladesh crisis, with a tape recorder given to him by Bob Dylan. He drove out to see the refugees from Bangladesh and wrote the poem *September on Jessore Road* which begins, 'Millions of babies watching the skies/ Bellies swollen, with big round eyes.'

in the end he doesn't seem to love being in the country, seeing it as more of a challenge than a pleasure, feeling 'very lucky' as he puts it, 'to have come through it all intact'. Unlike Ginsberg, Snyder complains, with little humour, about almost everything: about the food and about discomfort, about the lack of a proper system for numbering houses, and about the lack of toilet paper. He disapproves of cremation (a waste of wood); he is in constant fear of being cheated by rickshaw drivers and loses his temper repeatedly. He is disappointed by the lack of bars, of alcohol and of casual sexual intercourse. And he is rarely impressed by anything.

Snyder[17] had studied Zen Buddhism in Japan, and was on the look-out in India for fellow western practitioners of Buddhism. He is most excited to meet the German-Bolivian monk Lama Govinda, born Ernst Hoffman, living in the hills with his piano-playing Parsi wife; they discuss Tibetan meditation until Allen Ginsberg turns up and switches the subject to hallucinogenic drugs.[18] While at Sarnath, the site of the Buddha's first sermon, he met 'an English Lama' and writer, now known as 'Lobzang Jivaka', by whom he was unimpressed. He was, Snyder records, an Oxford graduate and a former doctor, who was 'sincere' but hadn't, in Snyder's view, really had enough experience of Tibetan meditation to write on

[17] Gary Snyder, from the West Coast, was the model for Japhy Ryder, the main character in Jack Kerouac's *The Dharma Bums*.

[18] Lama Anagarika Govinda was born in the German town of Waldheim in 1898 and encountered Buddhism through the works of Schopenhauer. He later believed he was a reincarnation of the poet Novalis (see page 244). He moved to south Asia in the late 1920s, teaching at Shantiniketan in the 1930s, and became a Tibetan Buddhist. As a German, he was interned by the British during the Second World War, and then moved, with his Parsi wife, to Crank's Ridge near Almora. The area around his home became known as Hippie Hill, and attracted many counter-culture superstars, including the LSD guru Timothy Leary and the psychiatrist RD Laing. The actress Uma Thurman, daughter of a Buddhist scholar, also lived here as a child, and according to locals, Bob Dylan, George Harrison and Cat Stevens all visited Crank's Ridge.

the subject. One feels Snyder might have jumped out of his skin if he had known Lobzang Jivaka's full story.[19]

There's a snarky side to Snyder, who is in competition with the world to prove how good he is at meditation and yoga, and to prove that Buddhism, particularly as practised in Japan, is superior to Hinduism. Snyder is the kind of person for whom the phrase 'irony by-pass' might have been invented — and his self-confidence must have caused some amusement among the Indians he met. He travels with Ginsberg and others to Rishikesh, which was not quite yet a hippie haven, and finds the Shivananda ashram 'vulgar' in tone and style, and full of 'duds'. And these duds, he sneers, don't even know about 'proper meditation posture'. They meet some 'matted haired, ash-smeared Shiva ascetics sitting under trees, quite motionless'. Ginsberg and his boyfriend, Peter, are impressed. Not Snyder, though, who describes how Peter 'would scarcely believe me when I told him how I could sit just as still as those fellers under the tree'.

Less than six years later, four youngish Liverpudlians also travelled to Rishikesh — an occasion that brought this riverside town of temples and ashrams to the attention of the world. The Beatles' interest in India had an unlikely beginning. Their second film, *Help!*, shot in 1965, is a slapstick comedy. It is, arguably, one of the silliest movies of all time, in which the almost plot-less plot revolves around a red jewelled ring worn by Ringo Starr.

---

[19] Snyder, for all his professed wisdom about everything, clearly had no idea of the real identity of Lobzang Jivaka. In fact, 'he' was the world's first modern female-to-male transsexual. She was born Laura Dillon in 1915 into an aristocratic Irish family. She studied, as Snyder correctly points out, at Oxford and practised as a doctor. She self-medicated herself with testosterone, and persuaded surgeons to perform a double mastectomy and then a phalloplasty on her. This involved the creation of a permanently semi-erect penis from a flap of stomach skin and flesh, and took thirteen operations to create. He fled to India when his story was splashed in the British and American press, became a Buddhist monk and died just three months after he met Snyder.

The film opens with preparations for human sacrifice in a temple somewhere in the east. There's a large multi-armed statue of a Kali-like goddess called Kaili, and a camp priest who is referred to either as Swami or Klang. Later, there is even a Beethoven-loving Bengal tiger hiding in the basement of a riverside pub in London. Although neither India nor Hinduism are mentioned in the film, there are plenty of references to the 'mystic east'. And the key scene, in terms of the wider Beatles' story, takes place in an Indian restaurant called 'Rajahama' (there's even a picture of the Taj Mahal on the walls), in which the cook, having performed a headstand, relaxes by lying down on a bed of nails. While the Beatles dine at the Rajahama, there's a group of Indian musicians playing in the background on a low stage; and it was here, during a break in filming, that George Harrison, 'the quiet Beatle', future lover of most things Indian, first picked up a sitar.

Later that year, Harrison played the sitar on the Beatles' hit *Norwegian Wood*, the start of a surge of interest in Indian music and instruments, which saw the sitar and the tambura being widely used by western pop musicians.[20] The Indian sitarist Ravi Shankar soon became Harrison's teacher and friend,[21] and in 1966, invited him and his wife, Pattie Boyd, to India, where they travelled, incognito, as Mr and Mrs Sam Wells, to Bombay, Kashmir and

[20] *Norwegian Wood* was the first commercial western popular music track to feature the sitar, though an earlier unreleased version of the Yardbirds' *Heart Full of Soul* has a sitar riff. The Rolling Stones' *Paint It Black*, released in 1966, also has a sitar riff played by Brian Jones — and the instrument would also be used by the Monkees, and the Kinks; while the tambura was used by the Beatles and Donovan. The latter would join the Beatles in Rishikesh in 1968. George Harrison's son, Dhani, was named after the sixth and seventh notes of the Indian classical scale.

[21] Ravi Shankar was already well known among western musicians, largely because of his collaborations with the classical violinist Yehudi Menuhin and the jazz saxophonist John Coltrane. Coltrane's second son, Ravi, also a saxophonist, was named after Ravi Shankar.

Benares. The visit unshackled Harrison, and provided an escape into anonymity and timelessness: 'It was the first feeling I'd ever had of being liberated from being a Beatle or a number . . . To suddenly find yourself in a place where it feels like 5000 BC is wonderful.' In Benares, he is fascinated, like Ginsberg, by the sadhus — and is aware of the Ginsberg connection. Harrison said:

> [In] the west, holy men would be called vagrants and be arrested, but in a place like India they roam around. They don't have a job, they don't have a Social Security number, they don't even have a name other than collectively — they're called *sannyasis*, and some of them look like Christ. They're really spiritual; and there are also a lot of loonies who look like Allen Ginsberg. That's where he got his whole trip from — with the frizzy hair, and smoking little pipes called chillums, and smoking hashish.

Hashish and other narcotics were part of the attraction of India, though Harrison later said that he got higher on meditation than on drugs. Harrison and the other Beatles would soon, under the influence of Maharishi Mahesh Yogi, at least temporarily forswear drug-taking.[22]

It was the Maharishi — founder of the Transcendental Meditation movement, and already the rest of the world's favourite Indian guru — who brought the Beatles to Rishikesh in 1968. Rishikesh had changed since the Beat poets were there; and the American tobacco heiress Doris Duke had funded the building of the Maharishi's sprawling ashram, officially the

[22] Pattie Boyd went to see the Maharishi at Caxton Hall. She then got George, Paul and John to go to a Maharishi lecture at the Hilton in London. They then all went to Bangor, and so did Ringo, Mick Jagger, Marianne Faithfull and Donovan. Cynthia Lennon was left behind because the security guard thought she was a fan and didn't let her on the train. While they were in Bangor their manager Brian Epstein died in London of a drink-and-drugs overdose.

Academy of Meditation, on forest land close to the banks of the Ganges. It was well guarded and the four Beatles, one Beach Boy, Donovan, and Mia Farrow and her sister, Prudence, were, for most of their stay, able to avoid the press. They were there to meditate, though some took this more seriously than others. Prudence Farrow was particularly obsessive. According to John Lennon, she became 'slightly barmy, meditating too long . . . if she'd been in the west, they would have put her away'. He wrote the song *Dear Prudence* ('won't you come out to play') about the attempts he and George made to get her to stop meditating for a bit. Ringo, on the other hand, was underwhelmed. He couldn't bear the food (he brought a suitcase of Heinz Baked Beans with him), and his wife, Maureen, couldn't stand the flies. They left early. John and George stayed on — but then left, dramatically, after rumours swept round the ashram that the Maharishi had made a pass at Mia Farrow. As they drove back to Delhi, John wrote another song, with the line, 'Maharishi, what have you done/ You made a fool out of everyone.' George persuaded him to change the word 'Maharishi' to 'Sexy Sadie', which became one of the most popular songs on the Beatles' *White Album*.

Each of the Beatles responded differently to their India experiences, though all claim to have enjoyed meditating. Ringo was not really interested and compared Rishikesh to 'a Butlins holiday camp'. Paul remained distant and stoical, rejecting the suggestion that he should give money to India's poor, saying, 'If we just give handouts to people, it'll just stop the problems for a day, or a week.' George remained committed to India, and eventually made his peace with the Maharishi. John didn't, but would still be writing songs about India just before his death in 1980, and he seems to have carried on resenting the Maharishi, seeing him as a manipulative fraud.

There was worldwide media coverage of the Beatles' visit to Rishikesh, though the reasons for the rupture with the Maharishi would only trickle out later. It was one of those essential moments of the late 1960s that have been caught forever in TV news coverage and by photographers. The Beatles, shot through a long-distance lens, walking through the trees in the Maharishi's ashram — George waving to the cameraman, the Maharishi giggling, the forest above Rishikesh, the snapshots of foreigners meditating, of the Beatles with garlands of flowers. These became powerful images of India, just as, through the mediation of the Beatles, the Maharishi and Ravi Shankar became the world's most famous Indians.[23] The image of India as a place of meditative relaxation, of spiritual harmony, caught hold of a generation of western teenagers, and of a few people from elsewhere in the world.

After the Beatles, Rishikesh would be flooded with hippies, drug-takers, Aquarians, beatniks, bohemians, freaks, neo-pagans, wastrels, sandal-wearers, Hare Krishnas, radicals, flower children, groovers and a few semi-respectable backpackers. A few are still there, some of them living in a late-sixties time-warp. But there are others there too. Rishikesh sells itself as the yoga capital of India, and as the best place in the country to go river-rafting. And it still attracts foreigners, more affluent these days, who want a week or two of ashram life, learning meditation or yoga; or the excitement of rafting down the fast-moving stretches of the Ganges, and getting very wet — which has become popular among Delhi-based expats.

The Maharishi left long ago, dying in Holland in 2008, reconciled by then with the surviving Beatles, Paul and Ringo

---

[23] By 1971, Indira Gandhi had joined their ranks. Prime minister since 1966, India's role in the Bangladesh crisis raised her profile internationally. Her opposition to American foreign policy in Asia made her many friends and many enemies. In the transcript of conversations released in 2005, President Richard Nixon referred to her as an 'old witch'. Nixon opined that 'the Pakistanis are straightforward and sometimes extremely stupid. The Indians are more devious, sometimes so smart that we fall for their line.' His national security adviser, Henry Kissinger, referred to Indians as 'bastards' and 'sons-of-bitches'.

— having earlier made his peace with George. His ashram in Rishikesh has long been closed, but was never dismantled. It's possible to sneak in, past a sleepily avaricious guard, and see what's left of the buildings where the Beatles once wandered. Inside, like some ancient ruin, the ashram is being swallowed up by the forests, the roots and branches of trees and bushes wrapping themselves around, and gently crushing, the brick and concrete that had served as a spiritual refuge. The fixtures and fittings have all been stripped out. But there remain strange beehive-shaped meditation cells; huge halls where meditation classes took place; smaller rooms where the guard, who has caught up with me, insists the Beatles once stayed — he names them John, Paul, Ringo. And asks for money. I tell him he has forgotten George, and give him nothing. The place, he insists, is now haunted by the ghosts of foreigners. I ask him to be silent for a moment, as if I might be able to summon up an echo of the past: a strummed guitar, or a plangent 'Om', or an irreverent giggle. But all I can hear is the chirruping of insects, and the tree-rustles and squeals of the monkeys who have taken over the ashram. The Maharishi's Academy of Meditation now belongs to the jungle.

A Fourteenth Intermission

I HAVE NOW lived in Delhi for more than a decade. My teenage daughter, Roxy, who has spent more than half her life here, keeps careful track of such things, reminding me on 5 January 2013 that it was the tenth anniversary of our arrival in Delhi. It is also more than a quarter of a century since I first came to India (and I have spent much more than half of those twenty-five-plus years living here). Prehistoric friends, ancient colleagues and distant family all associate me in a vague way with the country I have moved to. It seems to be the one thing my second cousins and my university acquaintances all know about me. And when I travel back to the UK, I am often informed in a solemn manner, 'You must love India.' And I'm not always quite sure how to respond, and if I even need to. I often just nod, slightly apologetically, and they will jump in with their suggestions of what I must love most in India: the food, the colours, spirituality, history, wildlife, mountains. My current favourite riposte is that India is perfect for anyone who is insatiably curious.

Occasionally I've come across foreigners who cannot abide India. Some just can't deal with the food, and even bring their own instead — like Ringo with his baked beans and Rossellini with his spaghetti.[1] Others simply wilt in the heat, or fall ill the moment they get off the plane, or can't manage the activation of all five of their senses at one time. I feel sorry for such people. It is a hard place to live in if you are obsessed by western ideas of hygiene,[2] and there are e-mail groups for expats living in Delhi

---

[1] I had a colleague who would bring a large case full of digestive biscuits — and she would live off these and hard-boiled eggs for a week.

[2] The hygiene argument is complex. Some Indians see the use of paper to clean one's bottom, and the use of a water-filled tub to clean one's body as examples of a western lack of hygiene. But many Indians were embarrassed

which have carried earnest discussions about which brands of Indian mineral water are safe for bathing babies and tips on how to deal with your maid's body odour. But the antipathy towards India can be more visceral. India can provoke feelings of anger, and even tirades of violent abuse. I'm a passive admirer of the folksy website www.oatmeal.com, run by the American cartoonist and humourist Matthew Inman. In 2008, he wrote a long blog about a brief visit to India. This is how the piece began.

> India is a nightmare. I'm a fairly open-minded guy and I know making generalizations about an entire country based on a tiny bit of experience is probably an unfair judgement, but fuck it — I'm gonna run with it: India is a nightmare. The week I spent in Delhi and Varanassi [sic] gave me enough empirical evidence to confidently label it as a sun-scorched, scabbed asshole of a country which, unless forcibly sent, I will never visit again.

And I have to admit that I, even armed with the entire resources of the Indian Ministry of Tourism and its Incredible India marketing team, would struggle to convince Inman otherwise. He is a lost case. And if his 2500-word article wasn't about the country I have settled in I might even accept that it was a rather impressive, almost admirable, example of sustained biliousness in print. He concludes with a series of curses:

> Being back in Seattle now, thousands of miles from rickshaws, the runs, and all the other sensory rape India had to offer, I feel righteous saying this: F**K you, India. May your rivers run black with the watery stool of a thousand culture-shocked tourists. May your cows get hit by trains. May your cockroaches choke under the waves of phlegm flooding your spit corners. And may I never, ever see you again.

and angry when a senior Indian Commonwealth Games official in 2010 appeared to defend the filth and human excrement found in athletes' rooms by saying westerners had 'different standards of hygiene from Indians'.

Inman is not alone in his views. In 2008, a Chinese-language blog with a series of photographs of bloated human corpses in the Ganges at Varanasi went viral. It begins with the words 'India is the dirtiest country I have ever been to,' and proceeds photographically to provide some very gruesome and vivid evidence. As the blog was shared on other websites, some more stomach-churning pictures were added, and the comments section turned into a tsunami of Indophobia. One reader described Indians as 'simply uncivilized, inhumane! I really think that they have not evolved fully! Savages!' Another said he would rather commit suicide than be sent by his company to work in India.[3]

The travel writer Matt Chua actually called his blog entry 'India . . . Why I won't be visiting again'. The article begins, 'I hate India. Having traveled more than my share of the world, India is the country I liked least, most wanted to leave, and least recommend to others. It is a place that is infinitely more beautiful in photos than reality, frustrated me at every turn, and did little to endear itself.' I'm unable to understand or excuse this kind of reaction. It baffles me, even though I do see that India can, at times, be an uncomfortable place for the faint-hearted, for the weak of stomach, for those who can't deal with uncertainty, for the hygiene-obsessive, or for the control freak. Ultimately, I find myself using a subterfuge or shorthand to explain away their vitriol, and arguing, a little too dismissively perhaps, that such people simply have an allergy to India. And there's nothing much to be done about an allergy, except avoid its cause.

[3] The blogger, a young woman, who goes by a pen name meaning 'pig afraid of fear', had slightly different intentions in writing her piece. She concludes it with an epiphany of sorts, arguing that 'only in the most disgusting of material surroundings, and the basest living conditions can we find the most profound spiritual enlightenment'. This does not seem to have been noticed by those commenting on her piece. The blog was translated into English for the website www.chinashack.com and has attracted an enormous amount of largely adverse criticism from Indian readers.

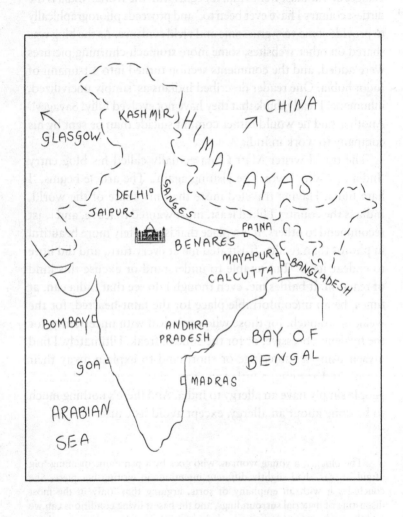

Chapter Fifteen: In which the Author considers the genealogy of Chicken Tikka Masala, confronts his colonial demons, and experiences an epiphany at the hands of a fortune-teller

WHEN I FIRST met my future wife in 1987, I persuaded her to come to my favourite Indian restaurant, the North Kensington Tandoori on Ladbroke Grove. She had never seen such a place. For me, though, it was just a traditional Indian establishment, with maroon flock wallpaper, dingy lighting, background sitar music, crimson napkins and images of the Taj Mahal — and (though I didn't realise this prior to this particular visit) not staffed by Indians, but by Bangladeshis. I was a regular, and would normally order chicken *dhansak* with *naan* bread. I thought this favourite dish of mine was adventurous, going beyond the usual samosas and onion bhajis, or tandoori chicken. As I ordered, Shireen pointed out that it was a little unusual to have *naan* with *dhansak*. And, when she saw the *dhansak* arrive on the table she was appalled. It was a creamy korma-like curry, cooked with pineapple. It bore no meaningful relationship to the *dhansak* I would later eat in my in-laws' Bombay home, a stewed and spiced combination of several types of lentils, with vegetables and meat, which has become the signature dish of the Parsi community. She interrogated the waiter, who turned out to know nothing of 'real' *dhansak*, and had come from the Sylhet region of northern Bangladesh. I tucked in, a little embarrassed. Shireen wasn't very hungry.

Indian cuisine has come a long way in the land of my birth. As a child growing up in London in the 1960s and 70s, I knew little about Indian food. There were a few Indian restaurants, but Chinese and Italian food was far more popular. My mother's only culinary nod towards India was the use of curry powder to liven up left-over meat. I knew what curry was, of course — and occasionally dishes masquerading as curry, often described adjectivally as 'curried', would appear on the menu of a desolate school dinner. There were TV jokes about curry, as a foodstuff that would either burn your throat, or give you the runs, or both; there was even a toe-curlingly awful comedy show called *Curry and Chips*,[1] which was taken off the air after complaints that it was racist. By my late teens, Indian restaurants had become places which young people, such as my friends and I, would frequent when we needed to sober up after a session at the pub. It was known as 'going for an Indian'. We'd compete to see who could eat the spiciest curry, usually a chicken vindaloo, something that, as I discovered years later, bore little resemblance to the real vindaloo,[2] a Portuguese-Goan speciality, cooked with vinegar. And my next Indian culinary adventure was with that other imposter: Anglo-Bangladeshi pineapple chicken *dhansak*. Only when I first travelled to Bombay in 1987 did I discover quite how delicious and extraordinarily varied Indian food can be.

An Indian foodie friend who visited the United Kingdom described Chicken Tikka Masala as a 'mystery of the Occident'. She was bemused by the ubiquity of a dish that sounded Indian

[1] Broadcast in 1969, *Curry and Chips* starred Spike Milligan who 'browned' up as a self-proclaimed Irish Pakistani called Kevin O'Grady. Milligan, who was born in India, teamed up again with his *Curry and Chips* co-star, Eric Sykes, for the pilot of another excruciatingly embarrassing comedy, called *Jewel in the Crown*, about an Indian restaurant of that name. It was deemed too racist ever to be broadcast; though scenes from it, as from *Curry and Chips*, can be viewed on YouTube.

[2] Vindaloo comes from the Portuguese *vinha d'alhos*, literally wine of garlic. In practice, *vinha d'alhos* in Portuguese cuisine is a marinade of wine vinegar, garlic and spices.

— but that was, in her view, quite blasphemously bland, and unknown in her homeland. Chicken Tikka Masala is so much more than just the most popular item of food at Indian restaurants in Britain. It is also a best-selling supermarket instant meal, a flavour of crisps, a kind of pasta sauce, a pizza topping and a sandwich filling. And it had also become, depending on who you listen to, either a British icon or the pride of Glasgow, and in either case a symbol of modern multiculturalism.

In 2009, a motion, signed by nineteen members of Parliament, fifteen of them from Scotland, was submitted for debate to the House of Commons:

> That this House records its appreciation of the culinary masterpiece that is Chicken Tikka Masala; notes that it is Britain's most popular curry; recognises that it was invented in the great City of Glasgow by Ali Ahmed Aslam, proprietor of the Shish Mahal restaurant in Glasgow's West End in the seventies; further notes that Glasgow is three times winner of the curry capital of Britain award; and supports the campaign for Glasgow to be given EU Protected Designation of Origin of this most popular dish.

The motion was not taken up for debate, and Chicken Tikka Masala was not given the protected status that has been accorded to Parma Ham or Cornish Clotted Cream. It needs no protection, and even if it was first concocted in Glasgow, it had already been raised informally to the status of Britain's national dish. That was an honour accorded by Robin Cook, the then foreign secretary, in a 2001 speech about the glories of British multiculturalism, designed to irritate conservative xenophobes, and devotees of either roast beef and Yorkshire pudding, or fish and chips. Cook proclaimed that:

> Chicken Tikka Masala is now a true British national dish, not only because it is the most popular, but because it is a perfect illustration of the way Britain absorbs and adapts external influences. Chicken Tikka is an Indian dish. The Masala sauce was added to satisfy the desire of British people to have their meat served in gravy.

The history of Chicken Tikka Masala is disputed and the subject of much modern mythology, but the dish probably didn't exist before the 1970s. The most popular tale, particularly in Scotland, is of a Pakistani chef at an 'Indian' restaurant in Glasgow heating up a tin of Campbell's Cream of Tomato Soup after a Scottish customer had complained about the lack of gravy on his chicken tikka.[3] It is possible to get more authentic Indian cuisine in Britain these days, though the vast majority of the nine-thousand-plus Indian restaurants in Britain serve Chicken Tikka Masala, and a similarly high percentage have cooks who came

---

[3] When news of the parliamentary motion referring to the Glaswegian origins of the dish reached India, several chefs and cookery experts argued that Chicken Tikka Masala actually dated back to the Mughal period — and was of Indian origin. One can only think these experts have never tried the tomato soup version of the dish. A survey by the *Real Curry Restaurant Guide* of forty-eight different British Chicken Tikka Masalas found that the only common ingredient was chicken. The fame of Chicken Tikka Masala has travelled far. The Hollywood actor Will Smith on visiting India for the first time said he was looking forward to tasting 'authentic' Chicken Tikka Masala. Tikka Masala (without the chicken) has also become a description of a way of cooking. There's even a restaurant run by an Englishman in Ecuador which serves Guinea Pig Tikka Masala.

not from India but from Bangladesh and Pakistan.[4]

In the 1980s, the British comedian Rowan Atkinson, the future Mr Bean, performed a solo sketch, known officially as *Guys After the Game*, but which would achieve YouTube fame as *The Indian Waiter*. Atkinson played the waiter, with a wretched Indian accent and a glitzy saffron tunic. In the sketch, Atkinson conjures up, in our minds' eyes, nine drunken Englishmen, who all try to sit down at a table for two. The waiter is overbearingly polite, of course, and informs them unctuously that the table is already booked. As they move to a larger table, one of them falls over, and Atkinson apologises for the floor, which he describes, with only the slightest of sneers, as 'deceptively flat'. He saves one of them from drowning in a pitcher of beer, and controls his irritation when forced to agree that seekh kebabs look like 'two little turds', and that shammi kebabs look like a cow-pat, only, he adds with a lip-curl, 'in smaller portions'. They do eventually manage to order a meal — four meat curries, one Bombay duck, four rice, four shammi kebabs, and a hot dog.

It's a performance which still makes me laugh, despite that appalling accent, both for the way in which Atkinson challenges the acceptable loutishness of the period — and for the way it tells part of the history of Indian food in Britain. It is a history that is important here because of the way that the adjective Indian came, by the 1980s, to designate, in Britain at least, not so much

[4] According to a 2006 survey by the British Hospitality Association, Chicken Tikka Masala was twice as popular as the two runners-up, Chicken Jalfrezi and Chicken Korma, followed closely by Lamb Madras. The original Chicken Tikka, without the gravy, was in eighth place.

a country or a people, but a food.[5] It was delightfully reversed in the new millennium when the British Asian comedy team behind the TV programme *Goodness, Gracious Me* performed a sketch called 'Going for an English', which involved their asking the waiter — whose name, James, they repeatedly mispronounced — for the blandest item on the menu, and then ordering twenty-four plates of chips.

The history of Indian food in Britain goes back a long way. Curry first appeared on British menus in the eighteenth century, and the first Indian restaurant, the Hindostanee Coffee House,[6] was opened by a man from Patna in London in 1810 (it closed a year later), while mulligatawny soup and kedgeree were adulterated imperial versions of simple Indian cuisine.[7] But

---

[5] Just as all south Asian food became Indian, among a smaller number of British xenophobes and racists, 'Paki' was used to describe all south Asians. To the dismay of many of those who fitted more refined stereotypes — the Hindu Gujarati corner-shop owner, the Sri Lankan Tamil petrol-pump operator, the Sikh bus driver and the Bangladeshi garment worker — they were all clubbed together as Pakis. Britain, of course, was not unique in this. Four days after the 9/11 attacks, an American Sikh was shot dead in Arizona by a gunman who wanted to kill some 'towel-heads'. There were a number of other incidents in subsequent years in which Sikhs were attacked by those who mistook them, presumably because of their turbans, for followers of Osama bin Laden.

[6] The Hindostanee Coffee House was set up by Sheikh Dean Mahomet from Patna, who then moved to Brighton with his English wife, Jane, and set up Mahomet's 'massage baths'. He introduced the notion of a 'shampoo' which then meant a massage, from the Hindi verb *champna* meaning to press. It first took on its modern meaning in the 1860s. Mahomet's grandsons included an Anglican vicar and a scientist who helped develop the first non-invasive blood pressure monitor. Veeraswamy's, the oldest surviving Indian restaurant in Britain, didn't open until 1926.

[7] Mulligatawny soup is usually made from chicken, rice and curry powder — but the name means pepper water in Tamil, and describes something closer to the tamarind-based broth known by lovers of Tamil food as *rasam*. Kedgeree made of fish, rice, eggs and a bit of curry powder began life as *kitchri*, a mix of rice and lentils usually served to the very young or the sick.

380

there was then something of a post-independence caesura. The great Indian culinary invasion of the 1970s and 80s should be seen rather differently — not as an imperial left-over, but as an unanticipated by-product of migration.

The key figures in the growth of the Indian food industry in Britain were not exactly from India. They were entrepreneurs of south Asian origin, pre-independence India certainly, but they had largely come to Britain from Bangladesh, Pakistan and east Africa — often fleeing from poverty and political turmoil. The restaurant business was an opportunity, even though most of them served food that bore little relation to what they would eat at home. The great British customer wasn't to know this — or, honestly, wasn't really interested. Indian restaurants, in the south of England, particularly London, tended to be run by Bangladeshis, while as one headed further north, the more likely they were to be run by people of Pakistani origin. To this day, about two-thirds of all Indian restaurants in Britain are run by people of Bangladeshi origin, mainly from the hills of Sylhet, where the traditional food is fish and rice — not the creamy north Indian hybrid for which their restaurants are best known.

There are many other examples of popular Indian fusion food from around the world (as well as a light sprinkling of Indian restaurants in all the world's great cities). In Germany there was the *currywurst*, or a sausage spiced with curry powder, while in Japan *karee pan* is a deep-fried doughnut-like bread roll with a curry filling; South Africa's *bunny chow* is a hollowed-out loaf of bread stuffed with curry. But these were almost always seen as extensions of the indigenous cuisine. In Britain, Indian food, despite its actual hybrid nature, was seen as a distinct cuisine from a foreign country, and one that was usually linked to, with cavalier imprecision, that part of the south Asian diaspora that came from India. This was a matter of some embarrassment to many visiting and migrant Indians. With food, as with television programmes, the British response to modern India took a peculiar, post-colonial form.

I hate *Top Gear*. For those who haven't been exposed to its dubious charms, *Top Gear* is a long-running BBC TV series about cars, which for me has come to epitomise the worst of British laddishness. It has three presenters, all white middle-aged men with paunches, who tease each other a lot, and use desperately contrived anthropomorphic mixed metaphors to describe new and ancient automobiles. When a car is first encountered it is usually discussed as a woman whose vital statistics and curves are assessed with a knowing sneer and a pat on the back fender. But the moment one of them gets into a car, and starts driving, it is somehow magically transformed into an ersatz penis. *Top Gear* is a simple and immensely successful programme, with an audience, I am assured, that is not entirely male.[8]

In 2011, the *Top Gear* team came to India, not long after I had rejoined the BBC, and I soon found myself in the uncomfortable position of being expected to defend one of the daftest programmes I have ever seen. The *Top Gear* trio pretended to be on a trade mission trying to sell British lawnmowers, trouser presses and hair products to the Indian public. And they were even waved off in Downing Street by the real-life British Prime Minister David Cameron, a close friend of the main presenter, Jeremy Clarkson. When they reached India they drove around Bombay, Jaipur, Delhi and into the Himalayas in some dodgy old British cars — a Rolls-Royce, a Jaguar and a Mini[9] — and complained a lot about the roads, and about Indian driving

[8] One faintly plausible reason for my hatred of *Top Gear* is that I don't drive. Friends who are fans of the programme have accused me of lacking in humour, and of having a sense of inferiority in relation to the stars of *Top Gear* because I haven't even passed a driving test.

[9] None of these companies is now British owned. Rolls-Royce and Mini are now part of the German company BMW, while Jaguar is part of the India-based Tata Group.

etiquette. It was a silly programme, and it was meant to be silly — but it also came across as rather patronising. Clarkson has a toilet seat fixed on the rear of his Jaguar, explaining that 'everyone who comes here gets the trots'; and a little later, drenched in perspiration, he declaims, 'In India you don't need your penis, because you drink and drink, and it just comes out as sweat.' All of this, and more, did not endear *Top Gear* to the Indian High Commission in London, which made a formal complaint to the BBC's director-general, saying, 'The programme was replete with cheap jibes, tasteless humour and lacked cultural sensitivity. This is not what we expect from the BBC.' Ominously, they said the BBC was in breach of an agreement under which permission had been given to film in India. A British Labour MP of Indian origin demanded an apology.

The BBC did not apologise, and went ahead with plans to re-broadcast the programme to Indian audiences on the BBC international entertainment channel. There was much talk of repercussions against the BBC, and even of demonstrations outside the BBC office of which I was the boss. I doubled the number of watchmen on duty, advised the local police about possible protests and asked for the BBC's name to be taken down from the front of the building. We waited. A certain siege mentality crept in, for which I take full and slightly embarrassed responsibility. The day of broadcast came. And it went. Nothing transpired; there was no diplomatic démarche, no demonstration. Nothing. No one in India seemed to care.

I was perhaps burdened by a sense of history. In 1970 the BBC was thrown out of India after a row about a film on Calcutta made by the French director Louis Malle. And there were other unforgotten events: in 1975 the BBC was forced to leave the country because it refused to accept censorship by the government; in 1984 the Delhi office was attacked by demonstrators protesting against a BBC radio interview with a Sikh separatist; in 1995 a cameraman was killed by a letter bomb in the BBC's Kashmir office. I think this is why I was so nervous about *Top Gear*.

The BBC's post-imperial relationship with India has been a complex one, and the 'Louis Malle affair' has to be seen in that context. The film itself certainly did linger on poverty, on the leprous, the deformed, the dying and the dead. It made the rich, as in a deliciously wicked scene at the Royal Calcutta Golf Club, look like heartless buffoons. The film was described by the Indian High Commission as 'derogatory to, and highly biased against India'. But the fault, if there was a fault, was only partially with the BBC, which had neither made nor commissioned the film. And by the time it was broadcast on the BBC it had already been shown on TV channels in the rest of Europe, and been nominated for the top prize at the Cannes Film Festival.[10] The row between the BBC and the Indian government quickly escalated. The BBC would neither apologise, nor would it promise not to show more of Louis Malle's programmes about India. And after a stand-up argument between a government official and the BBC correspondent (who was 'extremely abrasive' according to one of his own colleagues) it was decided to eject the BBC from India. An MP from the ruling Congress Party said the BBC was 'preaching a new kind of imperialism'.

Indian prickliness and the arrogance of foreign journalists in India have been constant themes of international coverage of the country over the last fifty years. But the BBC, on being allowed to return to India in 1972, made an inspired and unlikely choice as its new correspondent. Mark Tully was an India-born former personnel officer, with little journalistic experience, who was then working in a junior managerial role for the BBC in London. By

[10] Won by *If . . .* , a British movie that had nothing to do with the Kipling poem of the same name, but which was directed by the Bangalore-born Lindsay Anderson, who worked in military intelligence during the Second World War at the Wireless Experimental Centre in Delhi, the code-breaking India-based offshoot of Bletchley Park.

the 1990s, Tully would be India's best-known resident foreigner, and the most celebrated journalist in the country. He played a key role in transforming the BBC in India from being a relic of empire to being the country's most trusted provider of news. It would be hard to accuse Tully of cultural insensitivity. Indeed, for some in the BBC in the UK, and for other Delhi-based foreign correspondents, he had gone native, and was too close to the story. I worked in the shadow of Tully in the early 1990s, at the Delhi bureau of the BBC, and he became, after Tony Mango, the second of my foreign guides to India. I admired the manner in which he withheld early judgement, and the way he saw depth and complexity where other foreign correspondents saw shallow stereotypes and certainty. Tully, unlike many of the others, didn't seem to seek out stories that would reinforce existing foreign ideas about the country.

Tully was one of the interviewers for the 1974 BBC radio series, *Plain Tales from the Raj*, a title that evoked Kipling.[11] And it's possible to see the series as a precursor of what Salman Rushdie later christened the Raj Revival, in which, during the 1980s, India became a land of nostalgia, and, more controversially, a land of past glory — all part of a peculiarly British imagining of India. On one level, *Plain Tales from the Raj* was a more-than-worthy oral history project — a commendable attempt to capture, before they died, the memories of those British old enough to remember living as adults in Britain's Indian empire. Their accounts were often very touching and funny. But it was also uncomfortably nostalgic, and largely unreflective; a paean to a lost world, full of wondrous old things — bearers, chummeries and dacoits; balls, clubs and durbars. A world in which shouting at servants was normal, and where ayahs were told *not* to speak English so that their wards would not pick up their 'chee-chee' accents.

[11] Rudyard Kipling's first collection of short stories, *Plain Tales from the Hills*, was published in 1888, when Kipling was twenty-two years old.

There were occasional notes of regret — for the arrogance of the young British administrator, over the way Indians were excluded from most of their clubs; and there was one repentant British officer who had an Indian passenger thrown out of his train carriage — simply because he was an Indian. But part of my discomfort comes from the fact that no Indian voices are heard in the programme, nor are those of foreigners who weren't British — the Tony Mangoes of India. The producers would probably argue that this was the purpose of the programme — to record the voices and memories of a particular group, and it is true that this archive (the interviewees must all now be dead or well over a hundred years old) is of genuine historical importance. However, the overall tone of the interviewees is disconcertingly upbeat, sometimes self-justifying and boorish — as if it were the most natural thing in the world that a small nation off the north-west coast of Europe should rule a much larger country several thousand miles away. It's easy to understand why the series was so popular. The year 1974 was a hard one for Britain, with minority governments, a crippling miners' strike and the three-day week — and *Plain Tales from the Raj* captures what was seen by many as a golden age of British greatness.[12]

[12] The programme probably touched an even deeper vein of nostalgia for Victorian Britain. One interviewee, the historian and colonial administrator Philip Mason, described the life of the British in India as a 'fragment of the Victorian world — stranded in time, like a lost world'. The first radio series spawned a second one, and a book and, arguably, a growing interest in what was now firmly entrenched in the British mind as 'the Raj' — though the phrase had rarely been used in the colonial period.

Also broadcast in 1974 were the first episodes of *It Ain't Half Hot Mum*, an often puerile, and extremely popular long-running BBC television comedy set in a British army base in India, but largely filmed in the Home Counties. I was a teenage devotee of the programme — which came across to me as testament to a peculiarly British combination of incompetence and pluckiness. That teenage devotion became a matter of considerable embarrassment recently, when I watched some episodes again. The programme has not aged well. The BBC has chosen not to repeat the show

A full-blown Raj Revival took place in Britain in the 1980s,[13] and took the form of a number of popular TV shows or films set in India during the colonial period — and firmly established India, at least in the Anglophone world, as a haven of colonial nostalgia. These included *Gandhi*, the British film version of *A Passage to India* and two long-running TV series — *The Jewel in the Crown* and *The Far Pavilions*, both based on novels by English writers who had lived in colonial India.[14] David Lean, the director of *A Passage to India*, deliberately set out to make his adaptation of Forster's novel more friendly to the Raj. 'Forster was a bit anti-English, anti-Raj, and so . . . I intend to keep the balance more. I don't believe all the English were a lot of idiots. Forster rather made them so'; and he changed key parts of the storyline and the characterisation to make the British in India seem more likeable.

There were some very unpleasant British characters in both *The Jewel in the Crown* and *The Far Pavilions*, but overall it was possible to feel after watching either series that British rule in India wasn't so bad after all — and that the Raj might have

in recent times, apparently because of its insensitive or outdated attitude towards race and homosexuality. The sergeant major repeatedly refers to the soldiers as 'a bunch of poofs', while the only significant Indian character, an obsequious servant called Rangi Ram, is played by a white British actor, born in India, whose face was blacked up and who puts on a very silly Indian accent.

[13] An only slightly less romanticised vision of India was conveyed by the Festival of India held over a period of eight months in the UK in 1982. Indira Gandhi was there for the opening and closing of the festival, which was organised by the Indian government. Similar festivals were then organised in the USA, the Soviet Union and in France.

[14] Other films from this period that are at least partly set in India include the thirteenth James Bond film, *Octopussy*, with several Udaipur scenes, and *Indiana Jones and the Temple of Doom* (the second in that series), which was actually filmed in Sri Lanka, and in which Hindus are depicted as eaters of, *inter alia*, monkey brains. The far more thoughtful Merchant-Ivory film *Heat and Dust* also dates from this period.

The Far Pavilions

Ben Cross · Amy Irving

Omar Sharif · Sir John Gielgud · Christopher Lee · Rossano Brazzi

endured if it hadn't been for a few idiots on either side. Both stories majored on love stories that, just about, crossed the ethnic divide — two minor testaments to miscegenation. The British heroine of *The Jewel in the Crown* falls for an Indian who has been brought up in Britain, while the star-crossed lovers of *The Far Pavilions* are an English boy who grew up thinking he was an Indian, and an Indian princess who was quarter-Russian. And both series were adaptations of derivative novels: *The Jewel in the Crown* is best seen as a very readable if slightly flatulent tribute to *A Passage to India*, set in the years immediately before independence. Its author, Paul Scott — and the writers of the TV series — at least added some nuance to their characterisation of India and its people, even if none of the Indian characters are well developed.

The Far Pavilions, meanwhile, borrows its central story, its location and its period from *Kim*, but is written as an epic romance. For Salman Rushdie, the TV version of *The Far Pavilions* was 'a blackface minstrel show' which was both 'the purest bilge' and 'drivel' (the original novel got away lightly, as 'fibrous garbage'). I find it hard not to agree with Rushdie, but there is also no denying the immense popularity of both the TV series and the novel. However, *The Far Pavilions* deserves to be set apart from the other products of the Raj Revival for different reasons. *The Far Pavilions* signalled the return of Romantic fantasy to the Anglophone view of India — and could do so fluently because it was set in a period (the 1860s and 70s) that was, by the 1980s, outside the range of living memory. It was a post-Mutiny tale, in which the anxieties of that period no longer preyed on the minds of its audiences. In its flagrant disregard of historical accuracy, indeed any sort of accuracy, it defaults to an older model of imagining India. It aligns itself instead in its fantasies and absurdities, its stereotypes and motifs, with earlier continental European ideas of India.[15] A killer snake is dispatched even before the opening titles are over. It is full of hairy tribesmen and dancing girls and elephant processions; the two lovers are played by western actors who can't pronounce their own Indian names, and there are lots of amusingly evil Indians with large false moustaches. And, in that favourite nineteenth-century trope, the heroine is rescued by a white man from the funeral pyre of her husband. *The Far Pavilions* would later become a West End musical, and something of its spirit — far more so than with the other products of the Raj Revival — lives on in a variety of neo-Romantic western fantasies about India.

The 1970s were the heyday of the overland journey from Europe to the subcontinent. India was now a very long bus-ride away, a key destination on the hippie trail. There was nothing new to overlanding — this was how Alexander the Great, Ibn Battuta and Tom Coryate had all travelled eastwards, but in more recent centuries, the boat and then the airplane would become the more normal means of getting to India. Travelling by land, however, became a rite of passage for those who identified with the counter-culture — a wide range of people who wanted to take drugs, have adventures, seek spiritual solace, escape western materialism, or follow in the footsteps of the Beatles or Allen Ginsberg.[16] Many of the young visitors of the 1970s

---

[15] Ideas and imagery of the kind witnessed in the novels of Jules Verne, the films of Fritz Lang, or the novel and TV series of Salgari's *Sandokan*.

[16] The Beatles flew to India and Allen Ginsberg came by boat. The more affluent or less adventurous visitors continued to come by air — and in 1979 the Iranian revolution, and then the Soviet invasion of Afghanistan, meant that it was almost impossible to travel from Europe to India overland.

weren't terribly interested in India — their purpose was the achievement of getting there, and spending time with their fellow travellers. And on the whole their responses to India were not exactly original: they were preoccupied with poverty, their own health and surviving on very little money. There were a few who decamped to Goa, or the Himalayas, and stayed on. And some were so taken with Hindu spirituality that it became their life's calling, while for others it was a youthful dalliance. This was a time when *karma* and *mantra* and *guru* and *nirvana* became everyday words among the young.

Gita Mehta's *Karma Cola* caught the spirit of those times with her portrayal of bright-eyed, foolish foreigners who wander around India soaking up all that seems spiritual. She asks a Californian what he is doing in India. 'I am being,' he responds. She finds a Frenchwoman living under a tree in the jungle behind Delhi University — with a child fathered by a Hindu holy man. There is a Scandinavian woman who does nothing but hum for months on end, and there are western women in Goa who breast-feed monkeys. An American in Benares wants advice on how to control his sexual feelings and, as part of his lesson, is ejaculated on by a naked sadhu. An Englishman travels to Andhra Pradesh to find a holy man whose urine is like rose water — and is amazed to find that the would-be rose water smells and tastes like urine. And there are hippies who beg outside temples for money to buy drugs. Mehta's stories come across like ancient tall tales of India, but told, this time, of modern westerners.

In the early 1970s, a hill-dwelling Hindu holy man, Neem Karoli Baba, often referred to as Maharaj-ji, briefly replaced the Maharishi as the most-favoured guru among visiting and resident foreigners. He was particularly popular with Americans. Among his earliest western devotees was an eighteen-year-old blond surfer from Laguna Beach, California, called Michael Riggs, who, to this day, is a spiritual teacher known as Bhagavan Dass. In 1967, Riggs introduced Richard Alpert, a Harvard professor and LSD experimenter, to Maharaj-ji. Alpert was dubious, but Maharaj-ji was able to tell him the disease his mother died of, and to ingest LSD without any obvious effect. Alpert[17] decided he had found his guru, who gave him the name Ram Dass — and became the author of the remarkably eclectic *Be Here Now*, a best-seller of the 1970s. It begins as an autobiographical New Age paean to LSD and magic mushrooms, and describes Alpert's life-changing conversations with Maharaj-ji. The next part of the book consists of more than a hundred pages of brown paper, covered in words, and symbols and drawing in black ink. There is much meandering talk of 'cosmic consciousness', 'oceans of existence', 'freedom from attachment', and images of Hindu gods, of the Buddha, of Jesus and, of course, of Maharaj-ji. The final section called 'Cookbook for a Sacred Life' is full of tips, quotes, meditative techniques, yoga positions and advice on how to set up a spiritual community in the USA. It was an enormously influential book, said to have sold two million copies — and is still in print.

One of the earliest fans of *Be Here Now* was a long-haired, fruitarian college drop-out called Steve Jobs. He later said, 'It was profound. It transformed me and many of my friends.' And in 1974, he gave up his post as a junior technician at the video game company Atari — and headed to India where he immediately contracted both dysentery and scabies. His primary purpose in travelling to India was to meet Maharaj-ji, but when he reached his village in the foothills of the Himalayas, he discovered that the guru had died the previous autumn. He drifted around north India, hanging out with holy men, and occasionally losing his

[17] Alpert remains a spiritual teacher and lives in Hawaii. The ageless character Richard Alpert in the TV series *Lost*, adored by my children, is named after him. Alpert's character and role in the plot is, in turn, partly based on the Panchen Lama. The series is full of references to Hindu and Buddhist ideas and terminology (the Dharma initiative, the *dharmachakra* symbol, the concept of *karma* and the greeting *namaste*).

cool. He could never bear being ripped off. When Jobs returned to America, his hippie hair had all been shaved off, he was wearing Indian clothes — and his family failed to recognise him at the airport. Towards the end of his life, as he was dying of pancreatic cancer, Jobs reflected on his seven months in India, seeing them as having a 'big impact on my work'. He told his biographer that:

Coming back to America was, for me, much more of a cultural shock than going to India. The people in the Indian countryside don't use their intellect like we do, they use their intuition instead, and their intuition is far more developed than in the rest of the world. Intuition is a very powerful thing, more powerful than intellect, in my opinion.

Always a master of the sweeping generalisation, Jobs says that Indian villagers had never learned to think rationally, and that 'they learned something else, which is in some ways just as valuable but in other ways is not — that's the power of intuition and experiential wisdom'. That binary identification of the east with intuition and the west with rationality goes back to ancient times. It continues as a key motif of western views of eastern thought-processes. At least, small mercies, Jobs saw value and insight in what he described as the irrationality of the east, not ignorance or savagery — as others had done before him.

In the mid-1960s, two spiritually-minded Bengali gentlemen travelled, quite separately, from India to New York City. They set up movements, often referred to as cults, which helped give a new form to the Hindu-inspired American spiritual tradition that dated back intellectually to Emerson and Thoreau, and organisationally, to those early devotees of Swami Vivekananda at the very end of the nineteenth century. The 1970s and 80s were a time of cults, not all Hindu-inspired, but the preponderance of Indian leaders of New Age movements, and the distinctiveness of their dress code and their lifestyle, helped cement an American idea of India as a land of gurus and, a little later, as a land of yoga practitioners.

Sri Chinmoy was a supreme self-publicist, who worked briefly as a clerk at the Indian consulate in New York, before setting up a community of devotees in Queens. His was not the largest of the many US-based movements inspired by Indian belief systems, but it was the one that made the greatest efforts to nurture its relationship with the powerful and the famous. One of the key tasks of Sri Chinmoy's innermost circle of devotees was to elicit compliments about him from well-known people. At his memorial service in 2008, statements of condolence from Nelson Mandela, Bill Clinton and Mikhail Gorbachev were read out; while the musicians John McLaughlin, Carlos Santana and Roberta Flack had all been followers. Sri Chinmoy claimed to have written 1500 books, 115,000 poems[18] and 20,000 songs, and took a particular delight in breaking records. He was a prodigious public weightlifter, and used a mechanical device to convince people that he could power-lift more than anyone else

[18] An example of Sri Chinmoy's poetry: 'India is not just a place/ India is not just a people/ India is the celestial music,/ And inside that music/ Anybody from any corner of the globe/ Can find the real significance of life.'

ever, often using just one arm. There's a famous picture of him supposedly lifting more than seven thousand pounds, which would, if genuine, have been more than five times the world record. He made a practice of lifting baby elephants as well as a series of invited celebrities (including Steffi Graf, Sting, Richard Gere, Yoko Ono and Desmond Tutu) above his head. He became a public miracle-performer, an eastern prestidigitator whose Indian-ness was an explanation for his extraordinary gifts, or his magical trickery — depending on one's point of view.

Sri Chinmoy gave his followers Sanskrit names, and India was talked about as if it were a holy land. But he would not allow his American followers to travel there. One of them, Jayanti Tamm, of Estonian-American origin, describes how India — though she has never been there — felt like home. 'For the first quarter century of my life, I wore saris, sang Bengali songs, ate Indian food, bowed to Indian gods and goddesses, chanted from the Bhagavad Gita, and worshipped my guru.' Her real home was Greenwich, Connecticut. Sri Chinmoy told them stories of his encounters with tigers and monkeys and, she says, he deliberately 'kept India as some type of mythical place, we were allowed to partake in it from afar'. Long after leaving the cult, she considers herself Indian, though she is yet to go there.

When John Lennon made a cryptic reference to the Hare Krishnas in the song *I Am the Walrus*,[19] written in 1967, they were still an obscure movement, newly founded by a New York-based Bengali, Swami Prabhupada. By the early 1970s, partly because of George Harrison's decision to transfer his allegiance from the Maharishi to the Hare Krishnas, they were world famous. His chart-topping song *My Sweet Lord* was a hymn to Krishna, and used the Hare Krishna mantra, along with lots of

[19] The song contains the baffling lines, 'Semolina pilchard, climbing up the Eiffel Tower/ Elementary penguin singing Hare Krishna/ Man, you should have seen them kicking Edgar Allan Poe/ I am the eggman, They are the eggmen.'

Judeo-Christian hallelujahs. The Hare Krishnas, officially the International Society for Krishna Consciousness or ISKCON, had become ubiquitous at western airports and train stations, selling spiritual books and home-made biscuits, and preaching chastity outside marriage, vegetarianism, and the forsaking of drugs and alcohol. They danced and sang in public, and most of them dressed in a way that was immediately distinctive — with shaved heads and free-flowing orange clothes. Their happy earnestness[20] became a source of comic delight for film-makers in Woody Allen's *Hannah and Her Sisters*, for Cheech and Chong's *Up in Smoke* and for the *Airplane!* series.

Several of America's leading academic experts on India were originally Hare Krishnas. And the influence of the Hare Krishna movement extended elsewhere into the strange world of creationism and anti-Darwinian pseudo-science, with the publications of Michael Cremo (known by his fellow devotees as Drutakarma Dasa), who denies evolution, and who uses early Hindu texts such as the Puranas as part of his evidence that human beings existed before the dinosaurs.[21] ISKCON was

[20] In fact, all was not happy. After the death of Swami Prabhupada in 1977, his eleven anointed successors, all westerners, began pulling the organisation in different ways. One was murdered by a former devotee; another was accused of child sexual abuse and imprisoned for racketeering. The most important US-based Hare Krishna community at New Vrindaban in West Virginia was expelled from the movement for several years after high-profile court cases involving murder, drug-running, arms smuggling and paedophilia.

[21] Cremo, who calls himself a Vedic creationist, became a Krishna devotee after Hare Krishnas gave him a copy of the Bhagavad Gita at a Grateful Dead concert. He has written several books which aim to demonstrate that 'humans like ourselves have existed on the planet for tens of millions of years', and argues that evidence of this has been 'suppressed, ignored and forgotten because it contradicts generally held ideas about human evolution'. On his website, Cremo quotes the reaction of the anthropologist Richard Leakey to his book *Forbidden Archaeology*: 'Your book is pure humbug and does not deserve to be taken seriously by anyone but a fool.'

strongly identified inside the organisation and externally as a religious movement from India. And it undoubtedly grew out of a more genuinely Indian tradition than the Sri Chinmoy group, and some of the other Hinduism-inspired 'cults' that flourished in the west.

Although a Hare Krishna splinter group tried to make the organisation less distinctively Indian in their music and clothing, and more of an inter-faith movement closer to Christianity, India was much more than a distant and ancient holy land for most Hare Krishnas. The organisation's headquarters moved from the US to Mayapur, north of Calcutta, where a largely Indian congregation of devotees is presided over by 'His Holiness Jayapataka Swami', widely known as JPS, but born Gordon Erdman in 1949 in Milwaukee.[22] And just as Krishna devotion returned to India in a new avatar, mediated by the west, something similar happened with yoga.

The American writer and self-proclaimed spiritual teacher Philip Goldberg in his 2010 book *American Veda* advances the proposition that American culture is suffused with ideas that originally come from India. He slightly overstates his argument, but points to the continuing influence of Emerson and Thoreau, Swami Vivekananda and Ginsberg, as well as that host of New Age gurus and yogis, and fellow spiritual teachers — home-grown and Indian — who have played an important role in segments of the American population since the 1960s. Nowhere else in the world has 'spiritual India' received such a responsive welcome. There are many thriving Hare Krishna communities elsewhere in the world, and other Hindu-inspired groups exist in Europe and in Britain, but the impact has, it seems to me, been

[22] JPS has come a long way since his childhood in Milwaukee, as the son of a wealthy paint business owner. But Milwaukee has also come a long way. It's currently one of America's leading centres for Indian devotional singing or *kirtan*, under the stewardship of Ragani, born Julie Ann Hobing in Indiana, and introduced to *kirtan* by the yoga master Swami Rama.

less lasting. And the Americans I meet in India tend to be more respectful of Indian belief systems, often to the point of naivety, than visitors from other nations. But I too am here falling for the kind of generalisation which I lament in so many foreigners' accounts of India.

I've found it hard not to develop, over the decades, some crassly unscientific stereotypes of foreign visitors to India. There are the Brits who want to save the poor or search for the graves of their ancestors; the Americans who search for themselves and for enlightenment; the newbie journalists who search for the exotic stories they think their audiences want to watch, hear and read; the Italians and the French who search for a fantasy land of Maharajahs or happy village simplicity, or cheap gemstones; the east Asians and the Sri Lankans who search for anything Buddhist; the Australians who want adventure; the Pakistanis who search for ancestral homes and Sufi succour; the contemporary youngsters who seek work experience or simply the company of their peers; the big-talking entrepreneurs who imagine billion-dollar business opportunities; the spiritual seekers who search out and find a guru.

I sometimes feel fortunate that I first came to India almost by accident, with few expectations or prejudices. It was little more than an early chapter, or an intermission, in a love story. I seemed to glissade into an India that was unthreatening to my world-view, mediated in a gentle fashion by well-travelled Bombayites, and by that doyen of modern Indo-Greeks, Tony Mango. I was at the time more struck by the similarities with my London life, rather than the differences. It would be some years before I encountered a guru, or rode an elephant, or visited the Taj Mahal, or was cheated by a taxi driver, or saw a tiger, or fell seriously ill, or was entertained by a snake charmer, or even tried to buy a train ticket. Most foreigners have at least one of these experiences on that first visit. Instead I had the softest of landings, cosseted by my future in-laws, bloated with wonderful food, watching the waves from an elegant beach-side house in one of the biggest cities in the world.

I did soon begin to encounter many other Indias — largely through my work and through travel. And I encountered many other Indians too, performing their 'million mutinies' — the phrase VS Naipaul would use, in his more respectful, less scatological third book on the subject, to describe the apparent chaos of India. A billion mutinies might now be more appropriate. I have met many, many thousands of Indians, from all parts of this subcontinent — and yet at the same time have met just the tiniest, statistically insignificant proportion of its population. And I need to remember this, and so do we all perhaps, when we are drawn towards generalisation and stereotyping. I have now, inadvertently, developed a little sermon for newcomers to India. In this sermon I talk of many Indias, and then I tell my listeners to think of India not as a country but as a continent. Expect, I say to them, the differences that you might find within Africa or within Europe (between, say, Denmark and Albania, or Scotland and Greece). And then try out your favourite sweeping India generalisation by replacing the word 'India' with the word 'Europe', and then see how meaningful that generalisation is. And India, I continue earnestly, has on its own, a population that is larger than Europe, or Africa, or the Americas. China, I concede, has more people, but, I ask, rhetorically, is it as varied? And I continue, in this vein, until my listener finds some excuse to leave. Sometimes I have found myself exaggerating slightly, arguing that India is even more than a continent. It's a world of its own. Planet India, perhaps.

The enormous scale of India is important. It seems both large enough and varied enough for most things imaginable on this earth to be possible in just one country. Whatever you are searching for: great food, spiritual learning, a good holiday, narcotic experiences, snowy mountains, adventure, a job, tropical jungle, love of any kind, or even the happy and not-so-happy poor. And it's because (almost) everything is possible, that visitors continue to have such idiosyncratic fantasies and opinions and nightmares about India as a country, as if one tiny part stood for the whole. And this notion of scale and variety, turned about, helps me to understand why I love living here so much. For India makes the rest of the world feel small and tame and uniform and peripheral by comparison. India has everything that is old, and everything that is modern, and everything in between. It has quite enough to challenge and surprise me intellectually, aesthetically and existentially for many lifetimes. I have never been bored in India.

Recently, I was walking back to my flat in Panchsheel Park, troubled by family matters and work idiocies, groggy with influenza and bearing some cough linctus purchased from a local apothecary. A man with a red Rajasthani turban came up to me. He informed me, in broken English, that he was a fortune-teller. I nodded politely and walked on, as I do on such occasions. But a friend, a foreigner in Delhi, had told me a few days earlier how she had had her fortune told, and that it had been entertaining if not entirely accurate. She had ticked me off, in her disarming way, for being sniffy about such tiny things. How could I live in India and not have my fortune told? And I remembered her words, and stopped in my tracks, and turned my head. He scuttled back towards me, with a smile upon his face. He told me first that I was not well. I was very impressed by this, as the sick often are by such perspicacity in relation to their woes, only realising after our encounter that I looked like death and was carrying a bottle of cough syrup. It then became a bit hit-and-miss. He said, correctly, that I had two children. But they were, he insisted, both girls. And he informed me that I was from America, and that I had been married twice. I did not tell him that he was mistaken.

Then he wrote something down on a piece of paper, crumpled it up, and placed it in my hand. 'Don't open it yet.' He asked me my favourite colour, and I said purple, and he looked disappointed. He said choose another, and I said violet. He said choose another, and then I chose blue. Then he asked me to choose a number from 1 to 5 and he made me choose each until only 3 was left. He then made me open the paper and written on it were 'blue' and '3'. He pretended to look triumphant, but I think he was a bit fed up with me by then. He asked me for three hundred dollars, and I gave him one hundred rupees — about two dollars — which, however, seemed like quite a lot of money. He became theatrically angry, throwing my money on the ground and then picking it up again, and trying to get me to take it back. I stood my ground. And then he said some words that have remained with me. 'You will die in India,' he said.

Now, this story can be read in many different ways. Least interesting is my hypochondria, or my scepticism about fortune-telling. Or even my deliberate unwillingness to give the most likely, most pleasing, most complicit answer — a symptom of my 'oppositional' quality, as a boss of mine once put it. More interesting is that I was reminded again of what it might be like to be a foreigner coming to India for the first time — and how strangely disquieting this incident might seem. But let me also, for one moment, try to see it from the point of view of the fortune-teller. For him I was just another foreigner, a tourist to be jostled gently into a modest redistribution of a tiny percentage of his wealth. He must have met other, less oppositional, white people who answered 'blue' and '3', and even if they didn't, would hand over large (to him) sums of foreign money. I had not revealed myself, at any point, as a long-term resident of India or as a Hindi-speaker (I often don't — and I do take great pleasure in being able to eavesdrop on what Hindi-speakers are saying about me). And so his parting curse must be seen as less an act of verbal violence and more as a final attempt to get me to hand over more money. To put the fear of death into me. And to get me thinking, 'Why not? Why burden my weary life with a curse?', and thereby to get me digging into my pockets to find a little more money for a poor man.

Except, and this was the crux of the incident for me, by then I was thinking of other things. I was thinking that actually I would quite like to die in India. Not yet. Not for a long while. But, yes, by the ocean, or in the foothills of the Himalayas. His curse had been transformed into a promise — one that gave me pause, and led me to smile, and made my current sea of troubles less hard to bear. And maybe, I told myself, I should leave, settle somewhere else for a while, try out some other land that is less all-consuming. But I will return, to live out my years and, perchance, to die. For only by then will it be my time to enter a genuinely undiscovered country.

Apologies and Acknowledgements

THIS IS A book that tells its own story, as well as mine — and that of many foreigners who came to love or hate India. It began as a conversation (with Tony Mango, my wife's step-father, who died soon after, and to whom this book is dedicated), and it became an idea, a talk, and an essay — before turning into this intermittent history and memoir. It conceals and reveals — and a careful reader will note how the domestic circumstances of the author mutate over the course of its writing. And it is a book whose caesurae and interstices enlarge themselves as the book progresses.

For the pre-Columbian chapters, there are preciously few sources — and the named foreigners who visit, or have something to say about India, are easy to count, and almost impossible to ignore. Later on, the reverse is true. And by the nineteenth century there is an almost overwhelming wealth of source material. It is possible, therefore, that some readers may feel a little cheated, when they search for, and fail to find, their favourite India-visiting foreigner, or foreigner-invented Indian.

And for this reason I feel the need to precede my words of gratitude by saying sorry. Apologies then to the aficionados of, among others: the Maharajah of Gaipajama, Che Guevara, Little Black Sambo, Meera from Little Britain, Geeta from East Enders, Apu Nahasapeemapetilon, Enid Blyton, Emily Eden, Julia Roberts, Raj Koothrappali, Agnes Smedley, Hrundi V Bakshi, Korla Pandit, Elihu Yale, Hope Savage, Fanny Parkes, the Abyssinians of Janjira and Sachin, Hezekiah Butterworth, Henry Maine, the Sidis of Gujarat, Voltaire, the Great Oom, Kelly Kapoor, the Jews of Kerala, Vasily Vereshchagin, Max Reisch, Yvonne Maday de Maros, the Afghans and the Armenians of Calcutta, Malik Ambar, Maud Diver, Abraham Rogerius,

Tom Legge, Alain Danielou, Benoît de Boigne, Lord Curzon, Roberto Calasso, Werner Herzog, and those two precocious young witches, Padma and Parvati Patil. And apologies also to all those who hoped to find a narrative that talked instead about Indian ideas and experiences of the rest of the world. That book needs to be written.

There are many more thanks than apologies. My gratitude in particular to Romila Thapar and to John Keay whose histories of India have guided this work, and who took the trouble to read some or all of my words, and comment wisely — and point out a few terminological inexactitudes, solecisms and outright errors. Apart from the hundreds of primary sources that I've referred to in the text, I've relied on the works of many scholars, and many secondary sources. These include, for the early period, Grant Parker's *The Making of Roman India* and Yukteshwar Kumar's *A History of Sino-Indian Relations*. The writings of Sanjay Subrahmanyam, author of several fine books of history, including his magisterial biography of Vasco da Gama, helped steer me through the early European and Mughal period, as did Donald Lach's multi-volume *Asia in the Making of Europe*, while the works of Raymond Schwab (*The Oriental Renaissance*), Kate Teltscher (*India Inscribed*) and Maya Jasanoff (*Edge of Empire*) were of particular value for the eighteenth and early nineteenth century. So too — over a broader period — were Partha Mitter's superb *Much Maligned Monsters: A History of European Reactions to Indian Art,* and Ronald Inden's *Imagining India.*

There is a sudden mushrooming of scholarship that relates to British rule in India in the late eighteenth century and the nineteenth century. The work of Bernard Cohn (*Colonialism and Its Forms of Knowledge*), Vasudha Dalmia (*Orienting India*), Gauri Viswanathan (*Masks of Conquest*) have all been important to me, as have the more traditional histories of Lawrence James (*The Raj: The Making and Unmaking of British India*), and David Gilmour (*The Ruling Caste: Imperial Lives in the*

Victorian Raj). Two of William Dalrymple's histories — *White Mughals* and *The Last Mughal* — were invaluable (as were his bibliographical advice and his book-lending generosity).

For the twentieth century, the writings of Ramachandra Guha — as well as books by Sunil Khilnani (*The Idea of India*), and Pankaj Mishra (*From the Ruins of Empire*) have been of particular help. Other noticeably well-thumbed books are Pavan Varma's *Being Indian* and *Becoming Indian*, Anthony Copley's *A Spiritual Bloomsbury: Hinduism and Homosexuality*, Dilip Padgaonkar's *Under Her Spell: Roberto Rossellini in India,* Philip Goldberg's *American Veda*, Deborah Baker's *A Blue Hand: The Beats in India,* Hugh Purcell's *After the Raj,* Mrinalini Sinha's *Specters of Mother India,* Gerald Horne's *The End of Empires: African Americans and India, India through the Lens* edited by Vidya Dehejia, *The Hindus: An Alternative History* by Wendy Doniger and the complete 1887 *Imperial Gazetteer of India* left to me by Tony Mango.

There is a full set of references and a comprehensive bibliography at sammillerindia.com

My researches were helped and hindered at several stages by Facebook friends — who responded energetically, and not always accurately, to my requests for help with information and translation. I'd like to single out my friend and former BBC colleague Bernard Gabony for repeatedly providing the most amusing and irrelevant answers. This book has benefitted from many conversations over the decades with other BBC friends in the UK, in India, and the rest of the world. My most recent colleagues — at BBC Media Action in India — deserve a special mention as do all of those who have had the misfortune to be my boss.

And now that list of those who have helped me in the writing of this book, probably in ways that they have forgotten, or never knew about in the first place. Pan Singh Bisht, Shireen Vakil Miller, Ranjana Sengupta, Rahul Noble Singh, Catherine Goodman, Natalia Leigh, Benedict Leigh, Sarnath Banerjee,

Anita Roy, Karuna Nundy, William and Olivia Dalrymple, Aditya Pande, Tyrion Lannister, Georgie Pope, Sukanya Ghosh, Monica Chadha, Andrew Whitehead, Valeria Corvo, Sachin Mulji, Mohammed Hanif, Sue Preston, Lois Preston, Jorge Roza de Oliveira, Ferzina Banaji, Iris DeMent, Ananya Vajpeyi, Mirza Waheed, Nick Booker-Soni, Omair Ahmed, Tim Mackintosh-Smith, Anu Mukherjee, Naoshirvan Vakil, Anuradha Awasthi, Penny Richards, Prachi More, Lucy Peck, Edward Snowden, Sonali Gupta, Brinda Chugani, Nazes Afroz, Aradhana Seth, Jeroo Mango, Vikram Seth, William and Anjali Bissell, Viva Kermani, Kate Wolf, Sagarika Ghose, Rajdeep Sardesai, Tom Howells, Annabel Barber, Rob Lynes, Chloe Paidoussis, Aashish Yadav, Alice Helme, Simone Mezzedimi, Sara Castellani, Alan Sorrenti, Gurcharan Das, Alex Oosterwijk, Tony White, Naveen Sharma, Shreyasbhai, Deepak Mehta, Rohinee Ghosh, Peter Beland, Toby Sinclair, Naresh Fernandes, Bahram and Arti Vakil, Mala and Tejbir Singh, Annette Ekin, Clementina Lakra, Naomi Spencer, Raj Kumar Sharma, Naval Chopra, Pradip Krishen, Radharani Mitra, Jivi Sethi, Richard Harris, Sidharth Bhatia, Slaid Cleaves, Kaushik Ramaswamy, Ferida and Noni Chopra, Will Sweetman, Sandra Babli, Ratish Nanda, Sruthi Gottipati, Gautham Subramanyam, Madhup Mohta, Mark Tully, Gillian Wright, Stephen Sackur, Chelsea Manning, John Elliott, Jonathan Shainin, Mike Bryan, Heather Adams, Adam Brookes, Mark Magnier, Karan Ma, Andy Bell, Ann Cambier, Roy Wadia, Sunetra Sen Narayan, Padma Rao, Vineeta Dwivedi, Tinku Ray, Diana Melly, Natalia Antelava, Tabish Khair, Michael Perry, Seema Chishti, Andrea Spalinger, Meru Gokhale, Bani Abidi, Michael Wood, Patralekha Chatterjee, Madhu Jain, Rachel Dwyer, Rafil Kroll-Zaidi, Sunil Arora, Joseph Miller, Stringer Bell, Daniel Miller, Behroze Gandhy, Dorota Wąsik, Mihir Sharma, Christine Rai, Shantum Seth, Abbas Nasir, Carmen Gonzalez, Laura Marling, Amelia Gentleman, Indi Hazra, Reena Aggarwal, Eloise Carbert, Raghu Karnad, Alexandra Pringle,

Dora Miller, Ian Strathcarron, Anant Raina, Niranjani Iyer, Tim Dee, Siddhartha Swarup, Shimon Mercer-Wood, Shilpa Kannan, Richard Goodwin, Hugh Barnes, Pascale Harter, Chris Cramer, Christabel Holland, Daisy Goodwin, Sage Mehta, Chandra Sekar, Suman and Manju Dubey, Christina Noble, Catrin Ormestad, Cordelia Jenkins, John Otway, Mandakini Dubey, Urmila Jagannathan, Moska Najib, Miniya Chatterji, Daniel Lak, Josh Ritter, William Crawley, Patrick French, Karolina Sutton, Georgia Miller, Ardashir Vakil, Deepika and Gautam Mehra, Adam Roberts, Andrew North, all the members of the Delhi Poets Society, the staff at the library of the School of Oriental and African Studies, the producers of the BBC radio series *In Our Time* and *Witness*, and those namesakes of mine from Paradise Fears, *Cardiac Arrest*, and the world of speedway.

Thank you also to those most directly involved with the publication of this book. The Penguin team: Nandini Mehta, Chiki Sarkar, Arpita Basu, Tara Khandelwal, Pallavi Agarwala, Gavin Morris, Tara Upadhyay and R Ajith Kumar, the long-distance compositor. And in the UK: Dan Franklin at Jonathan Cape, and my agent, David Godwin. And a special thanks to Additi Seth who helped compile the references and bibliography that can be accessed at sammillerindia.com.

My parents, Jane and Karl Miller, have read every word of this book at least twice. I have usually taken their advice. And it is thanks to them there are fewer references to animal and human pudenda than would have otherwise been the case. This book would also, but for their intervention, have been a little more winsome.

I would like, as I did once before, to blame any errors on my computer-sharing children, Zubin and Roxy. But they have their own laptops these days and therefore I may have to take full responsibility. And there is one 'error' I have deliberately inserted as a little joke. If you are the first to spot it, tell me — you will be rewarded appropriately.

Index

417

Copyright Acknowledgements

Grateful acknowledgement is made for permission to reprint the following material:

Sam Miller: Photographs on pages 1, 23 (photo on left), 27, 38, 39, 51, 55, 68, 70, 80, 93, 132, 151, 175, 185, 186 (photo on left), 195, 205, 221, 232, 241, 261, 345.

Nazes Afroz: Photograph on page 5.

Naoshirvan Vakil: Photographs on pages 9 and 10.

Geena Goodwin: Photograph on page 34.

Chris Cramer: Photograph on page 57.

Annu Matthew: Photographs on page 102.

Courtesy of the National Museum: Painting on page 147, *Portrait of Babur.*

Dora Miller: Painting on page 198. Original painting by Ruth Collet.

Author's family collection: Photograph on page 200.

The Bridgeman Art Library: Photograph on page 223.

Kevin Moore, mooretoons.com: Illustration on page 227.

Sanjay Jha: Photograph on page 342.

Homai Vyarawalla: Photograph on page 347, published in *India in Focus: Camera Chronicles of Homai Vyarawalla.*

Grove Press: Drawing on page 363.

www.vintage-books.co.uk